PRAXIS® MATHEMATICS
Content Knowledge (5161)

Sandra Rush, M.A.

Research & Education Association

Research & Education Association
61 Ethel Road West
Piscataway, New Jersey 08854
Email: info@rea.com

Praxis® Mathematics: Content Knowledge (5161) Book + Online, 3rd Edition

Printed in the United States of America

Library of Congress Control Number 2016954067

ISBN-13: 978-0-7386-1212-6
ISBN-10: 0-7386-1212-X

REA® is a registered trademark of
Research & Education Association, Inc.

+ Scatter Plot · UPMA 10·12·18

Contents

R/3/8
D
I
IV
68%

Rev 3/8
68% I -
(D)

32% D -

68% I -

Chapter 7: Calculus 249
- 7.1 Limits 249
- 7.2 Derivatives and Differentiation 254
- 7.3 Integrals 273
- Practice Exercises 288
- Practice Solutions 291

Chapter 8: Probability and Statistics 293
- 8.1 Probability 293
- 8.2 Expected Value 308
- 8.3 Counting Principle 310
- 8.4 Statistics 311
- 8.5 Comparing Data Sets 324
- 8.6 Normal Distributions 330
- Practice Exercises 343
- Practice Solutions 346

Chapter 9: Discrete Mathematics 349
- 9.1 Sequences and Series 349
- 9.2 Set Theory 358
- 9.3 Binary Relations 363
- 9.4 Logic 366
- 9.5 Counting Techniques 372
- Practice Exercises 381
- Practice Solutions 383

PART III: PRACTICE TESTS

Praxis Math Content Knowledge Practice Test 1 387
- Practice Test 1 Answer Sheet 388
- Practice Test 1 389
- Answer Key 397
- Answers and Explanations 398

Praxis Math Content Knowledge Practice Test 2 407
- Practice Test 2 Answer Sheet 408
- Practice Test 2 409
- Answer Key 417
- Answers and Explanations 418

Praxis Math Content Knowledge Practice Test 3 ..... *available online at www.rea.com/studycenter*

Glossary 425

Index 447

Self-Assessment Guides for Practice Tests 1 and 2 459

About the Author

Sandra Rush is a bestselling author acclaimed for making mathematics easier to grasp. She has taught math and physics at both the secondary and college levels. As an undergraduate majoring in math at Temple University, Ms. Rush tutored members of the men's basketball team as well as students at Philadelphia public schools, which sparked her interest in teaching. After contemplating a career in the space sciences and receiving her master's degree in ionospheric physics from UCLA, she found fulfillment in teaching in the classroom environment as well as in individual tutoring. Ms. Rush has pursued her academic career in Massachusetts, Colorado, and Arizona. She has written test-preparation guides for all ages, with her approach to books continually informed by her one-on-one tutoring and coaching.

Author Acknowledgments

This book is the effort of many people, even though my name, as the author, stands alone on the cover. Acknowledgment is due to the publisher, Research & Education Association, especially to Larry B. Kling, Director of Editorial Services, and to Diane Goldschmidt, Managing Editor. I have had a professional relationship for many years with these two principals of REA, and I certainly do appreciate the support and autonomy they provided to me from concept through production of this book. In addition, Kathy Caratozzolo is to be commended for typesetting the book as well as working so well with the difficulties involved with presenting the ubiquitous mathematical equations and figures into a readable text.

I would be remiss to not mention Mike Reynolds, who recognized, through my editing work for REA, that I actually should try writing. He encouraged me to author math prep texts such as this one, and I have enjoyed this change in career tremendously.

Dedication

This book is dedicated to you, the reader, a future teacher of a most important subject and one that I love. As I have acknowledged many times in my career, what a profound and lasting influence great teachers have on their students. Keep that thought in mind as you enter your rewarding career as a math instructor.

About REA

Founded in 1959, Research & Education Association (REA) is dedicated to publishing the finest and most effective educational materials—including study guides and test preps—for students of all ages. Today, REA's wide-ranging catalog is a leading resource for students, teachers, and other professionals. Visit *www.rea.com* to see a complete listing of all our titles.

Publisher Acknowledgments

Technical Reviewer: Stu Schwartz

Indexer: Sandra Rush

Typesetting: Caragraphics

REA Test Prep Team

Publisher: Pam Weston

VP, Editorial: Larry B. Kling

VP, Technology: John Paul Cording

Managing Editor: Diane Goldschmidt

Copywriter: Kelli A. Wilkins

Cover Design: Jennifer Calhoun

PART I:
Praxis Math Content Knowledge Introduction

Getting Started

AN OVERVIEW OF THE TEST

Used in more than 30 states and the District of Columbia, the Praxis Mathematics Content Knowledge (5161) test is by far the most common teacher-certification test in the United States for prospective secondary math teachers.

The 150-minute test contains 60 questions. Question types include selected-response (some with more than one answer), numeric-entry, drag-and-drop, and text-completion questions covering two wide-ranging content areas:

- **Content Category I:** Number and Quantity, Algebra, Functions, and Calculus (approximately 41 items)

- **Content Category II:** Geometry, Probability and Statistics, and Discrete Mathematics (approximately 19 items)

There's no doubt about it: The test is a mental workout, requiring you to make educated guesses, distinguish patterns, employ logic, construct simple proofs, pull together strands from various areas of mathematics, distinguish between viable and nonviable solutions, and develop and use mathematical models to solve real-world problems. Beyond that, you may encounter some questions that the test developer, Educational Testing Service, is trying out for future tests and will therefore not count toward your score.

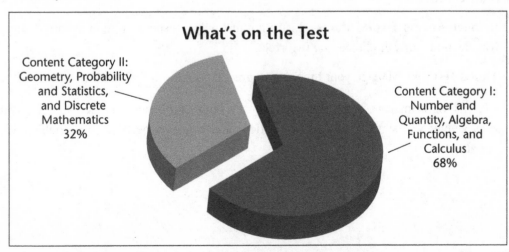

What's on the Test

Content Category II: Geometry, Probability and Statistics, and Discrete Mathematics 32%

Content Category I: Number and Quantity, Algebra, Functions, and Calculus 68%

How to Use This Book + Online Prep

This Book + Online prep will equip you to address the full array of question types and the complete range of difficulty you'll face on the Praxis Math Content Knowledge test.

Developed with the needs of teacher candidates like you in mind, this book, along with REA's online diagnostic tools, helps you customize your prep so you can make the most of your study time. Use all of it or just what you need to brush up in select areas.

Our Praxis Mathematics Content Knowledge Book + Online Prep package includes:

- Expert test tips and strategies

- Focused content review developed just for the Praxis Mathematics Content Knowledge (5161) test

- An in-depth tutorial on how to get the most out of the Infinity Softworks on-screen calculator

- Practice exercises on every topic

- Advice on how to solve math problems quickly

- An online diagnostic test to help you pinpoint where you need to spend your valuable study time

- Three full-length practice tests (two in the book and one online)

Test Yourself at the Online REA Study Center

The REA Study Center (*www.rea.com/studycenter*) is where you'll find the online material that accompanies this book—**the diagnostic test and a third full-length practice test**.

We know your time is precious and you want an efficient study experience. Our online content gives you feedback on where you stand right from the start.

- **Automatic Scoring**—Find out how you did on your test, instantly.

- **Diagnostic Score Reports**—Pinpoint the areas that challenge you the most, so you can study effectively.

- **Detailed Answer Explanations**—Learn not just why a response option is correct, but also why the other answer choices are incorrect.

- **Timed Testing**—Manage your time as you practice, so you'll feel confident on test day.

The Praxis Mathematics Content Knowledge test is computer-based, so practicing online at the REA Study Center will simulate test-day conditions and help you become comfortable with the exam format.

Five Steps to Success

We suggest five simple steps to help ensure your success on test day.

Step One: *Take REA's Praxis Math Diagnostic Test*

To get you started, we've included a diagnostic test at the online REA Study Center. Our customized diagnostic tools will show you how to spend your time and focus your study, highlighting the areas where you need the most help.

Step Two: *Evaluate Your Strengths and Weaknesses*

Check your diagnostic score report. Wherever you discover weak spots, you'll know where you need to extend your review. But even where you're already strong, be sure to read our answer explanations. This is a prime opportunity to reinforce key concepts and hone your skills.

Step Three: *Create Your Customized Study Plan*

Based on your diagnostic feedback, you'll know where to focus your prep. We suggest you start your preparation at least five weeks before test day. This will give you plenty of time to study the review materials and take the practice tests.

Step Four: *Review the Content*

Improve your weak areas by reviewing the appropriate content areas in this book.

Step Five: *Take the Practice Tests*

With three full-length REA practice tests, this Book + Online prep will thoroughly test your subject knowledge and build your test-day confidence.

To be assured you're on the path to success on the Praxis Math Content Knowledge test, you should aim to earn a score of at least 70% correct on your practice tests. Think of this as a good approximation of a passing score. We also encourage you to take the interactive practice tests available from ETS. For details visit *www.ets.org/praxis*.

Now let's turn to the nuts and bolts of what you need to do now through test day.

First things first.

REGISTERING FOR THE TEST

Setting Up Your Praxis Online Account

To register for the Praxis 5161, you must first create a Praxis account by setting up a user name and password. Go to *www.ets.org/praxis.* You must provide a valid mailing address, a valid email address, and an accepted form of payment (credit card, debit card or PayPal® account). In addition, for security reasons, you will be asked to select a security question. Remember the answer that you provide to that question.

If you forget your user name and/or password, click the "Forgot your user name or password?" link under "Returning Users" on the Praxis sign-in page (*www.ets.org/praxis*). You will be prompted to enter information about yourself, and to answer the security question you selected when creating your account. For security reasons, user names or passwords are not sent via email, so you will have to create a new password.

You must log into your Praxis account online for almost all interactions regarding registering, ordering test materials, making any necessary changes to or updating the personal information you provided, and viewing or ordering your scores.

Options for Registration

Once you have your Praxis account, you can register by mail, phone, or online. There is a $35 surcharge to register by phone, but there is no extra fee for registration by mail or online. You need to determine whether your state requires the Praxis Math Content Knowledge test (go to *http://www.ets.org/praxis/states*). Then find out where and when the Praxis 5161 test will be given in your area (see *http://www.ets.org/praxis/register/centers_dates*). Choose the date and time that is compatible with your schedule. ETS provides real-time seat assignments. You will be advised of seat availability when you select a test center. You must complete the registration process, including payment, and check out to guarantee your seat assignment.

 Do not wait until the last minute to register for the test. You need to register well ahead of the test date to guarantee your seat. Go to *www.ets.org/praxis.*

If you register by mail (ETS-Praxis, PO Box 382065, Pittsburgh, PA 15251-8065) or by phone (800-772-9476), ETS will mail you an admission ticket. If you register online through your Praxis account (*www.ets.org/praxis*), your admission ticket will not be mailed to you. You can always print your admission ticket through your Praxis account. Pay for the test on your Praxis account. Your test scores will not be released until your account is paid in full.

Tickets are not required for admission—they are provided only for the test-taker's information. However, the information on the ticket is what is in the ETS system for your account, so if there is an error on your admission ticket, such as a simple misspelling, corrections may be made online. After any change, including a change in location made by ETS, print an updated admission ticket.

 Be sure to log into your Praxis account three days prior to your appointment to confirm the test center's reporting location, which is subject to change.

If you find it necessary to change your test center, test date, or test time for a current test registration or to cancel your registration, you can do this up to three days prior to the test date not including the day of your test for a $40 fee online by logging in to your Praxis account or by telephone (800-772-9476).

If you make a change, however, ETS cannot guarantee that your requested testing time or test center will be available. If you completely cancel your original test by the appropriate deadline, however, you may be eligible for a refund of 50 percent of your test fees. If you are absent from the test (without canceling), your fees are automatically forfeited.

 Remember that you must make changes to your registration at least three full days before your test date, not including the day of your test, or your fees will be forfeited.

Ordering Materials

You can order test prep materials, such as the ETS Interactive Practice Test or Praxis webinars described in the section "Preparation for the Test" in this chapter, and view your ordering history through your Praxis account.

Changing Your Personal Information

Use your Praxis account to provide demographic information about yourself, to update your personal information or profile, or to make corrections.

Viewing Your Scores

You can view your scores, order additional score reports, or select recipients for your test scores (if applicable) through your Praxis account.

PREPARING FOR THE TEST

You are expected to know the math to get to the point of calculating the answer, for which the Infinity Softworks on-screen graphing calculator is invaluable to find exponents, roots, trigonometric values, and logarithms, and to solve equations. In addition, the graphing feature of the online calculator provides a means to easily graph and analyze functions as well as generate a table of values for a function. We'll run through all the features of the calculator in Chapter 2.

 Test taker-supplied calculators are not permitted for tests that offer on-screen calculators.

Review the math topics presented in the chapters of this book. The Praxis 5161 test is computer-based, but other formats are possible for test-takers approved for accommodations. You can access the online calculator to help answer any question, but the majority of questions can be answered without using this calculator. It is a good idea to get the 90-day trial online graphing calculator from Infinity (*http://www.infinitysw.com/ets*) before you start these chapters so you can determine what types of questions require using the calculator and how to do that quickly and efficiently.

Infinity's URL also provides a link to the manufacturer's manual and four online video tutorials on its usage. Read the calculator chapter in this book for an overview of the Infinity Softworks graphing calculator and easy-to-follow instructions for its use, including many screenshots to help you follow the instructions. It is up to you to allow yourself plenty of time to become familiar with the online calculator. The 90 days that Infinity Softworks gives you to learn how to use the calculator is not excessive.

With the wealth of material presented in this book, it's a good idea to make your first stop our online diagnostic test at *www.rea.com/studycenter*. Once you discover your weak points, you'll be in a good position to brush them up one by one. To aid you in this process, this book is fully indexed.

You can obtain free or paid books from ETS at *https://www.ets.org/praxis/prepare/materials/5161*. The ETS Interactive Practice Test for Content Knowledge is a full-length interactive practice test that consists of one set of authentic test questions in an environment that simulates the computer-delivered test, including a timer. You can move easily from question to question just like on the real test. After completing the practice test, you can see the correct answers as well as their explanations and you can view your results by content category. The ETS Interactive Practice Test is available for either 90 days from initial use or up to 10 total uses. There is only one version available for the Praxis 5161, so purchasing more than one Praxis 5161 practice test will not give you new or additional practice questions.

ETS offers free webinars (*https://www.ets.org/praxis/prepare/webinars*) that deliver in-depth information and demonstrations about ETS test preparation products and services. Each live webinar is interactive, so you have an opportunity to ask questions. View the schedule for more information regarding the live webinars.

WHAT TO EXPECT ON TEST DAY

You should plan to arrive at the test site at the time noted on your admission ticket. If you drive to the site, be sure you understand where to park—you cannot leave the test, once started, to "feed the meter." You do not have to have your ticket to be admitted to the test site, but you must have a photo ID that contains your name, signature, and photograph. You must present this as soon as you arrive at the test site. Requirements may vary from site to site; see *www.ets.org/praxis*.

You cannot bring food, drinks (including water bottles), scratch paper, study materials, or cell phones into the testing center—only your ID. Your pockets must be empty; leave your cell phone, calculator, and watch at home or store them in a locker at the site or in your car. Phones, watches, or other electronic, photographic, scanning, recording, and listening devices are strictly prohibited in the test center. Possession of any of these devices at the testing center will result in your being dismissed from the test, your test scores from all tests taken that day will be canceled, and you will forfeit your test fees. In addition, the device is subject to confiscation. For more information, see *https://www.ets.org/praxis/test_day/bring*.

Many testing sites are Prometric testing centers, which typically have lockers. The designation STN in front of a testing center name indicates an educational institution or testing center similar to Prometric, but it may not have lockers or storage facilities.

After you have identified yourself, you will be escorted to a test center administrator (TCA) for the check-in procedure. The administrator will check your photo ID, and you should be prepared for the ID procedure to also include fingerprinting, photographing, or some other form of ID verification, although this secondary verification is not always deemed necessary. To ensure security, prior to entering the testing room, you must show that your pockets are empty, and you may even be subjected to a handheld metal detector. Then you must write and sign a confidentiality statement and a test-taker roster.

The administrator will explain the testing procedures and rules for the exam and answer all of your questions. The administrator will provide everything you need during the exam, including scratch paper and pencil.

If you think you will need tissues during the two-and-a-half-hour test time, ask the TCA for a couple before the test begins. You cannot bring your own.

During the Test

The TCA will then escort you to your assigned test station and computer. Each test station has a video camera that is continually monitored by a TCA, so be aware that your every move is recorded. Get familiar and comfortable with your computer and mouse. Put the scratch paper and pencil that the TCA gave to you in a convenient location. When the session begins, you will be shown several screens. Click CONTINUE to go from one screen to the next. The first screen contains your personal data (name, ID, title of test) and your photo. Be sure that the information is correct and then log in. (If it is in error, raise your hand and the TCA will come to you.)

The next set of screens present general directions and testing tool information, including test navigation and how to answer various types of questions, as well as how to mark specific questions so you can come back to them during the test. Also included are directions for accessing the specific test and math resource information, such as the math reference sheets and the online graphing calculator. The last screen is a confidentiality agreement. When you click CONTINUE after this last screen, the test (and the clock) will begin.

A TCA will walk around the room during test time. If you have any questions during the test, raise your hand and the TCA will come to you to help you. Most centers do not offer a break during the test, even though it is 150 minutes long. If you need to take a break, the clock will not stop. You will need to sign out and back in again, so be sure to take your photo ID with you. You may even need to go through another security procedure (empty pockets, metal detector) before reentering the testing room.

Main Computer Functions

The Navigation bar at the top of the screen has buttons for REVIEW, MARK, HELP, BACK, and NEXT. The main window contains the question and answer choices (if applicable). To answer a selected-response question, click on your choice; to deselect it, click on it again; to change your choice, just click on a different choice and your first selection will automatically be deselected.

To go to the next question, click NEXT; to go to a previous question, click BACK. The NEXT and BACK buttons move only one question at a time.

 Watch out! If you double-click, you may skip past a question.

If you want to mark a question to review later, click on the MARK button at the top of the screen. To unmark a marked question, click MARK a second time.

At any time, the REVIEW button will reveal a screen with the status of each question: whether it is answered, not answered, or not yet seen. You may have to scroll the screen to see the whole review. The MARKED column in the review shows which questions you have marked for review. The last question is shown as highlighted. To go to a particular question, click on Go To Question at the top of the REVIEW screen. To go back to the question before you clicked the REVIEW button, click RETURN.

The HELP button takes you to information on the testing tools, such as How To Answer, How To Scroll, General Directions, and other resources that are available to you, which includes the math reference sheets and a calculator button to access the online calculator. The test clock does not stop when you are using the "Help" function.

The clock, which appears in the upper right hand corner of the screen below the Navigation buttons, tells you how much time is left. If you want to hide the clock, use the HIDE TIME button. To display it again, click SHOW TIME. At five minutes before the deadline, the time display will blink for a few seconds and then remain visible for the rest of the test. When time is up, a message "Your time for answering the questions in this section has ended" appears on the screen.

If you have finished the test and you still have time remaining, you will have the option of going to the last question (RETURN) or going to the REVIEW screen.

 Be careful. Clicking CONTINUE after the last question will end the test, even if you still have time.

If time runs out before you finish the test, the test will end automatically. You will get a message that says, "Your time has ended. Click CONTINUE to go on."

Scoring

When the test has ended, clicking CONTINUE takes you to the REPORT or CANCEL SCORES screen, which gives you either option. Consider your choice here very carefully, even though you have only two minutes to do so, because once you make this choice you cannot change it. If you fail to make your choice in time, the scores are automatically part of your record. If you choose to cancel your scores, they cannot be viewed, and no scores will be reported to you or to any institution or agency that you had designated. Your canceled scores cannot be retrieved or reinstated, and you will not be entitled to a refund of the test fee. After you have made your choice, click the NEXT button and then confirm your choice by clicking OK.

After you confirm your decision, the session will end, and you will receive the message, "Your test session is now complete." You will be asked to click CONTINUE to go on. The next screen will display your raw (unadjusted and unofficial) scores. Remember that these are not the adjusted scores that will be sent to you and your designees; they are just your raw scores, which are simply the number of questions answered correctly.

Adjusted scores, also called scaled scores, are equated to a scale that ETS uses to translate raw scores to scaled scores. The easier the questions are on a given test form, the more questions must be answered correctly to earn a given scaled score.

To avoid confusion between the adjusted (scaled) and unadjusted (raw) scores, ETS reports the adjusted scores on a score scale that makes them clearly different from the unadjusted scores. Note that ETS does not set passing scores for the Praxis tests. States, institutions, and associations that require the tests set their own passing scores. The most up-to-date score requirement information is located at *https://www.ets.org/praxis/states*.

ETS recommends that the passing score on this test should be 32 out of a possible 50 raw-score points. This equates to 64%, or a scaled score of 160 on the final Praxis test scale, which runs from 100 to 200. We recommend that your goal should be at least 35 correct on each of our practice tests, ⌐→ out of 50 equivalent to at least 70% correct on test day.

Passing score information for the score recipients you listed when you registered appears on your score report. If you test in a state with automatic score reporting, you will receive passing score information for that state. You can access your adjusted test scores via your Praxis account. This service is free of charge and replaces a mailed paper score report. Adjusted scores will be available approximately 10 to 16 business days after the testing window closes. The reporting dates vary based on the type of test you take. See *https://www.ets.org/praxis/scores/get* for more information.

Click CONTINUE to end the test session. Take everything, including the scratch paper and pencil, back to the check-in area, where you can sign out and retrieve any personal items you have stored.

Praxis tests can be retaken once every 21 days, not including the initial test date.

All About the Online Calculator

Infinity Softworks is the provider of the online graphing and scientific calculator technology for ETS's computer and internet-based testing platforms. This chapter provides an overview of the use of this calculator, which is an essential aid for the Praxis Mathematics Content Knowledge (5161) test.

The test assesses your knowledge of a wide variety of mathematical topics. Each problem requires you to know (1) what the question is asking and (2) how to get the correct answer. The rest of this book addresses the first of these requirements, but the second requirement—getting the correct answer—depends in many cases on knowing how to use the online calculator. The importance of this knowledge cannot be overemphasized, and it is the mission of this chapter to help you learn it.

The online calculator provided to you on the test may have features that are different from calculators with which you are familiar. This chapter presents step-by-step, easy-to-follow instructions and notes accompanied by many screenshots. In addition, the use of the calculator to solve several examples is presented at the end of this chapter.

Reserve the use of the online calculator, however, for those calculations that you cannot do in your head or quickly on the scratch paper provided for your use during the test. In the interest of time, it should not be used to do basic math (addition, subtraction, multiplication, or division) that you can quickly do on paper. Sometimes calculation is not necessary to answer a question, so remember to read the entire question before you attempt to find a numerical answer.

Use the calculator mainly for reference (e.g., for evaluating exponents, roots, trigonometric functions, and logarithms). The calculator is essential for quickly solving equations, graphing and analyzing functions, or generating a table of values for a function.

The calculator can be accessed for your use at any time during the exam. It appears when you call it out by clicking the ONLINE CALCULATOR button at the top of the screen. The calculator disappears from the computer screen, however, when you go to the next question, but you can call it out again if needed.

Go to *http://www.infinitysw.com/ets* to register for a 90-day trial of the graphing calculator. This URL also provides a link to Infinity Software's manual for the graphing calculator, as well as four online video tutorials on its usage. Any of the three sources (manual, tutorials, and this chapter) provide the information you need. This chapter has the additional benefit of Hints and Notes to help you use the calculator efficiently to save time during the test as well as to avoid pitfalls that will cost you time.

The Infinity Software calculator manual is also available at *infinitysw.s#.amazonaws.com/ets/ets_calculator_manual_pdf*, and the tutorials are also available at *www.infinitysw.com/exam/tutorials*.

The best way to learn the functions of the calculator is to use the trial version. A lot! Don't fall into the pitfall of thinking "I have 90 days to try it out, so what's the rush?" To ensure you're ready for test day, immediately start to learn how to use this specific calculator. It takes time, and it is better to have free time at the end of the trial period than to not have enough time to learn everything when the 90 days are up. Learning by hands-on "trial and error" is more memorable than anything you read on paper, especially if you just read it and don't experience it. So read the rest of this chapter with the trial calculator on-screen, and you will learn how to manipulate it faster, saving you time on the actual 150-minute test.

THE BASICS

Standard Keypad

The calculator will appear as shown in Figure 1. The window has two panes: the lower pane is the input pane, and the upper pane is the output pane.

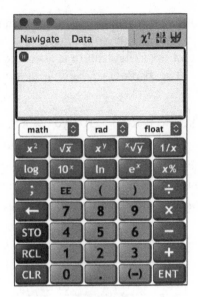

Figure 1

The number keys (the light gray keys in the middle of the calculator) and the function keys (the last five keys in the right column) stay the same for all calculations. They should look familiar because they are the same as on most calculators. The (−) key in the last number row means "negative," not "minus," and is used to indicate a negative value rather than subtraction. However, in addition, subtraction, multiplication, and division of numbers, this distinction isn't as important as when working with equations.

The back button on the keypad ← deletes anything in front of the cursor. You can also use the computer keyboard Backspace button. To clear the current input (in the lower pane), press the CLR (clear) button once. If you press CLR again, it will delete the display in the upper pane.

During the calculator trial period, most keypad buttons include a tip that is revealed when the cursor is on a particular function key. If you use your mouse to hover over the EE key, for example, you will see the following tip:

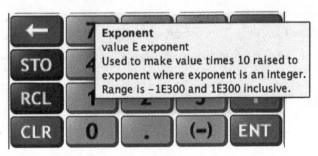

Exponent
value E exponent
Used to make value times 10 raised to exponent where exponent is an integer.
Range is −1E300 and 1E300 inclusive.

Figure 2

Tips do not show during the test, but use them as needed during the trial period to become familiar with the functions of each key and option. Move the cursor over any button to show its tool tips. This feature is available *only* on the trial version of the calculator—*it will not be available during the actual exam.*

As an example of the ⎡EE⎤ key, to insert 7×10^5, you would choose 7, ⎡EE⎤, and 5 from the keypad and then enter it by using the ⎡ENT⎤ button to show the result, 700,000 (see Figure 3). Notice that what you input appears in the bottom pane of the window, and the answer appears on the right of the top pane of the window. Thus, the bottom pane is for input and the top pane is for output (the input at the top left of the pane and the answer at the bottom right).

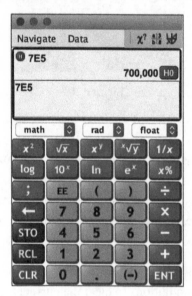

Figure 3

Storing and Recalling

The graphing calculator has 10 memory locations available, numbered 1–10. You can store or recall expressions in these locations. To store an expression in the input area (or its value), select ⎡STO⎤ and the number of the desired location. If there is no expression in the input area, the last result will be stored.

To store an expression or value in a memory location that you plan to recall, select STO after the calculation, and the expression will be stored in a designated location (automatically set as 0 through 9). To recall a stored value, select RCL and choose the memory location you want. It will recall this value to the current cursor position.

OPTIONS

Mode Choices

Three choices appear on the keypad just below the window, the first of which offers four mode choices: math, trig, number, and boolean (Figure 4).

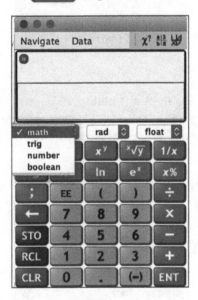

Figure 4

math : The input keys change to common mathematical functions, such as powers, roots, reciprocals, logs, and percentages (Figure 5).

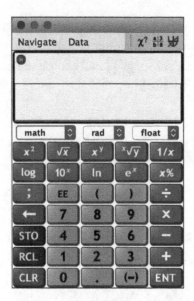

Figure 5

 Be careful when using the e^x button. If you want to evaluate $3e^x$, you must enter a multiplication sign (*) as follows: $3*e^x$ because the calculator will interpret it as a general exponent and return a message "Missing exponent value."

trig: The input keys change to common trigonometric functions, their inverses, and π (Figure 6). Only **sin**, **cos**, and **tan** are shown, since the other trig functions can be found by using the reciprocals of these functions. The labels for the inverse trig functions are **asin**, **acos**, and **atan**.

Figure 6

number : The input keys change to operations on numbers (Figure 7): abs (absolute value), nPr (permutation), nCr (combination), fact (factorial), int (greatest start with a letter; this same function occurs with My Data in the "Navigate" drop-down menu).

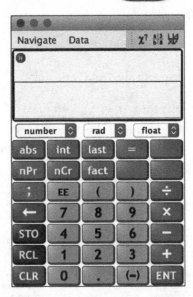

Figure 7

boolean : The input keys change to Boolean relationship functions (Figure 8), and the results are either "True" or "False." Read the explanations for these buttons by using your mouse to hover over them.

Figure 8

The translations of the Boolean keys are:

== indicates "equals"

!= indicates "not equal to"

> , >= , < , and <= indicate, respectively, "more than," "more than or equal to," "less than," and "less than or equal to."

&& and || indicate, respectively, "and" and "or"

Figure 9 shows inputs and results for || (A), && (B), == (C), and >= (D). Note that the output is either "True" or "False." Also note the parentheses in (A) and (B); without the correct punctuation, the result is "Missing or invalid operator," or a similar warning.

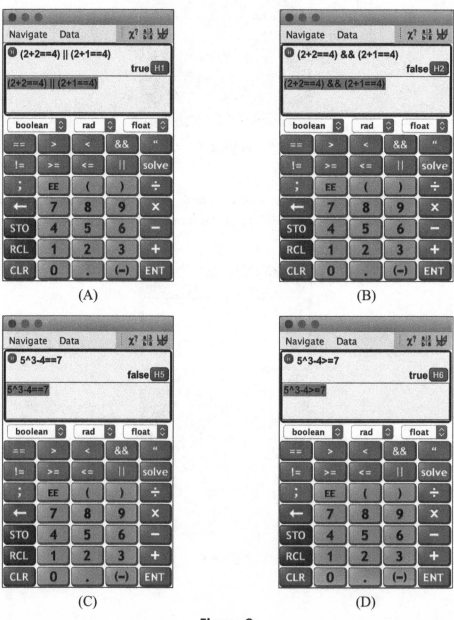

(A)

(B)

(C)

(D)

Figure 9

In boolean mode, the solve key options include solve ("expression"; "variable"). It is important that you enter the quotation marks and semicolon, as shown; these punctuation marks are part of the boolean keypad.) (The same function occurs with Solver.)

Other Choices

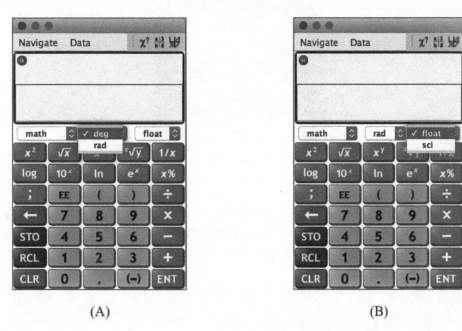

(A)   (B)

Figure 10

Figure 10 shows the next two drop-down menus above the keypad for angle measure and number type. When in the trig mode (A), choose deg for degrees or rad for radians. When in the number mode (B), choose float for numbers with a floating decimal point or sci for scientific notation. Note that in scientific notation, the letter E (keypad EE) is used for 10 to a power. For example, 3.4E7 = 3.4×10^7.

NAVIGATE AND DATA

Navigate

An important button on the calculator appears on the menu bar at the top. It is the Navigate button. The drop-down menu for the Navigate button contains four choices, History, Solver, My Data, and My Graphs, as shown in Figure 11.

Figure 11

History : Provides access to a list of previous calculations. You can access your previous calculations by selecting the small blue history circle in the upper left corner of the upper pane.

Solver : Gives numerical solutions to equations

My Data : Lists assigned variables

My Graphs : Creates and displays the types of equation to graph.

These last three choices are also available as icons (Figure 12) on the top right corner of the calculator for (left to right): Solver , My Data , and My Graphs . You can choose any of these three choices by clicking on its icon or by choosing it via Navigate . These three choices are discussed in detail later in this chapter.

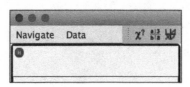

Figure 12

History

You can access your previous calculations by selecting the history circle in the left corner in the upper window. See, for example, Figures 9A–9D, where the history positions are H1, H2, H5, and H6, respectively. The [History] window that pops up displays the calculation and the result. The H1 History button in Figure 9A says it is in History position 1. If you want to retain your work in History, press [Done] (at the bottom of the screen). You will then be returned to the last screen. Press [Clear] if you want to erase all of it, and you will be prompted with "Are you sure you want to clear the History?" before it clears everything.

Data

Next to the [Navigate] button is the [Data] button, which clears memory, history, data, etc. It is not used to input data, as such, which is the function of the [My Data] button, described below. For example, choosing the [Data] button and selecting Clear History will delete everything from the current history, including the History values from Figures 9A–9D.

Do not confuse the [Data] button with the [My Data] button.

ENTERING DATA

To evaluate an expression, make sure the mode is correct. Then input your data by using either the calculator keypad or your computer keyboard, then select [ENT] on the calculator or Enter on the computer. The expression and answer will appear on the online calculator with either input method (or any combination). For example, in [math] mode, press [log] on the calculator, and log(value) appears in the lower window. Then enter your value, let's say 7.282, press [ENT], and the answer (0.862250674598) along with the input appear in the upper window (Figure 13).

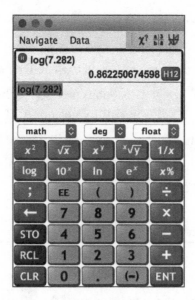

Figure 13

Watch out! If you type "log 7.282" on your computer keyboard (not calculator) during the test, you will get the message "Unknown variable" because you must use the `log` button on the calculator to enter the value for which you want the log to base 10. Similarly, do not type "ln" on your computer keyboard during the test—you must use the `ln` button on the calculator to enter the value for which you want the natural log.

Which is better—keypad or keyboard? This is an individual choice. If you use the keypad of the online calculator exclusively, that works fine, but it does take up a bit of time. If you use the computer keyboard, you have to watch out for functions (such as log, ln, EE) that are automatic from the calculator keypad but not recognized from the computer keyboard.

A third method is to use both hands at the same time. This takes some time to get used to, but it works this way: Use your left hand for inputting numbers, and maybe **Enter** from the computer keyboard, and use your right hand for inputting all of the functions. This saves time because you aren't manipulating the mouse and clicking among the numbers. Your right hand is on the mouse and your left hand is on the number bar of the computer, and they work in concert with each other. Although this is a hybrid method, it works and is quick.

Of course, if you are used to using the calculator *with a mouse*, go for the all-keypad method. Alternatively, if it is second nature for you to use the computer keyboard, and you use * for multiplication, / for division, ^2 for squared, hyphen for minus, and sqrt for square root, etc., use the all-keyboard method but watch out for the functions that will give you an ERROR message if you don't remember to use parentheses in the right places.

NAVIGATION

Solver

Solver is used to find numerical solutions to an equation with one or more variables. Access Solver from the Navigate menu, or you can simply choose the $\chi^?$ icon at the top right corner of the calculator screen.

To use Solver, enter your equation in the top pane, and then fill in the known data once it appears in the lower pane (see example in Figure 14). The window will list all variables under **Name**, and you fill in the known values in the **Value** column (here it is $x = 2$), and select the ? button in the **Solve** column for the variable you want to evaluate. When you select the ? button, the calculated value for that variable will appear in the **Value** column.

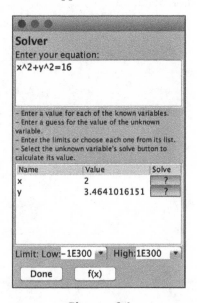

Figure 14

If necessary, you can set your limits at the bottom of the screen in the boxes labeled **Limit: Low** and **High**. (A similar choice of solve is also available in the boolean menu.)

To aid in entering your equation in Solver, you can choose functions from the drop-down menus for f(x) at the bottom of the Solver screen (Figure 15). These functions are a listing of the same functions that appear on the keyboard when you choose from the four modes at the beginning of a session. Figure 15 shows the functions available for the four choices under f(x): Math (A), Number (B), Trig (C), and Boolean (D).

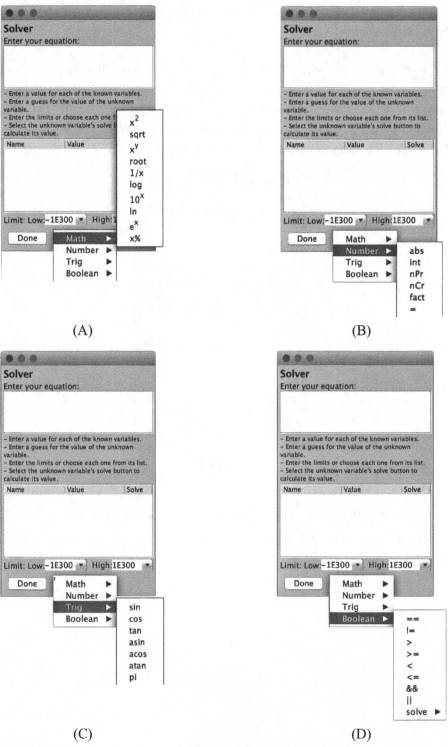

Figure 15

To input an equation in [Solver], be sure get the functions from [f(x)] on the [Solver] screen.

My Data

My Data displays all of the assigned variables in the calculator. You can access [My Data] under the [Navigate] menu, or you can simply choose the icon at the top right corner of the calculator screen.

As shown in Figure 16A for the equation entered in [Solver] (see Figure 14), [My Data] automatically enters the variables and their values (Figure 16B).

(A)   (B)

Figure 16

To create a new variable, select New at the bottom of the My Data screen. Enter the name in the Name column, and either a number or expression for the variable in the Value column. The expression should be entered via the calculator keypad or computer keyboard. These values can be used anywhere for performing calculations. Choose Clear if you want to erase all of it. You will then be prompted "Are you sure you want to clear My Data?" before it clears everything. Choose Done if you want to retain it, and you will be returned to the main screen.

You don't have to use just single letters for names, so if you called your new variable Bob with a value of sqrt(3), then the expression Bob^2 and Enter evaluates that expression and yields 3 as the answer. Be aware that the name you use for your variable is case-sensitive.

Do not use "pi" or "e" as variables since they already have values assigned to them. Also, it isn't wise to use the variables "x," "y," or "t" because they are used by the Graph Analysis mode.

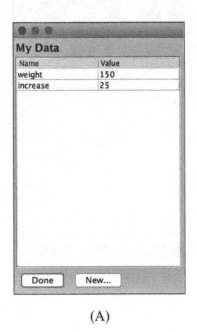

(A)

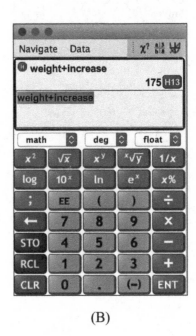

(B)

Figure 17

The variables you enter and their values will stay in the History. In Figure 17A, the first variable is weight and the second variable is increase. Then, if at any time you want the sum of the two, enter weight + increase, as shown in Figure 17B, choose ENT, and the value will be displayed in the upper pane. For multiple values, use names such as weight1, weight2, etc.

My Graphs

You can access [My Graphs] by choosing the **Navigate** menu and then choose [My Graphs], or you can simply choose the graph icon [graph icon] at the top right corner of the calculator.

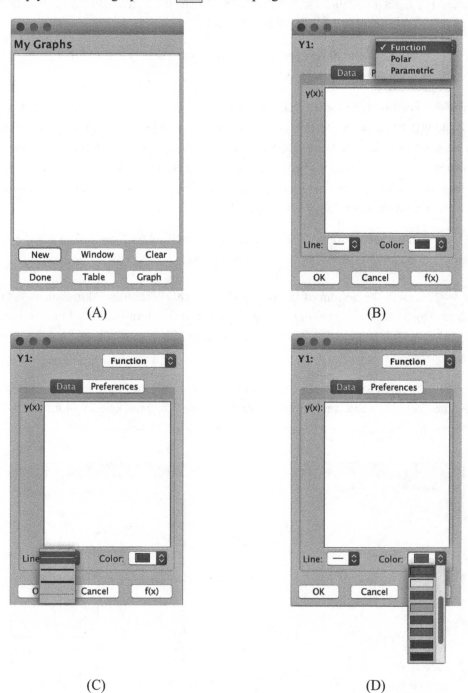

(A)

(B)

(C)

(D)

Figure 18

To enter an expression to be graphed, select New at the bottom of the screen (Figure 18A) to get the next screen (Figure 18B). The Function drop-down menu at the top right corner of the screen allows you to select the type of expression to be graphed: Function , Polar , or Parametric .

Function: For regular equations in the Cartesian coordinate system, such as y(x) = 3x + 4; y is the dependent variable and x is the independent variable.

Polar: For equations in the polar coordinate system, such as r(t) = 3 cos t; r is the dependent variable and t is the independent variable.

Parametric: For two (or more) equations that are defined with the same parameter, such as x(t) = t − 2 and y(t) = t²; x and y are the dependent variables and t is the independent variable. When a parametric function is graphed, the graph is the resultant equation when the parameter is eliminated. For example, for the equations here, t can be rewritten as t = x + 2, which yields the following equation for y in terms of x (eliminating t): y = (x + 2)². The window for a parametric function has two panes, one for x(t) and one for y(t).

The Line menu at the bottom of the screen (Figure 18C) offers four choices for the weight of the line (single thick, double thick, triple thick, and dotted.

The Color menu at the bottom of the screen (Figure 18D) presents color choices for the line. Sixteen colors (including black) are offered (note the bar at the right margin of the color palette to see more options). Colors appear as shades of gray in this book, but will be actual colors on the calculator.

If you are graphing more than one graph on the screen, be sure they are easily distinguishable from each other by at least choosing different colors. Different line thickness will further distinguish the two graphs, but it's a good idea to use color as the major distinguishing feature.

(A)

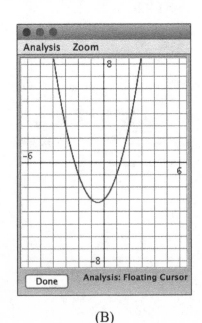

(B)

Figure 19

Enter your function in the window next to y(x) and then press OK (see Figure 18B). In the next window, you will see that the calculator uses Y1 for the function. For example, after you enter x^2 + x − 3 next to y(x), and click **OK** at the left bottom of the window to save it, this function is automatically added to the listing of **My Graphs**, which appears in a new window as Y1 (Figure 19A). If you have multiple functions to graph, pressing NEW will allow you to enter them, and they will be called Y2, Y3, etc.

The **My Graphs** window is handy because you can double-click any function to change any mistake you might have made when entering the function. That function will go back to the original screen on which you entered the function in the first place (see Figure 18) so you can change it. You can also change the line and color here if you want to. When you are satisfied with the function, click **OK**, which brings you back to **My Graphs** (see Figure 19A). Click **Graph** at the bottom of the screen and a graph of the function will appear in a new window (Figure 19B).

Note that equations and values from **My Graphs** are also available elsewhere in the calculator. **My Data** displays analysis results from the graph view as x and y. You can even do math with the variables x and y because their values are saved in the calculator. Once an expression has been defined in **My Graphs**, its name can be used throughout in functions on the calculator. For example, if you define Y1 as **sqrt(x)/2**, you can just enter Y1 in the **Math** window of **Solver** and the calculator will do the calculation as though you had entered **sqrt(x)/2**. So if you enter only Y1(4), the answer will be 1, since $\sqrt{4}$ / 2 = 1.

The **Graph** window (Figure 19B) allows you to analyze the graph of your function by selecting choices from the **Analysis** and **Zoom** options at the top of the window.

The **Analysis** options and certain **Zoom** options require user interaction, and may not be available on the actual online test. Only the available modes will be displayed on the online test. All of the options are listed here, and you should at least be familiar with them.

Analysis has the following options: Floating Cursor, Trace/Evaluate, Zero, Minimum/Maximum, and Table.

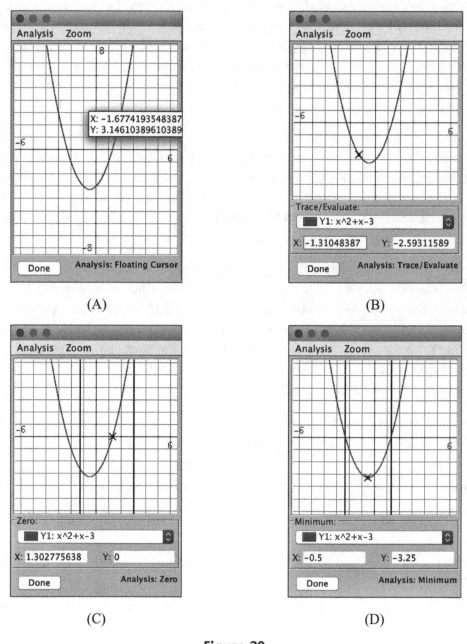

(A)   (B)

(C)   (D)

Figure 20

Floating Cursor (Figure 20A): Trace the cursor along the graph, and the values of **x** and **y** at each point are displayed at that point.

Trace/Evaluate (Figure 20B): Click on any point on the graph and its **x**- and **y**-values are displayed in boxes at the bottom of the screen. Just drag the cursor along the curve. This option also allows you to enter a numerical value for **x** at the bottom of the page and the corresponding **y** value will automatically show.

Zero (Figure 20C): Click anywhere on the graph and a vertical line appears. Drag that line to the right, and any values for which $y = 0$ in that interval will be marked; the value of x will be displayed in the boxes at the bottom of the window. This procedure has to be repeated for each zero.

Minimum/Maximum (Figure 20D): Similar to **Zero**—drag a line left to right and the minimum/maximum point in the interval between these two x values is marked, with the x- and y-values displayed in boxes at the bottom of the window. The graph displayed in Figure 20D has only a minimum. The procedure would have to be repeated for each minimum/maximum.

Table: Displays a table of points on the graph (see Figure 21).

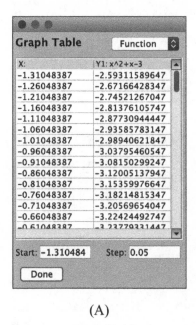

(A)   (B)

Figure 21

The table has a default spacing of 0.05 and a default starting point (see Figure 21A). By double-clicking on the [Start] window, you can change the starting point to another value (such as 0, see Figure 21B). By double-clicking on the [Step] window, you can change the x intervals. Be sure to choose [Done] so these values are displayed in the table. You can scroll down the table using the bar on the right-hand side to see more data points than fit on the one screen.

[Zoom] (at the top of the graph; see Figure 19B) has the following options: Box, In, Out, Previous, Default, Trig, Square, and Window.

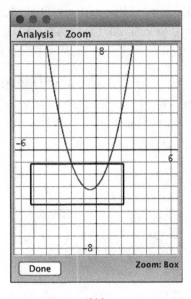

(A)

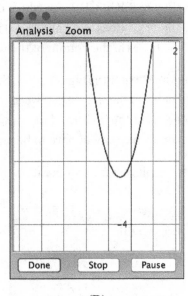

(B)

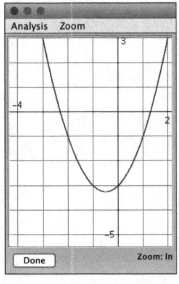

(C)

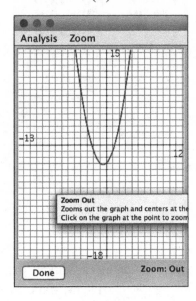

(D)

Figure 22

Box (Figure 22A): Allows a specific region of the graph to be magnified. Place your cursor on the upper left corner of the desired area to be magnified and drag to the lower right corner, which will form a box; the interior of that box will be magnified on the next screen (see Figure 22B).

Zoom In/Out: The [Zoom] scale is usually 2 but can be changed by going to the Window Settings options that appear when you select Window under the [Zoom] menu. Zoom In (Figure 22C) and Zoom Out (Figure 22D) are shown for the original graph shown in Figure 19B.

 The Zoom In/Out feature may not be operable on the test, in which case use Window under the [Zoom] menu and change the X and Y Maximum and Minimum values to larger numbers (e.g., ±20 for x and ±30 for y). See Window below.

Previous: Returns to the previous graph Window Settings.

Default: The default settings are ±6.5 for the x-axis and ±8.5 for the y-axis, the x scale and y scale set to 1 (meaning they are equal), and a zoom scale of 2. These settings can be changed by accessing Window Settings when you select Window on the [Zoom] menu.

Trig: Adjusts the graph window to ±2π for the x-axis with a scale of π/2. The y-axis is not changed from the default ±8.5.

Square: Changes the x and y ranges so the change of x is the same as the change of y. The idea is to make the grid square so circles look circular.

Window: Changes the view window explicitly. (This change can also be accessed in [My Graphs].) To change the area, use the Window Settings options that appear when you select Window. You can change X Minimum, X Maximum, Y Minimum, and Y Maximum by just entering new values. When you select [Save], a new view appears with the new window.

 The Window Settings option can be used instead of the Zoom In/Out option.

Graphing More Than One Function

Suppose you want to graph two or more equations on the same coordinate system to see points of intersection or other features. Choose [My Graphs], then select [New] for each function. The calculator uses Y1 for the first function, Y2 for the second, etc. Work with each function individually as discussed in the last section.

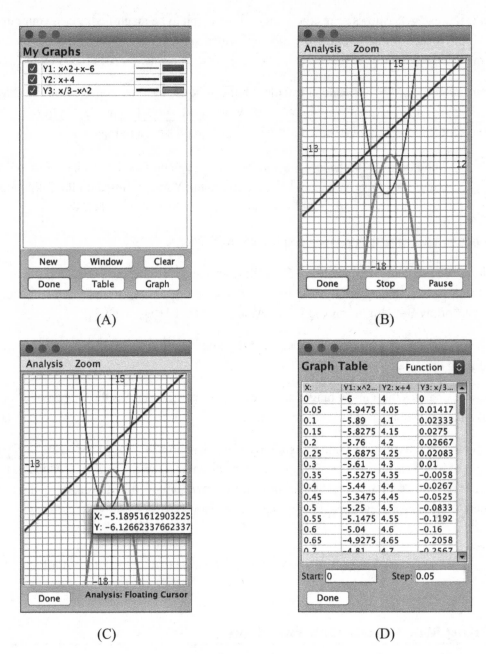

Figure 23

Notice in Figure 23A that the equations listed on the My Graphs screen are checked. Only checked equations will be graphed, so be sure to check which functions you want to graph together on the My Graphs page. To graph them, select the Graph button at the bottom right of the screen, and the graph will immediately be displayed, showing all of the checked functions on one coordinate system (Figure 23B). The Analysis and Solver drop-down menus at the top of the screen allow for interaction with the graph. The Floating Cursor or Intersection options (see below) can be used to find the x- and y-values at the points of intersection (see Figure 23C).

The Analysis and Solver menus for graphing more than one function have the following additions:

Intersection: Allows you to find a point of intersection of two graphs. Simply click the cursor somewhere to the left of the point of intersection and drag that line to the right to the point of intersection. The x and y values of the point of intersection within that interval are then displayed at the bottom of the page.

Table: Can be accessed from the Analysis menu or from My Graphs. When you select Table, the table will list values for each graph individually on the same page (Figure 23D).

Expression names can be used to define new graphs. On the My Graphs page, for example, if Y2 is defined as sin 2x and Y3 is defined as x/4, a new graph Y4 can be defined as Y2(Y3(x)). Be sure to select OK to put it in memory. When you select Y4, the graph will be that of $\sin2(x/4) = \sin(x/2)$. This feature is used for nested functions.

HOW THE ONLINE CALCULATOR CAN GET SOLUTIONS QUICKLY

You must realize that the calculator will not *solve* the Praxis 5161 problems for you. It will not do the mathematical thinking that is required. What it will do is finish the problem by performing the required calculations quickly, provide values for mathematical and trigonometric functions, and draw graphs according to your input parameters. You still have to know the math—that is why there are more chapters to this book than just this one.

The following problems are presented with two solutions—with and without using the online calculator. Using the calculator is not mandatory to get a solution, but you will realize that it is a time-saver and ensures accuracy.

1. Find the numerical value of cot 405°.

Answer: 1

Without calculator:

If you sketch the angle, you can see that it ends up in the first quadrant. Subtract 360° from the angle, and the result is 45°, so cot 405° = cot 45°, and since it is in the first quadrant, the signs will be the same (they are all positive in the first quadrant). Since $\cot \theta = \dfrac{1}{\tan \theta}$, you need only to find tan 45°, which is 1, so cot 45° is also 1, and thus cot 405° = 1.

With calculator:

Since cot A = 1/tan A, enter 1/tan (405) in trig mode.

2.   Find the value of x, in degrees, in the following equation: $\sqrt{1 - \sin x} = \frac{1}{2}$. Round to the nearest integer.

Answer: 50

Without calculator (until the end):

$$\sqrt{1 - \sin x} = \frac{1}{2}$$

$1 - \sin x = \frac{1}{4}$ (Square both sides)

$\sin x = \frac{3}{4}$ (Combine like terms, multiply equation by –1)

$x = \arcsin \frac{3}{4} = 48.59$ (Use calculator)

$x = 49$ (Round the answer to an integer)

With calculator:

Use [**Solver**], but be sure the **trig** mode on the computer is set for **deg**. Enter the equation, using the **f(x)** feature for square root (**math** mode) and sin (**trig** mode) and click the **?** under **Solve** for **x**. The answer is immediate: 48.5903778907, rounded to 49.

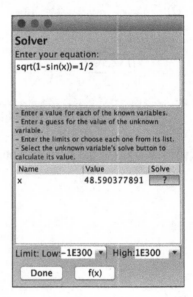

3.   If $\cos x = \dfrac{1}{9}$, the positive value of $\sin\!\left(\dfrac{1}{2}x\right)$ is

   (A) $\pm\dfrac{2}{3}$

   (B) $\dfrac{4}{9}$

   (C) $\dfrac{4}{3}$

   (D) $\dfrac{2}{3}$

Answer: (D) $\dfrac{2}{3}$

Without calculator:

$$\sin\!\left(\frac{1}{2}x\right) = \pm\sqrt{\frac{1-\cos x}{2}} = \pm\sqrt{\frac{1-\left(\frac{1}{9}\right)}{2}}$$

$$\pm\sqrt{\frac{8}{9}\div 2} = \pm\sqrt{\frac{8}{18}} = \pm\sqrt{\frac{4}{9}} = \pm\frac{2}{3}.$$

The question asks for the positive value, so the answer is $\dfrac{2}{3}$.

With calculator:

From the first equation, $x = \arccos(1/9)$. Substituting this value into the second equation in Solver yields an answer of .66666666667, which is recognized as 2/3.

4. Find the positive values of x less than 360° that satisfy the equation $\dfrac{2 + 3\tan x}{\tan x} = 5$.

    (A) 45°

    (B) 225°

    (C) 45° and 225°

    (D) 45° and 315°

Answer: (C) 45° and 225°

Without calculator:

$$\frac{2 + 3\tan x}{\tan x} = 5$$

$$2 + 3\tan x = 5\tan x$$

$$2 = 2\tan x$$

$$1 = \tan x$$

Tangent is positive in the first and third quadrants, so arctan 1 is 45° and 225°.

With calculator:

Use [Solver] to find the principal value of x, but since the problem asks for "the positive values of x less than 360°," you have to remember that the other value is positive, so it must be in the third quadrant, or 225°.

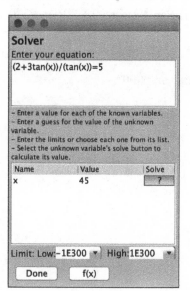

5. Find the values of θ, $0° < \theta < 360°$, that satisfy $3 + 2(\cos^2 \theta - 1) = \cos \theta + 1$. Enter *all* correct answers.

    A   60°

    B   90°

    C   270°

    D   300°

Answer: A 60°, B 90°, C 270°, and D 300°

Without calculator:

$$3 + 2(\cos^2 \theta - 1) = \cos \theta + 1$$
$$3 + 2\cos^2 \theta - 2 = \cos \theta + 1$$
$$2 \cos^2 \theta - \cos \theta = 0$$
$$\cos \theta(2 \cos \theta - 1) = 0$$

For $\cos \theta = 0$, arccos $0 = 90°$ and $270°$.

For $(2 \cos \theta - 1) = 0$, $\cos \theta = \dfrac{1}{2}$, and arccos $\dfrac{1}{2} = 60°$ and $300°$.

With calculator:

Use [Solver] to input the equation, which yields an answer of 60°. The question asks for all of "the values of θ, $0° < \theta < 360°$," so you must include the angles in each quadrant for which 60° is the reference angle.

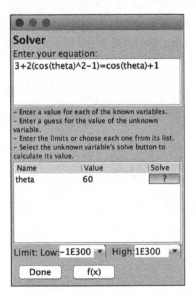

6.   As the sine of an angle decreases from 0 to –1, the tangent of that angle $\left\{\begin{array}{c}\text{increases}\\\text{decreases}\\\text{stays the same}\end{array}\right\}$.

Answer: increases

Without calculator:

Look at the graphs of sine and tangent. Be sure to use the trig option. The sine of an angle decreases from 0 to –1 in Quadrant III. In Quadrant III, the tangent of an angle increases from a value of 0.

With calculator:

To look at the graphs together, enter Y1: sin x and Y2: tan x by using the f(x) for trig in My Graphs (top figure). Choose Graph at the bottom of the page and go to Zoom to change to Trig so the horizontal axes are in quadrants (bottom figure). Then look at the graphs. where sine decreases from 0 to –1.

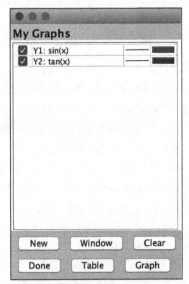

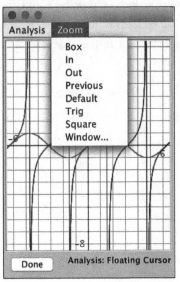

7. If $\cos x = \dfrac{2}{3}$, the value of $\cos 2x$ is

(A) $\dfrac{4 - \sqrt{5}}{9}$

(B) $\dfrac{4 + \sqrt{5}}{9}$

(C) $\dfrac{1}{9}$

(D) $-\dfrac{1}{9}$

Answer: (D) $-\dfrac{1}{9}$

Without calculator:

The Praxis online formula sheet doesn't give the formula for $\cos 2x$, but it does give the formula for $\cos (x \pm y)$, and we can get the double angle formula from that by making $y = x$. The formula for $\cos (x + y) = \cos x \cos y - \sin x \sin y$, which becomes (when $y = x$) $\cos 2x = \cos^2 x - \sin^2 x$. To find $\sin x$, use the Pythagorean formula and the fact that $\cosine = \dfrac{\text{adjacent}}{\text{hypotenuse}}$, as follows . In the given right triangle, $\cos x = \dfrac{2}{3}$, so we can say the hypotenuse is 3 and the adjacent side is 2, and then use the Pythagorean formula, to find b, the side opposite angle x by solving $b^2 = 3^2 - 2^2$, or $b = \sqrt{5}$. So $\sin x = \dfrac{\sqrt{5}}{3}$. Now we have enough to find $\cos 2 = \cos^2 x - \sin^2 x = \left(\dfrac{2}{3}\right)^2 - \left(\dfrac{\sqrt{5}}{3}\right)^2 = \dfrac{4}{9} - \dfrac{5}{9} = -\dfrac{1}{9}$.

With calculator:

Change the first equation to $y = \text{arccos}(2/3)$. Here we changed x to y, but it can be called anything as long as it is the same in the second equation, which now becomes $\cos 2y = \cos(2\text{arccos}(2/3))$. Enter it in [Solver] to get -0.11111111111, which is the decimal equivalent of $-1/9$, which is also the only answer choice that is negative.

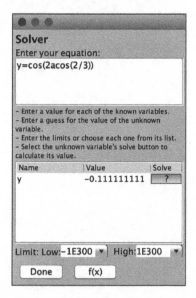

8. The length of a rectangle exceeds its width by 11 feet. If the length is decreased by 5 feet and the width is increased by 2 feet, a new rectangle is formed that has the same area as the original rectangle. What is the width of the original rectangle? _____ feet

Answer: 4

Without calculator:

Let the width of the original rectangle be x feet. Then the length is $(x + 11)$ feet, and the area is $x(x + 11)$ square feet. The new rectangle has width $(x + 2)$ feet and length $(x + 11 - 5)$ feet, and its area is $(x + 2)(x + 6)$ square feet. The two areas are equal, so the problem is to solve the following equation for x, the width of the original rectangle in feet:

$$x(x + 11) = (x + 2)(x + 6)$$
$$x^2 + 11x = x^2 + 8x + 12$$
$$3x = 12, \text{ or } x = 4$$

With calculator:

Just enter the data (length × width) onto the Solver on the calculator.

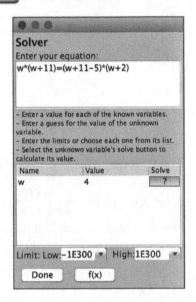

9. The denominator of a fraction is 1 less than 4 times the numerator. If the numerator is doubled and the denominator is increased by 6, the value of the resulting fraction is $\frac{2}{5}$. What is the original fraction?

    (A) $\frac{2}{5}$

    (B) $\frac{4}{19}$

    (C) $\frac{5}{19}$

    (D) $\frac{10}{19}$

A: (C) $\frac{5}{19}$

Without calculator:

The original fraction is $\dfrac{x}{4x-1}$. The changes make the new fraction $\dfrac{2(x)}{(4x-1)+6} = \dfrac{2}{5}$, which can be solved for x to find the original fraction.

$$\frac{2(x)}{(4x-1)+6} = \frac{2}{5}$$
$$10x = 8x + 10$$
$$2x = 10$$
$$x = 5$$

So the original fraction is $\dfrac{2(xx)}{4x-1} = \dfrac{5}{4(5)-1} = \dfrac{5}{19}$.

With calculator:

Use My Solver to find the value of x for x/(4x-1), and then substitute it into that fraction to get 5/(20–1) = 5/19:

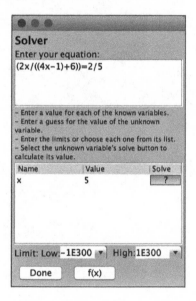

10. How many points of intersection are there between $x^2 + y^2 = 4$ and $y = x^2 - 8$?

    (A) 0

    (B) 1

    (C) 2

    (D) 3

Answer: 0

Without calculator:

To find points of intersection, solve the equations simultaneously. Rewrite $y = x^2 - 8$ as $x^2 = y + 8$. Then substitute this into the first equation to get an equation with only one variable:

$$(y + 8) + y^2 = 4$$
$$y^2 + y + 4 = 0$$

which has no real roots, so there is no point of intersection and the answer is 0.

With calculator:

You can graph both equations on one graph to see that they won't intersect, but you don't even have to go that far. Just graph the second equation $y = x^2 - 8$, and you should recognize $x^2 + y^2 = 4$ as a circle with center at 0 and radius 2, so you can just visualize it on the graph below to see that there are no points of intersection. (Note: If you graph both equations on the same graph using the calculator, you will see this also, but you will spend unnecessary time entering the equation for the circle.) Although the calculator can solve $x^2 + y^2 = 4$ (see Figure 14 for an example), to graph a equation, it must be in the form of $f(x)$, so you would have an extra step of converting the circle equation to $y = \sqrt{4 - x^2}$.

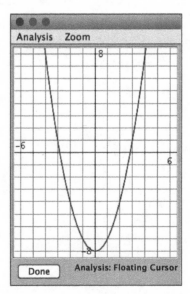

PART II:
Praxis Math
Content Knowledge
Review

Diagnostic Test
To focus your study, go to the online REA Study
Center to take the Diagnostic Test.

(www.rea.com/studycenter)

CHAPTER 3

Refresher on Number and Quantity

This review chapter presents the vocabulary and hints for information you probably already know but might need some reminders.

3.1 THE NUMBER LINE

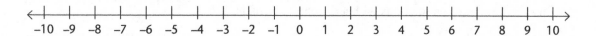

The **number line** actually goes on forever in both directions, so the line above is just part of it. Between the numbers shown on this line are actually infinitely many numbers, such as fractions and decimals. Any number is smaller than all of the numbers to the right of it and larger than any number to the left of it. Therefore, all positive numbers are larger than any negative number.

You should know the following symbols: < (less than), > (greater than), ≤ (less than or equal to), ≥ (greater than or equal to), ≠ not equal to.

 Hint: To remember whether the symbol means less than or greater than, look at the symbol: the quantity on the smaller side of the symbol is less than the quantity on the larger side.

The sentence "all positive numbers are larger than any negative number" can be symbolized as

positive numbers > negative numbers   or   negative numbers < positive numbers

For example, −3,678,295 < 20.

Notice also on the number line that as the numbers get farther from zero, the digits increase. This is obvious on the positive side of the number line, but negative larger digits are less than negative smaller digits. For example, $-983 < -900$ because -983 is farther from 0.

3.2 THE COMPLEX NUMBER SYSTEM

Complex numbers have two parts: a real part plus an imaginary part, which can be symbolized as $a + bi$, where a and b can be positive, negative, or zero. All real numbers can be thought of as complex numbers with $b = 0$.

3.2.1 Real Numbers

The set of all **real** numbers has various components. The two main components are the set of all **rational** numbers, Q, which are numbers that can be written as fractions or repeating or terminating decimals, and the set of all **irrational** (not rational) numbers, S, such as π or nonrepeating decimals, such as the value for $\sqrt{2}$. All real numbers are included on the number line.

The set of rational numbers is further separated into the set of all **natural** numbers, $\mathbb{N} = \{1, 2, 3, \ldots\}$, which are part of the set of all **whole** numbers, W = $\{0, 1, 2, 3, \ldots\}$, which are part of the set of all **integers**, $\mathbb{Z} = \{\ldots, -3, -2, -1, 0, 1, 2, 3, \ldots\}$. Fractions are rational numbers; they just aren't integers, which means they aren't necessarily whole or natural numbers, either (although all integers can be written as fractions with a denominator of 1).

3.2.2 Imaginary Numbers

It makes sense that numbers that aren't real are called **imaginary**. These numbers are of the form bi, where b stands for any number and i is an imaginary unit such that $i^2 = -1$. Since there is no real number that can equal a negative value when it is multiplied by itself, the unit i is imaginary. Its value is $\sqrt{-1}$.

The imaginary part of any complex number can be written in terms of i. Therefore, $\sqrt{-9} = \sqrt{9 \cdot (-1)} = 3i$ and $\sqrt{-8} = \sqrt{4 \cdot 2 \cdot (-1)} = 2\sqrt{2}i$. Imaginary numbers and i are discussed in more detail in Chapter 4, Section 4.5.2 on complex conjugates and Section 4.6.2 on quadratic equations.

3.3 CLOSURE OF RATIONAL AND IRRATIONAL NUMBERS

A set of numbers is said to be **closed** for a specific mathematical operation on members of a set (such as the addition of two rational numbers or the multiplication of two irrational numbers) if the result is itself a member of the set. See Section 9.3 in Chapter 9.

For example, the set of integers is closed under addition, subtraction, and multiplication, but not division. This is the same as saying that if you add, subtract, or multiply any two integers, you get an integer, but if you divide some integers, for example, $7 \div 5$, the result is a fraction, not an integer. You need only one example not to work to say it lacks closure. This "exception to the rule" is called a **counterexample** and is enough to prove a statement false.

 Watch out for the phrase "8 divides 2," which looks like it means 2 divides into 8, but the meaning of "divides" in this phrase means "is a divisor of," which isn't true (8 is not a divisor of 2). Instead, "2 divides 8," meaning 2 is a divisor of 8 (or is a factor of 8), is correct.

The set of rational numbers is closed under addition, subtraction, multiplication, and division (with the exception of division by 0, which is undefined and therefore neither rational nor irrational). The closure of rational numbers is straightforward. However, the set of irrational numbers is *not* closed for any of the operations. A counterexample for closure, for example, involves $(2 + \sqrt{3})$ and $(2 - \sqrt{3})$, which are both irrational. Addition gives an answer of 4 (rational); subtraction of either from itself gives an answer of 0 (rational); multiplication gives an answer of 1 (rational); and division of either by itself gives an answer of 1 (rational).

3.4 PROPERTIES OF REAL NUMBERS

3.4.1 Addition

3.4.1a Commutative Property of Addition

An example of the **commutative property of addition** is $3 + 5 = 5 + 3$. The name commutative comes from the word *commute*, which means to change position (like commuting to school—going from home to school). Changing the position of the numbers does not affect the answer. This property extends to adding any string of numbers:

$$3 + 5 + 6 = 5 + 3 + 6 = 6 + 3 + 5$$

and so on.

EXAMPLE 3.1

Add $6 + (-5) + 7 + 5$

SOLUTION 3.1

13. Rearrange, or "commute," the numbers to make the addition easier: $6 + (-5) + 7 + 5 = 6 + 7 + 5 + (-5) = 6 + 7 + 0 = 13$. Section 3.4.2 shows that subtraction is not commutative, but this is addition in which one of the numbers happens to be a negative.

3.4.1b Associative Property of Addition

In addition, we can also group numbers by using parentheses. So we can say, for example:

$$3 + (5 + 6) = (3 + 5) + 6$$

as well as a whole lot of other variations of the numbers and groupings. This grouping property has the name **associative property of addition** because we are associating numbers with other numbers in different groups.

3.4.1c Identity Property of Addition

When a number and its additive identity are added, the number doesn't change. Thus, the **additive identity** (also called the **identity element for addition**) is 0 for all real numbers, and $a + 0 = a$ for all a.

3.4.1d Inverse Property of Addition

The **inverse** of an operation "undoes" the operation and the result is the identity element for that operation, which is 0 for addition. Addition and subtraction are inverse properties, so the **additive inverse** of a is $-a$, and $a + (-a) = 0$.

3.4.2 Subtraction Properties

Because the order in which the numbers appear makes a difference in subtraction (that is, which number is subtracted from which), the operation of subtraction isn't associative or commutative. For example, $7 - 4 \neq 4 - 7$ and $(5 + 2) - 3 \neq 3 - (5 + 2)$. The inverse of subtraction is addition, so the additive inverse of $-a$ is a, and $-a + (a) = 0$.

3.4.3 Multiplication Properties

3.4.3a Commutative Property of Multiplication

Just as for addition, multiplication can be done in any order (called the **commutative property of multiplication**). So $3 \times 8 = 8 \times 3$. And $3 \times 5 \times 2$ is the same as $3 \times 2 \times 5$ or $5 \times 3 \times 2$ or any other order of these three numbers. The products are the same.

3.4.3b Associative Property of Multiplication

The associative property allows us to "group" numbers in multiplication. This grouping has the name **associative property of multiplication**, and it makes finding the product easier.

EXAMPLE 3.2

Multiply $25 \times 7 \times 4$.

SOLUTION 3.2

700. If we see that $25 \times 4 = 100$, the problem is really the same as $7 \times 100 = 700$. Compare that to multiplying $(25 \times 7) \times 4 = 175 \times 4$, or worse yet, $25 \times (7 \times 4) = 25 \times 28$. They all give the same answer, but the first solution is much easier.

3.4.3c Distributive Property of Multiplication

Another property of multiplication is that $6(3 + 4) = (6 \times 3) + (6 \times 4)$. This is called the **distributive property** of multiplication over addition because multiplication by 6 is "distributed" to each number being added in the parentheses. Of course, the problem shown here is more easily done as $6 \times 7 = 42$.

Sometimes you can recognize a common factor in an addition problem for which the reverse of the distribution property presented above can be useful. The distributive property and its reverse come in handy in some complicated problems, especially in algebra, as shown in Chapter 4.

EXAMPLE 3.3

Leroy bought 12 pencils for 6 cents each. When he told his mother about his purchase, she thought it was such a bargain that she bought 88 more for the class. How much did they spend together?

SOLUTION 3.3

$6.00. One way to do the problem is straightforward: $6(12) + 6(88)$, which will give the answer with some unnecessary multiplication. If you realize that $12 + 88 = 100$, the reverse of the distribution property gives $6(12) + 6(88) = 6(12 + 88) = 6(100) = 600$ cents $= \$6.00$. Much easier.

3.4.3c Identity Property of Multiplication

When a number is multiplied by its multiplicative identity, the number doesn't change. Thus, the **multiplicative identity** is 1 for all real numbers, and $a \times 1 = a$ for all a.

3.4.3d Inverse Property of Multiplication

The inverse of an operation "undoes" the operation and the result is the identity element for that operation, which is 1 for multiplication. Multiplication and division are inverse properties, so the inverse of a is $\dfrac{1}{a}$, and $a \times \left(\dfrac{1}{a}\right) = 1, a \neq 0$.

3.4.4 Division Properties

Just as for subtraction, where the order of the terms makes a difference, order makes a difference for division. Obviously, the answer for $4 \div 2 \; (= 2)$ is different from the answer for $2 \div 4 \left(= \dfrac{1}{2}\right)$. The commutative and associative properties don't work for division. The inverse of division is multiplication, so the inverse of $\dfrac{1}{a}$ is a, and $\dfrac{1}{a}(a) = 1, a \neq 0$.

3.5 ORDER OF OPERATIONS

The order of operations makes a difference in calculations, as shown in this section. Operations must be done in the following order to get the correct answer:

- *Parentheses:* Parentheses say "do me first." In other words, evaluate what is in the parentheses ( ) or brackets [ ] or braces { }, working from the inside out, until they are all gone.

- *Exponents:* Evaluate any part of the expression that contains exponents next.

- *Multiplication and Division:* Do any multiplication and/or division in order from left to right.

- *Addition and Subtraction:* Do any addition and/or subtraction in order from left to right.

The order of operations is often remembered by the mnemonic word **PEMDAS**, in which each letter stands for one of the above operations in order. (A **mnemonic** is a method to help memory—it doesn't even have to be a real word.) A mnemonic sentence for the same order of operations is the sentence "**P**lease **E**xcuse **M**y **D**ear **A**unt **S**ally," which uses the first letter of each word. You just have to remember what operations they stand for.

So even if the string of operations doesn't have parentheses or exponents or division or subtraction, and we want to evaluate $7 \times 2 + 4 \times 2$, PEMDAS tells us to do the multiplication first, and then the addition:

$$7 \times 2 + 4 \times 2 = 14 + 8 = 22.$$

If the operations were done as they appear, without regard to the order of operations, the incorrect answer would be $7 \times 2 + 4 \times 2 = 14 + 4 \times 2 = 18 \times 2 = 36$.

3.6 TYPES OF NUMBERS

3.6.1 Odd and Even Numbers

An **even** number is an integer that is divisible by 2. An **odd** number is an integer that is not divisible by 2. The odd and even designations hold for positive as well as negative numbers.

Be careful when finding two consecutive even or odd numbers. In both cases, even for odd numbers, just add 2 to the previous number. For consecutive even numbers starting with −6, for example, the numbers are −6, −4, −2, 0, 2, 4, 6, 8, . . . (notice that 0 is an even number). For consecutive odd numbers starting with −7, the numbers are −7, −5, −3, −1, 1, 3, 5, 7, . . .; in other words, you still add 2 to each odd number to get the next odd number.

If you add two even numbers or two odd numbers, the result is always an even number. However, the sum of an even and an odd number is always odd. These facts hold for subtraction of two numbers as well.

For multiplication, the rule is that if one of the multipliers is even, the product is always even. The only way to get an odd product is to multiply an odd number by an odd number. This is true for a whole string of numbers: If any one of them is even, the product is even. Therefore, $7 \times 6 \times 5 \times 4 \times 3 \times 2 \times 1$ must be an even number. If you took out the 4 and 2 and multiplied $7 \times 6 \times 5 \times 3 \times 1$, you still get an even number, although there are more odds than evens. If you now took out the 6 from this product, getting $7 \times 5 \times 3 \times 1$, there would be no evens, and the product would be odd.

 (Hint:) Rather than trying to memorize that an even plus an even gives an even, an odd plus an odd gives an even, etc., just figure it out, should the question come up, by using just the first five natural numbers, 1, 2, 3, 4, and 5, as your guide: $1 + 2 = 3$, $2 + 4 = 6$, $1 + 3 = 4$, etc.

3.6.2 Factors, Multiples, and Primes

Counting numbers are the set of numbers that we use to learn how to count: 1, 2, 3, 4, 5, and so on. They are also called natural numbers or positive integers. Some of these numbers can be expressed as a multiplication of other counting numbers, which are called **factors** of that number. For example, the three sets of factors of 12 are 2 and 6, 3 and 4, and 1 and 12.

Likewise, a number can have an infinite number of **multiples**, which are the numbers obtained when the number is multiplied by integers. For example, the multiples of 3 are . . . , –9, –6, –3, 0, 3, 6, 9, . . .

A **prime** number is not divisible by any positive number except 1 and itself. The first several prime numbers are 2, 3, 5, 7, 11, 13, 17, and 19—no positive numbers divide into any of these numbers.

EXAMPLE 3.4

What are the next three prime numbers after 19?

SOLUTION 3.4

23, 29, 31. We know that none of the even numbers can be prime, so we just try to factor each of the natural numbers that are greater than 19 and odd: 21, 23, 25, 27, 29, 31. If any is factorable it cannot be prime.

The only even prime number is 2, which is a factor of all the other even numbers.

3.6.3 Composite Numbers and Prime Factorization

All non-prime numbers are called **composite** numbers, and they may be divisible by several numbers. For example, the number 4 is the first composite number, and it is divisible by 1, 2, and 4 because $2 \times 2 = 4$, and $1 \times 4 = 4$. All even numbers (except 2, which is prime) are divisible by 2, so all even numbers are composite numbers.

The composite factors of a composite number can themselves be factored, and this factoring can be performed over and over until there are no more composite factors. This is the operation called **prime factorization**—when all of the factors of the original number are prime numbers.

EXAMPLE 3.5

What are all of the prime factors of 24?

SOLUTION 3.5

2 and 3. If the number is even, the first prime factor must be 2, and then use 2 as a factor as many times as necessary, then try the other numbers from 3 up. $24 = 2 \times 12 = 2 \times (2 \times 6) = 2 \times 2 \times 2 \times (2 \times 3)$, so the prime factors are 2 and 3. No other prime numbers divide evenly into 24.

3.7 FRACTIONS, DECIMALS, AND PERCENTAGES

3.7.1 Overview and Vocabulary

Decimals, fractions, and percentages are all closely related. For example, to say that 5 is half of 10 can also be represented as $.50 \times 10$, $\frac{1}{2} \times 10$, or 50% of 10. This chapter discusses each of these types of calculations. The information presented in this section is preliminary to discussing dimensional analysis, which is presented in Section 3.10.1.

Values between the integers on the number line represent **fractions** of the space between two integers. The parts of the fraction are the **numerator** (on the top) and the **denominator** (on the bottom).

All fractions can be converted into **decimals** by simply dividing the numerator by the denominator. Rational decimals either **terminate**, such as $\frac{1}{2} = .5$, or **repeat**, such as $\frac{1}{3} = .33\overline{3}$. The bar over the last 3 indicates that the 3 is repeated forever. Sometimes the repeating part of the decimal is more than just the last number. For example, any fraction with 7 in the denominator is a decimal with a group of several repeating numbers, such as $\frac{1}{7} = 0.142857\overline{142857}$. Sometimes it may not be easy to see the repeat pattern; here, it didn't occur until the seventh decimal place.

Fractions are **reducible** if the numerator and denominator have factors in common that can cancel out. For example, $\frac{16}{24}$ can be reduced because 2 is a common factor (since both parts are even numbers): $\frac{16}{24} = \frac{2 \times 8}{2 \times 12} = \frac{8}{12}$. But the same is true for $\frac{8}{12} = \frac{2 \times 4}{2 \times 6} = \frac{4}{6}$, and yet again, $\frac{4}{6} = \frac{2 \times 2}{2 \times 3} = \frac{2}{3}$. How much easier would this have been if we recognized that 8 was a common factor in the first place: $\frac{16}{24} = \frac{8 \times 2}{8 \times 3} = \frac{2}{3}$.

The word *decimal* comes from the Latin word that means "10." Our counting system as well as our monetary system are based on the number 10. Decimals indicate parts of units, with placeholders of tenths, hundredths, thousandths, and so on. The decimals appear after a decimal point (.) and get smaller as the numbers go to the right, starting at tenths, then hundredths, thousandths, etc. Note that there is no corresponding "unit" designation after the decimal point.

A **mixed number** consists of an integer part and a fractional or decimal part. For example, the mixed number $17\frac{2}{3}$ is read as "seventeen and two-thirds," and the mixed number 365.421 is usually read as "three hundred sixty-five point four, two, one." Often the decimal portion is read as a whole number (421 here) with the designation of the smallest measure (thousandths); thus, this can also be read as "three hundred sixty-five and four hundred twenty-one thousandths."

To convert decimals to fractions, just divide the numbers by the smallest decimal measure, which is thousandths here. For example, $.421 = \dfrac{421}{1000}$, which may not necessarily be reducible.

Fractions and decimals can be converted to **percentages**. The word *percent* comes from *per hundred* because "cent" refers to 100 (100 cents in a dollar, 100 years in a century, etc.). So a percentage is just a way to express a fraction with 100 as the denominator. In fact, the percent sign (%) came into use as a shorthand for 1/100, with the two 0s in the % sign being the two 0s in the number 100.

To convert a fraction to a percentage, convert it first to a decimal. To convert a decimal to a percentage, the decimal movement is to the right. For example, .23 is 23%, .675 is 67.5%, and .04 is 4%.

Hint: If you remember that .50 is 50%, you shouldn't get confused about which direction to move the decimal point.

Converting percentages to decimals just involves dropping the percent sign and moving the decimal point in the percentage two places to the left: two places because hundredths has two placeholders, to the left because the decimal equivalent is 100 times smaller than the percentage number. Confusion may arise when you have to fill in "phantom" places with zeros, such as in 3%, which equals .03, or when the percentage is itself a decimal, such as 1.2%, which is .012. But the rule doesn't change—move the decimal point two places to the left when converting percentages to decimals.

To convert a percentage to a fraction, drop the percent sign and multiply by $\dfrac{1}{100}$. Therefore, 20% means $20 \times \dfrac{1}{100} = \dfrac{20}{100} = \dfrac{1}{5}$, and 100% means $100 \times \dfrac{1}{100} = \dfrac{100}{100} = 1$, the whole thing.

EXAMPLE 3.6

Revise once again.

The batting average for a baseball player is expressed as the decimal equivalent (rounded to three decimal places) of the percentage of base hits to the number of times at bat (not counting walks, sacrifices, or being hit by the ball). Therefore, at a rookie's first time at bat, he can end up with a batting average of .000 if he doesn't get a hit or 1.000 if he does get a hit. (That is where the expression "batting 1000," which means "perfect," comes from.) For the rest of a player's career, the batting average is somewhere between these extremes.

a. The scoreboard indicates that the third batter's average is .250. After this time at bat, his batting average changes to .235. Did he make a hit?

    b. Juan has been at bat 55 times, and his batting average is .291. How many base hits has he made?

    c. If he made no base hits in the next game but was at bat three times, what would his batting average be?

SOLUTION 3.6

    a. No. If he made a hit, his batting average would increase.

    b. 16. Batting average $= \dfrac{\text{base hits}}{\text{number of times at bat}} = \dfrac{\text{base hits}}{55} = .291$. Therefore the number of base hits is .291(55), which rounds to 16.

    c. .276. Batting average $= \dfrac{\text{base hits}}{\text{number of times at bat}} = \dfrac{16}{58} = .276$.

3.7.2 Fractions

3.7.2a Multiplying and Dividing Fractions

This section and the next one on addition and subtraction of fractions are brief primers on operations on fractions. **Multiplication of fractions** is the easiest of these operations, so let's start with that. Division of fractions is just like multiplication.

Generally, when you multiply two or more fractions, you multiply the numerators to get the numerator of the answer, and then you multiply the denominators to get the denominator of the answer.

Multiplication of fractions is simplified by using **cancellation**, which is canceling the same factors in the numerator and denominator, as shown in Section 3.7.1 in the discussion of reducible fractions. Any factor in the numerator of a fraction that is a multiple of a value that is in the denominator of the fraction can be canceled by dividing that common value into both until it cannot be reduced any further.

For example, $\dfrac{24}{35} \times \dfrac{5}{36} = \dfrac{12 \times 2}{35} \times \dfrac{5}{12 \times 3} = \dfrac{2}{5 \times 7} \times \dfrac{5}{3} = \dfrac{2}{7} \times \dfrac{1}{3} = \dfrac{2}{21}$. In this example, 12 is a common factor of 24 in the numerator and 36 in the denominator, and 5 is a common factor of 5 in the numerator and 35 in the denominator. If, instead of 12 being recognized as a common factor the common factor used was 6, it would be obvious that the remaining numerator and denominator would be even and thus have 2 as a common factor. Cancellation might take a few easy steps—but it's better than multiplying lots of numbers out unnecessarily. A lot of cancellation can be done mentally.

The important part of cancellation is that the common factor must be a factor in the numerator *and* the denominator, and you can cancel it only once. This procedure is also called **simplifying the fraction**.

Multiplication of **mixed numbers** that have an integer part and a fraction part often is easier if you convert the mixed numbers to improper fractions. **Improper fractions** are fractions with a numerator greater than the denominator, such as $\frac{3}{2}$. The method for the conversion is essentially to convert the whole number part into a fraction with the same denominator as the fraction part and then add this result to the fraction. Thus, $3\frac{1}{4} = \frac{12}{4} + \frac{1}{4} = \frac{13}{4}$. The middle step of this conversion is usually incorporated into a one-step procedure by just multiplying the whole number by the denominator and adding it to the numerator to get the numerator of the improper fraction: $3\frac{1}{4} = \frac{12+1}{4} = \frac{13}{4}$, where the middle part is done mentally.

Division of fractions is the same as multiplying by the reciprocal (fraction formed by switching the numerator and denominator). This is easy to remember if you think of dividing, let's say, a dozen doughnuts between two hungry football players—it's the same as multiplying 12 by the reciprocal of 2, or $12 \div 2 = 12 \times \frac{1}{2} = 6$. Therefore, to divide by a fraction, just flip it over and multiply. Remember to convert any mixed number to an improper fraction first. For example,

$$2\frac{6}{7} \div 1\frac{3}{7} = \frac{20}{7} \div \frac{10}{7} = \frac{20}{7} \times \frac{7}{10} = \frac{2(10) \times 7}{7 \times 10} = \frac{2 \times 1}{1 \times 1} = \frac{2}{1} = 2$$

Whew! That example seems like a lot of math because it involves knowing not only to convert mixed numbers to improper fractions, and knowing to use the reciprocal of the divisor, but also factoring and canceling. However, many of the steps should have been done mentally, so actually there would be only one step written out before getting the answer.

3.7.2b Adding and Subtracting Fractions

This section is just a brief primer on the basics of adding and subtracting fractions.

The most important rule about **adding or subtracting fractions** is that the denominators of the terms must be the *same*. Then you simply add or subtract the numerators and keep the denominators the same. For example, $\frac{1}{7} + \frac{4}{7} = \frac{5}{7}$ and $\frac{7}{8} - \frac{2}{8} = \frac{5}{8}$.

If the denominators are not the same, you must find the **common denominator**, which is based on two facts that we will use again in dimensional analysis and unit conversion, presented in Section 3.10.1.

1. Any number divided by itself equals 1.

2. Multiplication by 1 doesn't change the value.

For example, $\frac{1}{7} + \frac{2}{5} = \frac{1}{7}\left(\frac{5}{5}\right) + \frac{2}{5}\left(\frac{7}{7}\right) = \frac{5}{35} + \frac{14}{35} = \frac{19}{35}$. In this calculation, the common denominator of 35 was found by multiplying the denominators together, which works every time. Then each term is multiplied by a fraction with the same numerator and denominator (so it is equal to 1 and doesn't change the value of the term) so that the denominator will equal the common denominator. Thus, the term with 7 in the denominator is multiplied by $\left(\frac{5}{5}\right)$ and the term with 5 in the denominator is multiplied by $\left(\frac{7}{7}\right)$.

The most efficient common denominator is known as the **lowest common denominator** (LCD), which is the lowest number all denominators can divide into. For example, to add $\frac{5}{27} + \frac{7}{54}$, a common denominator is, of course, 27×54, but the *lowest* common denominator is just 54. Both 27 and 54 divide evenly into 54, or said another way, both 27 and 54 are factors of 54. Then we have $\frac{5}{27} + \frac{7}{54} = \frac{5}{27}\left(\frac{2}{2}\right) + \frac{7}{54} = \frac{10}{54} + \frac{7}{54} = \frac{17}{54}$. Subtraction of fractions is done the same way: $\frac{5}{27} - \frac{7}{54} = \frac{5}{27}\left(\frac{2}{2}\right) - \frac{7}{54} = \frac{10}{54} - \frac{7}{54} = \frac{3}{54} = \frac{1}{18}$. Notice that the answer here is simplified at the end because 3 is a common factor of the numerator and denominator, so it can be canceled.

3.8 POWERS

Powers have to do with multiplication. They are a shorthand for repeated factors. **Exponents** indicate the power, or the number of repeated factors. We can write $2 \times 2 \times 2 \times 2 \times 2 \times 2 \times 2 \times 2$ as 2^8, which we say is "2 to the eighth power." The 8 is an exponent and the 2 is called a **base**.

2^8 means there are eight 2's multiplied together. This is not the same as 2 multiplied by itself eight times—if you count, there are only seven "×" signs.

Two particular powers are quite important: 2 and 3. An exponent of 2 is almost always called **squared** rather than "to the second power," and an exponent of 3 is almost always called **cubed** rather than "to the third power." These names derive from the geometry of squares and cubes, as shown in Chapter 5, Sections 5.5.5 and 5.11.1e, respectively. Exponents are used a lot in algebra, the topic of Chapter 4. We discuss the basics of exponents here.

The powers of 0 and 1 are special. Anything to the 0 power equals 1. *Anything.* So $10^0 = 1$ and $524^0 = 1$ also. Anything to the first power is itself. That makes sense from the definition of power. So $10{,}524^1 = 10{,}524$, and $0^1 = 0$.

0^0 is indeterminate because 0^0 can't equal 1 and 0 at the same time. (The value of 1 is due to $n^0 = 1$ for all values of n, and the value of 0 is due to the definition of powers of 0, or $0^n = 0$ for all n.) The word **indeterminate** is used in math when something has one value at one time and also has another value at the same time.

3.8.1 Common Powers

To save time during the test, become familiar with the following powers, but don't necessarily take the time to memorize them because you can always figure them out by multiplication or by using the online calculator.

$2^2 = 4$	$2^3 = 8$	$2^4 = 16$	$2^5 = 32$	$2^6 = 64$	$3^2 = 9$	$3^3 = 27$
$4^2 = 16$	$5^2 = 25$	$6^2 = 36$	$7^2 = 49$	$8^2 = 64$	$9^2 = 81$	$10^2 = 100$

3.8.2 Properties of Powers Rules

1. Product of powers property: To multiply two quantities with the same base, add their exponents.

$$2^2 \times 2^3 = 2^{2+3} = 2^5$$

2. Power of a power property: To find a power of a power, multiply the exponents.

$$\left(2^2\right)^3 = 2^{2 \times 3} = 2^6$$

3. Power of a product property: To raise a product to a power, raise each factor to that power.

$$(2 \times 3)^2 = 2^2 \times 3^2$$

4. Quotient of powers property: To divide two quantities with the same base, subtract the exponents.

$$\frac{2^5}{2^2} = 2^{5-2} = 2^3$$

5. Power of a quotient property: To raise a quotient to a power, raise each factor to that power.

$$\left(\frac{2^3}{3^2}\right)^4 = \frac{\left(2^3\right)^4}{\left(3^2\right)^4} = \frac{2^{12}}{3^8}$$

6. Negative exponent property: Negative exponents are the reciprocals of the positive exponents.

$$2^{-3} = \frac{1}{2^3}$$

The examples for each of the six power rules involve the number 2 (and 3) as bases. This is a helpful way to remember the rules because the lower powers of 2 (and 3) are familiar to you. If you momentarily forget what to do with the exponents in, for example, rules 1 and 2, just use 2 as a base: $2^2 \times 2^3 = 2^{2+3} = 2^5$, which is the same as $4 \times 8 = 32$, and $\left(2^2\right)^3 = 2^{2 \times 3} = 2^6$, which is the same as $4^3 = 64$, to remind you whether to add or multiply the exponents.

3.8.3 Scientific Notation and Orders of Magnitude

Scientific notation makes working with very large and very small numbers much simpler. Scientific notation uses powers of 10 to rewrite numbers that are either too big or too small to be conveniently written as decimals. A number in scientific notation consists of the product of a number with only one digit before the decimal point times a power of 10. To make the numerical part have only one digit before the decimal point, the existing decimal point usually has to be moved left or right. The power of 10 part indicates how many places the decimal point was moved from its original position. There are two steps to convert to scientific notation:

1. Move the existing decimal point so that it is after the first digit. In scientific notation, the number part is a decimal whose absolute value is between 1 and 10 (including 1 but not including 10).

2. Count the number of spaces the decimal point was moved. This is the power of 10. If the decimal point is moved to the left, the power of 10 is positive; if the decimal point is moved to the right, the power of 10 is negative.

For example, we can write the distance from Earth to the Sun, which is 93,000,000 miles, as

$$9_\uparrow 3000000._\uparrow = 9.3 \times 10^7,$$

where the little arrows show that the original decimal point at the end of the whole number 93,000,000 is moved seven spaces to the left to go between the 9 and 3 since the absolute value of the number part must be <10.

Likewise, very small numbers such as the weight of an electron, which is .00055 atomic mass units (1 amu is roughly the mass of a proton or neutron), can be written as

$$._\uparrow 0005_\uparrow 5 = 5.5 \times 10^{-4},$$

where, again, the little arrows show that the original decimal point is moved, this time four spaces to the right to go after the first 5 since the number part must be <10.

One advantage of having numbers in scientific notation is that they make comparisons of **orders of magnitude** easy to see. If numbers differ by one order of magnitude, one of them is about ten times the quantity of the other. If values differ by two orders of magnitude, they differ by a factor of about $10^2 = 100$. So when comparing very large or very small numbers, comparing the powers of 10, even ignoring the number part of the notation, gives a good idea of how much the two numbers differ.

For example, if you want to compare the distance from Earth to the Sun to the distance of a light-year represented in miles, we could compare 93,000,000 miles to 5,859,000,000,000 miles, or 9.3×10^7 to 5.859×10^{12}, from which we can see that the light-year is 5 orders of magnitude (or the order of $10^5 = 10,000$ times) greater than Earth's distance from the Sun. Note that to be precise, the real answer is $6.3 \times 10^5 = 63,000$, but difference in the order of magnitude, 5 (the exponent of 10), gives the scale of the difference.

In general, an increase of n orders of magnitude is the equivalent of multiplying a quantity by 10^n. Thus, 1234 is one order of magnitude larger than 123.4, which in turn is one order of magnitude larger than 12.34.

Similarly, a decrease of n orders of magnitude is the equivalent of multiplying a quantity by 10^{-n}. Thus, .5678 is one order of magnitude smaller than 5.678, which in turn is one order of magnitude smaller than 56.78.

Note that 942 and 672 are on the same order of magnitude (2), even though they are not equal.

3.9 RADICAL EXPRESSIONS

Radicals are the inverse of powers. Remember that the inverse of an operation "undoes" the operation. Whereas powers are indicated by an integer exponent, radical expressions are indicated by a radical sign, $\sqrt[n]{\ }$, where n can be any positive number, or a fractional exponent, such as in $4^{\frac{1}{2}}$ or $(1-a)^{\frac{2}{3}}$, as explained below. Therefore, if $4^4 = 64$, then $\sqrt[3]{64} = 4$.

The radical expression $\sqrt[k]{a}$, expressed as the kth root of a, consists of the **radical**, $\sqrt{\ }$; the **radicand**, a; and the **index**, k. Square roots are often indicated by a radical without an index.

For even or odd k, if a is positive, the value of the radical is positive: $\sqrt{16} = 4$ and $\sqrt[3]{27} = 3$. If k is odd and a is negative, the value of the radical is negative: $\sqrt[3]{-8} = -2$, since $(-2) \times (-2) \times (-2) = -8$. However, if a is negative, any root for which the index k is an even number will produce an imaginary answer involving $i = \sqrt{-1}$, as was discussed in Section 3.2.2 on imaginary numbers; for example, $\sqrt{-9} = 3i$. If $a = 0$, the value of the radical is 0.

A **fractional exponent** indicates a root, with the denominator being the root and the numerator being the power. For example, $4^{\frac{1}{2}} = \sqrt{4^1} = \sqrt{4} = 2$ and $8^{\frac{2}{3}} = \sqrt[3]{8^2} = \sqrt[3]{64} = 4$.

3.9.1 Common Radicals

To save time during the test, become familiar with the following radicals, but don't necessarily take the time to memorize them because you can always use your calculator. The square roots that equal whole numbers are square roots of **perfect squares**, defined as numbers for which the square root is an integer.

$$\sqrt{4} = 2 \quad \sqrt{9} = 3 \quad \sqrt{16} = 4 \quad \sqrt{25} = 5 \quad \sqrt{36} = 6 \quad \sqrt{49} = 7 \quad \sqrt{64} = 8 \quad \sqrt{81} = 9 \quad \sqrt{100} = 10$$

$$\sqrt[3]{8} = 2 \quad \sqrt[3]{27} = 3 \quad \sqrt[4]{16} = 2 \quad \sqrt[5]{32} = 2 \quad \sqrt[6]{64} = 2$$

The square roots of numbers between the perfect squares 1, 4, 9, 16, 25, 36, 49, 64, 81, and 100 are not integers and in fact are irrational numbers.

3.9.2 Simplifying Radical Expressions

The rules for simplifying radical expressions are based on the inverses of the rules for powers.

1. Product of roots property: To multiply two quantities with the same index, multiply their radicands.

$$\sqrt{20} \times \sqrt{5} = \sqrt{20 \times 5} = \sqrt{100} = 10$$

2. Root of a product property: If the radicand can be factored, the root of the radicand is equal to the product of the roots of the factors. The indices must match.

$$\sqrt{36} = \sqrt{4 \times 9} = \sqrt{4} \times \sqrt{9} = 2 \times 3 = 6$$

$$\sqrt{200} = \sqrt{100 \times 2} = \sqrt{100} \times \sqrt{2} = 10\sqrt{2}$$

Or a combination of rule 1 and rule 2:

$$\sqrt[4]{32} \times \sqrt[4]{8} = \sqrt[4]{256} = \sqrt[4]{16 \times 16} = \sqrt[4]{16} \times \sqrt[4]{16} = 2 \times 2 = 4$$

3. Multiplication of radicals: Use the commutative property to rewrite the multiplication.

$$3\sqrt{2} \times 4\sqrt{5} = (3 \times 4)(\sqrt{2} \times \sqrt{5}) = 12\sqrt{10}$$

4. Quotient of roots property: To divide two quantities with the same index, divide their radicands.

$$\frac{\sqrt{50}}{\sqrt{2}} = \sqrt{\frac{50}{2}} = \sqrt{25} = 5$$

5. Root of a quotient property: If the radicand can be written as the division of two numbers, the root is equal to the quotient of the roots of the numerator and denominator. The indices must match.

$$\sqrt[3]{\frac{8}{27}} = \frac{\sqrt[3]{8}}{\sqrt[3]{27}} = \frac{2}{3}$$

6. Division of radicals (the indices must match):

$$\frac{8\sqrt{15}}{4\sqrt{5}} = \frac{8}{4} \times \frac{\sqrt{15}}{\sqrt{5}} = 2\sqrt{3}$$

7. Addition and subtraction of radicals: To add or subtract radicals, the radicands and indices have to be the same.

$$6\sqrt{2} + 3\sqrt{2} = 9\sqrt{2}$$

but $\qquad\qquad 3\sqrt{2} - 2\sqrt{5}$ cannot be combined

By combining the rules, many radical expressions can be simplified. For example, even though the expression $3\sqrt{2} + 5\sqrt{32}$ looks at first to be an addition of unlike radicals, which cannot be done (according to rule 7), it actually can be simplified by using rule 2 and then rule 7:

$$3\sqrt{2} + 5\sqrt{32}$$
$$= 3\sqrt{2} + 5\sqrt{16 \times 2}$$
$$= 3\sqrt{2} + 5\sqrt{16} \times \sqrt{2}$$
$$= 3\sqrt{2} + 5 \times 4 \times \sqrt{2}$$
$$= 3\sqrt{2} + 20\sqrt{2}$$
$$= 23\sqrt{2}$$

Here, every step is shown, but most steps are done mentally. Notice on the third and fourth lines that the multiplication is done before the addition, following PEMDAS (see Section 3.3).

EXAMPLE 3.7

Simplify the expression $\sqrt{15} \times \sqrt{12}$. Leave your answer in radical form.

SOLUTION 3.7

$6\sqrt{5}$. The product of two radicals equals the radical of the product of the radicands, which then can be factored: $\sqrt{15} \times \sqrt{12} = \sqrt{15 \times 12} = \sqrt{180} = \sqrt{36 \times 5} = \sqrt{36} \times \sqrt{5} = 6\sqrt{5}$.

3.9.3 Approximating Radicals

We know or are familiar with the values of many rational radicals, such as $\sqrt{4}$ and $\sqrt{49}$, but what about the others, which may be irrational or rational, such as $\sqrt{7}$ or $\sqrt{110}$? Sure, we can use our calculators to get the value, but we should know enough to at least approximate the values. This approximation is based on the fact that we can establish a range of values from the "perfect" radicals above and below the radical of interest. "Perfect" radicals means radicals of **perfect squares**, which are numbers that have whole number roots, such as 1, 4, 9, 16, 25, and so on.

We can approximate $\sqrt{7}$ by knowing it must be between $\sqrt{4}$ and $\sqrt{9}$, which, of course, equal 2 and 3. So our first approximation of $\sqrt{7}$ is that it is greater than 2 but less than 3. If we want to be even more specific, we can select a best-guess answer to the tenths place by surmising that since 7 is closer to the upper limit 9 than it is to the lower limit 4, $\sqrt{7}$ is closer to 3 than it is to 2. In fact, 7 is $\frac{3}{5}$, or 0.6 of the way closer to 9, so let's use 2.6 as our first guess. We calculate $(2.6)^2 = 6.76$ to see how close we are, and then we calculate $(2.7)^2 = 7.29$. By using this best-guess method, we try $2.65^2 = 7.02$ and $2.64^2 = 6.97$. So we can say that, to the nearest tenth, $\sqrt{7} \approx 2.6$.

3.10 QUANTITY

Any **quantity** has two parts: the numerical part and the unit, or dimensional, part. For example 8 hours has the numerical part 8 and the unit *hours*. Often, the quantity has the unit as a rate, such as manufacturing 24 widgets in an 8-hour day, written as $\frac{24 \text{ widgets}}{8 \text{ hours}}$, which simplifies to $\frac{3 \text{ widgets}}{1 \text{ hour}}$, or 3 widgets per hour.

3.10.1 Dimensional Analysis

Dimensional analysis allows **unit conversion** to an equivalent unit of measure based on known equivalencies such as 1 minute = 60 seconds, 1 foot = 12 inches, 1 pound = 16 ounces, and so on. Dimensional analysis sets these equivalences up as ratios (or fractions) that equal 1. Thus, when any dimension is multiplied by any of these equivalences, the value is unchanged. The rules discussed earlier in Section 3.7.2 on fractions are also the rules used in dimensional analysis.

A typical problem in dimensional analysis asks "How many seconds are there in a week?" To find the answer, figure out what unit(s) you want to end up with in the answer. In this case, for example, it is seconds per week, or $\frac{\text{seconds}}{\text{week}}$. Write down the dimensional ratios you know that relate to the problem. (You may need to look up a few conversion factors.) There are two methods to start the problem.

For the first method, pick a starting ratio that you know as a fact. In this case, you may start with the fact that 1 week has 7 days, which can be written as either $\frac{1 \text{ week}}{7 \text{ days}}$ or $\frac{7 \text{ days}}{1 \text{ week}}$. Both of these equal 1, so choose the one that allows you to cancel out any units you don't want and still be left with "week" in the denominator. Continue in this manner until you are left with only the units you do want. The unit conversion here is from minutes to weeks. The solution for this problem looks like this:

$$\frac{7 \text{ days}}{1 \text{ week}} \times \frac{24 \text{ hours}}{1 \text{ day}} \times \frac{60 \text{ minutes}}{1 \text{ hour}} \times \frac{60 \text{ seconds}}{1 \text{ minute}}$$

$$= \frac{7 \times 24 \times 60 \times 60 \text{ seconds}}{1 \text{ week}} = 604,800 \frac{\text{seconds}}{\text{week}}$$

In the second method, you start with the ratio $\frac{60 \text{ seconds}}{1 \text{ minute}}$, and the math goes in reverse with the same result.

3.10.2 Quantitative Reasoning and Problem Solving

The example of finding how many seconds in a week shows quantitative reasoning. **Quantitative reasoning** is defined as using basic mathematical skills, understanding elementary mathematical concepts, and having the ability to model and solve problems with quantitative methods. In short, quantitative reasoning is equivalent to "doing math correctly." In fact, **problem solving** can be thought of similarly.

This entire book, and in fact all of the math that you encounter, involves quantitative reasoning and problem-solving skills. Even though a person can be taught the various algorithms for doing math, the skill to solve any math problem can be acquired only by experience. Practice, practice, practice!

EXAMPLE 3.8

Charene opened a food truck business to sell wraps on the street. On day 2, her business earned $112. On day 5, the business earned $367. Charene assumes that the earnings will continue to increase at the same rate. How much will the business earn on day 10?

SOLUTION 3.8

$792. Determine the daily increase in the first three days (days 2 to 5) by calculating $\frac{\$367 - \$112}{3} = \$85$ per day. Then from day 5 to day 10 (5 days), the total increase is 5($85) = $425. Added to the income on day 5, day 10's earnings are thus $367 + $425 = $792.

Example 3.8 involves an arithmetic sequence, which is described in full in Section 9.1.1. But it is solved here by using reasoning skills alone.

3.11 MEASUREMENT

We already have encountered measurement units in the examples in this chapter. Basically, there are two systems of units in use in the United States: (1) the **US standard** (or customary) system and (2) the **metric system**, also known as the International System of Units (SI). The metric system is used outside of the United States and in the scientific, medical, and international trade communities; the US standard system is the primary system used in the United States.

3.11.1 Measurement Equivalences

Since the system in common use in the United States is the US standard system, let's start with that. The US system is based on a British system that dates back to centuries before the United States even became a nation. The conversion numbers within the US system can be unwieldy and not necessarily easy to remember (for example, 1 mile = 5280 feet, 1 yard = 3 feet, 1 foot = 12 inches).

Measurement is basically of three kinds:

- Length, such as inch, foot, yard, mile.

- Weight, such as ounce, pound, and ton.

- Volume, such as cubic inches, cubic feet, and cubic yards; also, teaspoons, tablespoons, cups, pints, quarts, and gallons (the latter are used for liquid measures as well as for agricultural products, such as a quart of strawberries).

Volume (the amount of space an object takes up) is technically different from capacity (the amount of space that is available), although the two terms are sometimes used interchangeably.

The metric system is based on the number 10.

- Length, based on the meter.

- Weight, based on the gram.

- Volume, based on the cubic meter (volume) and the liter (capacity).

The names of these basic units are then combined with prefixes that tell how many times 10 the value is:

- milli-, meaning one-thousandth.

- centi-, meaning one-hundredth.

- kilo-, meaning times one thousand.

- mega-, meaning times one million.

- giga-, meaning times one billion.

Measurements in the metric system consist of combining the prefixes with the basic units, such as centimeters, kilograms, or milliliters. Some common metric combinations are

- millimeter = one-thousandth of a meter

- centimeter = one-hundredth of a meter

- kilometer = a thousand meters

- cubic centimeter is the same as one milliliter = one-thousandth of a liter

- milligram = one-thousandth of a gram

- kilogram = one thousand grams

The important thing is that you have a sense of the size of these units, such as knowing that the length of a piece of writing paper should be measured in inches (or maybe feet) rather than yards or miles. Or that the weight of a baseball is measured in ounces (or fractions of a pound), but never in tons, and that your weight can be measured in kilograms (a kilogram is a little more than two pounds). Or that a bathtub has a capacity of about 200 liters (a liter is a little more than a quart).

A good way to get a sense of metric units is to become aware of the metric units for the every-day things you use or food you eat. Almost everything sold in the United States has its metric equivalent written on the package. Some examples may help in remembering metric units:

- Length

  ▸ A meter is a little more than a yard.

  ▸ A millimeter is the size of a pin head.

  ▸ A centimeter is less than four-tenths of an inch, since a common conversion is 1 inch = 2.54 centimeters.

  ▸ A kilometer is about five-eighths of a mile, or a little more than a half mile.

- Weight

  ▸ A gram is about the weight of a paper clip.

  ▸ A milligram is so tiny that you cannot see it; capsule pills often contain 1000 milligrams.

  ▸ A kilogram is a little more than 2 pounds, which is the weight of a pineapple, for example.

- Volume

  ▸ A liter is about a quart.

  ▸ A cubic centimeter is about the size of a sugar cube.

3.11.2 Precision and Accuracy

Precision and accuracy are often confused with one another. The difference between them is subtle but important. They both have to do with comparison of measured values.

- **Precision** compares measured values to each other.

- **Accuracy** compares measured values to a true value.

An excellent way to remember the difference between precision and accuracy involves a bull's-eye target. The arrows of an *accurate* archer fall very near the bull's-eye. However, an archer can be precise and not accurate. The arrows of a *precise* archer all fall in the same place, even if it is far from the bull's-eye.

Another example is a field-goal kicker in American football who always kicks to the left of the goal posts instead of between them. He is precise, but not accurate! His team wants him to be precise *and* accurate.

As a general rule, the **degree of accuracy** is a half-unit on each side of a measure. So if you are measuring in inches, the degree of accuracy is a half-inch on either side of your measurement. Therefore, degrees of accuracy vary according to the instrument and scale of the measurement.

3.11.3 Rounding

Rounding an answer comes up frequently with decimals, although any number can be rounded. As an example, when something costs $24.95, we often say it costs $25. In this case, we rounded off to the nearest unit (dollar).

The method for **rounding** is to look at the next digit after the place value that we want to round. If it is less than 5, we just drop that digit and all the digits to the right (inserting zeros if necessary). If it is 5 or more, we add "1" to the digit to be rounded and again drop the digits to the right. This method works whether the number is a whole number or a decimal number. You just have to know which digit is being rounded.

For example, 1,346 rounded to the nearest hundred would be 1,300 because we look at the 4—the digit to the right of the "hundreds" digit 3. Since 4 < 5, we leave the 3 alone and fill in zeros for the rest of the placeholders. It is important to look only at the number one digit to the right of the one to be rounded and ignore the others to the right of it. A common mistake in rounding off is to start at the rightmost digit instead of the digit just one place to the right of the one being rounded.

For example, to round 1,346 to the nearest hundred, if we started at the 6 and rounded the 4 up to 5 (since 6 > 5), we would have 1,350, and then the answer we would get for the nearest hundred would be 1,400, not the correct answer of 1,300.

When dividing decimals, carry out the division to the next digit after the one to be rounded. For example, if we were dividing $125.32 by 7, the answer, according to the calculator, would be $17.90285714; however, because this is money we would look only at $17.902 (ignoring the other numbers) and round to the nearest cent, or $17.90. If the question had asked for the answer to the nearest dollar, we would carry the division only to $17.9 and then round up to $18.

Be careful when rounding, though. If you round early in a calculation, the answer may end up being way off. In fact, these type of errors are so common that they have a name, **rounding errors**. A well-known example of this type of error is provided by the Vancouver stock exchange index. When it began in 1982, the index was given a value of 1000.000. After 22 months of computing the index and rounding to three decimal places at each trade, which occurred about 3,000 times a day, the index stood at 524.881 despite the fact that its true value should have been 1009.811. Needless to say, that stock exchange index is no longer in existence.

EXAMPLE 3.9

Round 245.829 to

Rev.

    a. the nearest hundredth

    b. the nearest tenth

    c. the nearest hundred

SOLUTION

Look only at the digit to the right of the one being rounded to get

    a. 245.83

    b. 245.8

    c. 200

3.11.4 Estimation

We already did some estimation when we discussed finding the square roots of numbers that aren't perfect (Section 3.9.3), so we have a general idea of what estimation means: a rough calculation of the value, number, or quantity. It is "good enough," "close enough," and works if you don't need the exact answer. However, it is useless if it has no valid basis or is too broad, such as, "I estimate the population of the city to be more than a thousand."

Often, estimation is based on rounding to the nearest hundred, thousand, and so on, and is expressed in terms such as "not more than," or "approximately."

Estimation is helpful when taking a test because, even using a calculator, mist~~~~ entering the data. If you have an estimation of what the answer should be—even ~~~~ park" estimation (in the vicinity of the correct answer)—you can catch errors b~~~~

Estimation is related to rounding. For example, if you want to buy 7 items that cost $2.~~~~ can quickly estimate the cost by rounding $2.95 to $3.00, and know that the total will be around $21.00. This is only one example of the usefulness of estimation. Now, the accuracy of an estimation is something else.

3.11.5 Absolute and Relative Error

Any measurement made with a measuring device is approximate. If you measure the same object two different times, the two measurements may vary, if only slightly. This variation, or uncertainty in measurement, is termed an error, but this error is not the same as a mistake. It does not mean that the answer is wrong. This error in measurement is a mathematical way to show the uncertainty in the measurement due to the measuring device. It is the difference between the result of the measurement and the true value, and it is usually very small.

Two types of error that are essential in the knowledge of the scientific world are absolute error and relative error. The difference between them is important.

Absolute error is the amount of physical error in a measurement. For example, let's say a yardstick is used to measure a given distance and the measurement is done rather hastily. However, it is still good to $\pm\frac{1}{8}$ inch, the smallest unit of measurement on that yardstick. This is the absolute error of that measurement, or the actual amount you could be "off," or mistaken by, in a measurement.

Relative error compares the absolute error against the size of the thing being measured. For example, an absolute error of one inch makes a bigger difference if the thing being measured is approximately 12 inches long than it does in a measurement of something that is approximately 120 feet long. In other words, relative error is an indication of how good a measurement is relative to the size of the thing being measured. The formula for relative error is the absolute error divided by the measurement. The **percent error** is the relative error expressed in terms of percentage.

For example, let's say that two students measure two different objects with a tape measure with the smallest unit of $\frac{1}{8}$ inch. That is the absolute error. One student measures the height of a room and gets a value of 9 feet. The other student measures the height of a small box and gets 9 inches. Clearly, the overall accuracy of the ceiling height is much better than that of the 9-inch box. The comparative accuracy of these measurements can be determined by looking at their relative error percentages:

The relative error percentage of the ceiling height is:

$$\left(\frac{1}{8} \text{ inch} \div 9 \text{ feet}\right) \div 100 = \left(\frac{1}{8} \div 9(12)\right) \div 100 = \left(\frac{1}{8} \times \frac{1}{108}\right) \div 100 \approx \frac{.001}{100} \approx .00001\%$$

The relative error of the box height is

$$\left(\frac{1}{8} \text{ inch} \div 9 \text{ inches}\right) \div 100 = \left(\frac{1}{8} \times \frac{1}{9}\right) \div 100 \approx \frac{.014}{100} \approx .00014\%$$

Clearly, the relative error in the ceiling height is considerably smaller than the relative error in the cylinder height even though the amount of absolute error $\left(\pm\frac{1}{8} \text{ inch}\right)$ is the same in both cases.

Note that the symbol $\approx$ (meaning "approximately equal to") is used in these calculations. That is because the values are rounded, and when rounded values are used in calculations the answer is not precise.

3.12 VECTORS AND MATRICES

3.12.1 Vectors

So far, we have worked with **scalar** quantities, which are quantities that have only magnitude. **Vectors** are quantities that have both magnitude and **direction**. Vectors go in only one direction, so they can be written as a column or row of numbers. Vectors are useful in translations (see Section 5.9.1), displacements, velocities, forces, and other quantities that depend on direction.

3.12.2 Matrices

A vector is a row (or column) of an array called a matrix (plural, matrices), which is a rectangular array of numbers. A matrix is denoted by square brackets around **elements**, or entries, which make up the matrix. A matrix is described by the number of rows (M) and columns (N) as an (M × N) matrix. Vectors are a subclass of matrices, so every vector is also a matrix. A vector is a 1-dimensional matrix, either a vertical vector (M × 1) or horizontal vector (1 × N).

A square matrix has as many rows as columns. For example,

$$\begin{bmatrix} 1 & 3 \\ 4 & 2 \end{bmatrix}$$

is a 2 × 2 matrix, meaning it has two rows and two columns. Its value is determined, not surprisingly, by evaluating its **determinant**, which has the same elements as the matrix, but now it is written between two vertical lines, not brackets, to indicate that it is being evaluated:

$$\begin{vmatrix} 1 & 3 \\ 4 & 2 \end{vmatrix}$$

Even though the determinant symbols look like absolute value signs, determinants are not absolute values, and their values can be negative.

A 2×2 determinant is evaluated by multiplying the elements in the main diagonal (upper left downward) and subtracting the value of the multiple of the other diagonal from the value from the first diagonal. This specific order, which numerically follows the elements in this example determinant, is important because we are subtracting, and subtraction is not associative—it makes a difference which value is subtracted from which value. The value for the determinant $\begin{vmatrix} 1 & 3 \\ 4 & 2 \end{vmatrix}$ is

$(1)(2) - (3)(4) = 2 - 10 = -8. \quad -10$

Start at the upper left corner. That will also be the order when we cross-multiply proportions in Section 4.2.3b.

3.12.3 Applications of Matrices

Matrix mathematics has many applications, among them a systematic way for mathematicians, scientists, and engineers to represent groups of equations, similar to what is presented in Section 4.2.7d in Chapter 4. Matrix arithmetic embedded in graphic processing algorithms, especially to render reflection and refraction, are mainstays in video games. For example, in the Cartesian x-y plane, the matrix $\begin{vmatrix} 0 & -1 \\ 1 & 0 \end{vmatrix}$ reflects an object vertically. In a video game, this would render the upside-down mirror image of a dungeon reflected in a lake. And computer animation is based on matrix mathematics.

Many internet and computer programming companies also use matrices as data structures to track user information, perform search queries, and manage databases. In the world of information security, many public key cryptosystems are designed to work with matrices over finite fields, in particular those that are designed with speed of decryption as a goal. In fact, one of the most important uses of matrices is encryption of message codes, including sensitive and private data. Matrices also are the base elements for robot movements.

So even though we are surrounded by applications of matrix mathematics, few of us recognize it or consciously apply it in our day-to-day lives. Section 4.2.7d in Chapter 4 shows how matrices are used to solve simultaneous equations.

Practice Exercises

1. The number 18

    (A) is real.

    (B) is complex.

    (C) can be written as a fraction.

    (D) All of the above descriptions are true.

2. A certain brand of canned soup usually sells for $1.99 a can. If they are on sale at 3 cans for $4.50, how much would a customer save on 24 cans?

    (A) $36.00

    (B) 49 cents

    (C) $11.76

    (D) $1.47

3. During the month of September, a certain farmer sold 4,837 cows, 7,952 chickens, and 1,848 more rabbits than chickens. If these are the only animals sold, how many animals did he sell in September? _____

4. Arrange the following fractions in order from smallest to largest: $\dfrac{17}{24}, \dfrac{27}{48}, \dfrac{7}{12}, \dfrac{2}{3}, \dfrac{5}{8}$.

    (A) $\dfrac{27}{48}, \dfrac{17}{24}, \dfrac{7}{12}, \dfrac{2}{3}, \dfrac{5}{8}$

    (B) $\dfrac{27}{48}, \dfrac{7}{12}, \dfrac{2}{3}, \dfrac{5}{8}, \dfrac{17}{24}$

    (C) $\dfrac{27}{48}, \dfrac{2}{3}, \dfrac{5}{8}, \dfrac{7}{12}, \dfrac{17}{24}$

    (D) $\dfrac{27}{48}, \dfrac{7}{12}, \dfrac{5}{8}, \dfrac{2}{3}, \dfrac{17}{24}$

5. Sixteen percent of the 300 people who showed up at a rally registered to vote that day. When election day came, 75% of those registered people actually voted. How many of these new registrants voted?

(A) 225

(B) 36

(C) 48

(D) 300

6. The positive square root of a real number is $\left\{ \begin{array}{c} \text{always} \\ \text{sometimes} \\ \text{never} \end{array} \right\}$ less than the number.

7. Express $\sqrt{-9} + 4i$ as a single term.

(A) $\sqrt{-11}$

(B) $7i$

(C) $\sqrt{-13}$

(D) They cannot be combined into a single term.

Solutions

1. (D) All of the above descriptions are true. The number 18 is real because it is an integer. It is complex because all real numbers can be thought of as complex numbers with $b = 0$. It is a fraction because all integers can be written as fractions with a denominator of 1.

2. (C) $11.76. At the original price, 24 cans would cost $47.76. At the sale price, the cost would be $\left(\dfrac{24}{3} \right) \times \$4.50 = \$36.00$. The savings is $11.76. Another way to calculate the sale price is to multiply the cost per can by 24: $\left(\dfrac{\$4.50}{3} \right) \times 24 = \$36.00$.

3. 22,589. Just add the number of animals, realizing that there are $(7,952 + 1,848)$ rabbits.

4. (D) $\dfrac{27}{48}, \dfrac{7}{12}, \dfrac{5}{8}, \dfrac{2}{3}, \dfrac{17}{24}$. Convert all of the fractions to their equivalents with the LCD of 48: $\dfrac{34}{48}, \dfrac{27}{48}, \dfrac{28}{48}, \dfrac{32}{48}, \dfrac{30}{48}$, respectively, which is $\dfrac{27}{48}, \dfrac{28}{48}, \dfrac{30}{48}, \dfrac{32}{48}, \dfrac{34}{48}$ in order from smallest to largest. Then just reduce these back to their lowest terms for the answer: $\dfrac{27}{48}, \dfrac{7}{12}, \dfrac{5}{8}, \dfrac{2}{3}, \dfrac{17}{24}$.

5. (B) 36. The number who actually voted was 75% of the 16% of the 300, which equals $(.75)(.16)(300) = 36$.

6. Sometimes. An example when this is true is $\sqrt{4} = 2$. An example when it is false is $\sqrt{\dfrac{1}{4}} = \dfrac{1}{2}$. Remember that the words "real number" mean any integers, fractions, terminating and repeating decimals, as well as negatives and positives.

7. (B) $7i$. $\sqrt{-9} = \sqrt{9 \times (-1)} = \sqrt{9} \times \sqrt{-1} = 3i$. Then $3i + 4i = 7i$.

Algebra 4

4.1 EXPRESSIONS

Algebra involves equations or inequalities, which can be thought of as the sentences of algebra. Equations, in turn, involve **expressions**, which are equivalent to phrases in any language. The difference between equations and expressions is the verb. Sentences must have verbs. The verbs in mathematical statements are the relation symbols. These statements or expressions are not given to you algebraically in many cases; instead, you are given information and you have to "translate" that information into expressions to make up the equations to solve problems.

Examples of expressions are "a number less than 15," and "7 less than a number." Neither of these expressions contains a verb so they are not equations. They can become equations, however, with the inclusion of a relation, such as "What number is 8 less than 15?" and "What value is 7 less than 24?" As shown below, these two equations are $x = 15 - 8$ and $y = 24 - 7$.

 Any letter (or even a word) can be used as the unknown in algebra.

4.1.1 Translating from Words to Algebra

The following list shows how words translate into symbols to write an algebraic expression. These are the more common words and phrases; the context of the sentence gives hints for others.

1. The words *is* (or any variation of it), *cost*, and *is the same as* mean equals and should be substituted by an equal sign (=).

2. The words *what* or *how much* (or a similar question) mean the unknown, so replace them with a variable—*x, y,* or whatever you choose. The equation you construct will find the value for this variable.

3. *Sum, plus, in all,* or *combined* mean addition (+).

4. *Difference, less than, how much more, exceeds,* or *minus* mean subtraction (–).

5. *Product, times, area,* or *of* (e.g., *half of*) mean multiplication (×).

6. *Quotient, distribute,* or *per* mean division (÷).

7. *Decreased by* often indicates subtraction (–).

8. *Increased by* often indicates addition (+).

9. *At least* indicates equal to or more than (≥).

10. *At most* indicates equal to or less than (≤).

Of course, *equals, less than,* and *more than* indicate +, <, and >, respectively.

As stated above, equations are expressions with a verb, so equations are complete sentences, just written in algebraic symbols with letters for the unknown quantities. For example, "What is the difference between 32 and 28?" translates into the equation $x = 32 - 28$? This same question could have been posed as "Chary needs 32 ounces of liquid for a recipe, but she has only 28. How many more ounces does she need?" The equation is the same, but more thinking is involved.

Equations can take information from more than one sentence in a problem. For example, "Jordan has 7 marbles. He gives 3 to a friend. How many marbles does Jordan have left?" These three sentences end up with one equation: $7 - 3 = m$, where m is the number of marbles Jordan has left.

Often the question in an algebraic problem asks, "What is . . . ?" "How many are . . . ?" "The amount left was . . . ?" and so forth. These all involve various forms of the word "is," which stands for the equal sign.

EXAMPLE 4.1

Cassandra wants to spend no more than $100 ordering shirts from an online company. The company charges a $5 shipping fee for any order and $15 per shirt. What is the inequality for all possible numbers of shirts x that Cassandra can buy?

SOLUTION 4.1

$5 + 15x \leq 100$. The words "no more than 100" translate into ≤ 100.

4.1.2 Relations of Expressions to Numbers

Expressions have properties just as numbers do because expressions actually are describing numbers. As a review, the real number properties discussed in Section 3.4 of Chapter 3 include

- commutative property of addition and multiplication

- associative property of addition and multiplication

- distributive property of multiplication

- identity property

- inverse property

All of these properties hold for expressions. For example, using the first three properties:

Commutative property of addition	$(x + 3) + 2(y - 6) = (3 + x) + 2(y - 6)$
Commutative property of addition	$= 2(y - 6) + (3 + x)$
Distributive property	$= 2y - 12 + 3 + x$
Associative and commutative properties of addition	$= x + 2y - 9$

The next section on equations shows the importance of the last two properties, identity and inverse.

Since expressions are actually taking the place of numbers, **rational expressions** have the same properties as rational numbers. According to the definition of *rational*, rational expressions are expressions that can be written in fraction form, where the numerator and denominator are themselves expressions. Rational expressions are closed under addition, subtraction, multiplication, and division, just as rational numbers are. The restriction that the denominator $\neq 0$ holds as well.

Likewise, the basic arithmetic operations of addition, subtraction, multiplication, and division, as discussed in Chapter 3, hold for expressions.

4.2 LINEAR EQUATIONS

So far, we have talked about solving equations with one unknown to the first power, so the answer is one number. Equations with two unknowns, usually x and y each to the first power, are known as **linear equations** because the unknown values that make these types of equations true form a line when graphed on an xy-coordinate system (see Section 4.2.4).

4.2.1 Creating Equations from Expressions

Algebra involves **equations**. The word *equations* has the same root as the word *equal*, and that is what equations are all about. Whatever is on one side of the equal sign must equal what is on the other side. So if you add something to one side, you must also add it to the other side. The same is true for subtracting, multiplying, dividing, taking roots, or raising to powers. Working with any of these operations in an equation usually depends on inverses.

4.2.2 Using Inverses in Solutions

Remember, addition and subtraction are inverses; multiplication and division are inverses; and in higher-order equations, powers and roots are inverses. For the solution of a linear equation, we want one variable (usually y) alone on one side of the equal sign and the other unknown (usually x) and numbers on the other side. To do that, we use inverses. Remember that whatever you do to one side of an equation must be done to the other side.

For example, consider the equation $(4y + 2) = 3(x - 3)$.

First, use the distributive property to get rid of the parentheses: $\quad 4y + 2 = 3x - 9$

Next, to get y on one side of the equation, add the inverse of $+2$: $\quad 4y + 2 - 2 = 3x - 9 - 2$

Combine the number terms: $\quad 4y = 3x - 11$

Finally, to get y alone, use the inverse of multiplying by 4: $\quad \dfrac{4y}{4} = \dfrac{3x - 11}{4}$

Simplify the equation: $\quad y = \dfrac{3x}{4} - \dfrac{11}{4}$

Every step is spelled out here, but most of the steps are usually done mentally.

4.2.3 Ratio, Proportion, Mean, Variation

4.2.3a Ratio

A **ratio** is a way of comparing two quantities. Ratios can be expressed as fractions, decimals, or by two numbers separated by a colon. For example, let's say the ratio of the length to the width of a bathmat is 3 feet to 2 feet. This can be written as 3:2, $\dfrac{3}{2}$, or even that the length is 1.5 times the width.

As another example, Bill's age is triple his son Will's age. The ratio of Bill's age to Will's age is 3 to 1, or $\dfrac{3}{1}$. The ratio of Will's age to Bill's age is $\dfrac{1}{3}$. It is very important to state the ratio in the correct order. It would make no sense in this case to say that the ratio of the son's age to the father's age is 3:1.

4.2.3b Proportion

A **proportion** is the equivalence of two ratios. For example, if Will's age is 10 years, then Bill is 30 years old. This calculation can be done mentally, but formally the proportion for this situation is

$$\frac{3}{1} = \frac{\text{Bill's age}}{10} = \frac{30}{10}$$

It is important to put "like" quantities in like places in a proportion. On the left-hand side of this proportion, the numbers represent Bill's age on top and Will's age on the bottom. So the right-hand side should be the same: Bill's age on top and Will's age on the bottom. The proportion works out because indeed $\frac{3}{1}$ does equal $\frac{30}{10}$.

Often, however, the numbers aren't as easy as this. Then we would set up a proportion, fill in all of the known values and use the proportion to find the missing value. Luckily, algebra comes to the rescue and makes a complicated-sounding problem easy to do. We want to get the unknown value that we are trying to find alone on one side of the equation. This is done by **cross-multiplication**, which ends up with a short equation in which the unknown has a multiplier. Then we divide both sides of that equation by the multiplier of the unknown (remember, division is the inverse of multiplication), and you get the unknown quantity right away.

For example, let's do the Bill-Will example above by using cross-multiplication. We are asked to find Bill's age knowing that Will's age is 10 and Bill's age is triple that. The proportion is

$$\frac{3}{1} = \frac{x}{10}.$$

where x is Bill's age. Just like it sounds, cross-multiplication means multiplying in the shape of a cross, where the two multiplications equal each other.

$$\frac{3}{1} \diagdown \frac{x}{10}$$

$$3 \times 10 = x \times 1$$

$$x = 30.$$

Although it doesn't make a difference with cross-multiplication, you should get in the habit of starting from the top left corner so that when you evaluate matrices (where the starting point does make a difference), you already are used to starting at the top left corner. Matrices are discussed later in Section 4.3 as a method of solving equations.

4.2.3c Means and Extremes of a Proportion

In any proportion of the form

$$\frac{a}{b} = \frac{c}{d}$$

b and c are called the **means** of the proportion, and a and d are called the **extremes** of the proportion. A basic property of a proportion is that the product of the means is equal to the product of the extremes, or $a \times d = b \times c$, as shown above.

To compare two fractions, set them up as a proportion and multiply the means and the extremes. If these two results match, the fractions are equal. If the product of the extremes is greater than the product of the means, the left-hand fraction is larger; conversely, if the product of the means is greater than the product of the extremes, the right-hand fraction is larger. For example, comparing $\frac{3}{4}$ and $\frac{2}{3}$, the product of the extremes is 9 and the product of the means is 8, so $\frac{3}{4} > \frac{2}{3}$.

In a true proportion, the product of the means equals the product of the extremes.

4.2.3d Variation

Another type of relationship between two variables that involves proportions is called **variation**. In this relationship, the product is a constant. With **direct variation**, when one variable increases, the other increases in proportion so that the ratio between the variables is unchanged. The general equation for direct variation between two variables is

$$y = kx$$

where x and y are the variables and k is the constant of variation. A classic example of direct variation is speed and distance. The formula for distance is $d = rt$, where r is speed, and t is time. In the same amount of time (so t takes the place of the constant k), we intuitively know that in a given time, if you go faster, you go farther, so as r increases, so does d.

EXAMPLE 4.2

The growth of a particular strain of bacteria varies directly with the temperature. When the temperature is 100 degrees, there are 20 million bacteria. How many millions of bacteria are there when the temperature is 150 degrees?

SOLUTION 4.2

30. Using direct variation, we first have to find the constant of variation, k, in the relationship $B = kT$, which we can find from the given information that at a temperature (T) of 100 degrees, there are 20 million bacteria (B). Since the question

asks for *how many millions* of bacteria there would be, we can use 20 (millions of bacteria) in our calculation. Therefore,

$$k = \frac{B}{T} = \frac{20}{100} = 0.2 \,.$$

Then the final equation to find how many millions of bacteria there are when the temperature is 150 degrees is $B = kT = (.2)(150) = 30$. The answer is 30 rather than 30 million because the question asks for *how many millions* of bacteria there would be.

Example 4.2 brings up several facts:

1. In many cases, you have to first find the constant of variation before you find the answer.

2. Here we used T and B instead of x and y. We can use any letters as the variables.

3. Instead of using 20,000,000, we just used 20, but we have to remember that the answer is in millions of bacteria. It just makes the calculation easier.

Example 4.2 could also have been set up as a proportion problem:

$$\frac{100}{20 \text{ million}} = \frac{150}{B}$$

$$100B = 3000 \text{ million}$$

$$B = 30 \text{ million}$$

With **inverse variation**, when one variable increases, the other decreases in proportion so that the product of the variables is unchanged. The general equation for inverse variation between two variables is

$$y = \frac{k}{x}, \text{ or } xy = k$$

where k, again, is the constant. So the bigger x becomes, the smaller y becomes, and vice versa. An example of an inverse relation is the amount of gas used to heat a home versus the temperature outside. As the temperature falls, the amount of gas used increases.

4.2.4 Graphing on the Coordinate Plane

First, let's look at the coordinate system called the **Cartesian coordinate system**. The **domain** axis (usually the x-axis) runs horizontally and the **range** axis (usually the y-axis) runs vertically. The axes (plural of *axis*) divide the coordinate system into four quadrants, usually labeled counterclockwise with Roman numerals from the upper right quadrant. The point where the axes meet is called the **origin**.

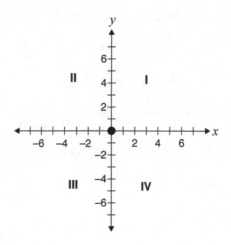

4.2.4a Ordered Pairs

We can locate points (called **coordinates**) and the lines and curves that these points form on the Cartesian coordinate system. The coordinates are of the form (x, y) or (domain, range), and because order makes a difference in how we write coordinates, they are also called **ordered pairs**. The coordinates of the origin are usually $(0, 0)$. Note that in Quadrant I, all x and y values are positive; in Quadrant II, x is negative and y is positive; in Quadrant III, x and y are both negative, and in Quadrant IV, x is positive and y is negative.

The **ordered pair** $(x, y) = (3, 4)$ is plotted as a point 3 units to the right of the origin and 4 units up from it. Each labeled point is unique, meaning in this case that there is only one point that can be labeled $(3, 4)$. The point $(-3, 4)$ would be in Quadrant II.

4.2.4b Table of Values

Now let's look at the linear equation $y = 2x + 3$ and how it is graphed on the coordinate system. Usually, the x value is the independent variable, which means we can plot a bunch of (x, y) points, with the y values depending on what we choose (arbitrarily) as the x value. We can keep track of these points by putting them in a **table of values**.

How many points should we plot? For a linear equation, connecting just two points will make a line, but to make sure one of those two points wasn't in error somehow, plot a third point. All three points should be **collinear** (along the same line). If they aren't, you have to go back and correct your error. A safety net is to plot four points. If there is an error, it will show up as a point not on the line that contains the other three points.

x	y
0	3
1	5
2	7
−1	1

The values for y came directly from substituting each x value into the equation $y = 2x + 3$. It is usual for the first value for x to be 0 because that makes calculation of y the simplest. The other values for x are picked arbitrarily.

The corresponding points to plot on the graph are thus (0, 3), (1, 5), (2, 7), (−1, 1). The graph looks like

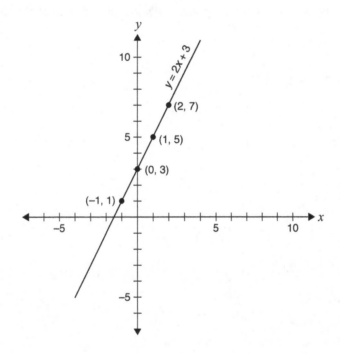

4.2.4c Constraints

Constraints on either the domain or range of a relation can be stated in several ways. Think of a constraint as a restriction on the value of a variable. Constraints on the domain translate through the relation into constraints on the range. Constraints are indicated by using inequalities or interval notation.

- **Inequalities** such as $-5 < x \leq 4$, which means "all values of x greater than -5 and less than or equal to 4." An example of a further constraint to only integers is the set notation $\{x \in \mathbb{Z} \mid -5 < x \leq 4\}$, where $\mathbb{Z}$ is the set of integers (see Chapter 3, Section 3.2.1).

- **Intervals** describe specific sets of numbers and are very useful when discussing domain and range. "The domain is $(-5, 4]$" is the same thing as $-5 < x \leq 4$ in **interval notation**. It simply shows the upper and lower bounds of the interval. An open constraint, indicated by a parenthesis, means up (or down) to the value indicated (the same as < and >). A closed constraint, indicated by a bracket, means to include that value (the same as ≤ and ≥). Intervals can be completely closed, completely open, or a combination, as in $(-5, 4]$, which means all of the numbers from -5 to 4, *except -5*.

In reality, a line contains an infinite number of points, and for the majority of them x is not an integer. For linear equations, x usually has any real value, denoted as $(-\infty, \infty)$. Whenever interval notation to $-\infty$ or ∞ is indicated, parentheses are used because the variable cannot actually reach infinity.

Graphically, a constraint may confine the graph to one, two, or three quadrants. Or a constraint may truncate (or end) the graph at a certain point. Let's look at the graphs of two examples.

EXAMPLE 4.3

Rev. Graph $y = x + 2$, $x > 3$.

SOLUTION 4.3

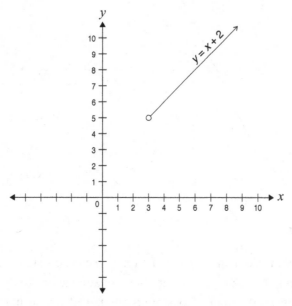

For the graph of $y = x + 2$, $x > 3$, the constraint is $x > 3$, so the graph will appear only in the first quadrant because if $x > 3$, then $y > 5$. Make a table and determine at least three points to form the line, but end the line at the point (3, 5), and in fact make an open circle at that point. The open circle says that the line gets as close as possible to (3, 5), but the actual point is not part of the graph. If it were, the circle at (3, 5) would be filled in. Note that we draw a circle because a point cannot be drawn that would show whether it was filled in or not, but the circle is supposed to represent just one point.

$\mathcal{R}^2$ **EXAMPLE 4.4**

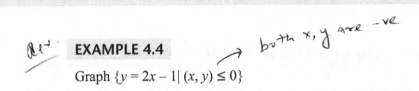
both x, y are –ve

Graph $\{y = 2x - 1 \mid (x, y) \leq 0\}$

SOLUTION 4.4

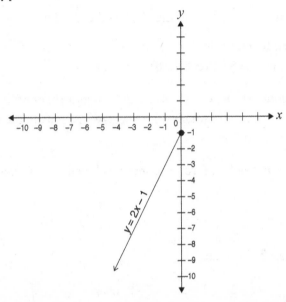

$\{y = 2x - 1 \mid (x, y) \leq 0\}$ means the graph appears only in the third quadrant, which is the only quadrant for which x and y are both less than 0. The "or equal to" part of the constraint means that the point on the axes that form the boundary of Quadrant III are included.

4.2.4d Absolute Value

A special kind of constraint that we encounter is the absolute value. **Absolute value** is used for expressing distance, and is indicated by two vertical bars $|\ |$. The value of the expression inside the absolute value signs is changed to a positive value. For example, $|-6| = 6$, $|3 + 4 - 2 - 8| = 3$.

When absolute value appears in an equation or an inequality, we must evaluate the expression inside the absolute value signs as a negative as well as a positive quantity, so we end up with two separate equations. This can be seen when solving the simple equation $|x| = 4$. The value of x can be either positive or negative, yielding two answers: $x = 4$ or -4. Likewise, $|3x - 2| = 7$ has two solutions, one for $(3x - 2)$ being positive, or simply $3x - 2 = 7$, and one for the case when $(3x - 2)$ is negative, which is the equation $-(3x - 2) = 7$, or $-3x + 2 = 7$, which is completely different from the positive case.

To solve any equation involving absolute value, isolate the absolute-value expression and then split the equation into two possible cases, one for the expression inside the absolute value sign as given and another for the expression preceded by a minus sign.

4.2.5 Slope-Intercept Form of a Linear Equation

Linear equations can be written in many equivalent forms. The two forms that are used most often are:

- The **standard form**, $Ax + By = C$, where A, B, and C can be any numbers.

- The **slope-intercept form**, $y = mx + b$, where m is the **slope** (see Section 4.2.5a), and b is the y-intercept of the line (see Section 4.2.5b).

We can use basic algebra to change any linear equation into either of these forms. For example, consider the equation $4x + 2 = 2y - 7$, which we recognize as a linear equation because it involves two variables raised to the first power.

To write this equation in standard form, use inverses by simply subtracting $2y$ from each side to get

$$4x + 2 - 2y = 2y - 7 - 2y, \text{ or } 4x - 2y + 2 = -7$$

and then subtract 2 from each side to get

$$4x - 2y + 2 - 2 = -7 - 2, \text{ or } 4x - 2y = -9$$

which is in standard form with $A = 4$, $B = -2$, and $C = -9$. Note that both sides of this equation can be multiplied by -1 to get an equivalent equation in standard form, $-4x + 2y = 9$.

 Hint: Sometimes multiplying an equation by -1 is handy to eliminate working with a lot of minus signs; this is especially true when all the terms in a linear equation are negative.

To write $4x + 2 = 2y - 7$ in slope-intercept form, use the following steps:

1. Move the y term to one side of the equation by doing whatever algebra is needed (e.g., using inverses):

$$4x - 2y = -9$$

$$4x + 9 = 2y$$

2. Now get y alone by using the multiplicative inverse, dividing both sides by the coefficient of y.

$$\frac{4x + 9}{2} = \frac{2y}{2}$$

$$\frac{4x}{2} + \frac{9}{2} = y$$

3. Simplify the equation (and switch sides if necessary, just so it is in slope-intercept form and easier to recognize).

$$2x + \frac{9}{2} = y$$

$$y = 2x + \frac{9}{2}$$

This equation is in the form $y = mx + b$, with the slope $m = 2$, and the y-intercept $b = \frac{9}{2}$. Now let's discuss what each of these values means.

4.2.5a Slope

Any point on the line that represents a linear equation on a graph is a solution to the linear equation. The values of the point (x, y) don't have to be integers, but for every x there is one and only one value of y that is a solution to the linear equation. The line itself tells us about the relationship between x and y, such as how quickly y changes in relation to x (the rate of change of the relationship). This is called the **slope** of the line. Formally,

$$\text{slope} = \frac{\text{change in } y}{\text{change in } x} = \frac{\Delta y}{\Delta x}, \text{ where } \Delta \text{ is a Greek letter that signifies "change."}$$

Slope is sometimes stated as

$$\text{slope} = \frac{\text{rise}}{\text{run}} \text{ or "rise over run."}$$

If you pick any two points on a line to find the slope, that fraction (the slope) doesn't change its value.

 Remember that the slope always has the change in y as the numerator.

The slope of a line can be positive or negative. If the slope is positive, the line goes up to the right; if it is negative, the line goes down to the right. If the line is parallel to the x-axis, y doesn't change, so the slope of a horizontal line is 0 (this is not the same as "no slope"). If the line is parallel to the y-axis, x doesn't change, so a vertical line is infinitely steep and has no slope. This is seen by the fact that division by 0 (the change in x) is undefined.

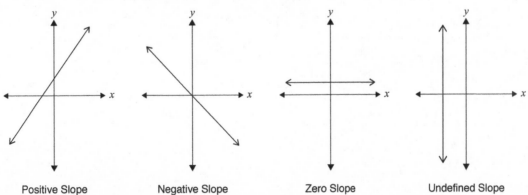

Positive Slope   Negative Slope   Zero Slope   Undefined Slope

4.2.5b y-Intercept

Obviously, many lines can have the same slope (see the graphs below of $y = x + 5$, $y = x$, and $y = x - 4$, which each have a slope of 1). Then what distinguishes the graph of one line from another? The answer is where it crosses the y-axis, the point called the **y-intercept**. That pins down exactly where the line is graphed.

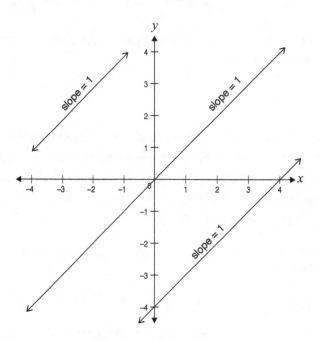

The value of x at the y-intercept is 0.

In our example of $y = 2x + \dfrac{9}{2}$, we found that the slope is 2. That means for every change of 1 unit for x, the change in y is 2 units (because $2 = \dfrac{2}{1}$). The slope is positive, so it goes up to the right. We also found that the y-intercept occurs at the point with coordinates $(0, \dfrac{9}{2})$. Therefore, the graph of our original equation, $4x + 2 = 2y - 7$, is shown next. First, the point of the y-intercept is graphed, and then points that are 1 unit away in the x-direction and 2 units away in the y-direction are graphed and finally the line connecting the points is drawn.

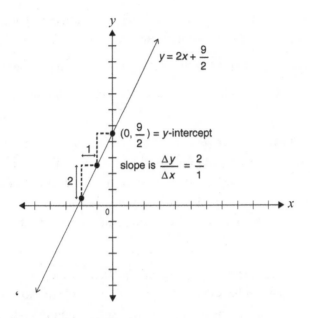

4.2.6 Ways to Solve a Linear Equation

In summary, there are two basic ways to solve a linear equation.

- Algebra, by using the properties and operations discussed in Chapter 3, especially Section 3.4, and in this chapter, Section 4.1, on expressions, which hold for algebra.

- Graphing, where every point on the line is a solution to the equation.

4.2.7 Systems of Linear Equations

Systems of equations are a group of two or more equations that share one solution. Since they all have the same solution at the same time, they are often called **simultaneous equations**. An important rule with systems of equations is that you must have as many equations as variables. If the variables in the equations are x and y, you need two equations to find the one ordered pair that is a solution for both. If the variables in the equations are x, y, and z, you need three equations to find the one set of values for x, y, and z, that is a solution to all three equations.

Any point on a line is a solution to the equation of that line. When two lines cross, and they intersect in only one point, that point is a solution to the equations of both lines. Likewise, if three lines intersect in only one point, that ordered pair is a solution for all three lines. We use this fact to solve systems of linear equations—to find the one ordered pair that works for all linear equations involved.

See Pg 5-7 in Blue Regis. (BR)

Every system of equations falls into one of the following categories:

- **Consistent equations.** These are equations whose graphs intersect at a common point, the solution for all of the equations. These can be solved algebraically and graphically, as well as by using matrices (Section 4.2.7d).

- **Inconsistent equations**. These are equations whose graphs are parallel lines. This means they never intersect so there is no solution that holds for all of the equations. For example, $x + 7y = 6$ and $x + 7y = 10$ are parallel lines (they have the same slope, which is $-\frac{1}{7}$). Notice that they are inconsistent because $x + 7y$ cannot have two different values, 6 and 10, at the same time.

- **Dependent equations**. These are equations whose graphs are the same line. One equation is actually equal to the other equation multiplied (or divided) by the same quantity on both sides. Since they are the same line, they have an infinite number of the matching ordered pairs, so they have an infinite number of solutions, just like any single line. For example, $x + y = 3$ and $2x + 2y = 6$ are dependent because the second equation is just twice the first equation.

The following discussion pertains to consistent equations, which are the only ones that have one solution. These equations can be solved algebraically (by substitution or addition or subtraction), by graphing and finding the point of intersection, or by using matrices, which is a variation of the algebraic method.

4.2.7a Solving Systems of Equations by Substitution

Among the several ways to solve systems of equations, substitution is the most straightforward, especially for two equations and two unknowns. The method involves the following steps:

1. If you can, rewrite one of the equations so that one variable is written in terms of the other.

2. Substitute this value in the other equation and solve the resulting equation.

3. Substitute the value of the variable found in step 2 into one of the original equations and solve the resulting equation for the other variable.

EXAMPLE 4.5

Solve the system of equations $x - 2y = -7$ and $7x + 5y = 8$.

SOLUTION 4.5

$(-1, 3)$. The first equation can be rewritten as $x = 2y - 7$. If we substitute that value for x in the second equation, we get

$$7(2y - 7) + 5y = 8,$$

which is now one equation with one unknown, so it is solvable.

$$14y - 49 + 5y = 8$$

$$19y = 57$$

$$y = 3$$

To get the value for x, substitute $y = 3$ into either of the original equations:

$$x - 2y = -7$$

$$x = 2y - 7$$

$$x = 2(3) - 7 = -1$$

If we used the second equation instead to find x, we would get the same result:

$$7x + 5y = 8$$

$$7x = -5y + 8$$

$$x = \frac{-5y + 8}{7}$$

$$x = \frac{-5(3) + 8}{7}$$

$$x = \frac{-15 + 8}{7} = \frac{-7}{7} = -1$$

Always try to choose the easiest of the equations; obviously, that would be the first one for the equations in Example 4.5.

Coin problems seem complicated unless you realize that the value for each denomination should be written in the same units, usually cents. So n nickels are worth $5n$ cents, d dimes are worth $10d$ cents, and q quarters are worth $25q$ cents. Usually the total number of coins is given as well as a value for the worth of all coins together.

EXAMPLE 4.6

195

A purse contains 3 more nickels than dimes. The value of the coins is $1.95. How many coins of each type are there?

SOLUTION 4.6

12 dimes, 15 nickels. Since there are two unknowns, there should be two equations. First, for the number of coins, 3 more nickels than dimes means $n = d + 3$. Now, for the value (in cents): $5n + 10d = 195$. So these are the two simultaneous equations, and we can substitute the first equation into the second to get numbers for n nickels and d dimes.

$$5(d + 3) + 10d = 195$$

$$5d + 15 + 10d = 195$$

$$15d = 180$$

So there are $d = 12$ dimes, and thus $n = d + 3 = 15$ nickels.

4.2.7b Solving Systems of Equations by Addition or Subtraction

Solving simultaneous equations by addition or subtraction actually involves the following properties:

- The algebraic associative, commutative, and distributive properties.

- The fact that equals added to or subtracted from equals are equal. In other words, if $a = b$, and $c = d$, then $a + c = b + d$ and $a - c = b - d$, where a, b, c, and d can stand for either numbers or equations.

- If an equality is multiplied through by the same number on both sides, the result is also an equality.

Efficiently solving systems of equations by addition or subtraction requires practice, but it works all the time and doesn't involve fractions along the way, which sometimes happens with the substitution method. The addition or subtraction method involves the following steps:

1. If necessary, multiply one or more of the equations by numbers that will make the coefficients of one unknown in the resulting equations numerically equal. You could multiply different equations by different numbers, but often one equation is left unchanged.

2. If the signs of equal coefficients are the same, subtract the equations, otherwise add them. The result is one equation with one unknown.

3. Solve that equation and, as was done in the third step of the substitution method, substitute the value into the other equation(s) to find the unknown that was first eliminated.

EXAMPLE 4.7

Use the addition or subtraction method for the same set of equations used in Example 4.5:

$$x - 2y = -7$$
$$7x + 5y = 8,$$

SOLUTION 4.7

$(-1, 3)$. Multiply the first equation by 7 and subtract the second equation from it to eliminate the x's. Note that the second equation is left as it was, although it could have been multiplied through by -1, and then the two equations would be added. The result is the same. Here we use subtraction, term by term:

$$7x - 14y = -49$$
$$7x + 5y = 8$$
$$-19y = -57$$
$$y = 3$$

The rest of this solution is the same as was found by the substitution method in Example 4.5.

4.2.7c Solving Systems of Equations by Graphing

Graph each equation on the same set of axes. The ordered pair of the point of intersection of the drawn lines is a simultaneous solution for the equations, which corresponds to the answer that would be found analytically. This method takes more time and is less accurate than analytical solution protocols, especially if the solution involves numbers that are not integers.

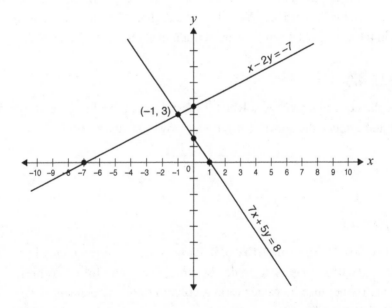

Of course, if the two lines are inconsistent (parallel), they don't intersect and there isn't a solution, and if the lines are dependent, there are an infinite number of points in common because they are the same line.

4.2.7d Solving Systems of Equations by Using Matrices

Solving systems of equations by using **matrices** is related to solution by addition or subtraction because the elements in the matrix are the values of A, B, and C in the standard form of the equations that are manipulated in the addition/subtraction method.

As shown in Chapter 3, Section 3.12.2, a **matrix** is simply a way to organize data in columns and rows. A matrix can easily be evaluated by finding its **determinant**, a special number that can be calculated from a **square matrix**, which has the same number of rows and columns. The determinant is useful for solving systems of equations.

To review from Chapter 3, Section 3.12.2, the determinant of a matrix has the same elements as the matrix, and its value is found by multiplying the elements in the main diagonal, which starts at the upper left corner. and then subtracting the product of the elements in the second diagonal. This specific order is important because subtraction is not associative—it makes a difference which value is subtracted from which value. Always start at the upper left corner.

 Hint: The order of the diagonals used to evaluate the determinant is the same order as used for cross-multiplication in proportions (see Section 4.2.3b in this chapter): Start with the upper left element ↘ and then the upper right element ↙ thus forming an **X**.

Since linear equations have only two variables, we will be working with two equations, and 2×2 (read as "two-by-two") matrices. We will evaluate three determinants that come from the A, B, and C values in the equations when they are written in standard form, $Ax + By = C$.

EXAMPLE 4.8

Let's use the equations that we solved by substitution, the addition and subtraction method, and graphically above. They are already in standard form.

$$x - 2y = -7$$

$$7x + 5y = 8$$

SOLUTION 4.8

$(-1, 3)$. The first determinant, let's call it det D, is the one formed only by the A and B values of the equations. Next to det D, write a column of the C values, called a column matrix because its values form a column only one element wide. We will be working with det D, and using the column matrix only for constructing the other two determinants from our system of equations, called det D_x and det D_y.

$$\det D = \begin{vmatrix} 1 & -2 \\ 7 & 5 \end{vmatrix} \qquad \text{column matrix} = \begin{bmatrix} -7 \\ 8 \end{bmatrix}$$

The second determinant, det D_x, is formed by replacing the A values (x coefficients) in det D with the column matrix values. Similarly, the third determinant, det D_y, is formed by replacing the B values (y coefficients) in det D with the column matrix values.

$$\det D_x = \begin{vmatrix} -7 & -2 \\ 8 & 5 \end{vmatrix}$$

$$\det D_y = \begin{vmatrix} 1 & -7 \\ 7 & 8 \end{vmatrix}$$

Now we are ready to get values for x and y that are solutions to both equations. The way to do this is to evaluate the following determinants:

$$x = \frac{\det D_x}{\det D} = \frac{\begin{vmatrix} -7 & -2 \\ 8 & 5 \end{vmatrix}}{\begin{vmatrix} 1 & -2 \\ 7 & 5 \end{vmatrix}} = \frac{-35 - (-16)}{5 - (-14)} = \frac{-19}{19} = -1$$

$$y = \frac{\det D_y}{\det D} = \frac{\begin{vmatrix} 1 & -7 \\ 7 & 8 \end{vmatrix}}{\begin{vmatrix} 1 & -2 \\ 7 & 5 \end{vmatrix}} = \frac{8 - (-49)}{5 - (-14)} = \frac{57}{19} = 3$$

We get the same values, $x = -1$ and $y = 3$, as before, except this time we used the "magic" of matrices and their determinants. It's not truly magic because it is based on math, but it seems like it is. The name for this method is **Cramer's Rule**, and it simply states that

$$x = \frac{\det D_x}{\det D} \text{ and } y = \frac{\det D_y}{\det D},$$

where D is the determinant of the coefficients of the left sides of the equations, D_x is det D with the x coefficients replaced by the C values in the column matrix, and D_y is det D with the y coefficients replaced by the C values in the column matrix.

For a set of equations to be solved by using Cramer's Rule, D must not equal 0 since division by zero is not allowed. Any matrix that has a nonzero determinant is called **invertible**. So the first step in solving a system of equations by Cramer's Rule is to evaluate the determinant D. If it is not invertible (meaning its value is 0), stop right there—it cannot be solved by using Cramer's Rule. The system is either inconsistent or dependent, meaning there is no single point that satisfies both equations.

 Matrices may be used to solve any system of equations that have as many equations as unknowns, thus forming a square matrix. The method is identical to what is shown above for a 2 × 2 matrix, except that evaluating a higher order matrix is a little more involved than multiplying in an "**X**" format.

4.3 LINEAR INEQUALITIES

Inequalities are solved the same as equalities (equations) except for one important difference. When you multiply or divide an inequality by a negative number, the inequality sign is reversed. Thus, to solve $2x > 4$, you would divide both sides by 2, and get $x > 2$. But if the inequality was $-2x > 4$, and you divide both sides by -2, the answer becomes $x < 4$. The graph of $-2x > 4$ would have an open circle on the number line at 4, since this inequality does not include 4, and the line would be bold from 4 left to $-\infty$ (indicated by an arrow at the end of the number line).

For linear inequalities with two variables, the rule is the same: treat as an equality but reverse the inequality if the calculation involves multiplication or division by a negative number. Now, whereas the solutions to a linear equation are represented by a line with every point on the line being a solution to the equation, the solutions to linear inequalities are all points that make the inequality true, which is a half-plane that may or may not include the line. If the inequality indicates "or equal to" ($\leq$ or $\geq$), then the line is included and is drawn as a solid line; if the inequality doesn't include the line ($<$ or $>$), then the line is dashed.

So the graph of the solution of a linear inequality has only two steps:

1. Graph the line. Make it dashed or solid, according to the inequality sign.

2. Choose a point on either side of the line. (Usually the origin $(0, 0)$ is a good choice since the math is easier.) If that ordered pair makes the inequality true, shade that side of the line; if not, shade the other side.

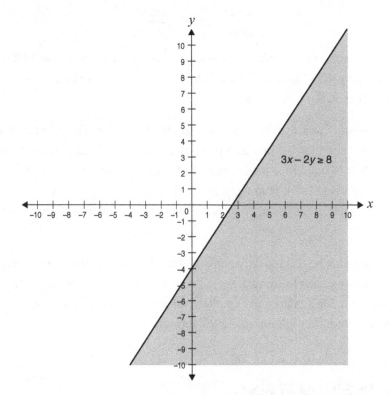

The area for solutions to systems of inequalities is restricted to the overlap, or intersection, of the shaded areas of each inequality.

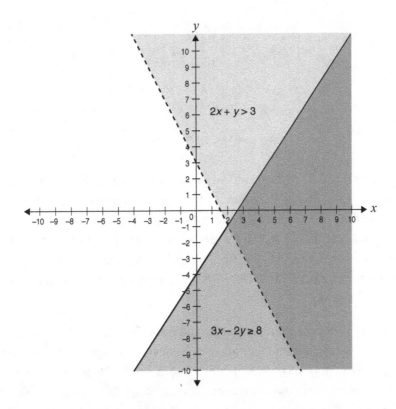

4.4 MULTIPLYING BINOMIALS

Binomials are the sum or difference of two terms, such as $x + 3$ or $y - 4$. Here, we are interested in multiplying two binomials that contain unknowns to only the first power. This multiplication has a lot of uses and implications.

4.4.1 F-O-I-L Method

Let's use the two binomials $(x + 6)(2x + 3)$ to illustrate the multiplication of binomials. One way to do this is by longhand—multiply $(2x + 3)$ by x and then multiply $(2x + 3)$ by $+6$ and combine like terms. A similar method, called the **F-O-I-L method**, is easier to remember. F-O-I-L is a **mnemonic**, a word to remember something. The letters in F-O-I-L stand for

First-Outside-Inside-Last

This means that when we multiply two binomials, such as $(x + 6)(2x + 3)$, we multiply the first terms, then the outside terms, then the inside terms, and finally the last terms and then add all of the results. The following example of F-O-I-L uses our specific binomials because it is easier to understand that way, but F-O-I-L works for binomials with any coefficients and any constants.

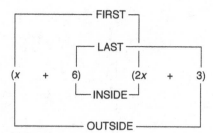

The first terms (F) are x and $2x$, the outside terms (O) are x and 3, the inside terms (I) are 6 and $2x$, and the last terms (L) are 6 and 3. When we multiply each of them, in F-O-I-L order, we end up with the product of the two binomials. Here, when we multiply the first terms we get $2x^2$, when we multiply the outside terms, we get $3x$, when we multiply the inside terms, we get $12x$, and when we multiply the last terms, we get 18. Then when we add it all up, we get the product: $2x^2 + 3x + 12x + 18$, which equals $2x^2 + 15x + 18$. This trinomial has a specific name; it is called a quadratic, the topic of Section 4.5.

If the two binomials have the same first terms and the second terms differ only in sign, then the outer and inner products cancel each other out and the answer is only the difference of the F and L terms. For example, $(3x + 5)(3x - 5) = 9x^2 - 15x + 15x - 25 = 9x^2 - 25$. So if you recognize two binomials as the sum and difference of the same terms, you can write the answer directly, eliminating the inner and outer products, $(3x + 5)(3x - 5) = 9x^2 - 25$. Remember that the last term is always negative. The reverse of this process, called the difference of two squares, is discussed in Section 4.5.1.

4.4.2 Complex Conjugates

Complex conjugates are pairs of complex numbers such that the real parts are the same and the imaginary parts differ only in sign, such as $a + bi$ and $a - bi$. When we multiply a complex number by its conjugate, the complex parts cancel each other out. The longhand version is as follows:

$$(a + bi)(a - bi) = a(a) + a(-bi) + bi(a) + bi(-bi) = a^2 - abi + abi - b^2i^2 = a^2 + b^2$$

But if we look at the product $(a + bi)(a - bi)$ as a special case of multiplying two binomials with the first terms being the same and the second terms differing only in sign, as discussed in the preceding paragraph, and use the FOIL method, we get the same result: The abi terms drop out because they appear only in the inner and outer products of F-O-I-L. The answer is the difference of F and L in the F-O-I-L calculation, but watch out! Those last terms contain $i^2 = -1$, so the last term of the multiplication of complex conjugates is positive because a negative (from F-O-I-L) times a negative (from i^2) equals a positive. Therefore,

$$(a + bi)(a - bi) = a^2 + b^2$$

This fact is useful for rationalizing a fraction, which involves removing a radical from the denominator of a fraction. Similarly, since a complex number involves a radical, it also has to be rationalized because radicals should not appear in the denominator of a fraction.

EXAMPLE 4.9

Rationalize the fraction $\dfrac{3}{1+\sqrt{2}}$.

SOLUTION 4.9

$-3+3\sqrt{2}$. To eliminate the radical in the denominator, multiply the entire fraction by the fraction with the conjugate of the denominator over itself (so it is equal to 1), as follows:

$$\frac{3}{1+\sqrt{2}} = \frac{3}{1+\sqrt{2}} \times \frac{1-\sqrt{2}}{1-\sqrt{2}} = \frac{3-3\sqrt{2}}{1-2} = \frac{3-3\sqrt{2}}{-1} = -3+3\sqrt{2}$$

EXAMPLE 4.10

Rationalize the fraction $\dfrac{2-3i}{1+4i}$.

SOLUTION 4.10

$-\dfrac{10}{17} - \dfrac{11}{17}i$. Multiply the numerator and denominator of the fraction by a fraction with the complex conjugate of the denominator in its numerator and denominator $\left(\text{because } \dfrac{1-4i}{1-4i} = 1 \right)$:

$$\frac{2-3i}{1+4i} \times \frac{1-4i}{1-4i} = \frac{(2-3i)(1-4i)}{1^2 + 4^2} = \frac{2-3i-8i+12i^2}{17} = \frac{2-11i-12}{17} = -\frac{10}{17} - \frac{11}{17}i$$

 With a *complex* conjugate, we still have an i term, but it is only in the numerator.

4.4.3 Binomial Theorem

4.4.3a General Formula

The **binomial theorem,** stated in general terms, is:

$$(x+y)^n = x^n + \frac{n}{1}x^{n-1}y + \frac{n(n-1)}{1 \times 2}x^{n-2}y^2 + \ldots + y^n,$$

where n is the power of the binomial, and the binomial formula finds any power of a binomial without multiplying at length. So for $(x+y)^2$, $n = 2$, and immediately can write

$$(x+y)^2 = x^2 + 2xy + y^2$$

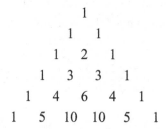

→ Do Qs on Pascal's △.
• $(x+y)^n$ expansion has $n+1$ terms.

4.4.3b Pascal's Triangle

But not all binomials are so simple. Luckily, the binomial theorem is simplified by looking at a very interesting triangle called **Pascal's triangle** (named after seventeenth century mathematician, Blaise Pascal, although it had been used hundreds of years before Pascal by mathematicians in China, India, Persia, and Europe). The first part of Pascal's triangle looks like the following:

$$
\begin{array}{ccccccccccc}
& & & & & 1 & & & & & \\
& & & & 1 & & 1 & & & & \\
& & & 1 & & 2 & & 1 & & & \\
& & 1 & & 3 & & 3 & & 1 & & \\
& 1 & & 4 & & 6 & & 4 & & 1 & \\
1 & & 5 & & 10 & & 10 & & 5 & & 1 \\
\end{array}
$$

We can continue to add rows to this triangle because the method is that all the edges are 1's, and all the numbers in the middle are the sums of the two numbers above them. You should see that the next row would be

$$
\begin{array}{ccccccc}
1 & 6 & 15 & 20 & 15 & 6 & 1
\end{array}
$$

Hint: If you remember that Pascal's triangle starts with 1 $\overset{1}{}$ 1 and each succeeding row starts and ends with a 1 and is formed by adding the two numbers from the row above it, you can always construct the triangle, especially when confronted with a binomial raised to any power.

It's that simple, yet Pascal's triangle is a very powerful tool. Among other uses, it determines the coefficients that arise in binomial expansions. The first row of the triangle is row 0, the next is row 1, then row 2, etc. These row numbers correspond to the power of a binomial.

NOTE The second number of each row tells which row it is. For example, the 5th row is 1 5 10 1 0 5 1, and gives the coefficients of the terms in a binomial raised to the 5th power.

For an example, let's consider the expansion $(x + y)^3 = x^3 + 3x^2y + 3xy^2 + y^3$. We see that the coefficients of the terms are 1, 3, 3, 1, which is row 3 in Pascal's triangle (remember that the top row is row 0). The second step in writing the expansion of $(x + y)^3$ using Pascal's triangle is to fill in the powers of the terms of the binomial (here, they are x and y). Start with the highest power of x, which is 3 here, and the lowest power of y, which is 0 (remember that $y^0 = 1$). Then just decrease the x powers and increase the y powers in each term. The sum of the exponents in each term equals the power of the binomial. This is better shown by example, using the same binomial, $(x + y)^3$.

1. Since this is a third-order binomial, go to row 3 on Pascal's triangle, 1 3 3 1, which also shows that there will be four terms, $(x + y)^3 = 1\underline{\quad} + 3\underline{\quad} + 3\underline{\quad} + 1$.

2. Now fill in the x's, starting with x^3, and the y's, starting with y^0. Notice that the sums of the exponents always add to 3 here.

$$(x + y)^3 = 1x^3y^0 + 3x^2y^1 + 3x^1y^2 + 1x^0y^3$$

3. Simplify the answer by getting rid of the 1's and 0's. In reality, you wouldn't even be writing these anyway: $(x + y)^3 = x^3 + 3x^2y + 3xy^2 + y^3$.

This method works with any binomial to any power. Just substitute the first term for x and the second term for y, as shown in Example 4.8. This will take two steps: (1) writing the expansion according to the rules for Pascal's triangle, and (2) simplifying each term. There is no adding of like terms or multiple multiplications by the binomial. There is only following the rule.

EXAMPLE 4.11

Find $(2x - 3)^4$. (This binomial has a coefficient with the first term and a negative second term, so it is as complicated as you will encounter on a test.)

SOLUTION 4.11

$16x^4 - 96x^3 + 216x^2 - 216x + 81$. Of course, you can multiply $(2x - 3)^4$ manually, but in the time it takes to set up that calculation, you can just write the answer by using Pascal's triangle. Row 4 is 1 4 6 4 1, so the solution would start as follows, substituting $(2x)$ for x and (-3) for y in the steps using Pascal's triangle:

$$(2x - 3)^4 = 1(2x)^4 + 4(2x)^3(-3) + 6(2x)^2(-3)^2 + 4(2x)(-3)^3 + (-3)^4$$

Notice that the coefficients are 1 4 6 4 1, so there are five terms. The first term has $(2x)$ to the 4th power and each succeeding term has $(2x)$ to one lower power; also, the first term has (-3) to the 0 power (since that equals 1, we don't have to write it) and each succeeding term has (-3) to one higher power. Now we just have to do the multiplication term by term in each of the five terms:

$$(2x - 3)^4 = 16x^4 + (4)(8)(-3)x^3 + (6)(4)(9)x^2 + (4)(2)(-27)x + 81$$
$$= 16x^4 - 96x^3 + 216x^2 - 216x + 81$$

EXAMPLE 4.12

What is the third term of the expansion of $(x - y)^5$.

SOLUTION 4.12

First, go to the third term of row 5 of Pascal's triangle, which is 10. That is the coefficient. Since this is the third term, the power of x is 3, so the power of $(-y)$ is 2, since the exponents must add up to 5. Thus, the third term of $(x - y)^5$ is $10x^3y^2$. Notice that the minus sign, which belongs to y disappears because $(-y)$ is to an even power. How much simper this is than doing the multiplication longhand, combining like terms, and then counting over to the third term!

4.5 QUADRATIC EQUATIONS

A **quadratic equation** is an equation in which the unknown is squared and there is no higher power of the unknown. It is okay if there are no lower powers of the unknown (in other words, no "x" term or no "pure number" term). Examples of quadratic equations include $x^2 + x - 6 = 0$, $x^2 - 9 = 0$, and $x^2 + 3x = 0$.

Quadratic equations always have two solutions for the value of x (even though at times they are the same value twice). The general form of a quadratic equation is $ax^2 + bx + c = 0$, where b and c can be any numbers, even 0. If $a = 0$, though, the equation is no longer a quadratic—according to the definition, there has to be an x^2 term. If $a = 0$, it is a linear equation.

4.5.1 Solving a Quadratic Equation

A quadratic equation can be solved graphically, by using matrices, or algebraically. Graphically, a quadratic is a parabola, which is discussed in Section 5.8.2a in Chapter 5, and the solutions (there are two) are the points where the graph crosses the x-axis, similar to the case for linear equations. These points are called the **zeros** or **roots** of the quadratic equation, or the values for which the quadratic equation has a value of zero.

The algebraic solutions to a quadratic equation are based on a simple fact: if two factors are multiplied together and the product is 0, then either one or both of the factors must equal 0. There aren't any two nonzero numbers whose product is 0. Period.

The algebraic solutions to a quadratic equation are usually found by writing the quadratic expression on one side of the equal sign and 0 on the other. To make calculations easier, be sure to clear the equation of fractions, if there are any, by multiplying through by the common denominator.

If we can find two factors for a quadratic expression, the solution to the quadratic equation is found by setting each of the factors equal to 0 and solving for the unknown variable. Each of the factors will contain the unknown to only the first power (e.g., x). Solving each of these gives two roots (solutions, or zeros) for the quadratic equation. Four methods to solve a quadratic equation by factoring include the following:

1. **Difference of two squares**. If the quadratic equation is the difference of two squares (a perfect square, a minus sign, and another perfect square, with no x term, e.g., $x^2 - 25 = 0$), the factors are the sum and difference of the square roots, here the factors are $(x - 5)(x + 5)$. In this case, setting each factor equal to 0, we get, $x = +5$ or -5, written as $x = \pm 5$, since $\pm$ means plus or minus.

    If $b = 0$ in the general equation and it isn't obvious that the equation is the difference of two squares, simply isolate x^2 on one side of the equal sign and then take the square root of each side of the equation. For example, for $9x^2 - 8 = 0$, rewrite it as $x^2 = \dfrac{8}{9}$, so $x = \pm\sqrt{\dfrac{8}{9}} = \pm\dfrac{2\sqrt{2}}{3}$. This is the basic reasoning for method #4 below.

2. **Common factor**. This method involves recognizing that there is a common factor in each term. For equations without the constant (c) term, the common factor is x. For example, $x^2 + 3x = 0$ has x as a common factor, and the two factors are x and $x + 3$. Setting each factor equal to 0 yields roots of $x = 0$ or -3.

3. **Factoring into Binomials**. Factoring a quadratic equation of the general form $ax^2 + bx + c = 0$ involves finding two binomials that are factors of the quadratic. This is the reverse, of course, of finding the product of two binomials by the F-O-I-L method. This involves finding factors of the product ac that add up to b. This method is by trial and error because ac can have many factors that have to be checked to see if they add up to b. Don't forget to consider all of the combinations of positives and negatives. Rewrite the original problem with the middle term split into the two factors of ac that add up to b. Then split the four terms into two sets of two terms, and factor each by grouping. Use the reverse of the distributive law to find the two factors of the quadratic. Once you have the two binomial factors, the solutions are found by setting each binomial equal to 0. See Example 4.16.

Method #3 above may sound a little different from other methods for factoring a quadratic into binomials, but it has the advantage of finding the factors more quickly than traditional trial-and-error methods when $a \neq 1$ (see Example 4.16). However, when $a \neq 1$, the quadratic formula (Section 4.5.2) is usually the best way to find the roots of a binomial.

4. **Completing the Square**. Basically, this is a method to "force" an equation into a form that essentially is the equality of two squares, which is solved by taking the square root of each side. This method actually works for any quadratic but it can be more cumbersome than the three preceding methods. However, it is useful in some situations, such as converting from the general to the standard form of the equation of a conic section (see Section 5.8.2).

This method involves several steps but it isn't difficult. Follow the steps to solve the equation $3x^2 + 2x - 1 = 0$ by completing the square.

a. Make sure the coefficient of the square term is 1. If it isn't, divide the equation through by the coefficient of the square term.

b. Put the constant by itself on the other side of the equal sign.

c. Take half the coefficient of the term that is to the first degree and square it, and add it to both sides of the equation.

d. Express the left-hand side as the square of a binomial and simplify the right-hand side.

e. Take the square roots of both sides of the equation and simplify. Don't forget the plus or minus sign on the right side of the equation.

EXAMPLE 4.13

Find the roots of $3x^2 + 2x - 1 = 0$ by completing the square.

SOLUTION 4.13

$\frac{1}{3}, -1$. Follow the five steps listed to complete the square:

a. Dividing $3x^2 + 2x - 1 = 0$ by 3 gives $x^2 + \frac{2}{3}x - \frac{1}{3} = 0$.

b. $x^2 + \frac{2}{3}x = \frac{1}{3}$

c. Complete the square on the left hand side by squaring one-half of the coefficient of x, or $\left(\frac{1}{2} \times \frac{2}{3}\right)^2 = \frac{1}{9}$

d. Adding $\frac{1}{9}$ to both sides of the equation gives: $\left(x^2 + \frac{2}{3}x + \frac{1}{9}\right) = \frac{1}{3} + \frac{1}{9}$.

e. $\left(x + \frac{1}{3}\right)^2 = \frac{4}{9}$

f. $x + \frac{1}{3} = \frac{\sqrt{4}}{\sqrt{9}} = \pm\frac{2}{3}$, or $x = \left(\pm\frac{2}{3}\right) - \frac{1}{3}$, or $x = \frac{1}{3}, -1$.

No matter what method you use, be sure to check your answers by substituting the roots, or the values found for x, into the original equations.

EXAMPLE 4.14

Solve the quadratic equation $d^2 - \frac{9}{16} = 0$.

SOLUTION 4.14

$\pm\frac{3}{4}$. This quadratic is the difference of two squares, since 9 and 16 are both perfect squares. One way to solve for d is to use the difference of squares formula, which results in $\left(d + \frac{3}{4}\right)\left(d - \frac{3}{4}\right) = 0$, or $d = \pm\frac{3}{4}$. Alternatively, clear the equation of fractions by multiplying through by 16 to get $16d^2 - 9 = 0$, which is clearly the difference of two squares, which factors into $(4d + 3)(4d - 3) = 0$ or $d = \pm\frac{3}{4}$.

EXAMPLE 4.15

Solve the equation $3x^2 = 9x$.

SOLUTION 4.15

0, 3. Rewrite the equation as $3x^2 - 9x = 0$. Because this quadratic doesn't have a c term, it should have a common factor involving x. Indeed, the common factor is $3x$, and if this is factored out of both terms, the result is $3x(x - 3)$, which results in solutions of $3x = 0$ and $x - 3 = 0$, or $x = 0, 3$.

EXAMPLE 4.16

Solve the equation $x^2 - 2x = 15$.

SOLUTION 4.16

–3, 5. First, write the equation in the general form of $ax^2 + bx + c = 0$ by moving the 15 to the left side of the equation: $x^2 - 2x - 15 = 0$. Then solve the equation algebraically by finding two numbers whose product is –15 and sum is –2. The possibilities for a product of –15 are 3 and –5, –3 and 5, 1 and –15, and –1 and 15. Only the first of these (3 and –5) has a sum of –2, so the quadratic becomes $(x + 3)(x - 5) = 0$. Setting each of these factors equal to 0 gives the solution $x = -3$ or $x = 5$.

EXAMPLE 4.17

Solve $2(x^2 + 1) = 5x$.

SOLUTION 4.17

$2, \frac{1}{2}$. First, write the equation in the general form of $ax^2 + bx + c = 0$:

$$2x^2 + 2 = 5x$$

$$2x^2 - 5x + 2 = 0$$

So the problem is to find two numbers whose product is $ac = 4$ and sum is $b = -5$. The possibilities for $ac = 4$ are 2 and 2, –2 and –2, 4 and 1, and –4 and –1. Here –4 and –1 fulfill the criteria. Rewrite the original equation with the middle term ($-5x$) split into two terms that add up to $b = -5$ and use the distributive property:

$$2x^2 - x - 4x + 2 = 0$$

$$x(2x - 1) - 2(2x - 1) = 0$$

$$(x - 2)(2x - 1) = 0$$

Set each factor equal to 0 to find the two solutions to the quadratic.

$$(x - 2) = 0 \Rightarrow x = 2 \text{ and } (2x - 1) = 0 \Rightarrow x = \frac{1}{2}$$

4.5.2 Quadratic Formula

The quadratic formula can find the roots for *all* quadratic equations and, although the formula looks complicated, it is in many cases easier than the factoring methods discussed in Section 4.5.1. All quadratic equations of the form $ax^2 + bx + c = 0$ can be solved by using the **quadratic formula**.

$$x = \frac{-b \pm \sqrt{b^2 - 4ac}}{2a}$$

Note the following details about this useful formula:

- The value of a cannot be 0, both because if $a = 0$, the equation would be linear and not quadratic, and because division by 0 is undefined.

- The formula contains a $\pm$ sign, which gives the two roots that all quadratic equations have.

- The formula involves a square root. The value under the square root sign, $b^2 - 4ac$, is called the **discriminant**.

The discriminant describes the roots, so often it is a first step when solving quadratic equations.

- If $b^2 - 4ac > 0$, both roots are real and easily found by using the quadratic formula. The graph of this function crosses the x-axis at exactly two places.

- If $b^2 - 4ac = 0$ (that is, if $b^2 = 4ac$), the two roots are real and identical and equal to $\frac{-b}{2a}$. When two roots are identical, they are called **double roots**. An example of this case is the quadratic equation $x^2 + 6x + 9 = 0$, with a double root of –3. The graph of this function touches the x-axis at only one point (it is **tangent** to the x-axis).

- If $b^2 - 4ac < 0$, the roots are not real; they are **imaginary**, and thus **complex** (see Section 3.2). Complex roots always come in pairs, so if one root is $6 + 3i$, the other root is $6 - 3i$, its **complex conjugate** (see Section 4.4.2). When graphed, this type of function does not cross the x-axis.

In addition,

- If $b^2 - 4ac$ is a perfect square, the roots are rational, and if $b^2 - 4ac$ is positive and not a perfect square, the roots are irrational.

Important things to watch out for when using the quadratic formula include:

- When determining what a, b, and c are, remember to include their signs.

- The factor $2a$ divides into the whole numerator, not just one of the terms. A common mistake is to divide it only into the square root term and to forget about the $-b$ term that is also in the numerator.

- Following the order of operations, check out the discriminant first. That will tell whether the roots are real or imaginary.

- The quadratic equation gives roots, not factors, so if you are using the quadratic equation as a tool for factoring, the last step after finding the roots is to then write the factors. For example, if the roots of an equation are 3 and –4, the factors are $(x-3)$ and $(x-(-4)) = (x+4)$.

 (Hint:) All quadratic equations can be solved by using the quadratic formula, which is not provided on the Praxis formula sheets, but important enough to memorize it.

EXAMPLE 4.18

Use the quadratic formula to find the roots of $3x^2 + 2x - 1 = 0$, the equation for Example 4.13. Compare the two sets of answers.

SOLUTION 4.18

For this equation, $a = 3$, $b = 2$, and $c = -1$. Then

$$x = \frac{-b \pm \sqrt{b^2 - 4ac}}{2a} = \frac{-2 \pm \sqrt{4 - 4(3)(-1)}}{2(3)} = \frac{-2 \pm \sqrt{16}}{6} = \frac{1}{3}, -1,$$

which is the same as the solution to Example 4.13.

4.5.3 Linear Quadratic Systems

Do its As on internet

Just as was the case for systems of linear equations, systems of quadratic and linear equations, called **linear quadratic systems**, are a group of two or more equations that share solutions.

And like systems of linear equations, linear quadratic systems can be solved either algebraically or graphically. There are several algebraic choices:

- Rearrange each equation so they each equal y alone. Then set them equal to each other and solve the resulting quadratic equation for x the usual way. Then substitute the x value into the linear equation (either will work, but linear is easier) to find y.

- Rearrange only the linear equation to get an equation for y in terms of x (or x in terms of y). Then substitute this equation into the quadratic equation. The result is a quadratic equation that can be solved the usual way. Again, substitute this value into the linear equation to find the other unknown.

- Also do system of Quadratic Inequalities. As in Laptop Praxis folder.

Graphic solutions involve the intersection of the graphs of the linear equation (a line) and the quadratic equation (a parabola, or U-shaped curve). We already saw that systems of linear equations can be consistent (one solution), inconsistent (no solution), or dependent (infinite solutions). Like-wise, linear quadratic systems can have 0, 1, or 2 solutions (but obviously not an infinite number because a line is different from a parabola).

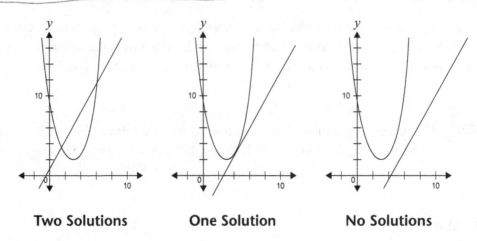

Two Solutions   **One Solution**   **No Solutions**

There are no solutions when the two graphs never intersect and there are two solutions when they do intersect, which is the usual configuration. But don't forget that there can also be just one solution if the line meets the parabola at a single point of tangency, or **tangent point**.

4.6 POLYNOMIALS

A **polynomial** is defined as an expression of more than two algebraic terms that contain different powers of variable(s). Thus, a quadratic is a type of polynomial. The **degree** of a polynomial is the largest exponent of the variable.

4.6.1 Roots of a Polynomial

The **Fundamental Theorem of Algebra** states:

> Any polynomial of degree n has n complex roots in the form of $a + bi$, which are either all real, all imaginary, or a combination of real and imaginary roots.

As Section 4.5 shows, quadratics are equations of degree 2 with 2 roots. The roots of a polynomial can be real, such as a root of 4, and/or imaginary, such as a root of $4 + 2i$. Every **imaginary root** (of the form $a + bi$) is accompanied by its conjugate (here, $a - bi$). A **conjugate** is the result of changing the sign in middle of two terms; they don't have to be imaginary. For instance, if one root is $3 + \sqrt{2}$, another root must be $3 - \sqrt{2}$. Imaginary roots never appear alone, so a polynomial can have any even number of imaginary roots up to n, the degree of the polynomial, including 0 imaginary roots.

Finding the roots of a polynomial of degree $n > 2$ is not as straightforward as finding the roots of a quadratic, but some facts help to describe them:

1. From the Fundamental Theorem of Algebra, we automatically know that the total number of roots cannot exceed the degree of the polynomial.

2. Use **Descartes Rule of Signs** to determine how many of the roots can be positive real numbers and how many can be negative real numbers, and possibly determine how many other roots there are. This rule doesn't involve any real math—just an ability to count sign changes. Count the number of times the sign changes in the original equation—that is the maximum number of positive real roots. For the maximum number of negative roots, rewrite the equation with x replaced by $-x$ and count the sign changes. Again, subtract by two for possible imaginary roots. If there are any positive complex roots, since they come in pairs, the actual possibilities for positive *real* roots are the number you get, or two less (because two can be complex), or four less, etc., and the same is true for negative complex roots.

3. Similar to finding the factors for quadratics, we look at the first (highest-order) and last (constant) terms of the polynomial to determine possibilities for the real roots of the polynomial. Then we use the **Rational Roots Test** for a list of relatively easy *possible* numbers to try in the polynomial. Then if any make the polynomial equal to 0, that number is a root. Most of these possible zeros will not turn out to actually be zeros! If any of these numbers is ± 1, that is the easiest starting point.

The "formula" is to write out all of the factors of the constant term and all of the factors of the leading coefficient and then list all of the combinations of

$$\pm \frac{\text{factors of constant}}{\text{factors of leading coefficient}}$$

EXAMPLE 4.19

Determine the nature of the roots of the equation $x^3 + 4x^2 + 3x - 2 = 0$.

SOLUTION 4.19

Either one real positive root and two real negative roots, or one real positive root and two complex roots. The equation $x^3 + 4x^2 + 3x - 2 = 0$ has exactly three roots. There is only one sign change, from $+3x$ to -2, so there is a maximum of one positive real root. Replacing x with $-x$, we get $(-x)^3 + 4(-x)^2 + 3(-x) - 2 = 0$, and two sign changes, so there is a maximum of two negative real roots. Therefore, $x^3 + 4x^2 + 3x - 2 = 0$ has either one real positive root and two real negative roots, or one real positive root and two complex roots.

EXAMPLE 4.20

Find the roots of $x^3 + 4x^2 + 3x - 2 = 0$ using the information in Example 4.19.

SOLUTION 4.20

$x = -2, -1 + \sqrt{2}, -1 - \sqrt{2}$. The Rational Roots Test says that the possible real roots are $\pm\dfrac{2, 1}{1}$, or $\pm\dfrac{2}{1}, \dfrac{1}{1}$, or $+1, -1, +2, -2$. The easiest to try is $+1$: $(1)^3 + 4(1)^2 + 3(1)^1 - 2 \neq 0$. Note that we don't have to come up with a value—only whether it equals 0. So $+1$ is not a root. Next, we try -1, 2, and -2. It turns out that -2 does make the equation equal 0.

Once we have found a root, we can divide its factor $(x + 2)$ into the original equation to get a simplified equation to work with for the other two roots. This division can be done by long division or synthetic division (see Section 4.6.4). Here the simplified equation is the quadratic $x^2 + 2x - 1$, since $\dfrac{x^3 + 4x^2 + 3x - 2}{x = 2} = x^2 + 2x - 1$, so we actually can get the other two roots of the equation by using the quadratic formula on $x^2 + 2x - 1$.

$$x = \frac{-b \pm \sqrt{b^2 - 4ac}}{2a} = \frac{-(2) \pm \sqrt{(2)^2 - 4(1)(-1)}}{2(1)} = \frac{-2 \pm \sqrt{8}}{2} = -1 \pm \sqrt{2}$$

Thus, the roots of $x^3 + 4x^2 + 3x - 2 = 0$ are $x = -2, -1 + \sqrt{2}, -1 - \sqrt{2}$.

Polynomials of a power greater than 3, require repeating the procedure in Examples 4.19 and 4.20 for each successive quotient.

4.6.2 Polynomial Identities

You may already know some of the following common polynomial identities from having used them. They are not on the Praxis formula sheet.

$$(a + b)^2 = a^2 + 2ab + b^2$$

$$(a + b)(c + d) = ac + ad + bc + bd$$

$$a^2 - b^2 = (a + b)(a - b)$$

$$a^3 + b^3 = (a + b)(a^2 - ab + b^2)$$

$$a^3 - b^3 = (a - b)(a^2 + ab + b^2)$$

$$x^2 + (a + b)x + ab = (x + a)(x + b)$$

4.6.3 Factor Theorem and Remainder Theorem

The **Factor Theorem** can be stated in two equivalent ways:

For a polynomial $f(x)$, if $f(c) = 0$, then $(x - c)$ must be a factor of $f(x)$,

or

if $(x - c)$ is a factor of a polynomial $f(x)$, then $f(c) = 0$.

The **Remainder Theorem** states:

When a polynomial $f(x)$ is divided by a binomial $x - c$ the remainder r equals $f(c)$.

4.6.4 Long Division and Synthetic Division

Synthetic division is actually based on long division of a polynomial by a binomial. First let's look at the long division, which is very much like long division of numbers.

The following long division is included here only to illustrate how simple synthetic division is compared to long division. Let's divide $x^5 + x^4 - 6x^3 - 2x^2 + 10x - 12$ by $x - 2$:

$$
\begin{array}{r}
x^4 + 3x^3 \qquad\quad - 2x \quad + 6 \\
x - 2 \overline{)\, x^5 + \ x^4 - 6x^3 - 2x^2 + 10x - 12} \\
\underline{x^5 - 2x^4} \qquad\qquad\qquad\qquad\qquad \\
+3x^4 - 6x^3 \qquad\qquad\qquad\quad \\
\underline{+3x^4 - 6x^3} \qquad\qquad\qquad\quad \\
0 - 2x^2 + 10x \qquad\quad \\
\underline{- 2x^2 + 4x} \qquad\quad \\
+ 6x - 12 \\
\underline{+ 6x - 12} \\
0
\end{array}
$$

Whew! Now, let's do the same division using synthetic division. One of the rules for synthetic division is that the divisor must be a first-degree (linear) expression with 1 as the coefficient for x. So you can use synthetic division to divide by $x - 2$ (as we have here), or by any binomial such as $x + 6$, but not by $x^2 - 2$ nor by $2x + 5$. However, in the last case, you can use $x + \dfrac{5}{2}$ instead to make the coefficient of x equal to 1. This is okay, because the first step in synthetic division is:

1. Set the original divisor equal to 0, and use the value that makes that equation true. In our example, which is dividing $x^5 + x^4 - 6x^3 - 2x^2 + 10x - 12$ by $x - 2$, once we set $x - 2 = 0$, we know our "synthetic divisor" will be 2 (the solution to $x - 2 = 0$).

We use the factor (e.g., $x - 2$) in long division, but the root of the factor (e.g., 2) in synthetic division.

Next, to find the "synthetic dividend,"

2. Make sure the terms are in descending powers and merely write only the coefficients of all the terms in the polynomial, along with their signs, using 0 for any missing power.

For our example, then, we have the following setup for synthetic division:

$$2 \,\big|\, \quad 1 \quad\quad 1 \quad\quad -6 \quad\quad -2 \quad\quad +10 \quad\quad -12$$

3. Bring down the first number, multiply it by the synthetic divisor, and put that value in the next column.

4. Add the numbers in the next column, multiply this sum by the synthetic divisor, and put that value in the next column, and continue to the end.

For the same problem as the long division, this would look like:

$$
\begin{array}{c|cccccc}
2 & 1 & 1 & -6 & -2 & +10 & -12 \\
  & \downarrow & 2 & 6 & 0 & -4 & 12 \\
\hline
  & 1 & 3 & 0 & -2 & 6 & 0
\end{array}
$$

The last number, 0 here, is the remainder.

- If the remainder isn't 0, that divisor isn't a root of the original equation. You can then try another number, according to the Rational Roots Test.

- If the remainder equals 0, the divisor is a root of the original equation. Not only that, but the numbers in that last row are the coefficients of the polynomial that is a factor of the original polynomial.

Thus, for this sample problem,

$$x^5 + x^4 - 6x^3 - 2x^2 + 10x - 12 = (x - 2)(x^4 + 3x^3 - 2x + 6)$$

This last factor, $(x^4 + 3x^3 - 2x + 6)$, is the last row of the synthetic division, 1, 3, 0, –2, 6.

The quotient of long division by a possible factor is the "other factor" if the remainder is 0. In synthetic division, the last line can be translated into the "other factor" if the last number equals 0, and the synthetic divisor is a root.

EXAMPLE 4.21

Find all of the factors of $x^3 + 3x^2 - 10x - 24$.

SOLUTION 4.21

$(x + 2)(x + 4)(x - 3)$. Since the highest power of the polynomial is 3, there are at most three distinct roots, which means three factors. Use the Rational Roots Test to determine relatively easy *possible* numbers to try in the polynomial: $\pm\dfrac{\text{factors of constant}}{\text{factors of leading coefficient}} = \pm1, \pm2, \pm3, \pm4, \pm6, \pm8, \pm12, \pm24$, or all the factors of 24. This makes 16 possibilities, but remember we need to find only one to simplify the problem. Use Descartes Rule of Signs to determine how many of the roots can be positive real numbers and how many can be negative real numbers. Since there is only one sign change in the original equation, $x^3 + 3x^2 - 10x - 24$, there is a maximum of one positive real root. If x is replaced by $-x$, there are two sign changes, so there is a maximum of two negative real roots. Now we know we are looking for one positive and two negative real roots (or possibly one real positive and two imaginary roots).

We can either substitute the root into the equation, do long division, or do synthetic division, looking for a number that will make the value of the equation 0 or make the remainder in the division 0.

When we did the rule of signs using x and $-x$, we essentially were checking ±1, so now we check ±2. First let's check $x = 2$, and let's use synthetic division (although we could also use substitution or even long division):

$$
\begin{array}{r|rrrr}
2 & 1 & 3 & -10 & -24 \\
  & \downarrow & 2 & 10 & 0 \\
\hline
  & 1 & 5 & 0 & -24
\end{array}
$$

Since the remainder is –24, and not 0, let's go on to check –2 in the same way:

$$
\begin{array}{r|rrrr}
-2 & 1 & 3 & -10 & -24 \\
   & \downarrow & -2 & -2 & 24 \\
\hline
   & 1 & 1 & -12 & 0
\end{array}
$$

Success! One of the factors is $x + 2$, and the other factor is $x^2 + x - 12$, which is a quadratic that can easily be factored into $(x + 4)(x - 3)$. Then the three factors are $(x + 2)(x + 4)(x - 3)$. That means the three real roots of $x^3 + 3x^2 - 10x - 24$ are –2, –4, and 3, and there are one positive and two negative real roots, as predicted by the Descartes Rule of Signs.

NOTE The value of a polynomial $f(x)$ at a particular value of x is the remainder when $f(x)$ is synthetically divided by the value of x.

EXAMPLE 4.22

What is the value of $x^3 + 3x^2 - 10x - 24$ for $x = 2$?

SOLUTION 4.22

−24. We need go no further. In Example 4.21, we saw that there was a remainder of −24 when we synthetically divided by 2, so we know that is the value of the equation at $x = 2$.

Practice Exercises

1. If $f(x) = 3x^4 + 2x^3 + 4x$, what is $f(-5)$?

   (A) 2145

   (B) 1605

   (C) 69

   (D) −421

2. What must be the value of C for $x = 2$ to be a solution of $f(x) = x^6 - x^4 - 2x^3 + C$?

   (A) −32

   (B) 32

   (C) 0

   (D) 2

3. Find the solutions to the quadratic $x^4 - 16 = 0$.

   (A) ±4

   (B) ±2

   (C) ±2, ±4

   (D) ±2, ±2i

4. Reduce to lowest terms: $\dfrac{4-2x}{x^2-4}$.

 (A) $\dfrac{2}{x+2}$

 (B) $-\dfrac{2}{x+2}$

 (C) $\dfrac{2}{x-2}$

 (D) $-\dfrac{2}{x-2}$

5. Simplify $\dfrac{x+\frac{1}{2}}{x^2-\frac{1}{4}}$.

 (A) $\dfrac{2}{2x-1}$

 (B) $\dfrac{2}{2x+1}$

 (C) $\dfrac{4}{4x-1}$

 (D) $\dfrac{2}{2x^2-1}$

6. The factors of x^3-a^2x are: (Choose *all* that apply.)

 A x^2

 B x

 C $x+a$

 D $x-a$

7. In the equation $y=5-\dfrac{1}{x}$, as x decreases, y $\left\{\begin{array}{l}\text{increases}\\\text{decreases}\\\text{stays the same}\end{array}\right\}$.

→ Attn!

8. Write the equation of a straight line parallel to the line $2y-3x=8$ that has integer coefficients and a y-intercept of 5.

Rev.

 (A) $y=\dfrac{3}{2}x+5$

 (B) $2y-3x=8$

 (C) $2y=3x+5$

 (D) $2y=3x+10$

9. To rationalize the denominator of the fraction $\dfrac{5-\sqrt{2}}{5+\sqrt{2}}$, multiply the fraction by

(A) $5-\sqrt{2}$

(B) $\dfrac{27-10\sqrt{2}}{23}$

(C) $5+\sqrt{2}$

(D) $\dfrac{5-\sqrt{2}}{5-\sqrt{2}}$

10. Solve $3x^2 = 9x$

(A) $0, 3$

(B) $0, -3$

(C) $3, -3$

(D) $0, 0$

11. Find the roots of $2x^3 - x^2 - 2x + 1 = 0$.

(A) $1, \dfrac{1}{2}, -1$

(B) $-1, \dfrac{1}{2}, 1$

(C) $1, \dfrac{1}{2}, 1$

(D) $1, -\dfrac{1}{2}, -1$

Solutions

1. **(B)** 1605. The easiest way to find the value of a polynomial $f(x)$ at a particular value of x is to use synthetic division to find the remainder when $f(x)$ is divided by the value of x. For synthetic division, every power of x in $f(x)$ must have a coefficient, so for those that are missing (the x^2 and constant terms), use zeros in the synthetic division. Thus, $f(-5)$ is the remainder of the synthetic division $\dfrac{f(x)}{-5}$, or 1605:

-5	3	2	0	4	0
↓		-15	65	-325	1605
	3	-13	65	-321	1605

2. (A) -32. The value of $f(2)$ must be 0 for $x = 2$ to be a solution of $f(x)$. This value can be found in a couple of ways: Substituting $x = 2$ into $f(x)$ yields $f(2) = (2)^6 - (2)^4 - 2(2)^3 + C = 64 - 16 - 16 + C = 0$, or $C = -32$. Synthetic division, with the remainder equal to 0 would also work, but if the calculation is easy, as it usually is for low values of x, just go with the substitution.

3. (D) $\pm 2, \pm 2i$. If we look at this as the difference of two squares (the squares being x^4 and 16), then the factors are the sum and difference of the square roots, $(x^2 + 4)(x^2 - 4)$, but the last factor is itself the difference of two squares, so the factors of $x^4 - 16$ are $(x^2 + 4)(x + 2)(x - 2)$. In this case, we know two of the roots are $x = \pm 2$, but $x^2 + 4$ doesn't have any real roots because there isn't any number that, when squared, will yield -4. Such roots are imaginary, or $\sqrt{-4} = \pm 2i$. Since this is a fourth-degree equation, it should have four roots.

4. (B) $-x + \dfrac{2}{2}$. Rewrite the numerator so the first term is an x term and the common factors will more easily be seen. $\dfrac{4 - 2x}{x^2 - 4} = -\dfrac{2x - 4}{x^2 - 4} = -\dfrac{2\,(x - 2)^1}{(x + 2)\,(x - 2)^1} = -\dfrac{2}{x + 2}$. Remember to carry the minus sign before the fraction through to the end.

5. (A) $\dfrac{2}{2x - 1}$. One way to do this problem is to recognize that the denominator, $x^2 - \dfrac{1}{4}$, is the difference of two squares, so it can be factored into $\left(x + \dfrac{1}{2}\right)\left(x - \dfrac{1}{2}\right)$, and the first of these factors can cancel with the numerator, so the problem fraction reduces to $\dfrac{1}{x - \frac{1}{2}} = \dfrac{1}{\frac{2x-1}{2}} = \dfrac{2}{2x - 1}$. However, if you don't recognize this "shortcut," the usual way of dividing fractions works as well: $\left(x + \dfrac{1}{2}\right) \div \left(x^2 - \dfrac{1}{4}\right) = \left(\dfrac{2x + 1}{2}\right) \div \left(\dfrac{4x^2 - 1}{4}\right) = \left(\dfrac{2x + 1}{2}\right) \times \dfrac{4}{(2x + 1)(2x - 1)} = \dfrac{2}{(2x - 1)}$ after some cancellation. Another way to do this, which works with all complex fractions, is to multiply every term in the complex fraction by the LCD, which is 4 in this problem. The result is $\dfrac{4x + 2}{4x^2 - 1}$, which can be factored as $\dfrac{2(2x + 1)}{(2x + 1)(2x - 1)}$ and with cancellation, the final answer is $\dfrac{2}{2x - 1}$.

6. $\boxed{B}\,x$, $\boxed{C}\,x + a$, $\boxed{D}\,x - a$. The solution involves taking out a common factor and recognizing the difference of two squares: $x^3 - a^2 x = x(x^2 - a^2) = x(x + a)(x - a)$.

7. Decreases. As x decreases, the fraction $\dfrac{1}{x}$ increases. Since an increasing amount is subtracted from 5, $y = 5 - \dfrac{1}{x}$ decreases.

8. (D) $2y = 3x + 10$. If the line is parallel to the given line, they must have the same slope, so put the given line in slope-intercept form to determine the slope: $2y - 3x = 8$ becomes

$2y = 3x + 8$, which is $y = \dfrac{3}{2}x + 4$ in slope-intercept form, so the slope is $\dfrac{3}{2}$. Now that we have the slope and were given the y-intercept of 5, the equation of the requested line is $y = \dfrac{3}{2}x + 5$. But since the problem states that it should have integer coefficients, we must multiply through by 2 to get $2y = 3x + 10$.

9. (D) $\dfrac{5 - \sqrt{2}}{5 - \sqrt{2}}$. The value of the fraction in answer choice (D) is 1, so multiplying by it won't change the value of the fraction. Answer choices (A) and (C) will change the value of the fraction. Answer choice (B) is the value of the fraction when the denominator is correctly rationalized, but that isn't what the problem asks for.

10. (A) 0, 3

$$3x^2 = 9x$$

$$3x^2 - 9x = 0$$

$$3x(x - 3) = 0$$

$$3x = 0 \text{ or } x - 3 = 0$$

$$x = 0, 3$$

11. (A) $-1, \dfrac{1}{2}, 1$. If any of the possible roots are 1 or -1, try them first. Here, if we try $x = +1$ and use synthetic division (or divide $x - 1$ into the equation), we get

1	2	-1	-2	$+1$
	$\downarrow$	$+2$	$+1$	-1
	2	$+1$	-1	0

which shows that $x = 1$ is a root, and the quotient translates into $2x^2 + x - 1 = (2x - 1)(x + 1) = 0$. Setting each factor equal to 0 gives the other two roots, $x = \dfrac{1}{2}$ and $x = -1$.

Geometry

5.1 BASIC DEFINITIONS

5.1.1 Points

Let's start with the most basic geometric object—the **point**. A true point actually has no dimensions (no length, no width, no height). So two questions come to mind: (1) What good are points? (2) How we can draw them?

Points are used for defining positions, and we draw them as a dot, which even if we use the sharpest pencil, still looks like it has a tiny length and width or maybe looks like a really small circle. We talk about the position of a point when plotting ordered pairs on a graph.

Even though a point has no dimensions, it is real, it isn't invisible, and it's really useful. Points are the building blocks of all other geometric objects. The **distance between two points** (x_1, y_1) and (x_2, y_2) in the coordinate plane is given by the distance formula.

$$d = \sqrt{(x_1 - x_2)^2 + (y_1 - y_2)^2}$$

The distance from any point (x_1, y_1) on the coordinate plane **to a line** given by $ax + by + c$ is

$$d = \frac{|ax_1 + by_1 + c|}{\sqrt{a^2 + b^2}}$$

This formula is on the Praxis formula sheet.

5.1.2 Lines

When we string an infinite number of points together, we get a **line**, straight or curved. A line can be seen, and it has one dimension—length. Between any two points on a line, there is always another point, and so on and so on.

When we talk about lines, we should be precise about what we mean.

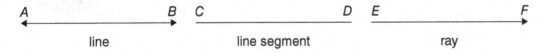

A line goes on forever in two directions. Of course, when we draw a line, we can't draw out to outer space, so we indicate that it goes on forever by putting an arrowhead on both ends, and by referring to it as $\overleftrightarrow{AB}$. Often, though, we are using **line segments**, which have endpoints and a definite length. They are usually named by their endpoints, such as line segment $\overline{CD}$ above. A **ray** is a special type of line that has an **endpoint** on one "end" and an arrowhead on the other, indicating that it really isn't ending in one direction, like $\overrightarrow{EF}$.

To get an idea of the infinite number of points on a line, line segment, or ray, draw a six-inch line segment and label the endpoints A and B. Now put a mark at the halfway point, called the **midpoint** (3 inches from either end). Let's close in on point B at the end of the line. From the midpoint you just indicated, make a mark halfway to point B, then halfway again, and again, and again. Keep doing this—will you ever reach point B? No, because even though the distance to B is getting smaller and smaller, there is always a point that will be the midpoint of the remaining distance. If we were to measure these distances precisely, we never get to point B because we can always take one-half of the last distance, and the measurement quickly becomes a decimal with lots and lots of zeros after the decimal point.

5.1.3 Angles

If we connect two rays at their endpoints, we form an **angle**. The place where the two endpoints meet is called the **vertex** of the angle. The sides of the angle, being rays, go off into space unless we put an endpoint on one or both of them.

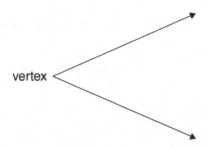

What distinguishes one angle from another is how wide open it is. The measurement of an angle is based on 360°, which is how many degrees there are in a circle. Indeed, if an angle has 360°, the sides are one on top of the other and they no longer look like an angle, they look like a ray.

5.1.3a Types of Angles

An angle that equals 90° is a **right** angle. The rays of a right angle are perpendicular to each other. Any angle that is less than 90° is called **acute**, and any angle greater than 90° and less than 180° is called **obtuse**.

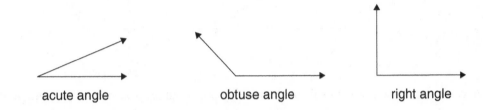

acute angle   obtuse angle   right angle

An angle of exactly 180° is called a **straight angle** because the rays form a straight line. An angle that is greater than 180° but less than 360°, is called a **reflex** angle, but we rarely encounter it.

straight angle

reflex angle

5.1.3b Angle Relationships

Relationships between angles mostly have to do with their measurements. **Adjacent angles** share a side. Any two angles that total 180° are called **supplementary**, and they need not be adjacent. If they are adjacent, their outer sides form a straight line. Likewise, any two angles that total 90° are called **complementary**, and they need not be adjacent. If they are adjacent, their outer sides form a right angle.

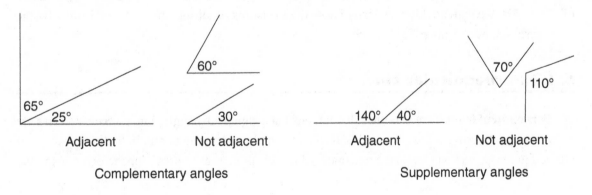

Adjacent   Not adjacent   Adjacent   Not adjacent

Complementary angles   Supplementary angles

5.2 PARALLEL AND PERPENDICULAR LINES

5.2.1 Parallel Lines

As we saw in Chapter 4, Section 4.2.7, two lines that never meet are called **parallel** lines. If parallel lines are crossed by another line, which is called the **transversal**, eight angles are formed.

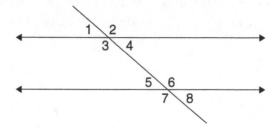

When two lines cross, the angles formed are either **supplementary** or they are **vertical angles**, which are equal angles opposite each other. The (adjacent) supplementary angle pairs in the figure above are $\angle 1$ and $\angle 2$, $\angle 3$ and $\angle 4$, $\angle 5$ and $\angle 6$, $\angle 7$ and $\angle 8$, $\angle 1$ and $\angle 3$, $\angle 2$ and $\angle 4$, $\angle 5$ and $\angle 7$, $\angle 6$ and $\angle 8$. The vertical angle pairs are equal $\angle 1 = \angle 4$, $\angle 2 = \angle 3$, $\angle 5 = \angle 8$, $\angle 6 = \angle 7$.

From these relationships, we can see, for example, that $\angle 1 = \angle 5$; these are called **corresponding angles** because they are in corresponding positions on the two parallel lines (the others are $\angle 2 = \angle 6$, $\angle 3 = \angle 7$, and $\angle 4 = \angle 8$). Likewise, we can see that $\angle 1 = \angle 8$ and $\angle 2 = \angle 7$, which are called **alternate exterior angles** because they are in corresponding positions on the two parallel lines: on *alternate* sides of the transversal and *exterior* to the parallel lines. $\angle 3 = \angle 6$ and $\angle 4 = \angle 5$, are called **alternate interior angles** because they are *interior* to the parallel lines and on *alternate* sides of the transversal in corresponding positions on the two parallel lines. The equal angles can be visualized quite readily.

So when two parallel lines are crossed by a transversal, we need the measure of only one of the eight angles formed to get the measures of all of them, since all of the angles are either supplementary or are vertical (equal) angles. In the figure above, for example, if we know the measure of $\angle 1$ is 75°, we can quickly and easily know the measures of all the other angles formed by the transversal—they are either 75° or 105°.

5.2.2 Perpendicular Lines

Perpendicular lines are two lines that intersect at a right (90°) angle. Since vertical angles are equal, the two lines form four 90° angles. Right angles play a prominent role in finding the areas of closed figures, as will be seen in the remainder of this chapter, as most areas depend on knowing the altitude of the figure. The **altitude** of a figure is a line that is perpendicular to one side of the figure and ends at the opposite angle (vertex).

5.2.3 Slopes of Parallel and Perpendicular Lines

If you know the slopes of two lines, you don't even have to graph them to see whether they are parallel or perpendicular. Put the equation of the line in slope-intercept form ($y = mx + b$), and compare the m values. Chapter 4, Section 4.2.7, showed that lines with the same slope are all parallel. The slopes of perpendicular lines also have a relationship: their slopes are negative reciprocals of each other.

EXAMPLE 5.1

Are the two lines given by $3x + 4y = 6$ and $3y - 4x = 7$ perpendicular?

SOLUTION 5.1

Put each equation in slope-intercept form:

$$3x + 4y = 6 \qquad\qquad 3y - 4x = 7$$

$$4y = 6 - 3x \qquad\qquad 3y = 4x + 7$$

$$y = -\frac{3}{4}x + \frac{3}{2} \qquad\qquad y = \frac{4}{3}x + \frac{7}{3}$$

The slope of the first line is $-\dfrac{3}{4}$ and the slope of the second line is $\dfrac{4}{3}$, which are negative reciprocals, so the lines are perpendicular.

Don't forget the negative part of negative reciprocals!

5.3 SEGMENTING LINES

5.3.1 Midpoint, Median, and Midsegment

Line segments can be divided into equal parts. If a line segment is divided into two equal parts, the point where they meet is called the **midpoint** of the line segment. That point is exactly halfway between the endpoints of the segment. Midpoints play a prominent role in finding the areas of closed figures as well as other attributes in geometry, as will be seen in the remainder of this chapter. The **median** of a triangle, for example, is a line that goes from the midpoint of one side of the triangle to the opposite vertex. A **midsegment** is a line that joins the midpoints of two sides of a triangle or a trapezoid.

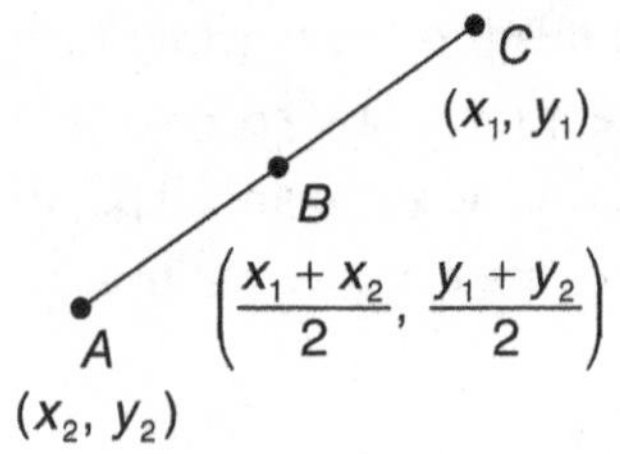

midpoint of a line

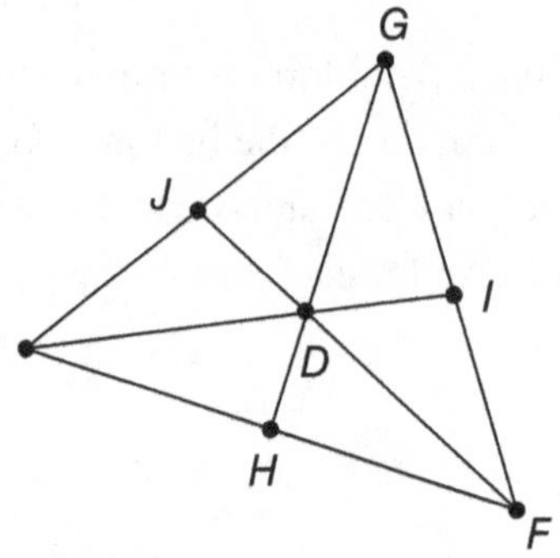

medians of a triangle

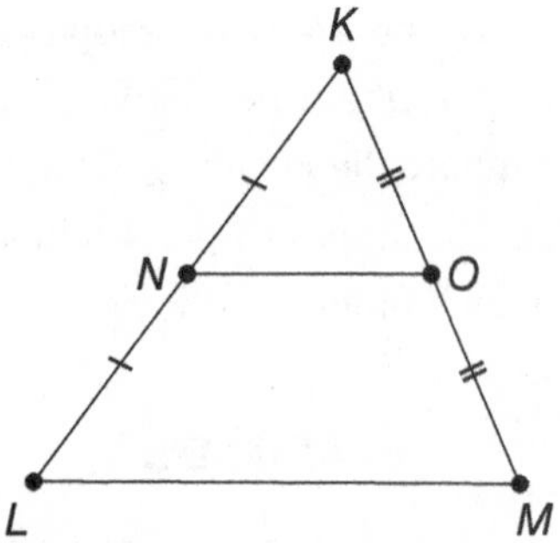

midsegment of a triangle

The formula for the midpoint of a line segment with endpoints (x_1, y_1) and (x_2, y_2) is the point with coordinates that are the average of the coordinates of the endpoints. For example, the midpoint of the line segment with endpoints (2, 6) and (4, 10) is calculated as

$$\text{Midpoint} = \left(\left(\frac{x_1 + x_2}{2}\right), \left(\frac{y_1 + y_2}{2}\right)\right) = \left(\frac{2+4}{2}, \frac{6+10}{2}\right) = (3, 8)$$

5.3.2 Dividing a Line Segment into Equal Parts

The midpoint divides a line segment into two equal parts, but what if we wanted three equal parts, or four, or seven? The formula for doing this is

$$(x, y) = (x_1 + k(x_2 - x_1), y_1 + k(y_2 - y_1))$$

where the endpoints are (x_1, y_1) and (x_2, y_2), and k is the fraction for the first point in the segmentation. For example, to divide a segment into five equal parts, use $k = \frac{1}{5}$ for the first point, and then use $k = \frac{2}{5}$ for the next point, and so forth. The arithmetic for this isn't difficult but it is very tedious. It's enough to know that any line segment can be divided into any number of equal parts accurately without guesswork.

NOTE: To divide a line segment into four parts, find the midpoint using the much easier midpoint formula, and then find the midpoints of the two half line segments.

5.3.3 Dividing a Line Segment by Using Ratios

To divide a line segment so that the parts are in the same ratio as another line segment, use perpendicular lines. The geometry for this will be evident in subsequent sections of this chapter, but for now it is sufficient to know that the following is possible. Say, for example, that we have a board with marks for where we want to attach hooks (not necessarily equally spaced). Then we discover that this board is too long (or too short), so we buy another board of the correct length but we still want the hooks to be marked with the same spacing ratio between the hooks. This can be done as shown in the figure below.

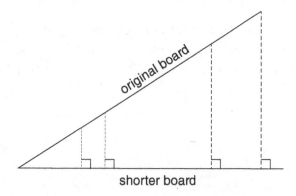

5.4 TRIANGLES

Triangles are formed when three line segments form a closed figure. They also have three angles, thus the name triangle. The sum of the angles in a triangle is 180°. The longest side is opposite the largest angle, and the smallest side is opposite the smallest angle. The sides of a triangle are designated by their endpoints (which are vertices of the triangle), or by a lowercase letter that matches the angle opposite that side, which is given as a capital letter.

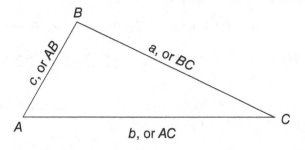

Triangles are one of the most important shapes in geometry. One of the useful properties of triangles is that they are rigid. That means that once you have three sides attached in a triangle shape, you cannot change it. You cannot make one of the sides longer, and you cannot make any of the angles larger without changing all the sides. This is why bridge supports have triangles as their major structure. Contrast this to a four-sided figure; if you push on one corner of a rectangle, for example, it can squish down to a parallelogram shape, even down to a line the length of two sides. That is why four-sided shapes in bridge supports have a diagonal bar—it converts them into two rigid triangles.

Another fact that has to do with a triangle's rigidity is that if only three measurements in a triangle are known, the remaining measurements can be determined by using trigonometry, discussed in Section 5.13 in this chapter. One exception is that if only the three angles are known, triangles of different sizes can be formed—this is discussed in Section 5.4.4 on similar triangles in this chapter.

The sum of the lengths of any two sides of a triangle must be greater than the length of the longest side, or we don't have a triangle (the two sides won't meet), as illustrated below. Another way to look at this rule is that the difference between the lengths of any two sides of a triangle must be less than the length of the shortest side.

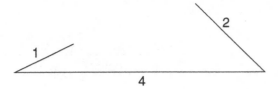

If all you know are the lengths of two sides of a triangle and nothing about the angles, you don't automatically know the third side of the triangle—it actually could be any length, depending on the angle between the two sides.

5.4.1 Types of Triangles

5.4.1a Classification by Sides

Triangles can be classified by their side measurements.

- **Scalene**: A triangle in which the lengths of all of the sides are different.

- **Isosceles:** A triangle with two equal side lengths. The two equal sides are called the **legs**, and the third side is called the **base**.

- **Equilateral**: All three side lengths are equal. The name comes from the two parts of the word: *equi* (equal) and *lateral* (sides).

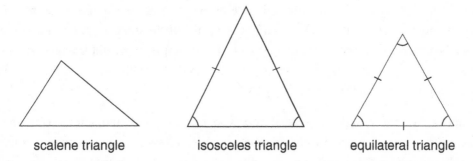

scalene triangle   isosceles triangle   equilateral triangle

 In the figures in this book, if sides are equal, they will be marked with the same tick marks (either one or two). Likewise, if angles are equal, they will be marked with the same angle marks. Right angles are marked with a small box.

5.4.1b Classification by Angles

The **base angles** in an isosceles triangle are equal. These are the angles that are across from the equal sides. An equilateral triangle is also called an **equiangular** triangle because if all three sides are equal, so are all three angles. The two parts of the word equiangular are: *equi* (equal) and *angular* (angles). The angles in an equilateral triangle are each 60° because there are three of them and they have to add up to 180°. Triangles are also classified by their angle measurements.

- **Acute**: All the angles are acute angles.

- **Obtuse**: One of the angles is an obtuse angle. There can be only one obtuse angle in a triangle because it uses up more than 90° of the total 180° in a triangle.

- **Right**: One of the angles is a right angle. This is such an important kind of angle that it deserves sections in this book all its own (Sections 5.4.1c–5.4.1f).

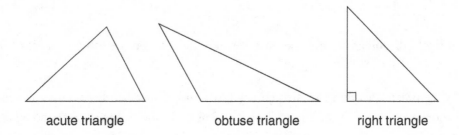

acute triangle   obtuse triangle   right triangle

5.4.1c Right Triangles

Right triangles are a special class of triangles because they are so common in our everyday life. They get their name from the fact that one of the angles is a right angle, or 90°, which means that two of the sides are perpendicular. Everyday examples of right triangles include a ladder propped against a house (the house is perpendicular to the ground) or a shadow cast by a tree (the tree is perpendicular to the ground).

In a right triangle, you need to know only one of the other angles to figure out the third angle because you know the right angle is 90° and the measures of the three angles in a triangle add up to 180°, so the other two angles must add up to 90°. For example, in a right triangle with one angle of 30°, the third angle is found by subtracting the other angle from 90°, so we get $90° - 30° = 60°$. This quick subtraction from 90° applies only to *right* triangles.

The sides of a right triangle are special, too. Knowing two sides and automatically being able to find the third side isn't possible with any other triangle, unless you also know one of the angles. But in a right triangle, you automatically know one of the angles—it is 90°.

5.4.1d Pythagorean Theorem

The formula for finding the third side of a right triangle if you know any of the other two sides is called the Pythagorean Theorem, which states:

The square of the hypotenuse is equal to the sum of the squares of the other two sides.

The **hypotenuse** of a right triangle is the side opposite the 90° angle. It is the longest side. The **legs** are the other two sides, and they aren't necessarily equal.

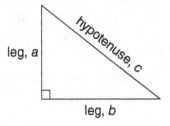

The formula for the Pythagorean Theorem is thus written as

$$c^2 = a^2 + b^2$$

Remember the Pythagorean formula because it is not included on the formula sheet of the Praxis test.

The Pythagorean Theorem can also be used to find the distance between two points on the Cartesian coordinate plane (see Section 5.1.1). The lengths of the two legs are found by calculating the absolute differences in the x values $|x_2 - x_1|$ and the y values $|y_2 - y_1|$. Then use these values as the a and b values, respectively, in the Pythagorean Theorem, and the c value will give the distance between the points. This can be seen in the following figure.

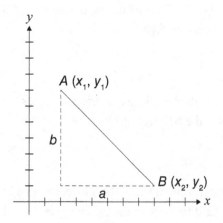

5.4.1e Pythagorean Triples

It is a good idea (and a time-saver on the test) if you know at least one of the **Pythagorean triples**. These are the sides of right triangles that are whole numbers, and thus don't involve a lot of math. The most popular is easy to remember. It is known as the 3-4-5 right triangle. Since $3^2 + 4^2 = 5^2$, the sides of this right triangle are indeed 3, 4, and 5.

Any multiple of the 3-4-5 right triangle (such as 6-8-10 or 9-12-15) is also a right triangle. So if we know that two legs of a right triangle are 6 and 8, we automatically know the third side (hypotenuse) is 10. Other Pythagorean triples are not as easy to remember as the 3-4-5. They are 5-12-13 and 8-15-17, and, of course, any multiples of them.

EXAMPLE 5.2

A ladder 10 feet long is propped 8 feet up on a house. How close to the foundation of the house is the base of the ladder?

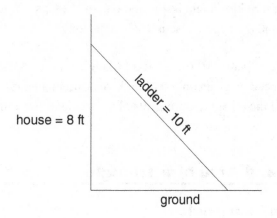

SOLUTION 5.2

6 feet. Since the house and its foundation form a right angle, we can use the Pythagorean Theorem, so $c^2 = a^2 + b^2$, or $10^2 = 8^2 + b^2$, and $b^2 = 36$. Thus, b, which is the

distance from the house to the base of the ladder, is 6 feet. This is double a 3-4-5 right triangle, so its sides are 6-8-10.

EXAMPLE 5.3

To drive to the ball game after work, Nick drives 8 miles north and then 15 miles west. How many miles is the ball field from Nick's workplace? ↳West from North ↳ Workplace

SOLUTION 5.3

17 miles. A sketch of the problem shows that it forms a right triangle in which the distance from the ball field to work is the hypotenuse. Use the Pythagorean Theorem: $c^2 = 8^2 + 15$. So the ball field is $\sqrt{289} = 17$ miles from Nick's workplace. This is a 8-15-17 right triangle.

5.4.1f Ratios of Sides of Right Triangle

In addition to knowing Pythagorean triples, which saves time when doing problems involving right triangles, two other triangles whose sides have memorable ratios are the 30°-60°-90° triangle and the 45°-45°-90° triangle.

- In the 30°-60°-90° triangle, the side opposite the 30° angle is half the hypotenuse and the length of the side opposite the 60° angle is the shortest side times $\sqrt{3}$. The ratio of the sides of any 30°-60°-90° right triangle, which is easy to remember, is 1-2-$\sqrt{3}$. So if you know that one angle of a right triangle is 30° and it has a hypotenuse of a units, you automatically know that the length of the shortest side is $\frac{a}{2}$ units, and the length of the other side is $\frac{a}{2}\sqrt{3}$ units.

- In a 45°-45°-90° triangle the legs are equal because it is not only a right triangle, but also an isosceles triangle. The sides of this triangle also have a memorable ratio: 1-1-$\sqrt{2}$. So if you know one angle of a right triangle is 45° and one of the legs is b units long, the other leg is also b units long, and the hypotenuse is $b\sqrt{2}$ units long.

 For both the 30°-60°-90° (or 1-2-$\sqrt{3}$) triangle and the 45°-45°-90° (or 1-1-$\sqrt{2}$) triangle, you need be given only one angle measurement and one side length to be able to find all of the other measurements of the triangle. Just remember which side is the hypotenuse (the longest side).

5.4.2 Perimeter and Area of a Triangle

5.4.2a Perimeter of a Triangle

The **perimeter** of a triangle is simply the sum of the side lengths. If the triangle is an isosceles triangle, two lengths will be the same. If it is an equilateral triangle, the perimeter is three times the length of one side, since they are all the same. For a right triangle, we may have to calculate the third side by the Pythagorean formula before we can add the three sides. So for any triangle with three sides, a, b, and c, the perimeter (P) is given by

$$P = a + b + c.$$

5.4.2b Area of a Triangle

The **area** of a triangle is one-half the base times the height (altitude) of the triangle. You can choose any of the three sides to be the **base**, although for an isosceles triangle it is easiest if it is the unequal side, and for a right triangle it should be one of the legs. The **height**, or **altitude**, is the perpendicular distance from the base to the opposite angle.

The tricky part to finding the area is determining the height of a triangle. It is equal to the length of one of the sides only if the triangle is a right triangle because the two legs are perpendicular. For any other triangle, it is not one of the other sides. The figure below shows the altitude for acute, isosceles, equilateral, and obtuse triangles. Note that for the isosceles and equilateral triangles, the altitude divides the base into two equal segments, and for the obtuse triangle, the altitude is actually outside the triangle itself.

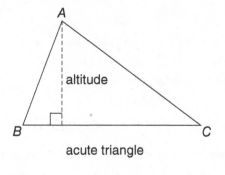

acute triangle

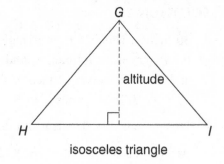

isosceles triangle

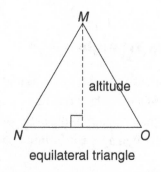

equilateral triangle

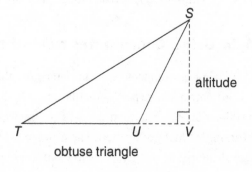

obtuse triangle

The formula for the area (A) of a triangle, where b is the base and h is the height to that base, is

$$A = \frac{1}{2}bh$$

Where did the $\frac{1}{2}$ come in? For any triangle, we can duplicate across any of the sides and we will end up with a four-sided figure in which the sides across from each other are equal. The area of this new four-sided figure (a parallelogram) is simply its base times its height (perpendicular distance between the two bases; see Section 5.5.2a). The two triangles are identical. The area of either triangle is one-half the area of the four-sided figure. So when you figure the area of a triangle, don't forget the $\frac{1}{2}$.

Even though a formula sheet is provided on the Praxis, formulas for two-dimensional areas are not listed there because you are expected to know them.

EXAMPLE 5.4

The longest side of a right triangle is 13 inches and the shortest side is 5 inches.

    a. What is the perimeter of the triangle?

    b. What is the area of the triangle?

SOLUTION 5.4

a. 30 inches. This is a right triangle, so the longest side is the hypotenuse. Use the Pythagorean formula to find the third side: $13^2 = 5^2 + b^2$. Then $b^2 = 144$, and the third side is 12 inches. The perimeter is then the sum of the sides, or $13 + 5 + 12 = 30$ inches. (Note that this is a 5-12-13 Pythagorean triple.)

b. 30 square inches. The legs of the right triangle are 5 and 12, as determined in part (a). Then the area is $\frac{1}{2}(5)(12) = 30$ square inches. Remember that area is measured in square units. Note that the area and perimeter are usually not the same number, even though they are in this example.

5.4.2c Using Coordinates to Find the Area of a Triangle

By using coordinates, we can determine the altitude (and hence the area) of a triangle. Since the coordinate axes are perpendicular to each other, the altitude of a triangle makes any triangle into two right triangles, and then the area of the original triangle is just the sum of the areas of the two right triangles that are formed. The altitude is found by using the Pythagorean formula on each of the resulting right triangles, as shown in Example 5.5.

EXAMPLE 5.5

Find the area of a triangle with sides 5, 7, and 10.

SOLUTION 5.5

Since triangles are rigid, there is only one triangle with sides 5, 7, and 10. It is easier, but not necessary, to visualize dividing the triangle into two right angles if it is drawn on coordinate axes. Here, however, we will just draw the triangle. Any side can be the "base"—let's use the longest side, and draw the altitude to it. Automatically, we have two right triangles with the same altitude (h) and with bases of x and $10 - x$.

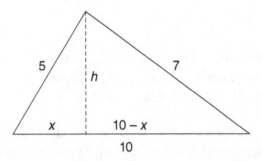

First, using the Pythagorean theorem on each of the smaller triangles yields

$$5^2 = h^2 + x^2 \text{ and } 7^2 = h^2 + (10 - x)^2.$$

Therefore, we have two equations with two unknowns, which can be rewritten as

$$h^2 = 25 - x^2 \text{ and } h^2 = 49 - (100 - 20x + x^2) = 49 - 100 + 20x - x^2.$$

Substituting for h^2 and eliminating the $-x^2$ terms on each side of the equation yields

$$25 = 49 - 100 + 20x, \text{ or } 20x = 76, \text{ and thus } x = 3.8.$$

To find h, the height of the original triangle with base 10, use $x = 3.8$ in the Pythagorean formula for either smaller triangle. Using the left triangle, we get $h^2 = 25 - (3.8)^2$, or (by using the calculator), $h = 3.25$. Thus, the area of the original 5-7-10 triangle is

$$A = \frac{1}{2}bh = \frac{1}{2}(10)(3.25) = 16.25 \text{ square units.}$$

Later in this chapter, Section 5.13.8d discusses Heron's formula, which computes the area of any triangle when all that is known are the three sides, but Solution 5.5 always works as well.

5.4.3 Congruent Triangles

Congruent figures are exactly the same size. Their orientation may be different, but their sizes (sides and angles) are correspondingly equal. The "correspondingly" refers to which sides are between which angles. The symbol for congruent is ≅. It is easy to see that $\triangle ABC \cong \triangle DEF$, but not as straightforward to see that $\triangle ABC \cong \triangle GHI$.

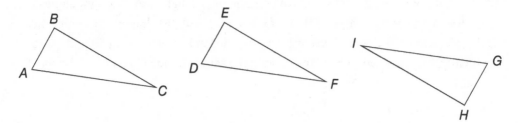

The angles and sides of congruent triangles appear in corresponding places when written out. For example, $\triangle ABC \cong \triangle DEF$ means that $\angle A = \angle D$, $\angle B = \angle E$, and $\angle C = \angle F$ and $AB = DE$, $AC = DF$, and $BC = EF$.

As a consequence of the rigidity of a triangle, there is one and only one triangle that can be drawn if two angles and the distance between them are known. As another example, if the lengths of two sides and the measure of the angle between them are known, the measures of the third side and the other two angles are fixed. The figure on the left below shows that if the lengths of sides DE and DF and $\angle D$ are known, there is only one way to form a triangle (draw EF). Likewise, if one side and two angles in a triangle are known, the lengths of the other two sides are predetermined. If we extend the two partial sides in the figure on the right below, they will meet at a point (let's call it T) that depends on $\angle R$ and $\angle S$. Thus, there is one and only one triangle that can be drawn if two angles and the distance between them are known.

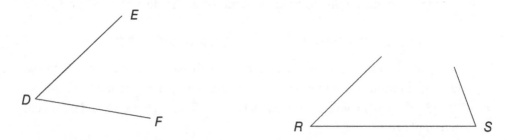

It makes sense, then, that if two angles and the distance between them are identical in two triangles, the triangles must be congruent. The same is true for a number of relationships between two triangles, as noted below, where S = side and A = angle, and, for example, ASA stands for two angles and the side between them. If the two angles and included side of one triangle are identical to corresponding two angles and the included side of another triangle, the two triangles are congruent. (The word "corresponding" indicates that the sides and angles mentioned must be in the same place relative to each other, as mentioned in the note above.)

For two triangles to be congruent, one of the following must be true.

- The three sides of one triangle are equal to the three corresponding sides of another triangle (known as SSS).

- Two sides and the angle between them on one triangle are equal to the corresponding two sides and angle between them of another triangle (known as SAS).

- Two angles and a side of one triangle are equal to the corresponding two angles and side of another triangle (known as ASA if the side is between the angles, or AAS if it is not between the angles).

- In a right triangle, if the hypotenuse and either of the legs are equal to the hypotenuse and either of the legs of another triangle. (Known as HL in some texts; this is a variation of SSS, since the third sides must also be equal from the Pythagorean Theorem.)

However, if two sides and an angle not between them on one triangle are equal to the corresponding two sides and angle not between them on another triangle, the two triangles might or might not be congruent. (That is why SSA is not a rule for congruence.)

Likewise, if the three angles of one triangle are equal to the corresponding three angles of another and nothing is said about the sides, the triangles are not necessarily congruent. However, they are similar, the subject of the next section.

5.4.4 Similar Triangles

Similar figures have equal corresponding angles, but the lengths of the corresponding sides are proportional, and not necessarily equal. The symbol for similarity is ~. Therefore, in the figure below, $\triangle JLK \sim \triangle MNP$, but $\triangle JLK$ is clearly not congruent to $\triangle MNP$.

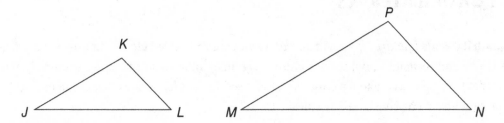

Since these two triangles are similar, we can deduce that $\angle J = \angle M$, $\angle L = \angle N$, and $\angle K = \angle P$ as well as that $\dfrac{JL}{MN} = \dfrac{LK}{NP} = \dfrac{JK}{MP}$. In fact we didn't even need the figures to state these equalities and proportionalities—we needed only to follow the corresponding places of the letters in $\triangle JLK \sim \triangle MNP$. And since the corresponding sides are in corresponding places when we write $\triangle JLK \sim \triangle MNP$, it is *not* true that $\triangle JLK \sim \triangle PMN$.

5.4.4a Proportions in Similar Triangles

The sides are not the only proportional parts in similar triangles. The altitudes to any side are also proportional (as long as we have the correct corresponding sides), and in fact so are the corresponding medians, midsegments, and angle bisectors (see Section 5.3.3a).

We already know that if two angles of one triangle are equal to two corresponding angles of another triangle, the triangles are similar because if we know two angles of a triangle, there is only one measure for the third angle. We can also prove two triangles are similar by proving two of the corresponding sides of each of the two triangles are proportional as long as their included angles are equal.

5.4.4b Scale Factors

Because all similar triangles have the same shape, the only thing that is different from one triangle to a similar triangle is its size. Imagine two triangles, one with a side of 1 inch and the other with a corresponding side of 2 inches. The **scale factor** between these two triangles is 2, the ratio of the sides. What about the areas of the two triangles? Since area involves the product of two dimensions ($\frac{1}{2} \times$ base $\times$ height), and each linear measure in the smaller triangle is scaled by 2 in the larger triangle, the area is enlarged 2×2, or 4 times.

If two two-dimensional figures have the same shape and are scaled by a factor of x, their areas are scaled by a factor of x^2. The fact that area measures are given in square units will remind you to square the scale factor.

5.5 QUADRILATERALS

Quadrilaterals (*quadri* = four and *lateral* = side) are four-sided closed figures. We are familiar with squares and rectangles, but there are infinitely many other quadrilaterals. Their only requirement is that they be closed and have four sides. Closed figures have sides that begin and end at the same point without crossing over any sides.

Three facts are true of all quadrilaterals:

1. The sum of the angles is $360°$.

2. The perimeter of a quadrilateral is the sum of the lengths of the four sides. So if the four sides have lengths a, b, c, and d, the perimeter is

$$P = a + b + c + d$$

3. In general, the area of any quadrilateral is based on the product of one side (called the *base*) times the perpendicular distance to the opposite side. This distance is called the *height* or *altitude*. So for a quadrilateral with base b and height h, the area is

$$A = bh$$

Five quadrilaterals are special due to certain facts about their angles and side lengths, as shown next.

5.5.1 Trapezoid

A **trapezoid** is a quadrilateral with only one special fact: Two of the sides are parallel. They don't have to be equal, and the other two sides don't have to be parallel or equal either.

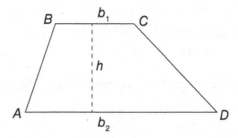

Trapezoid

5.5.1a Perimeter and Area

The *perimeter* of a trapezoid is just the sum of the sides ($AB + BC + CD + DA$, here). So for a trapezoid with four sides of lengths, say, $e, f, g,$ and h, the perimeter is

$$P_{\text{trapezoid}} = e + f + g + h$$

The area of any quadrilateral is based on the simple formula of base × height (also called altitude), but to find the area of a trapezoid, we have to consider the average of the two bases as the base in this calculation. Otherwise, the area would be two different numbers, depending on which of the parallel sides is considered to be the base. The height is defined as the perpendicular distance between the bases. The average of the two bases is their sum divided by 2. So the base to use for a trapezoid is $\frac{1}{2}(b_1 + b_2)$, where b_1 and b_2 are the lengths of the two parallel sides. Thus, the area of a trapezoid is given by

$$A_{\text{trapezoid}} = \frac{1}{2}(b_1 + b_2)h.$$

5.5.1b Isosceles Trapezoids

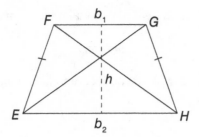

Isosceles Trapezoid

If the two nonparallel sides of a trapezoid are equal, the trapezoid has a special name: isosceles, just as for triangles. An **isosceles trapezoid** has two parallel sides (*FG* and *EH* in the figure above), and the other two sides are equal (*EF* = *HG*). The base is usually chosen to be the longest parallel side, and the base angles (the angles on either side of it) are equal ($\angle E = \angle H$), although it is also true that the other two angles are equal ($\angle F = \angle G$).

In addition, for an isosceles trapezoid, the *diagonals* (here they would be *EG* and *FH*) are of equal length.

5.5.2 Parallelogram

A **parallelogram** is a quadrilateral with two pair of parallel sides, as the name implies. In this case, it is a step up from the trapezoid because the other two sides are also parallel. So a parallelogram has two pair of parallel sides, and the parallel sides are equal to each other.

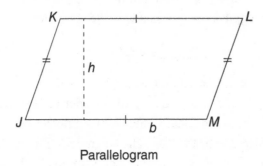

Parallelogram

5.5.2a Perimeter and Area

The *perimeter* of a parallelogram is still the sum of the lengths of all four sides. So the perimeter of the above parallelogram is *JK* + *KL* + *LM* + *MJ*. In general, if the lengths of the sides of a parallelogram are, say, *q*, *r*, *s*, and *t*, its perimeter is

$$P_{\text{parallelogram}} = q + r + s + t.$$

Since the sides opposite each other are equal as well as being parallel, $q = r$ and $s = t$, and the perimeter can be rewritten as

$$P_{\text{parallelogram}} = 2q + 2s = 2(q + s).$$

Thus, the perimeter of a parallelogram is twice the sum of the two unequal sides.

The *area* of a parallelogram is given by the general formula of base × height, where the height is perpendicular to the base:

$$A_{\text{parallelogram}} = bh$$

5.5.2b Additional Properties of a Parallelogram

1. The *diagonals* of a parallelogram bisect each other.

2. A new feature of the parallelogram is that the angles form two pairs, with the ones across from one another being equal ($\angle J = \angle L$ and $\angle K = \angle M$)).

3. The pairs of adjacent angles ($\angle J$ and $\angle K$, $\angle K$ and $\angle L$, $\angle L$ and $\angle M$, or $\angle M$ and $\angle J$ in the figure) add up to 180°, which means they are **supplementary** to each other.

5.5.3 Rhombus

If we add the condition that all four sides of a parallelogram are equal, then we have a **rhombus**. So a rhombus has all of the properties of a parallelogram plus the sides are equal.

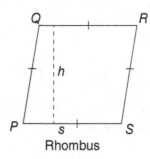

Rhombus

5.5.3a Perimeter and Area

In the figure of the rhombus above, $PQ = QR = RS = SP = s$. and the *perimeter* can be written as

$$P_{\text{rhombus}} = 4s$$

Likewise, the *area* of the rhombus is

$$A_{\text{rhombus}} = bh = sh,$$

where any of the sides can be used as the base, and the height drawn to each side is the same.

5.5.3b Additional Properties

The *diagonals* of a rhombus bisect each other (as they did for the parallelogram), but now they also are perpendicular to each other.

5.5.4 Rectangle

If, instead of saying the four sides of the parallelogram are equal, we say that the four angles are equal, we have a **rectangle**, which is a parallelogram with four equal angles.

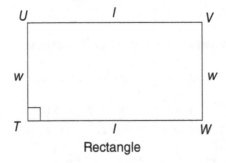

Rectangle

Thus, in the figure of the rectangle above, $\angle T = \angle U = \angle V = \angle W$, and since the angles of a quadrilateral add up to 360°, each of the four angles is 90°, or a right angle.

The opposite sides are equal, as in a parallelogram, but not all sides are equal (as they were in the rhombus).

5.5.4a Perimeter and Area

The *perimeter* is written as usual as

$$P_{\text{rectangle}} = TU + UV + VW + WT = 2l + 2w = 2(l + w).$$

Because all the angles are right angles, all sides l (length) are perpendicular to sides w (width), so they take the place of the base and height, and the *area* of the rectangle is

$$A_{\text{rectangle}} = bh = lw.$$

5.5.4b Additional Properties

The diagonals of a rectangle are equal, and they bisect each other (as they did for the parallelogram), but they are not perpendicular to each other—that was true only for the rhombus.

We can halve a rectangle in several ways, and the area of each half will always be half the area of the original rectangle, even though they may have different shapes.

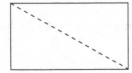 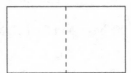 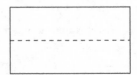

5.5.5 Square

Now we come to the most restrictive, but also the most popular, quadrilateral—the square. A **square** is a parallelogram with four equal angles and four equal sides. It can also be thought of as a rhombus with four equal angles or a rectangle with four equal sides.

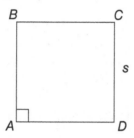

5.5.5a Perimeter and Area of a Square

Since a square is a rectangle with equal sides, its perimeter is

$$P_{\text{square}} = 4s,$$

and its area is

$$A_{\text{square}} = s^2.$$

5.5.5b Properties of a Square

The square has all of the properties of the parallelograms mentioned above, as shown in the following table.

Properties of the Square

Property of the square:	Same as property for:
Opposite sides are parallel	Parallelogram
All sides are equal	Rhombus
All angles are equal	Rectangle
Diagonals bisect each other	Parallelogram
Diagonals are perpendicular to each other	Rhombus
Diagonals have equal lengths	Rectangle

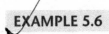

EXAMPLE 5.6

What is the value of x in the quadrilateral shown below?

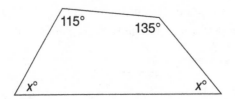

SOLUTION 5.6

55°. All of the angles in a quadrilateral total 360°. So we have

$$135° + 115° + x + x = 360°$$

$$2x = 110°$$

$$x = 55°$$

The problem is to find the value of x, not $2x$. Also, unless you are told what a figure is, don't assume it is what it looks like. This figure looks like a trapezoid, but it isn't; this figure is just a quadrilateral, as the problem states.

EXAMPLE 5.7

Which of the following rectangles have the same perimeter? (The figures are not drawn to scale; use the given measurements.)

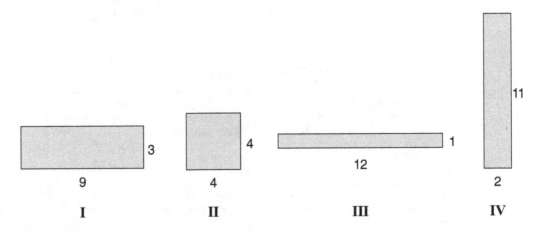

SOLUTION 5.7

III and IV. The perimeter of a rectangle is $P = 2(l + w)$. For figure I, $P = 24$; for II, $P = 16$; for III, $P = 26$; and for IV, $P = 26$.

5.6 POLYGONS

Polygons are closed, straight-line figures. The angle of a polygon is referred to as a **vertex**. Polygons are named for the number of their sides, which happens to be the number of vertices also. An aerial view of the government building called the Pentagon shows that it has five equal sides. A cell in a beehive or even the cross-sections of many wooden pencils are six-sided **hexagons**. The total number of degrees in polygons increases as the number of sides increases. The formula for the total number of degrees in a polygon is given by $(n-2)180°$, where n is the number of sides of the polygon. The sum of the angles is given in the following table to show how it increases with the number of sides. You can always figure that sum out because it increases by 180° for each side, and you know the sum for the triangle and quadrilateral already.

Name of Polygon	Number of Sides	Sum of Interior Angles
Triangle	3	180°
Quadrilateral	4	360°
Pentagon	5	540°
Hexagon	6	720°
Heptagon	7	900°
Octagon	8	1080°
Nonagon	9	1260°
Decagon	10	1440°
n-gon	n	$(n-2)180°$

5.6.1 Regular Polygons

Most polygons we see, such as those mentioned above, are **regular** polygons, meaning all the sides (and angles) are equal. But closed figures don't have to be regular. You can draw a figure of connected straight lines that aren't of the same length, and it is also a polygon. Equilateral triangles and squares are examples of regular polygons of three and four sides, respectively.

5.6.2 Perimeter and Area of Polygons

The *perimeter* of any polygon is the sum of the lengths of the sides—just add them up. It follows that the perimeter of a regular polygon is the length of a side multiplied by how many sides there are. For an irregular polygon, if any of the sides are unknown, they can be found by dividing the polygon into triangles and using the Pythagorean Theorem or trigonometry (see Sections 5.4.1d or 5.13) to find the missing side.

The *area* of an irregular polygon is more complicated; it can be found by dividing the polygon into a number of triangles and adding up their areas. But finding the area of a scalene triangle can be complicated, too, as was shown in Section 5.4.2 on triangles.

The area of a regular polygon, however, is derived from the fact that any regular polygon is made up of identical isosceles triangles, for which we can more easily determine the area. An example is a regular hexagon, shown below.

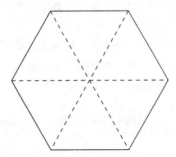

The area of this figure is 6 times the area of each triangle because it is a regular hexagon and the triangles are all equilateral. The formula for the area of a triangle involves not only the base (which is the side of the hexagon), but also the height to the base, or a perpendicular line from the center of the hexagon to a side. This line is called the **apothem**. So the area of any regular polygon is given by

$$A_n = n\left(\frac{1}{2}bh\right) = \frac{1}{2}ap \, ,$$

where a is the apothem and p is the perimeter, which is equal to n times any side.

Thus, the tricky part of finding the area of a regular polygon is finding the apothem. Consider only one of the triangles, and find the apothem in the same manner as we found the area (and thus the altitude) of any triangle by using coordinates earlier this chapter. But this time it is easier because the triangles in a regular polygon are all isosceles, and the apothem divides the base in half. In addition, we also know the central angle of the triangles that form the polygon, which is $\frac{360°}{n}$, where n is the number of sides of the polygon, and 360° is the total number of degrees of the central vertices. So, for example, finding the apothem reduces to finding the height BD of the right triangle on the right-hand side of triangle ABC, which is one of the triangles of an n-sided regular polygon with side length s. This involves trigonometry (see Section 5.13).

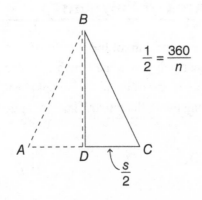

EXAMPLE 5.8

Find the area of a regular hexagon with side length 8.

SOLUTION 5.8

$96\sqrt{3}$. Since the triangles that form a regular hexagon are all equilateral, the apothem is the third side of a right triangle with hypotenuse 8 and base 4:

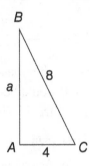

And we can just use the Pythagorean formula to find the apothem, a.

$$8^2 = a^2 + 4^2, \text{ so } a^2 = 48 \text{ and } a = \sqrt{48} = 4\sqrt{3}$$

Thus, the area of the hexagon is

$$A_n = \frac{1}{2}ap = \frac{1}{2}\left(4\sqrt{3}\right)(6\cdot 8) = 96\sqrt{3}$$

Can you see that if this was a pentagon, even if we knew each side length was 8, we wouldn't necessarily know the distances AB or BC without trigonometry?

EXAMPLE 5.9

Each side of the Pentagon building is 921 feet. What is the perimeter of the Pentagon?

SOLUTION

4,605 feet. Since the pentagon has five sides, its perimeter is 5 times the length of a side, or $5 \times 921 = 4,605$.

5.6.3 Diagonals of Polygons

A diagonal of a polygon is a line from any vertex to another vertex. The number of diagonals from any vertex is three fewer than the number of sides because the lines to the two adjacent vertices are not diagonals (they are sides of the polygon), and there is no line drawn from a vertex to itself. Therefore, the formula for the number of diagonals from any vertex of a polygon of n sides is $n - 3$. So for a pentagon, each vertex has $(5 - 2) = 3$ diagonals, as shown below.

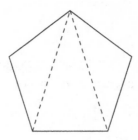

That would lead you to believe that a pentagon has 10 diagonals (2 for each of 5 vertices). However, a diagonal from vertex A to vertex B would be the same as one from B to A, so we must divide this result by 2 to eliminate all of the duplicates. Therefore, the total number of diagonals for any n-sided polygon is given by $\dfrac{n(n-3)}{2}$. For a pentagon, this would be $\dfrac{5(2)}{2} = 5$, as shown below. But don't be fooled into thinking the number of diagonals is always the number of sides. (Think of a quadrilateral; it has only two diagonals, not four.)

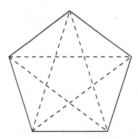

 A diagonal can be outside of the polygon if the polygon is **concave** (one of the angles is greater than 180°), even if it is a closed figure. By definition AC is a diagonal of polygon $ABCD$ because it connects two vertices.

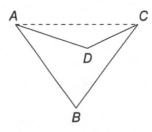

5.6.4 Congruent and Similar Polygons

Just as we saw for congruent triangles, two polygons are **congruent** if all of the pairs of corresponding angles and corresponding sides are equal. And just as we saw for similar triangles, two polygons are **similar** if all of the pairs of corresponding angles are equal and pairs of corresponding sides are proportional.

Therefore, all squares are similar to all other squares because they all have 90° angles and the sides of any square are equal, so the ratios between the sides of two squares will be constant.

 If the sides of two squares are in the ratio of $\frac{s_1}{s_2}$, their areas are in the ratio of $\left(\frac{s_1}{s_2}\right)^2 = \frac{(s_1)^2}{(s_2)^2}$.

EXAMPLE 5.10

A farmer has two square gardens. The smaller one has an area of 100 square feet, and one side of the larger garden is twice as long as a side of the smaller garden. What is the area of the larger garden?

SOLUTION 5.10

400 square feet. If the smaller square garden has an area of 100 square feet, then each side must be $\sqrt{100} = 10$ feet. Thus, the larger garden with dimensions twice as long must be 20 feet on a side, and its area must be $(20)^2 = 400$ square feet. Another way to look at this problem is that the ratio of the sides of the larger to smaller garden is given as $\frac{2}{1}$, so the areas must be in the ratio of $\left(\frac{2}{1}\right)^2 = \frac{4}{1}$, which would make the larger garden 400 square feet.

5.7 CIRCLES

5.7.1 Parts of a Circle

The circle is an important shape indeed. A **circle** is defined as all the points at a fixed distance from a certain point called the **center** of the circle, and usually designated by an O. The fixed distance from the center to the circle is called the **radius** of the circle. If we extend the radius across the center to the other side of the circle, we get the **diameter**, which is just twice the radius. The circle is usually named by its center, so this is circle O.

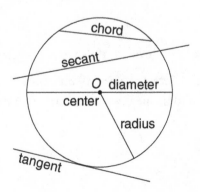

Three other lines in the figure of the circle are the chord, secant, and tangent. These lines can appear anywhere in relation to the circle and can have various lengths (unlike the radius and diameter, which are a specific length for each circle). These lines have important properties in relation to the circle and are defined as:

- **chord**: A line segment whose endpoints are on the circle. The longest chord in a circle is the diameter.

- **secant**: The extension of a chord in both directions. A secant intersects the circle at two points, whereas a chord's endpoints are on the circle.

- **tangent**: A line that touches the circle at just one point and all its other points are outside the circle. A radius drawn to the tangent at the point of tangency is perpendicular to the tangent.

5.7.2 Perimeter and Area of a Circle

An important value when talking about circles is the Greek letter pi (π), which is defined as the ratio of C, the **circumference** (perimeter) of the circle to d, its diameter, or $\pi = \dfrac{C}{d}$. So the circumference of a circle is given by

$$C = \pi d.$$

Since the diameter is twice the radius (r), $d = 2r$, the circumference can also be written as

$$C = 2\pi r.$$

Pi has a value of roughly 3.14. This ratio is the same for all circles, no matter how large or small they are. The Praxis test will indicate whether to use π as a decimal or to leave an answer in terms of π.

EXAMPLE 5.11

State the circumference of a circle of radius 4 inches

    a. in terms of π.

    b. to the nearest hundredth of an inch (use $\pi = 3.1416$).

SOLUTION 5.11

    a. 8π inches. Since $C = 2\pi r$, the circumference is $C = 2\pi(4) = 8\pi$ inches.

    b. 25.13 inches. Since $C = 2\pi r$, the circumference is $C = 2(3.1416)(4) = 25.1328$ inches, which is 25.13 to the nearest hundredth of an inch.

The **area** of a circle is given by

$$A = \pi r^2,$$

and its dimensions are in square units.

EXAMPLE 5.12

For a circle with a diameter of $\dfrac{2}{3\pi}$ units, what is

a. the circumference

b. the area

Leave the answers in terms of π.

SOLUTION 5.12

a. $\dfrac{2}{3}$ units. For the circumference, $C = \pi d$, so $C = \pi\left(\dfrac{2}{3\pi}\right) = \left(\dfrac{\pi}{1}\right)\left(\dfrac{2}{3\pi}\right)$ units. Can-

cel the π in the numerator and denominator to get $C = \dfrac{2}{3}$ units.

b. $\dfrac{1}{9\pi}$ square units. For the area, we must first find the value of r. Since $d = 2r$,

$r = \dfrac{1}{2}d = \dfrac{1}{2} \times \dfrac{2}{3\pi} = \dfrac{1}{3\pi}$. So the area is $A = \pi r^2 = \pi\left(\dfrac{1}{3\pi}\right)^2 = \dfrac{1}{9\pi}$ square units.

Be sure the circumference is always given in linear units and the area is given in square units.

EXAMPLE 5.13

The three circles pictured below have radii of 3, 4, and 5 inches. What is the perimeter of the triangle formed by connecting the centers of the circles?

SOLUTION 5.13

24 inches. The sides of the triangle are made up of the sum of radii of the three circles, or $3 + 4 = 7$, $3 + 5 = 8$, and $4 + 5 = 9$ inches. Then the perimeter is $7 + 8 + 9 = 24$ inches.

EXAMPLE 5.14

A circle is drawn inside a larger circle, as shown below. The smaller circle has a diameter of 4 and the larger circle has a diameter of 6. What is the area of the shaded portion?

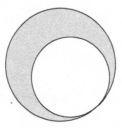

SOLUTION 5.14

5π. The larger circle has a diameter of 6, or a radius of 3, so its area is $\pi r^2 = \pi(3)^2 = 9\pi$. The smaller circle has a diameter of 4, or radius of 2, so its area is $\pi r^2 = \pi(2)^2 = 4\pi$. The shaded portion is the difference between the larger and smaller circle areas, or 5π.

A **semicircle** is a half circle. Its area is exactly one-half of the area of the full circle. The perimeter, however, is not one half of the circumference of the whole circle, which is seen in the following figure of a semicircle. On this figure, the perimeter is the round part (which is half of the circumference of the whole circle), plus the diameter, which is the straight part of the semicircle.

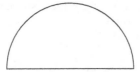

5.7.3 Arcs, Sectors, and Angles

5.7.3a Arcs

The portion of the circumference of a circle between two points is called an **arc**. An angle with its vertex at the center of a circle and two radii as its sides is called a **central angle**. The sum of the central angles in a complete revolution (or circle) is 360°.

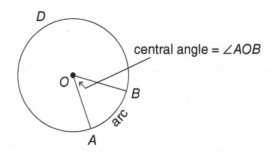

Arcs are designated by their endpoints with an arc sign over them; for the figure above, it would be the symbol $\overset{\frown}{AB}$. However, there are actually two arcs between points A and B in the figure, which we can designate as $\overset{\frown}{AB}$ and $\overset{\frown}{ADB}$, which are a minor arc (less than 180°) and a major arc (greater than 180°), respectively. An intervening point (here, D) avoids ambiguity about which arc is designated.

The measurement of the arc in degrees is the same as the degree measurement of the central angle drawn to it. The length of an arc is simply a fraction of the circumference, with the fraction being equal to $\dfrac{n}{360°}$, where n is the number of degrees in the arc and 360 is the number of degrees in the whole circle. Therefore, the length of an arc is given by

$$\text{length}_{\text{arc}} = \frac{n°}{360°}(\pi d) \text{ or } \frac{n°}{360°}(2\pi r)$$

EXAMPLE 5.15

Two 12-inch diameters in a circle meet at right angles. What is the length of the one of the minor arcs formed in this configuration (give the answer in terms of π)?

SOLUTION 5.15

3π. Any two perpendicular diameters divide the circle into four equal parts.

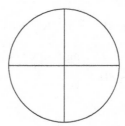

Therefore, each of the equal arcs is one-fourth of the circumference of the circle, or $\left(\dfrac{1}{4}\right)(\pi d) = \dfrac{\pi(12)}{4} = 3\pi$.

5.7.3b Sectors

The pie-shaped area of circle O is called a **sector** of the circle, where the straight sides are radii and the curved side is an arc. Therefore, the area of a sector is found similarly to the length of the arc:

$$A_{arc} = \left(\frac{n^\circ}{360^\circ} \right) (\pi r^2)$$

If you think of the hands of a clock to visualize central angles and arcs, be careful. Even though, since a clock shows 12 hours, and the angle between any two numbers on a clock is $(360^\circ \div 12) = 30^\circ$, the angle between the hands of the clock at 4:10 is not 60° (the angle between the 2 and the 4) because the hour hand will have moved beyond the 4, on its way to the 5.

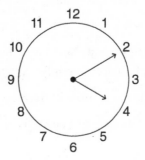

5.7.3c Circle Angles

Whereas the central angle is formed by two radii, the remaining angles within and outside a circle are formed by chords and tangents. The relations of their measures to their intercepted arcs depend on whether the vertex of the angle is on, within, or outside the circle. When not designated as a major arc, remember that "arc" refers to the minor arc.

- *Angles with a Vertex on a Circle.* The measure of an angle with its vertex *on* a circle is simply given by (m here is shorthand for "the measure of")

$$m(\text{angle}) = \frac{1}{2} m(\text{intercepted arc}).$$

These two cases are seen in the following figures, which show two secants (on the left) and a secant and a tangent (on the right).

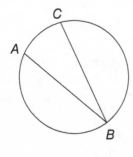

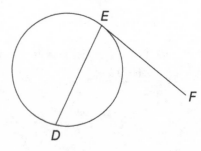

$$\angle ABC = \frac{1}{2} \overparen{AC} \qquad\qquad \angle DEF = \frac{1}{2} \overparen{ED}$$

- *Angles with a Vertex within a Circle.* An angle whose vertex is *within* a circle is formed by two intersecting chords. Its measure is given by half the *sum* of the intersected arcs, as shown below.

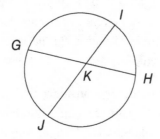

$$\angle GKJ = \angle IKH = \frac{1}{2}(\widehat{GJ} + \widehat{IH})$$

Can you see in this last figure that $\angle GKI = \angle JKH = \frac{1}{2}(\widehat{GI} + \widehat{JH})$?

- *Angles Outside a Circle.* Angles with a vertex outside a circle intercept two arcs, a smaller arc and a larger arc. The measure of any angles with a vertex outside the circle is equal to the *difference* of these two arcs, obviously (larger arc – smaller arc). For the three cases shown below (left: two secants; middle: secant-tangent; right: tangent-tangent), the general formula is

$$m(\text{angle}) = \frac{1}{2}m(\text{larger intercepted arc} - \text{smaller intercepted arc})$$

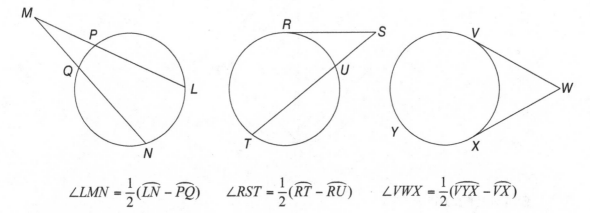

$$\angle LMN = \frac{1}{2}(\widehat{LN} - \widehat{PQ}) \qquad \angle RST = \frac{1}{2}(\widehat{RT} - \widehat{RU}) \qquad \angle VWX = \frac{1}{2}(\widehat{VYX} - \widehat{VX})$$

As you might have guessed from the last figure, the tangents from a point outside a circle are equal, or $VW = XW$. This is an important fact.

5.7.4 Inscribed Polygons

An **inscribed polygon** in a circle has all of its vertices on the circumference of the circle. In other words, every side of the polygon has to be a chord. The polygon doesn't have to be regular. For example, connect any three points on a circle to draw an inscribed triangle. This concept can be extended to as many points on the circle as you wish; the inscribed polygon is regular only if the points are evenly space along the circumference of the circle.

If a triangle is drawn inside a semicircle (or inside a circle with the longest side of the triangle being the diameter), it is a right triangle. This fact comes directly from the measure of an angle with its vertex on the circle. The intercepted arc is 180°, so the angle must be 90°.

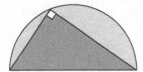

The number of inscribed polygons in the following figure of circle O with diameters MP and NQ is five, even though there are more than five polygons inside the circle. Only five of them have all of their vertices on the circumference of the circle (and thus are considered inscribed). The triangles that have O as a vertex are not inscribed because O is not on the circumference of the circle. In addition to the quadrilateral $MNPQ$, four triangles have vertices on the circle: $\triangle MNQ$, $\triangle NPQ$, $\triangle PQM$, and $\triangle PMN$.

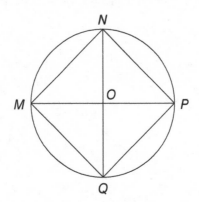

Rev

EXAMPLE 5.16

How many right triangles are in circle O above (they don't have to be inscribed angles)?

SOLUTION 5.16

Four. There only four right triangles that we are sure of: $\triangle MNQ$, $\triangle NPQ$, $\triangle PQM$, and $\triangle QMN$ are right triangles because they are inscribed in a semicircle, or their hypotenuse is a diameter of circle O. The four triangles with O as a vertex may or may not be right triangles if we aren't told that the diameters are perpendicular to each other. Don't assume facts unless you can prove them. In this figure, the angles at O look like right angles, but they could be 89° and 91°.

5.8 CONIC SECTIONS

A **conic section** is the intersection of a plane slicing through a cone, which is how it gets its name. Each of the conics is a set of points (**locus**) that obeys some sort of rule or rules. Conic sections include **circles**, **ellipses**, **parabolas**, and **hyperbolas**, depending on the angle of the slicing plane, as shown in the figures below.

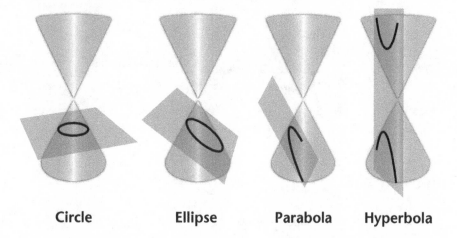

| Circle | Ellipse | Parabola | Hyperbola |

For the hyperbola, *two* cones are involved. The plane for the other conic sections slice through only one cone.

5.8.1 Graphs of Conic Sections

The graphs of conic sections are distinct. The following figures show the shape of the graph for each and some of the parameters, which are discussed in the following sections.

5.8.1a Parabola

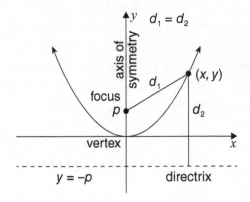

5.8.1b Hyperbola

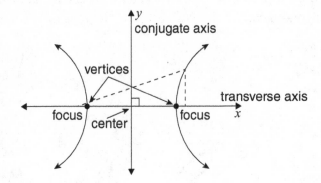

5.8.1c Ellipse

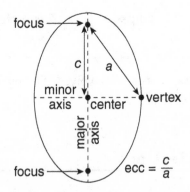

5.8.1d Circle

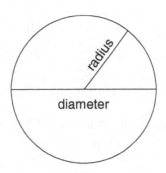

5.8.2 Equations and Parameters for Conic Sections

5.8.2a General Form of Equations for Conic Sections

The **general equation** that covers all second-degree equations is $Ax^2 + Bxy + Cy^2 + Dx + Ey + F = 0$, but $B = 0$ for conics, because conics have no xy terms.

So the **general equation for conics** is

$$Ax^2 + Cy^2 + Dx + Ey + F = 0$$

From this general equation, we can create general equations for the circle, ellipse, parabola, and hyperbola. So given a general equation, you can always figure out what the conic is from the following list and the flow chart that follows it.

- **Parabola.** This is the graph of a quadratic equation, which we saw in Chapter 4, Section 4.5. It has no y^2 term. This parabola opens vertically.

$$Ax^2 + Dx + Ey + F = 0$$

 For a parabola that opens horizontally—it looks like a vertical parabola (see Chapter 4) lying on its side—the equation would be $Ay^2 + Dx + Ey + F = 0$ with no x^2 term. However, this parabola is not a function (see Chapter 6), so we concentrate only on vertical parabolas here.

- **Hyperbola.** Note that the coefficients of x^2 and y^2 have different signs.

$$Ax^2 - Cy^2 + Dx + Ey + F = 0$$

 The equation xy = constant is actually a special case of a hyperbola that has only an xy term, no x^2 or y^2 terms, and the constant cannot equal 0. This is the graph of an inverse variation between x and y (see Section 4.2.3d). Here, we discuss only the general equation of the hyperbola shown above, but you should know that the other one exists.

- **Circle**. Note that the coefficients of x^2 and y^2 are equal.

$$Ax^2 + Cy^2 + Dx + Ey + F = 0, \text{ where } A = C$$

- **Ellipse**. Note that the coefficients of x^2 and y^2 are different, but have the same sign.

$$Ax^2 + Cy^2 + Dx + Ey + F = 0$$

The conics are presented here in this order because, given any general form of a conic, we can figure out which one it is by using the following "flow chart":

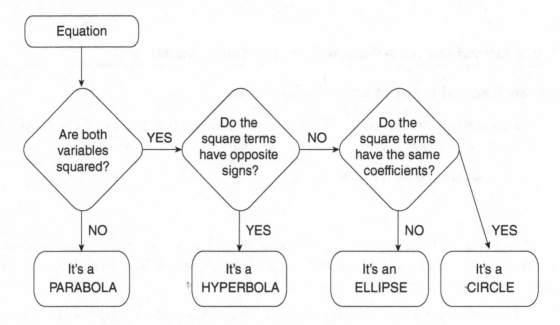

Therefore, for any conic equation in general form, you have to look only at the x^2 and y^2 terms to determine the general shape of its graph.

EXAMPLE 5.17

What conic section does the equation $x^2 + 4y^2 + 8x - 8y + 16 = 0$ represent?

SOLUTION 5.17

Ellipse. Right away you know it isn't a parabola because it has two "square" terms. Now all you have to do is look at the coefficients of x^2 and y^2; +1, and +4—they don't have different signs, so it's not a hyperbola, and they aren't equal, so it can't be a circle—it must be an ellipse.

5.8.2b Eccentricity of a Conic Section

Eccentricity is a measure of the curvature of a conic section. Specifically, it is the ratio of the distance of any point on the conic section from the focus to its distance from directrix. The **directrix** is a line in the plane (see the figures above), and the foci (plural of **focus**) are points in the plane (two for an ellipse and a hyperbola; one for a parabola). The eccentricity of a conic section describes the figure.

- Ellipse: Eccentricity varies from 0 to 1; the closer the eccentricity is to 1, the narrower is the ellipse.

- Circle: Eccentricity is 0 because the center and focus of the figure are the same point, so the distance between them is 0.

- Parabola: Eccentricity is 1 because the distance from the figure to the focus equals the distance from the figure to the directrix.

- Hyperbola: Eccentricity is greater than 1. The larger the eccentricity of a hyperbola, the straighter the curvature.

EXAMPLE 5.18

Describe the shape of the graph of the general equation $x^2 + 4x - y - 5 = 0$.

SOLUTION 5.18

First, since this equation has no y^2 term, it is a parabola. To find the standard form, move the y term to one side of the equation and complete the square of $(x^2 + 4x)$. Take half of the coefficient of x, square it, and add and subtract the result (4) to the equation. This yields $y = (x^2 + 4x + 4) - 5 - 4$ or $y = (x + 2)^2 - 9$, which is in the form $y = a(x - h)^2 + k$. Thus, the vertex is at $(h, k) = (-2, -9)$, the axis of symmetry is $x = -2$, and the parabola faces upward.

5.8.2c Standard Forms of Equations for Conic Sections

The values for all of the parameters for a conic figure are contained in the **standard form** of the equation, which can be obtained from the general forms discussed above. To summarize, the general form can quickly tell the shape of the conic just by looking at the coefficients of the squared terms, and the standard form can easily tell the parameters needed to sketch the conic. The two equation forms for a conic are related. In fact, the standard form is found by completing the squares in the general form (see Section 4.5.1 for the steps used in completing the square).

Now let's look at the standard forms for each of the conic sections. For all of the conic sections, the x-intercepts are found by setting $y = 0$, and the y-intercepts are found by setting $x = 0$.

- **Parabola**. The standard form for a parabola is $y = a(x - h)^2 + k$, where $x = h$ is the **axis of symmetry** and the point (h, k) is the **vertex**. The standard form of the equation for a parabola is derived from the general form by completing the square. The sign of a, the coefficient of x^2, tells whether the parabola opens up ($a > 0$) or down ($a < 0$).

The coefficient of x^2 in either the general or standard form is the same, so $A = a$, and the sign tells the direction of the parabola.

- **Hyperbola**. A hyperbola looks like two mirror-image parabolas, with each of its "arcs" bound by an asymptote. Hyperbolas have two asymptotes. The standard form of a hyperbola is $\dfrac{(x - h)^2}{a^2} - \dfrac{(y - k)^2}{b^2} = 1$, which is derived from the general form by completing the squares for x as well as y. To find the parameters of the hyperbola, it must be converted to standard form by completing the two squares (one involving the x^2 and x terms, and one involving the y^2 and y terms). Then the center is at (h, k). The orientation is determined by the placement of the a^2 term (remember, $a = A$ in the general form): if it is below the x^2 term, the axis of the hyperbola is horizontal; if it is below the y^2 term, the axis is vertical. Another way to determine the orientation is by the signs of the $(x - h)^2$ and $(y - k)^2$ terms: If $(x - h)^2$ is positive, the orientation is horizontal; if $(y - k)^2$ is positive, the orientation is vertical.

- **Circle**. The standard form of the circle is $(x - h)^2 + (y - k)^2 = r^2$. The point (h, k) is the center of the circle and r is the radius, which must always be a positive number. To get the standard form from the general form for a circle, complete the square twice, once for x and once for y. Rewrite any equation for a circle in standard form to find the center and radius readily.

- **Ellipse**. The standard form for a vertical ellipse is $\dfrac{(x - h)^2}{a^2} + \dfrac{(y - k)^2}{b^2} = 1$, which is derived from the general form by completing the squares for x as well as y. The point (h, k) is the center of the ellipse. Ellipses are like circles but with major and minor axes, which give them their oval shape. The value of a is half the length of the major axis, and the value of b is half the length of the minor axis. The ends of the major axis are considered the vertices of the ellipse. The orientation is determined by the relative sizes of a and b: If $a > b$, the orientation is horizontal, and if $b > a$, the orientation is vertical.

5.8.2d Summary

A summary of the terminology is presented in the following table.

Parameter	Circle	Ellipse	Parabola	Hyperbola
center	(h, k)	(h, k)	None	(h, k)
vertex		End of the major axis	Point at the "end": (h, k):	Turning point of a branch
focus, directrix, and eccentricity	Point and line from which distances are measured in forming a conic. The ratio $e = \dfrac{\text{focus to conic}}{\text{directrix to conic}}$, called the eccentricity, determines which conic it is.			
	$e = 0$	$0 < e < 1$	$e = 1$	$e > 1$
axis		Major axis is a line segment perpendicular to the directrix of an ellipse and passing through the foci; also called the principal axis of symmetry. The semi-major axis is half the major axis. Minor axis: a line segment perpendicular to and bisecting the major axis of an ellipse. The axes terminate on the ellipse at either end.	Axis of symmetry: Line perpendicular to the directrix and passing through the vertex.	Transverse axis: Line through the center and two foci; the axis through the center and perpendicular to the transverse axis is called the conjugate axis.

5.9 TRANSFORMATIONS IN THE COORDINATE PLANE

Transformation involves *translation* (moving an object left or right, up or down, but keeping the same orientation), *reflection* (moving the object across either axis), and *rotation* (turning the object). These mathematical transformations are useful in graphic arts, architecture, masonry, jewelry design, and many other occupations.

5.9.1 Translation

Translation means moving an object from one place to another. It doesn't change its size or orientation. You can think of a translation as sliding a penny across a table from one position to another without allowing it to rotate or flip over as you slide it.

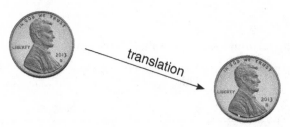

If the translation is vertical, or "up" or "down," the *x*-coordinate stays the same and the *y*-coordinate changes by the amount of the translation (+ for up and – for down). Similarly, if the translation is horizontal, or "left" or "right," the *y*-coordinate stays the same and the *x*-coordinate changes by the amount of the translation (+ for right and – for left). A translation at an angle, as in the figure above, is done in two steps, horizontal and then vertical (or vice versa).

EXAMPLE 5.19

Point P (5, −3) is plotted on the coordinate grid. If point S is 4 units above point P, what are the coordinates of point S?

SOLUTION 5.19

(5, 1). Here we aren't really physically translating point *P*, but using translation to figure where point *S* would be. The translation is up (*S* is above point *P*), so we add 4 to the *y*-coordinate. The coordinates of *S* are (5, 1), and point *S* is aligned in the horizontal direction above point *P*.

Sometimes the translation is actually two translations. Just do the first one, and then the second one starting from the new position.

EXAMPLE 5.20

Translate the point (3, −5) down 2 units and to the right 4 units. What are the coordinates of the translated point?

SOLUTION 5.20

(7, −7). Sketch the point and its translation on a graph.

Translating points isn't very complicated. A little more complicated is translating figures, such as triangles, but we can streamline that translation as well by looking at the vertices individually instead of thinking about the whole figure. A typical Praxis test problem shows a figure and then asks something about the new values if it were translated on the plane.

EXAMPLE 5.21

Triangle *ABC* is drawn on the coordinate plane, as shown below. If the triangle were translated down 4 units, what would be the new coordinate of point *A*?

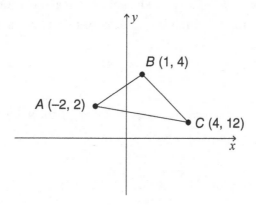

SOLUTION 5.21

(–2, –2). This problem is the same as if it had asked, "If the point (–2, 2) is translated down 4 units, what would be the new coordinates?" Don't let the fact that point *A* is part of a triangle throw you—it is asking only about point *A*. If we move point *A* down 4 units, we just move 4 units down for the new *y*-coordinate, and the *x*-coordinate remains the same. Four units down from 2 is –2, so the answer is (–2, –2). For this problem, it really doesn't matter where the rest of the triangle goes. It is asking only about point *A*.

Another variation of this sort of problem is to be given a choice of five graphed translations. Save time and trouble by first finding one point, which will probably eliminate one or two answer choices, and then look at the next point—most likely that's all that you would need to do. Only one of the remaining choices will match those two points. The idea is that you don't have to find all three points if you are given a choice of answers in graphed form.

As mentioned above, many test-takers get confused with transformations because they look at the whole picture and it's too many points to keep straight. The tactic should be to streamline the process as much as possible, saving time and frustration. This type of thinking is shown next for reflections and rotations.

5.9.2 Reflection

Reflection is just what it sounds like. If we placed a mirror on the reflection axis (usually, the *x*-axis, the *y*-axis, or the line *y* = *x*), we would see where the reflection of a point would go. But that isn't feasible in a test setting, nor is it easy to do anyway. The rule for reflection across an axis is: For a reflection across the *x*-axis, change the sign of the *y*-coordinate; for a reflection across the *y*-axis, change the sign of the *x*-coordinate.

If a point is reflected across the *x*-axis, which is essentially what we did in the last example, we know we are going up or down, depending on where the original point was. The reflected point must be in the opposite quadrant (up or down), the *x* value doesn't change, and the new *y* value is simply the opposite of the old *y* value.

EXAMPLE 5.22

Reflect the point $(4, -2)$ across the *x*-axis. What are the new coordinates?

SOLUTION 5.22

$(4, 2)$. Just change the sign of the *y* value.

Similarly, if the reflection is across the *y*-axis, the opposite quadrant is left or right, the *y* value doesn't change, and the new *x* value is simply the opposite of the old *x* value.

EXAMPLE 5.23

Reflect the point $(4, -2)$ (the same point) across the *y*-axis. What are the new coordinates?

SOLUTION 5.23

$(-4, -2)$. Just change the sign of the *x* value.

The rule for a reflection across the line $y = x$ is $(x, y) \rightarrow (y, x)$. Similarly, the rule for a reflection across the line $y = -x$ is $(x, y) \rightarrow (-y, -x)$. Look at the two graphs below to see that if we folded the graph along the line, the original *x* and *y* values will "land" as shown.

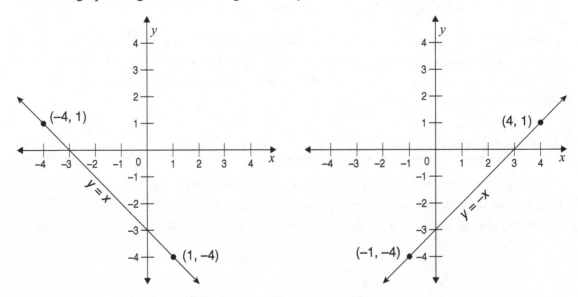

Again, if the problem presents a triangle and a line of reflection and wants ↑
triangle will look, the answers will probably be multiple-choice graphs. Th↗
tions, break this up into pieces (actually, individual coordinates). Look at on↗
sure the new positions have the same letter, probably with a prime. Eliminate any ↗
match up. Probably only two vertices are needed, and maybe not even two. Don't get conf↗
the sides of the triangle—it's the placement of the vertices that make the difference. Usually, th↗
correct answer choice is obvious early on by elimination.

Imp.

5.9.3 Rotation

Actually the hardest part of rotation problems is remembering what clockwise and counter-clockwise mean. **Clockwise** means what it sounds like: turning like a clock, from 1 to 2 to 3. The other way is called **counterclockwise**. Most rotation problems are clockwise.

Each quadrant is 90 degrees. Rotating a figure 90 degrees just means it will go into the next quadrant (clockwise) so, for example, from Quadrant I to Quadrant II; 180 degrees puts the figure halfway around (clockwise or counterclockwise), for example, from Quadrant I to Quadrant III; and 270 degrees goes three-quarters of the way around, for example, from Quadrant I to Quadrant IV. Rotating 270 degrees clockwise is the same as rotating 90 degrees counterclockwise, which will make visualizing simpler.

The visualization of a two-blade fan shown below (start anywhere and go in any direction) will help to locate a point on a figure that is being rotated. Notice two things: the point closest to the hub (intersection of the axes) remains closest to the hub. It doesn't flip over either vertically or horizontally. Likewise, the point that is farthest from the hub also just rotates as shown and is farthest from the hub in all rotations.

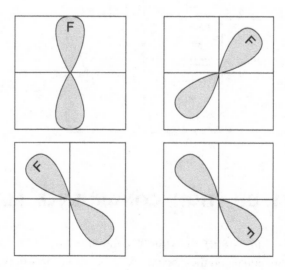

Concentrate on the part of the figure that is in one quadrant, even though the figure itself may cross over into other quadrants. As with the other transformations, look at one vertex of the figure at a time. The placement of the vertices is what makes the difference. Usually, the correct answer choice becomes obvious early on by elimination.

EXAMPLE 5.24

What is the orientation of the following figure when it has been rotated 270° clockwise?

SOLUTION 5.24

Imagine the original figure in the first quadrant. Then look at the point of the arrowhead in relation to what would be the hub (lower left corner). Go counterclockwise 90°, which is equivalent to what was asked, 270° clockwise. So the answer comes with the first tumble counterclockwise. This is the full rotation by 90° between pictures.

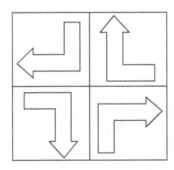

5.10 SIMILARITY, DILATION, CONGRUENCE, MAPPING

- **Similarity**: As noted previously in Sections 5.4.4 and 5.6.4, two figures are **similar** if their respective angles are equal and their respective sides are proportional. So they have the same shape but aren't the same size.

- **Dilation**: The proportionality of two similar figures is also the dilation of one to the other. For example, if two figures are similar and the ratio of their sides is 5, then the smaller is dilated by a **scale factor** (also called a **size transformation**) of 5 to get the larger one. A dilation can be a fraction, in which case the dilated figure is smaller than the original figure.

- **Congruence**: If the scale factor is 1, the two figures are **congruent**, meaning the respective angles are equal and the respective sides are equal.

- **Mapping**: According to *Webster's New World College Dictionary*, **mapping** is a transformation taking the points of one space into the points of the same or another space, which is what transformations are all about. Specifically, for dilations, each point is dilated to another point in the coordinate system.

EXAMPLE 5.25

$(1, 5)$

Map the points of triangle *ABC* with vertices at (1, 1), (4, 1), and (5, 1) onto a dilation *A'B'C'* with scale factor 2, translated one unit up and one unit to the right.

SOLUTION 5.25

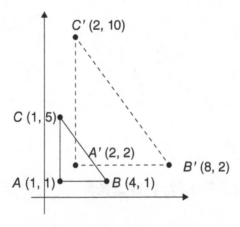

The mapping of a dilation by a factor of 2 preserves the similarity between the figures—the corresponding angles ($A \rightarrow A'$, $B \rightarrow B'$, $C \rightarrow C'$) are equal, even though their coordinates are doubled. The information "translated one unit up and one unit to the right" distinguishes the resulting triangle from the infinite number of other triangles that could be dilations of the original one by fixing one of the resultant vertices. The distances between the vertices, which are the lengths of the sides of the triangles, are doubled.

5.11 CONSTRUCTIONS

Constructions of shapes historically are done with a straightedge, a compass, and a pencil. A straightedge can be a ruler or anything that will allow you to draw a straight line. A compass is a device that allows construction of equal angles; it also measures equal distances. It is pictured in the figure below. Since constructions are mostly done by computer, we will review only one construction here to show how these tools are used and how the rules of geometry influence the construction.

We are going to draw the angle bisector of $\angle ABC$, or a ray that divides $\angle ABC$ in half. First use the compass to mark off equal lengths BD and BE on the rays of the angle. A compass will draw a perfect circle, but here we need only the parts of a circle that cross the rays of the given angle. The geometric rule here is *all radii of a circle are equal*, so the two marks on BA and BC are equidistant from point B. From those two points, mark off arcs of two circles with the same radius, as shown. Again, the geometric rule here is that the radii of equal circles are equal. Draw line BF from where these two arcs meet at point F to $\angle ABC$. $\angle ABF = \angle CBF$, which is the definition of angle bisector, because all points on BF are equidistant from the rays of $\angle ABC$.

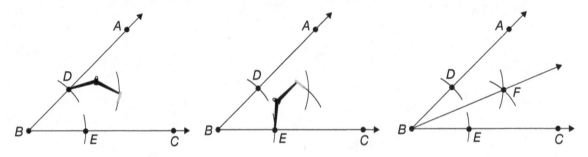

5.12 THREE-DIMENSIONAL FIGURES

Three-dimensional figures have depth in addition to length and width. Three axes for three-dimensional figures reflect these dimensions, even though it is drawn in two dimensions.

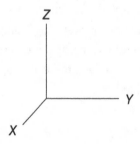

Another way to visualize how the three planes meet is to look at the corner of a room, where the two walls and the floor (or ceiling) form the three planes and the joints are the axes.

A three-dimensional figure drawn on a two-dimensional space shows solid lines to indicate edges that you actually see and dashed lines to indicate edges that are obscured from the two-dimensional perspective. **Edges** are the lines where two **faces** (flat surfaces) meet on a three-dimensional figure. **Vertices** are the points where three faces meet. On the figure shown below, the "main" face is shaded and the arrows indicate which way the figure is facing. It takes a while to get used to this way of looking at three-dimensional figures.

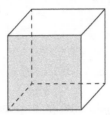

The Praxis formula sheet provides the formulas you will need to do most three-dimensional surface area and volume problems. Still, you need to know what these terms mean as well as what the variables in the given equation mean or the formulas won't be of any use to you. Therefore, this section on three-dimensional figures provides information to help you understand the Praxis formula sheet, but it isn't necessary to memorize the formulas. However, you should know the formulas for a rectangular solid (e.g., a brick).

The **surface area** of a three-dimensional figure is exactly what it sounds like. It is the total area of all the faces, even those you cannot see in the picture unless it is a specific shape (like a silo that you want to paint, so the bottom isn't considered). So for surface area, we need to remember the formulas for the areas of the two-dimensional faces that make up each three-dimensional figure. The surface area of a right rectangular prism (sometimes called a rectangular solid) can be thought of as the area of a shirt box that is covered by wrapping paper (with no overlapping).

Volume is how much space a three-dimensional figure takes up. It is sometimes confused with **capacity**, which is how much a three-dimensional figure can hold. The difference between the two is the thickness of the figure. Basically, for three-dimensional figures that have identical "tops" and "bottoms" (bases), volume is the area of the **base** (bottom or top) multiplied by the height of the figure.

The dimensions for each measure are shown in the following table. Often, the answer choices on the test will have the correct number, but different dimensions, so be sure to check both parts of the answer before making your choice. Note that the exponent matches the number of the dimension of the figure.

Unit	Dimension	Examples
Surface area	square units	ft^2, in^2, m^2, cm^2
Volume	cubic units	ft^3, in^3, m^3, cm^3

5.12.1 Right Prisms

One type of three-dimensional figure is known as a **right prism**. Examples of three right prisms are shown below.

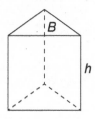 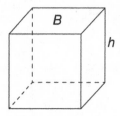 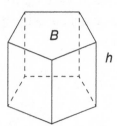

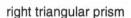

right triangular prism   right rectangular prism   right pentagonal prism

The bases of each are identical polygons, which can be regular polygons, as pictured above, but they don't have to be regular. The **faces** are perpendicular to the bases (which is why "right" is in the name—they meet the base at right angles). The faces in a regular right prism are rectangles. Each set of three edges meets at a point called the **vertex** (plural, vertices). Obscured in the figure, but something we can envision, are the diagonals of a right prism, which are not the diagonals of the faces; rather, they are diagonals that run internally from one corner to another opposite corner, as shown below.

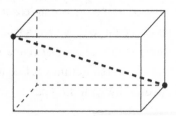

5.12.1a Surface Area of a Right Prism

As stated above, every right prism has one pair of identical faces, which are the polygon bases, and one set of lateral faces that are perpendicular to the bases. The surface area of a right prism is thus the sum of the areas of the two polygon faces and as many rectangles as there are sides in the polygon. The area of each base is usually designated as B, and the area of each lateral face is the height of the prism (h) times the length of the side of the polygon. Since there are as many of these lateral sides as there are sides of the polygon, when we add up all the sides, we essentially have the perimeter of the base (p) times the height (h). Thus, the surface area becomes

$$SA_{\text{right prism}} = ph + 2B.$$

This formula is not given on the Praxis formula sheet, but should be intuitive.

5.12.1b Volume of a Right Prism

The **volume** of a right prism follows the rule that volume is the area of the base times the height. The equation for the area of the base depends on what kind of polygon it is. The volume is thus

$$V_{\text{right prism}} = Bh$$

EXAMPLE 5.26

Find the surface area and volume of a $3 \times 4 \times 6$-inch right rectangular prism.

SOLUTION 5.26

108 in^2 and 72 in^3. The surface area is $SA = 2[(3 \times 4) + (3 \times 6) + (4 \times 6)] = 2(12 + 18 + 24) = 2(54) = 108$ square inches. For the same right rectangular prism, the volume is $V = (3)(4)(6) = 72$ cubic inches.

5.12.1c Cubes

Since a square is a rectangle with equal sides, a **cube**, which has twelve edges and six square faces (see the figure below), is included in this classification.

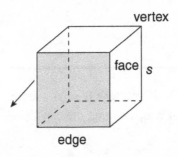

Therefore, the surface area of the cube is

$$SA_{\text{cube}} = 2s^2 + 2s^2 + 2s^2 = 6s^2$$

The volume of a cube comes from the volume of a rectangular solid with $l = w = h = s$. So

$$V_{\text{cube}} = s^3$$

Rev.

EXAMPLE 5.27

Kristen uses a plain wooden cube 18 inches on an edge as a plant stand.

a. She wants to cover it with a patterned adhesive paper, but first she must figure out how much paper she needs to buy. She wants to cover all the sides, including the bottom. How many square feet of paper does she need?

b. If the top of the cube is removable and the thickness of the cube is 1 inch all around, what is the capacity (in cubic inches) of the cube?

SOLUTION 5.27

a. 13.5 square feet. First of all, since the paper is sold in square feet, we should convert the 18 inches into 1.5 feet to make the final calculation easier. Then the square footage Kristen needs is $(1.5)^2 = 2.25$ square feet for each side times the number of sides in a cube (which is 6), or $6(2.25) = 13.5$ square feet of paper.

b. 4,096 cubic inches. The question asks for cubic inches, so we can leave the dimension of a side in inches. But here we need capacity, which is the "inside" volume. The inside "edge" of the cube is the outside edge minus 1 inch on each side, or $18 - 2(1) = 16$ inches. Then the capacity is given by $V = s^3 = (16)^3 = 4096$ cubic inches. Note that the capacity is different from the volume of a cube 18 inches on a side.

5.12.2 Cylinder

A **cylinder** is the shape of a can. If you take the cylinder apart, you will see that it consists of two round ends plus a rectangle that wraps around the can shape.

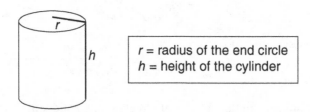

r = radius of the end circle
h = height of the cylinder

5.12.2a Surface Area of a Cylinder

The **surface area** of a cylinder is the area of the two circular ends, or $2(\pi r^2)$, plus the area of the rectangle for the "wrap." One side of this rectangle is the height of the cylinder, h, and the other side is the circumference of the circular end $(2\pi r)$, so the area of the rectangle is $2\pi rh$. Therefore,

$$SA_{\text{cylinder}} = 2\pi rh + 2\pi r^2$$

Hint: Think of a soup can with the label peeled off to see that the ends are two circles, and the label is the area around the cylinder. This image will help to see what the net of a cylinder is. Nets are discussed in Section 5.12.8a.

5.12.2b Volume of a Cylinder

The **volume** of a cylinder follows the rule that it is the area of the base (πr^2) times the height, *h*, so

$$V = \pi r^2 h$$

EXAMPLE 5.28

How much paper does Lisa need to put a label made from her own design on a can that is 6 inches high and has a diameter of 4 inches? (Use $\pi = 3.14$. Round your answer to the nearest square inch.)

SOLUTION 5.28

75 square inches. The label on the can is the same as the surface area of the side of a cylinder, which is actually a rectangle with a length that equals the circumference of the can and a width that is the height of the can. The circumference of a circle (in this case, the end of the can) is $C = \pi d = 4\pi$, so the dimensions of the label will be $A_{\text{rectangle}} = lw = (4\pi)(6) = 24 \times 3.14 = 75.36$, which rounds to 75 square inches. Note that the answer is 75 because the question asks for the answer to be rounded to the nearest square inch.

EXAMPLE 5.29

At 11 a.m., water starts to flow into a cylindrical storage tank that is 6 feet in diameter and 4 feet high. The water is coming into the tank at a rate of 20 cubic feet per hour.

a. Will the tank be above or below halfway full at 2 p.m.?

b. If the water flow into the tank is stopped at noon and a tap is opened at the bottom of the tank that lets water escape at the rate of 10 cubic feet per hour, how long will it take for the tank to empty?

SOLUTION 5.29

a. Above. The full capacity of the storage tank is given by $V = \pi r^2 h = \pi 3^2 (4) = 36\pi \approx 113$ cubic feet. Therefore, halfway full is ≈ 56.5 cubic feet. At 2 p.m., the flow of 20 cubic feet per hour has gone on for 3 hours, so 3(20) = 60 cubic feet have entered the tank, and the tank is more than half full.

b. 2 hours. The water is escaping at half the rate that it had been entering. At noon, that would have been 1 hour of filling, so it will take 2 hours to empty the tank.

5.12.3 Regular Pyramids

A **regular pyramid** is a three-dimensional figure in which one base is a regular polygon, the other end is a point that is above the center of the polygon, and all of the faces are identical triangles.

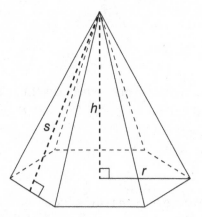

5.12.3a Surface Area of a Pyramid

The **surface area** of a pyramid is the sum of the areas of the base and the n triangles that form the sides, where n is the number of sides of the pyramid base. Obviously, if the base is a square, the sides are four triangles, and if the base is a triangle, three other triangles (not necessarily identical to the base triangle) form the sides.

A new measurement is introduced with figures that come to a point, the **slant height**, s, which is the measure from the point to the middle of a side of the base, as shown in the above figure. Since the base is regular (all sides are equal), the slant heights for all sides of a pyramid are equal. The area of each triangle is $\frac{1}{2}bs$, where b is a side of the base of the pyramid, and s is the slant height. Since there are n triangles, the sum of the triangle areas is $n\left(\frac{1}{2}bs\right)$, where nb is just the perimeter ($p = nb$) of the pyramid base. So the total area of all the sides is $n\left(\frac{1}{2}bs\right) = \frac{1}{2}ps$. The area of the base is defined as B, and is the area of whatever the base polygon is. The final equation is thus

$$SA_{\text{pyramid}} = \frac{1}{2}ps + B.$$

5.12.3b Volume of a Pyramid

The **volume** of a pyramid, instead of being Bh, as volume was for the prism, is now $\frac{1}{3}Bh$, where B is the area of the base and h is the perpendicular height from the base to the point (it is not the slant height). This factor of $\frac{1}{3}$ is used for all regular solids in which one "base" comes to a point.

$$V_{\text{pyramid}} = \frac{1}{3}Bh.$$

EXAMPLE 5.30

The Great Pyramid of Giza in Egypt has four sides with the following approximate measurements:

Height = 480 feet

Sides = 755 feet at the base

Slant height = 610 feet

a. What is the surface area of the Great Pyramid of Giza in Egypt?

b. How many acres does the pyramid cover? (An acre is equal to 43,560 square feet.) Give the answer rounded to the nearest whole number.

SOLUTION 5.30

a. 921,100 square feet. The surface area of a pyramid is $SA_{\text{pyramid}} = \frac{1}{2}ps + B$, but since the question asks for the surface area of the Great Pyramid, we exclude the base and the equation is just

$$SA_{\text{Great Pyramid}} = \frac{1}{2}ps,$$

where p is the perimeter of the base. Here the base is a square with side equal to 755 feet, so $p = 4(755) = 3020$ feet. The s in the pyramid equation is not a side, but the slant height, 610 feet.

$$SA_{\text{Great Pyramid}} = \frac{1}{2}(3020)(610) = 921,100 \text{ square feet}$$

b. 13. Asking how much area the pyramid covers is the same as asking for the area of the base. Since the base is a square, the area is found by squaring one of the sides of the base, which are also the bases of the triangles, 755 feet each. So the area of the base is $(755)^2 = 570,025$ square feet. To find out how big this is in acres, use the proportion $\frac{1 \text{ acre}}{43,560 \text{ square feet}} = \frac{x \text{ acres}}{570,025 \text{ square feet}}$, which, by cross-multiplication, yields $43,560x = 570,025$, and $x = \frac{570,025}{43,560} = 13.09$ acres, which rounds to 13 acres. Impressive!

5.12.4 Right Circular Cone

A **right circular cone** is like a cylinder that comes to a point. The measures of the surface area and volume are not as straightforward as they were for the other three-dimensional figures but similar to these measures in the pyramid, discussed above. The only difference between the right circular pyramid and cone is that the base is a circle and not a regular polygon.

5.12.4a Surface Area of a Right Circular Cone

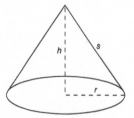

The surface area of a cone is the area of the base (circle) and the area of the "wraparound." This last area actually comes from the formula for the pyramid with a little imagination. Imagine that instead of, say, a square as the base of the pyramid, we have a regular polygon of 100 sides. The formula will still be the perimeter of the base times the slant height, right? Now imagine the number of sides on the base increases greatly—the base is coming very close to being a circle with that many sides, and the perimeter is coming very close to being its circumference. So instead of the pyramid's surface area of $\frac{1}{2}ps + B$ that we found for the pyramid in the last section, we substitute the circumference ($2\pi r$) for the perimeter p. Also, B, the area of the base, now becomes the area of a circle (πr^2). So we get $SA_{\text{cone}} = \frac{1}{2}(2\pi r)s + \pi r^2$, which simplifies to

$$SA_{\text{cone}} = \pi rs + \pi r^2,$$

which is the formula given on the Praxis formula sheet.

5.12.4b Volume of a Cone

The volume of a cone follows the same reasoning as for the pyramid, except that for the cone, the base is a circle of area πr^2. As mentioned before, the factor $\frac{1}{3}$ appears in the volume formula because the figure comes to a point. And the height is the perpendicular height h from the point to the circular base (not the slant height). So the volume of a cone is given by

$$V_{\text{cone}} = \frac{1}{3}\pi r^2 h,$$

which is the formula given on the Praxis formula sheet.

EXAMPLE 5.31

Approximate the volume of a right cone with a base of radius 8 inches and a slant height of 17 inches. Give your answer to the nearest hundredth, using $\pi = 3.1416$.

SOLUTION 5.31

1005.31 in³. The given information includes the slant height of the cone, but the formula for a right cone uses the altitude, or the perpendicular height from the point to the base. So first find the altitude h.

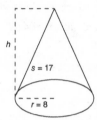

The height h, radius r, and slant height s form a right triangle, as shown. The Pythagorean formula or just the Pythagorean 8-15-17 triple yields a length of $h = 15$ inches. Therefore,

$$V_{cone} = \frac{1}{3}\pi r^2 h = \frac{1}{3}\pi(8)^2(15) = 320\pi = 1005.312$$

and the answer to the nearest hundredth is 1005.31 in³.

5.12.5 Sphere

A **sphere** is a three-dimensional figure in which every point on the surface of the sphere is the same distance, r (the **radius**), from a point called the **center** of the sphere. The idea is that it is like a three-dimensional circle.

A common example of a sphere is a ball. The reason spheres are so common in nature (a drop of water, for example, or the Moon) is that they have the smallest surface area for a given volume, so they have the least resistance to gravity. The formulas for the surface area and volume of a sphere have a factor of 4 in them that can be explained only by using calculus (see Chapter 7).

5.12.5a Surface Area of a Sphere

The **surface area** of a sphere is similar to the area of a circle (πr^2) with a factor of 4.

$$SA_{\text{sphere}} = 4\pi r^2$$

This formula is given on the Praxis formula sheet.

5.12.5b Volume of a Sphere

Likewise, the formula for the volume of a sphere is similar to the formula for the volume of a cone where the height is the radius r with a factor of 4:

$$V_{\text{sphere}} = 4\left(\frac{1}{3}\pi r^2\right)r = \frac{4}{3}\pi r^3$$

This formula is also given on the Praxis formula sheet.

EXAMPLE 5.32

A sphere is inside a cube so that it touches every side of the cube. If an edge of the cube is 10 inches, what is difference between the volumes of the square and the circle? (Use $\pi = 3.14$ and round your answer to the nearest hundredth.)

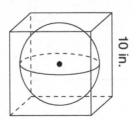

SOLUTION 5.32

476.67 cubic inches. The volume of the cube is $V_{\text{cube}} = s^3 = 1000$ cubic inches. The volume of the sphere is $V_{\text{sphere}} = \frac{4}{3}\pi r^3$, so we need to know the radius of the sphere. We know the diameter of the sphere because it has to be the same as the edge of the cube, or 10 inches. So the volume of the sphere is $V_{\text{sphere}} = \frac{4}{3}\pi r^3 = \frac{4}{3}\pi(5)^3 = \frac{4}{3}(3.14)(125) = 523.33\overline{3}$. The difference to the nearest hundredth is therefore $1000 - 523.33 = 476.67$ cubic inches.

5.12.6 Similarity and Congruence of Three-Dimensional Figures

The requirements for congruence and similarity of three-dimensional figures is the same as that for two-dimensional figures, only with another dimension added.

- Three dimensional figures are **congruent** if their corresponding angles (two-dimensional angles as well as vertices) are equal and their corresponding sides are equal.

- Three-dimensional figures are **similar** if their corresponding angles (two-dimensional angles as well as vertices) are equal and their corresponding sides are proportional.

From these definitions, we can arrive at the following generalities:

- All spheres are similar to all other spheres, and the proportionality constant is the ratio of their radii.

- Spheres are congruent to each other only if their radii are equal.

- All *regular* right prisms with the same number of sides are similar if their corresponding sides are proportional; for example, all cubes are similar to all other cubes.

5.12.7 Relationship between Volume and Density

To understand the relationship between volume and density, we must understand what mass is. **Mass** is simply the amount of matter in an object. We perceive it as the weight of an object; however, mass and weight are different, although related. Weight depends on the pull of gravity on an object, whereas mass stays the same. You may have heard that on the Moon you would weigh one-sixth of your weight on Earth, and that is true because gravity is much less there; your mass, though, would be the same. Someone who is obese on Earth will look the same on the Moon, obese and all—but will be able to move around better. Mass is measured in grams, kilograms, ounces, and pounds.

To get an idea of different masses, a cubic centimeter of foam is 0.03g, whereas for the same **volume** (cm^3), defined as the amount of space that an object occupies, that would be 2.3 g for concrete and 19.3 for gold. The differences are related to how closely the molecules are packed together, or the **density** of the object.

In symbols, the relationship among volume, density, and mass is

$$\text{density} = \frac{\text{mass}}{\text{volume}}, \text{ or } D = \frac{m}{V},$$

which can be rewritten as mass = density × volume. Thus, density and volume are inversely proportional: for a given mass, if density increases, volume decreases, and if volume increases, density decreases. If you add mass to an object without changing its volume, the object's density increases.

Interestingly, the density of aluminum is 2.7 g/cm³, a little more than concrete! We tend to think of aluminum as being light and concrete as heavy, but that is because we are used to seeing a tiny volume of aluminum (either as aluminum foil with hardly any thickness or as aluminum furniture, which is hollow). This shows how volume (or size) makes a difference in comparing two materials.

5.12.8 Relationship of Two-Dimensional to Three-Dimensional Figures

As stated earlier in Section 5.12, three-dimensional figures can be drawn on a two-dimensional paper. These are only representations of three-dimensional shapes. One way to go from a two-dimensional representation to a three-dimensional representation is through nets.

Another way to create a three-dimensional figure from a two-dimensional figure is by rotating it around any line in the Cartesian plane. In either case, the third dimension is depth.

5.12.8a Nets

Nets are two-dimensional patterns traced on paper, cut, and folded to make three-dimensional figures. So two-dimensional polygons can form a three-dimensional **polyhedron**. Conversely, a net is the shape that is formed by unfolding a three-dimensional figure. Classic examples of nets are shown in the table below.

Polyhedron Name	Net	Three-Dimensional Image
triangular prism		
square pyramid		

Polyhedron Name	Net	Three-Dimensional Image
cone		
cylinder		

5.12.8b Rotation and Slicing

Other ways that two-dimensional and three-dimensional shapes are related is through rotation (two-dimensional to three-dimensional) or slicing (three-dimensional to two-dimensional).

We will explore rotation further in Chapter 7, Section 7.3.7b. For now, we can picture how **rotation** is the method by which a circle can become a sphere, a rectangle can become a cylinder, or a triangle can become a cone.

rotate a circle to make a sphere

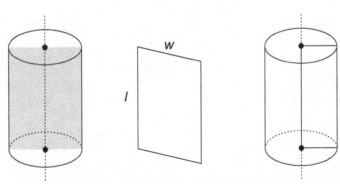

rotate a rectangle to make a cylinder

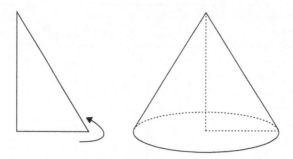

rotate a triangle to make a cone

The "**slicing**" of a cone, as discussed at the beginning of the Section 5.8, shows how a three-dimensional shape can reveal two-dimensional shapes.

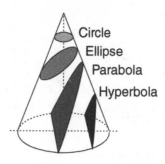

Circle
Ellipse
Parabola
Hyperbola

5.13 TRIGONOMETRY

5.13.1 Definitions of Trigonometric Functions

A right triangle is the basis for the definitions of the trigonometric (trig) functions. Because all right triangles with the same corresponding angles are similar, the ratios between any two sides of all right triangles are the same for a particular angle measurement. For $\angle\theta$, we can state these ratios in trigonometric terms, where *opposite* means the side opposite $\angle\theta$, and *adjacent* means the side adjacent to $\angle\theta$ (the other adjacent side being the hypotenuse). The hypotenuse is always opposite the right angle.

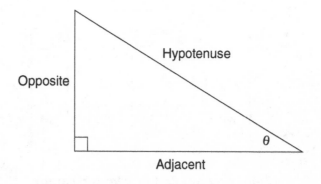

The three most important trigonometric functions are sine, cosine, and tangent (abbreviated as sin, cos, and tan, respectively).

$$\sin = \frac{\text{opposite}}{\text{hypotenuse}}$$

$$\cos = \frac{\text{adjacent}}{\text{hypotenuse}}$$

$$\tan = \frac{\text{opposite}}{\text{adjacent}}$$

The three other trig functions are simply reciprocals of these three, going in the direction tangent to sine. They are the cotangent (cot), secant (sec), and cosecant (csc).

$$\cot\theta = \frac{1}{\tan\theta} = \frac{\text{adjacent}}{\text{opposite}}$$

$$\sec\theta = \frac{1}{\cos\theta} = \frac{\text{hypotenuse}}{\text{adjacent}}$$

$$\csc\theta = \frac{1}{\sin\theta} = \frac{\text{hypotenuse}}{\text{opposite}}$$

The abbreviation for cosecant cannot be "cos" because that abbreviation is already used for cosine.

Only the values for sine and cosine are needed to get values for the rest of the functions since they are all related to those two functions:

$$\tan\theta = \frac{\sin\theta}{\cos\theta}; \quad \cot\theta = \frac{\cos\theta}{\sin\theta}; \quad \sec\theta = \frac{1}{\cos\theta}; \quad \csc\theta = \frac{1}{\sin\theta}$$

Keeping these definitions in mind, the other trigonometric functions can be derived rather than memorized.

5.13.2 Degrees and Radians

Angles are measured in degrees and also in radians. The formal definition of a radian is the measure of a central angle that intercepts an arc equal to the radius of the circle. (The name *radian* is a contraction of radius-angle.)

Since the circumference of a circle is $C = 2\pi r$, it makes sense that there are 2π radians in the circumference of a circle. So a circle measures $360° = 2\pi$ radians and therefore

$$1 \text{ radian} = \frac{360}{2\pi} \text{ degrees} \approx 57.296 \text{ degrees}$$

- To convert a degree measurement to radians, multiply by $\frac{2\pi}{360} = \frac{\pi}{180}$.

- To convert a radian measurement into degrees, multiply by $\frac{360}{2\pi} = \frac{180}{\pi}$.

Common conversions are

Degrees	Radians	Degrees	Radians
0	0	90	$\frac{\pi}{2}$
30	$\frac{\pi}{6}$	180	π
45	$\frac{\pi}{4}$	270	$\frac{3\pi}{2}$
60	$\frac{\pi}{3}$	360	2π

Radian measure is usually given in terms of π. It is customary to omit the word *radians* if an angle measure is given in terms of π.

5.13.3 Unit Circle

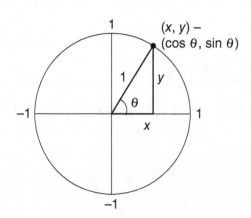

Any angle can be put in standard position in a **unit circle** (a circle with radius = 1) with its vertex at the center (0, 0). The standard position ray that lies along the positive x-axis intersects the circle at (1, 0). The terminal ray intersects the circle at some point (x, y). When the angle is graphed in the unit circle, the x-coordinate of the point of intersection of the terminal ray and the circle represents $\cos \theta$ and the y-coordinate of the point of intersection represents $\sin \theta$. The terminal side of the angle is the radius (= 1) to the point (x, y).

 On the unit circle, positive angles are graphed counterclockwise from the positive x-axis and negative angles are graphed clockwise from the positive x-axis.

An important and useful trigonometric identity comes from the Pythagorean Theorem and the unit circle:

$$x^2 + y^2 = 1$$

$$\cos^2 \theta + \sin^2 \theta = 1 \text{ or the more familiar } \sin^2 \theta + \cos^2 \theta = 1$$

The method for finding the sine and cosine of an angle by using the unit circle is outlined below for some common angles. This method is valid for all angles.

- The terminal ray of an angle that measures $\dfrac{\pi}{2}$ radians (or 90°) intersects the unit circle at (0, 1). Since (x, y) on the unit circle represents $(\cos \theta, \sin \theta)$, this means $\sin \dfrac{\pi}{2} = 1$ and $\cos \dfrac{\pi}{2} = 0$.

- The terminal ray of an angle that measures π radians (or 180°) intersects the unit circle at $(-1, 0)$, so $\sin \pi = 0$ and $\cos \pi = -1$.

- The terminal ray of an angle that measures $\dfrac{3\pi}{2}$ radians (or 270°) intersects the circle at $(0, -1)$, so $\sin \dfrac{3\pi}{2} = -1$ and $\cos \dfrac{3\pi}{2} = 0$.

- The terminal ray of an angle that measures 2π radians (or 360°) intersects the circle at (1, 0), so $\sin 2\pi = 0$ and $\cos 2\pi = 1$.

The following table lists the sine, cosine, and tangent of key angles in the first quadrant. The values are readily found by using the definitions of the functions and the facts that in a 30°-60°-90° triangle the side opposite the 30° angle is half the hypotenuse and the ratio of the sides is 1-2-$\sqrt{3}$, and in a 45°-45°-90° triangle the legs are equal and the ratio of the sides is 1-1-$\sqrt{2}$.

θ, degrees	θ, radians	$\sin \theta = \dfrac{\text{opposite}}{\text{hypotenuse}}$	$\cos \theta = \dfrac{\text{adjacent}}{\text{hypotenuse}}$	$\tan \theta = \dfrac{\sin \theta}{\cos \theta}$
0°	0	0	1	$\dfrac{0}{1} = 0$
30°	$\dfrac{\pi}{6}$	$\dfrac{1}{2}$	$\dfrac{\sqrt{3}}{2}$	$\dfrac{\frac{1}{2}}{\frac{\sqrt{3}}{2}} = \dfrac{1}{\sqrt{3}} = \dfrac{\sqrt{3}}{3}$
45°	$\dfrac{\pi}{4}$	$\dfrac{1}{\sqrt{2}} = \dfrac{\sqrt{2}}{2}$	$\dfrac{1}{\sqrt{2}} = \dfrac{\sqrt{2}}{2}$	$\dfrac{\frac{1}{2}\sqrt{2}}{\frac{1}{2}\sqrt{2}} = 1$
60°	$\dfrac{\pi}{3}$	$\dfrac{\sqrt{3}}{2}$	$\dfrac{1}{2}$	$\dfrac{\frac{\sqrt{3}}{2}}{\frac{1}{2}} = \sqrt{3}$
90°	$\dfrac{\pi}{2}$	1	0	$\dfrac{1}{0}$, undefined

The numerical values for sine, cosine, and tangent are programmed into most calculators, so it isn't necessary to memorize any of the values in the table above, but they occur so frequently that you should at least know how to get them from a sketch of the 30°-60°-90° or 45°-45°-90° triangle.

5.13.4 Inverse Trigonometric Functions

The notation for the **inverse** sine function is $\sin^{-1} x$ or arcsin x, read as "the angle whose sine is." The other trig functions with a –1 exponent also mean "the angle whose [function] is."

The notation $\sin^{-1}$ does not mean $\dfrac{1}{\sin}$; it means "arcsin" or "the angle whose sign is."

The Praxis formula sheet uses $\sin^{-1}$, $\cos^{-1}$, and $\tan^{-1}$ for inverse functions. On the calculator keys for the Praxis test, however, arcsin is abbreviated further to asin. (Similarly, acos means arccos and atan means arctan.)

Only **one-to-one functions** can have inverses, by definition (see Chapter 6, Section 6.5), so we confine the domain of $y = \sin x$ to the interval $-\dfrac{\pi}{2} \le \theta \le \dfrac{\pi}{2}$. Then sin x will pass the horizontal as well as vertical line test (See Chapter 6, Section 6.1.2), and is thus a one-to-one function with an inverse. Since arccsc and arctan are related to arcsin, they also have this restricted range. The other functions (arccos, arccot, arcsec) similarly have a restricted range of $0 \le \theta \le \pi$.

The principal value of an inverse function is less than 180°. Specifically,

- For a positive number, it is a positive angle in Quadrant I.

- For a negative number, it is a negative angle in Quadrant II for arcsin, arctan, arccot, and arccsc

- For a negative number, it is a positive angle in Quadrant IV for arccos and arcsec.

Thus, the principal value of $\arcsin\left(\dfrac{1}{2}\right)$ is 30° and not 150°; $\arcsin\left(-\dfrac{\sqrt{3}}{2}\right)$ is –60° and not 240°; $\arccos\left(-\dfrac{1}{2}\right)$ is 120° and not –120°.

EXAMPLE 5.33

Find the principal value of $\arcsin\left(\cos\dfrac{\pi}{6}\right)$.

SOLUTION 5.33

$\dfrac{\pi}{3}$. The cosine of $\dfrac{\pi}{6}$ is $\dfrac{\sqrt{3}}{2}$. So $\arcsin\left(\cos\dfrac{\pi}{6}\right) = \arcsin\left(\dfrac{\sqrt{3}}{2}\right) = \dfrac{\pi}{3}$.

NOTE This answer is given in radians because the problem is given in radians. An answer of 60° would also be correct, but it is better not to switch between the two systems. Be sure the online calculator is set to the desired system.

EXAMPLE 5.34

Zip line is always slant.

Rev. A ski resort has installed a zip line. The zip line is 1750 feet long and allows its rider to descend a vertical distance of 450 feet. What is the angle of declination to the nearest degree? (The angle of declination is the angle between the horizontal and the zip line.)

SOLUTION 5.34

Sketch the problem first:

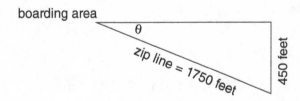

From the sketch, it is clear that $\sin\theta = \dfrac{\text{opp}}{\text{hyp}} = \dfrac{450}{1750} = \dfrac{9}{35}$. So the problem is to find $\arcsin\dfrac{9}{35} \approx 15°$.

Use the fraction and don't waste time finding the decimal equivalent for two reasons: (1) the calculator accepts fractions for inverse trig functions (and most everything else as long as you remember to include the fraction in parentheses, if necessary); and (2) finding the decimal equivalent of a fraction and rounding it in the middle of a calculation can introduce rounding errors in the result.

5.13.5 Algebra with Trig Functions

Trig functions (together with their angles) are treated the same as variables in an algebraic equation. As a start, use your knowledge of the following:

1. The fundamental Pythagorean identity from the unit circle: $\sin^2 a + \cos^2 a = 1$

2. The relationships (definitions) of the trig functions sin, cos, tan, cot, sec, and csc.

3. Knowledge of basic algebra and recognizing that $\sin \theta$ and $\cos \theta$ (as well as the other trig functions) take the place of the variables used in algebra.

4. Other trigonometric relationships that appear on the Praxis formula sheet, if needed.

For example,

$$\sin \theta + 3 \sin \theta = 4 \sin \theta$$

$$\cos^2 \pi = \cos \pi \times \cos \pi$$

are treated identically to

$$s + 3s = 4s$$

$$c^2 = c \times c$$

Note, however, that $\sin A + \sin 3A \neq \sin 4A$ because the angles are different, even though they are written in terms of the same angle ($A \neq 2A \neq 3A$).

EXAMPLE 5.35

Find acute angle x when $4 \cos^2 x = 1$.

SOLUTION 5.35

$60°$. Treat $\cos x$ as a variable, so $4 \cos^2 x = 1$ is the same as $\cos^2 x = \dfrac{1}{4}$. Take the square roots of both sides of that equation to get $\cos x = \pm \dfrac{1}{2}$. The problem asks for an acute angle, so $x = 60°$.

EXAMPLE 5.36

In right triangle ABC with right angle C, $c = 25.0$ and $A = 40°$. Find the other angle and the other two sides to the nearest tenth.

SOLUTION 5.36

$\angle B = 50°$; $a = 16.1$, and $b = 19.2$. To find $\angle B$, use the fact that the two acute angles in a right triangle are complementary. So $\angle A + \angle B = 90°$. Sketch the triangle. Since $\angle A = 40°$, $\angle B = 50°$. Use $\sin A = \dfrac{a}{c}$ to find a. With the given values and the calculator for the sines of the angles, $\sin 40° = \dfrac{a}{25}$, or $a = 25(\sin 40°) = 25(.6428) = 16.07$, or $a = 16.1$, rounded to the nearest tenth. Use $\sin B = \dfrac{b}{c}$ to find b. Then $\sin 50° = \dfrac{b}{25}$, or $b = 25(\sin 50°) = 25(.7660) = 19.15$, or $b = 19.2$, rounded to the nearest tenth.

EXAMPLE 5.37

A guy wire reaches from the top of a pole to a stake in the ground, 10 feet from the foot of the pole. The wire makes an angle of $65°$ with the ground. Find the length of the wire rounded to the nearest foot.

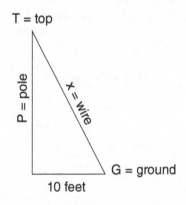

T = top

P = pole

x = wire

G = ground

10 feet

SOLUTION 5.37

24 feet. The function to use here is sine because the values that are needed to find x are given. We know the angle at T is $25°$, so the equation is $\sin 25° = \dfrac{10}{x}$, or $x \sin 25° = 10$, or $x = \dfrac{10}{\sin 25°}$. Use the calculator for $\sin 25°$, to find $x = \dfrac{10}{.4226} = 23.66$ feet, which is rounded to 24 feet.

 The height of the pole doesn't have to be known to solve this problem because once we know three angles of a triangle, we need to know only one side to fix the triangle, and we know that one leg is 10. We could then find the height of the pole by using the Pythagorean Theorem.

EXAMPLE 5.38

Simplify $\dfrac{\sec x}{\cot x + \tan x}$ to a single trigonometric function by using the relations among the functions.

SOLUTION 5.38

$\sin x$. First, rewrite the three trigonometric functions in terms of sine and cosine only: $\dfrac{\sec x}{\cot x + \tan x} = \dfrac{\frac{1}{\cos x}}{\frac{\cos x}{\sin x} + \frac{\sin x}{\cos x}}$. Then multiply the fraction through by the LCD

$(\sin x \cos x)$ to get $\dfrac{\sin x \cos x\left(\frac{1}{\cos x}\right)}{\sin x \cos x\left(\frac{\cos x}{\sin x}+\frac{\sin x}{\cos x}\right)} = \dfrac{\sin x}{\cos^2 x + \sin^2 x} = \dfrac{\sin x}{1} = \sin x$.

EXAMPLE 5.39

Find the angle θ that satisfies the equation $3(\sin\theta + 1) = \sin\theta + 4$ on the interval $\left[0, \dfrac{\pi}{2}\right]$.

SOLUTION 5.39

$\dfrac{\pi}{6}$. Treat this equation the same as the quadratic $3(x + 1) = x + 4$:

$$3(\sin\theta + 1) = \sin\theta + 4$$

$$3\sin\theta + 3 = \sin\theta + 4$$

$$2\sin\theta = 1$$

$$\sin\theta = \frac{1}{2}$$

Then $\theta = \dfrac{\pi}{6}$.

5.13.6 Special Cases

5.13.6a Reference Angles

Every angle whose measure is greater than 90° or less than 0° has a corresponding **reference angle**, which is the acute angle formed by the terminal side of the given angle and the negative or positive x-axis. This reference angle can be used to calculate the absolute trigonometric values for the given angle, and then, depending on the quadrant of the terminal side of the original angle and the trigonometric function, positive or negative values can be applied.

A simple sketch will show how to find the reference angle.

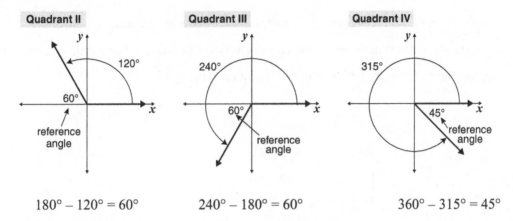

$$180° - 120° = 60° \qquad 240° - 180° = 60° \qquad 360° - 315° = 45°$$

Always start in Quadrant I and remember that each quadrant is 90° or $\frac{\pi}{2}$. Once you have the approximate position of the given angle, let's call it θ, its quadrant determines how you proceed. In general, the reference angle is the angle between the terminal ray of the given angle θ and the x-axis.

- For Quadrant II, the reference angle is the difference $180° - \theta$.

- For Quadrant III, the reference angle is the difference $\theta - 180°$.

- For Quadrant IV, the reference angle is the difference $360° - \theta$.

The x (cos) and y (sin) values are positive or negative depending on the quadrant. All trigonometric functions in Quadrant I are positive. The following table shows the signs of the trig functions in the four quadrants, but they can be figured out readily by determining the signs of x and y in each quadrant, remembering that $x =$ cos and $y =$ sin and remembering the relationships of the other four functions with relation to sine and cosine.

Reciprocal functions	Quadrant containing terminal side			
	I	II	III	IV
Sine and Cosecant	+	+	−	−
Cosine and Secant	+	−	−	+
Tangent and Cotangent	+	−	+	−

EXAMPLE 5.40

If $\tan\theta = -\dfrac{5}{12}$ and $\dfrac{3\pi}{2} < \theta < 2\pi$, evaluate $\sin\theta$.

SOLUTION 5.40

$-\dfrac{5}{13}$. From the preceding table, tangent is negative in the second or fourth quadrants, and the restrictions in the problem put it in Quadrant IV. Sketch the reference angle in the fourth quadrant with the information that $\tan\theta = -\dfrac{5}{12}$:

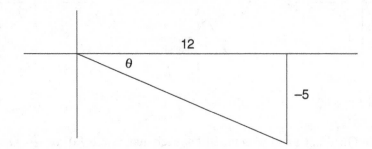

Find the hypotenuse and use that information to write sin θ. The Pythagorean formula gives the hypotenuse as $\sqrt{12^2 + 5^2} = \sqrt{169} = 13$; and the hypotenuse is always positive. This triangle is the 5-12-13 Pythagorean triple. So $\sin\theta = \dfrac{\text{opp}}{\text{hyp}} = -\dfrac{5}{13}$.

EXAMPLE 5.41

An airborne kite 80 feet high is staked to the ground by a string that forms a 50° angle with the ground. How long is this string to the nearest tenth of a foot?

SOLUTION 5.41

Sketch the information.

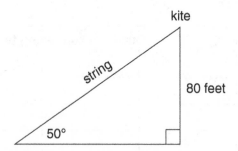

104.4 feet. The only trigonometric functions that relate an angle (50° here) and the side opposite and the hypotenuse are sine and cosecant. Since the calculator does not have a csc button, use sin. So $\sin 50° = \dfrac{80}{x}$, where x is the length of the string.

Then use the calculator to get $x = \dfrac{80}{\sin 50°} = 104.432583147 = 104.4$ feet.

Do not find sin 50° and divide that value into 80—just enter the fraction $\dfrac{80}{\sin 50°}$ into the calculator.

5.13.6b Angles Greater Than 360° (2π radians)

One full rotation of the unit circle is 360° or 2π radians. Since trig functions are cyclic, the trig functions for any angle are repeated in every rotation.

Change a given angle greater than 360° to an angle in the interval [0, 360°] (or [0, 2π]) by repeatedly subtracting 360° (or 2π) from the angle measurement until the difference is ≤360° (or ≤2π), which is an angle equivalent to the given angle. The given angle will have the same trigonometric values as this angle equivalent. If the equivalent angle is not in Quadrant I, figure out the reference angle as shown in Section 5.13.6a.

 This procedure is mostly unnecessary since most calculators are programmed to give the sine, cosine, and tangent of any angle, large or small, positive or negative.

EXAMPLE 5.42

What is sin 750°?

SOLUTION 5.42

$\dfrac{1}{2}$. Subtract 360° from 750°. The result is 390°, so repeat the process: 390° − 360° = 30°. Since 30° is in the first quadrant, the trig functions of 750° are the same as those for 30°, so $\sin 750° = \dfrac{1}{2}$.

5.13.6c Negative Angles

Change **negative angles** to an angle in the interval [0, 360°] (or [0, 2π]) by repeatedly adding 360° (or 2π) to the angle measurement until the difference is positive. That positive number is the coterminal angle for the given angle. **Coterminal** angles are two angles that share the same terminal ray. Coterminal angles differ by 360° or 2π radians. Therefore, −70° is coterminal with 290°; 45° is coterminal with 405°, 765°, and −315°, among others; and π radians is coterminal with 3π radians, 5π radians, and $-\pi$ radians, among others.

The given angle will have the same trigonometric values as its coterminal angle. If the coterminal angle is not in Quadrant I, figure out the reference angle as shown in Section 5.13.6a.

Sometimes it is easier to just sketch the negative angle—but remember to start at the positive *x*-axis and go clockwise because it is a negative angle.

EXAMPLE 5.43

Find $\cos(-330°)$.

SOLUTION 5.43

$\dfrac{\sqrt{3}}{2}$. Adding 360° to –330° yields 30°, so $\cos(-330°) = \cos(30°)$.

 $\text{Cos}(-330)°$ is not the same as $-\cos(330°)$, which is $-\dfrac{\sqrt{3}}{2}$.

5.13.7 Trigonometric Function Graphs

The trigonometric functions are examples of **periodic functions** because they repeat their output values at regular intervals, or periods. Other examples of periodic functions are sound waves, tides, and heartbeats. One complete repetition of the output values of a periodic functions is called a **cycle**. The **period** is the horizontal length of one cycle. For sine and cosine, the cycle and period can be seen as the rotation of the unit circle.

The following graphs of the six trigonometric functions show this periodicity. Also marked on the graphs are the ranges. For sine and cosine, the range is [–1, 1], and for the other four functions, it is (–∞, ∞). The domains for all trigonometric functions is (–∞, ∞) except for the asymptotes for the tangent and secant of $y = \dfrac{\pi}{2} + np$ and the asymptotes for the cotangent and cosecant of $y = np$.

 The asymptotes for tangent and secant are the values for which cosine = 0 since cosine is in the denominator of tangent and secant. Likewise, the asymptotes for cotangent and cosecant are the values for which sine = 0 since sine is in the denominator of tangent and secant.

 The graphs across from each other in the figures on the following page are reciprocals of each other.

$y = \sin x$

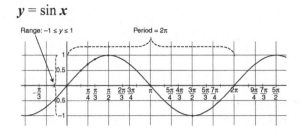

$y = \csc x$

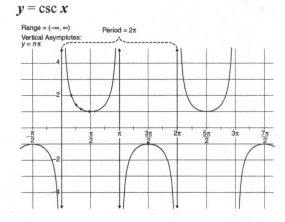

$y = \cos x$

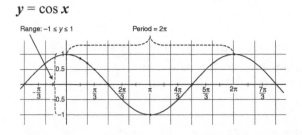

$y = \sec x$

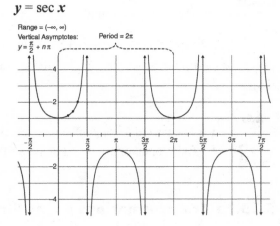

$y = \tan x$

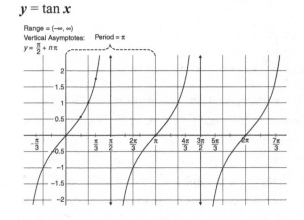

$y = \cot x$

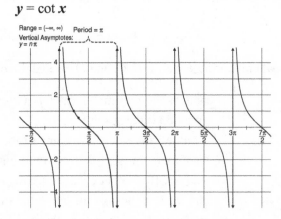

5.13.7a Transformations of Trigonometric Functions

Trigonometric function graphs follow the same basic transformation rules as transformations in the coordinate plane (see Section 5.9): shifting up, down, left, right; reflection about the axes; expanding and contracting.

In the first quadrant, as any angle A increases, the functions sin A, tan A, and sec A also increase, and the cofunctions cos A, cot A, and csc A decrease.

The one graph that is indispensable for graphing trigonometric functions is the sine curve. You can see that sine starts at (0, 0) (meaning the sine of 0 is 0), and that it has a period of 2π. Those facts are all you need, and everything else will fall into place. In fact, all of the trigonometric functions have cofunctions as follows (thus, the names cosine, cotangent, and cosecant).

The cofunctions (sine and cosine, tangent and cotangent, secant and cosecant) are related in an interesting way: for *complementary* angles, the function and cofunction are equal. That is, sin 30° = cos 60°, as seen in the table in Section 5.13.3. Likewise, tan 50° = cot 40° and sec 20° = csc 70°. These relationships are evident when looking at a right triangle.

Trigonometric functions can be transformed, just like other functions. We will use the sine curve for the following discussion, but the same rules for transformations apply to the other functions.

The period of tangent and cotangent is π, not 2π, so adjust the changes to the period (horizontal dilation and phase shift accordingly).

5.13.7b Transformations of the Sine Function

The general form for the equation of the sine function is

$$y = A\sin B(x - C) + D$$

where the values for A, B, C, and D change the basic $y = \sin x$ curve in some way.

   A changes the amplitude, which is a kind of vertical dilation. The **amplitude** of a periodic function is the absolute value of one-half the difference between the highest and lowest y values. Instead of the graph of the sine function having an amplitude of 1 (meaning its maximum is +1 and its minimum is –1), the graph will now "bounce" between $+A$ and $-A$. If no other changes are made, changing the amplitude has the effect of changing the steepness of the curve because now it has to go A units in the same horizontal distance. If A is positive, that's all that changes—how high ($|A| > 1$) or low ($|A| < 1$) the curve goes. The higher A is, the steeper the curve, and the closer A is to 0, the flatter the curve. If A is negative, the curve also flips over the horizontal axis.

B changes the **period** of the curve, but the change is actually the reciprocal of the horizontal dilation. The period of sin *x*, instead of being 2π or $360°$, will now be $\dfrac{2\pi}{B}$ or $\dfrac{360}{B}$. If *B* is less than 1 (in other words, a fraction), it has the effect of stretching the graph out, and if it is greater than 1, it has the effect of pulling the graph tighter. To visualize the effect of *B*, consider that for $B > 1$, the period is $\dfrac{1}{B}$ times what it was without this horizontal dilation. In other words, *B* tells how many complete cycles the curve will make in the space that originally had only one. If $B < 1$, the curve becomes more elongated.

C is a **horizontal translation**, or a **phase shift** to the left ($C < 0$) or right ($C > 0$) with no dilation. Note that in the general equation, *C* is *subtracted*, so keep your signs straight—it is the value of *C* (not −*C*) that determines left or right shift. Trigonometric cofunctions are related to each other through phase shifts of $90°$, or $\dfrac{\pi}{2}$. For example, $\sin\left(x + \dfrac{\pi}{2}\right) = \cos x$ and the shift is to the left because $C = -\dfrac{\pi}{2}$ here. Likewise, $\cos\left(x - \dfrac{\pi}{2}\right) = \sin x$ and the shift is to the right because $C = +\dfrac{\pi}{2}$ here. In general, phase shifts can have any value.

D is a **vertical shift**, up (if $D > 0$) or down (if $D < 0$). The whole graph, is raised or lowered. In other words, this is a vertical translation with no dilation. The midline of the graph, which is the horizontal line about which the graph of a periodic function oscillates, becomes $y_{new} = y_{old} + D$. For example, the midline of the sine or cosine graphs would change from $y = 0$ to $y = D$.

Hint: For an easy way to remember the direction of a horizontal shift, use a standard sine curve and determine by how many units $(0, 0)$ has moved to the right or left.

For an easy way to visualize vertical shift, just renumber the *y*-axis so the line $y = 0$ becomes $y = D$ and renumber the other values on the *y*-axis accordingly.

For an easy way to visualize a change in period (*B*) for the sine function, renumber the *x*-axis so $x = 2\pi$ becomes the new value *Bx*, and renumber the other values on the *x*-axis accordingly.

EXAMPLE 5.44

Describe the graph of $y = 3\sin 2\left(x - \dfrac{\pi}{4}\right) + 1$.

SOLUTION 5.44

The reference graph is $y = \sin x$. The transformed graph is shown below it.

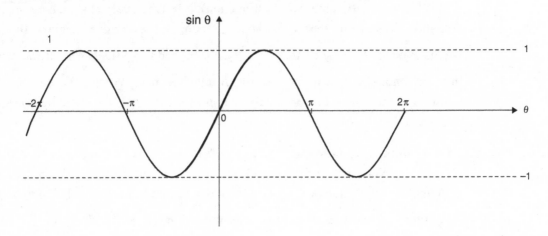

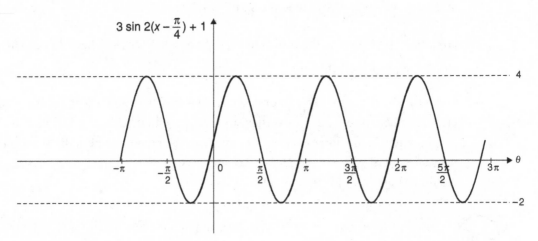

EXAMPLE 5.45

What is the period of $5 \sin\left(\dfrac{x}{3} + \pi\right)$?

SOLUTION 5.45

6π, or $1080°$. The only number you have to look at for the period is the coefficient B in the general form $y = A \sin B(x - C) + D$, which is $\dfrac{1}{3}$ because $5\sin\left(\dfrac{x}{3} + \pi\right) = 5\sin\dfrac{1}{3}(x + 3\pi)$. This means that the cosine curve completes only $\dfrac{1}{3}$ of its period in 2π, and the whole period is therefore $3(2\pi) = 6\pi$. The coefficient $A = 5$ adjusts the amplitude from 1 to 5 units, and $C = 3\pi$ added to the argument is simply a phase shift; neither of these changes the period.

5.13.8 Finding the Area of a Triangle

Earlier in this chapter, we found the areas of several triangles. The formula for the area of a triangle is

$$A = \frac{1}{2}bh,$$

where b is the base of the triangle and h is the perpendicular distance from the base to the opposite vertex. For right triangles, the two legs can be considered as the base and the height, so the area is simply half the product of the lengths of the two legs.

For triangles that aren't right triangles, we may be able to form two right triangles by drawing the height and using the Pythagorean Theorem to find the areas of the two right triangles whose sum is the area of the whole triangle. Or we can graph the triangle if we know enough about the vertices and find the area that way.

But what if none of these methods works? What if, for example, all we know are two sides and the angle between them? Or all we know are the three sides of a triangle? Can we get enough information about an acute or obtuse triangle to find the area or the missing side(s) or angle(s)?

The answer is yes, by using trigonometry.

5.13.8a SAS—Area of a Triangle

To find the area of a triangle if all we know are two sides and the included angle, we use the basic equation, $A = \frac{1}{2}bh$, and a sketch of the triangle to guide our solution. Let's say we know sides a and b and the included angle C. First, draw the height, h, to side b (shown by a dashed line).

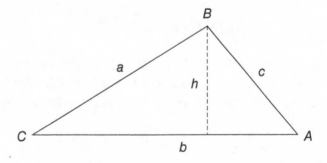

By using trigonometry, and looking at only the left triangle formed by h, we see that $\sin C = \dfrac{h}{a}$, or $h = a \sin C$. So now for Area $= \frac{1}{2}$(base) $\times$ (height), we have

$$\text{Area} = \frac{1}{2}ab\sin C.$$

This formula for finding the area of any triangle when you know only two sides and the included angle is sometimes called the ***a-b-C* formula**. However, since the assignment of letters was arbitrary, it is also true that Area $= \frac{1}{2}bc\sin A$ and Area $= \frac{1}{2}ca\sin B$. Just be sure that the angle you are using is the one between the two sides.

EXAMPLE 5.46

In triangle ABC, $a = 9$, $b = 8$, and $\sin C = \frac{5}{12}$. What is the area of triangle ABC?

SOLUTION 5.46

15. Area $= \frac{1}{2}ab\sin C = \frac{1}{2}(9)(8)\frac{5}{12} = 15$

5.13.8b SAS—Law of Cosines

We can use the Pythagorean Theorem ($c^2 = a^2 + b^2$) to find the third side of a right triangle. But what if we want to find the third side of a triangle that isn't a right triangle? The law of cosines makes that calculation fairly simple. All you need to know are the lengths of the other two sides and the angle between them, just as for the area formula in Section 5.13.8a. It is important that the angle between the sides is the known angle because those two sides could be two sides of an infinite number of triangles, depending on how close or far apart they are, but by specifying the exact angle between these two sides, there is only one triangle possible. That's why SAS works for proving two triangles are congruent (see Section 5.4.3).

The formula for the law of cosines looks like the Pythagorean Theorem, but the last term is a kind of "correction" term to compensate for the fact that this isn't a right triangle.

$$c^2 = a^2 + b^2 - 2ab\cos C$$

Just like the case for the area formula in the last section, since the assignment of letters was arbitrary, it is also true that $a^2 = b^2 + c^2 - 2bc\cos A$ and $b^2 = a^2 + c^2 - 2ac\cos B$. Again, just be sure that the angle you are using is the one between the two sides. The law of cosines is on the Praxis formula sheet.

5.13.8c ASA—Law of Sines

If we know two angles of any triangle, we can compute the remaining angle by simply subtracting their sum from 180°, the total number of degrees in a triangle. Knowing the three angles in a triangle, though, doesn't tell us the size of the triangle. There are infinitely many similar triangles with any particular configuration of angles. However, if we know just one side, the size of the triangle is locked in—there is only one triangle that has those three angles and that side. That's why SAS works for proving two triangles congruent. Of course, which side is known is important.

Knowing which angle is opposite the known side, we can use the law of sines to find the other two sides. This is because the ratios of the sides of a triangle and their opposite angles are constant in any triangle. The law of sines states this relationship as:

$$\frac{\sin A}{a} = \frac{\sin B}{b} = \frac{\sin C}{c}$$

Thus, if you know the three angles (even if you are given only two of them, you can find the third) and only one side, you can find the other two sides by successive use of the law of sines. and therefore you have the complete triangle. The law of sines is on the Praxis formula sheet.

5.13.8d SSS—Area of a Triangle

If you know the lengths of the three sides of a triangle, the angle measurements are locked in (that's why SSS for congruence works). So even if you don't know what any of the angles are, you can still calculate the area of the triangle, even if it isn't a right triangle. **Heron's formula** has been known for about 2,000 years, and it is just a two-step process:

1. Calculate the **semiperimeter** s (half the perimeter of the triangle with sides a, b, and c)

$$s = \frac{a+b+c}{2}$$

2. Then calculate the area of the triangle with sides a, b, and c using the value for s:

$$A = \sqrt{s(s-a)(s-b)(s-c)}$$

EXAMPLE 5.47

What is the area of the equilateral triangle with a side = 5 units? Round your answer to the nearest integer.

SOLUTION 5.47

11 square units. First, recognize that since this is an equilateral triangle of side 5 units, every side = 5 units. Find $s = \frac{5+5+5}{2} = 7.5$. Then substitute it into Heron's formula:

$$A = \sqrt{s(s-a)(s-b)(s-c)} = \sqrt{7.5(2.5)(2.5)(2.5)} = 10.8253175473 \approx 11$$

Note that rounding should wait until the last step, even though it doesn't change the answer in this case. The calculator can find the square root of the product of the four numbers directly, so you don't have to actually figure what 7.5(2.5)(2.5) (2.5) is. Of course, to do the rounding at the end, we look only at 10.8 and ignore the other numbers. They were included here to show that the calculator will come up with an answer to the square root right away without any intermediate number. Rounding before the end of the problem can introduce errors of overestimation or underestimation.

5.13.9 Pythagorean Identities

First, let's distinguish between an identity and an equation. **Equations** can be proven to be true or untrue, based on the values of the variable(s). **Identities**, however, are statements that are always true. Even though they contain an equal sign, they are not exactly equations, they are statements. This is an important distinction.

The most useful of the Pythagorean identities is

$$\sin^2\theta + \cos^2\theta = 1,$$

and its variations, $\sin^2\theta = 1 - \cos^2\theta$ and $\cos^2\theta = 1 - \sin^2\theta$.

This identity derives immediately from the equation for the unit circle, $x^2 + y^2 = r^2 = 1$, since a radius of 1 is the definition of a unit circle (see Section 5.13.3). To review, at any point (x, y) on the unit circle, where θ is an angle in standard position, $x = \cos\theta$ and $y = \sin\theta$. Thus, $x^2 + y^2 = 1$ is equivalent to $\cos^2\theta + \sin^2\theta = 1$, or the more familiar $\sin^2\theta + \cos^2\theta = 1$.

The other Pythagorean identities can be derived from this basic identity, by using the definitions of the six basic trigonometric functions and a little algebra. Remember that any trigonometric function can be treated as an unknown in an algebraic equation (see the Section 5.13.5).

For example, if we divide the basic Pythagorean identity by $\cos^2\theta$ (here we are using only algebra), we get

$$\frac{\sin^2\theta + \cos^2\theta = 1}{\cos^2\theta} = \frac{\sin^2\theta}{\cos^2\theta} + \frac{\cos^2\theta}{\cos^2\theta} = \frac{1}{\cos^2\theta}$$

$$= \left(\frac{\sin\theta}{\cos\theta}\right)^2 + \left(\frac{\cos\theta}{\cos\theta}\right)^2 = \left(\frac{1}{\cos\theta}\right)^2.$$

By using the definitions of the functions $\tan\theta = \dfrac{\sin\theta}{\cos\theta}$ and $\sec\theta = \dfrac{1}{\cos\theta}$, we get the second Pythagorean identity:

$$\tan^2\theta + 1 = \sec^2\theta,$$

and its variation: $\tan^2\theta = \sec^2\theta - 1$.

Likewise, if we divide the basic Pythagorean identity by $\sin^2 \theta$ (again, using only algebra), we get

$$\frac{\sin^2 \theta + \cos^2 \theta = 1}{\sin^2 \theta} = \frac{\sin^2 \theta}{\sin^2 \theta} + \frac{\cos^2 \theta}{\sin^2 \theta} = \frac{1}{\sin^2 \theta}$$

$$= \left(\frac{\sin \theta}{\sin \theta}\right)^2 + \left(\frac{\cos \theta}{\sin \theta}\right)^2 = \left(\frac{1}{\sin \theta}\right)^2 .$$

Using the definitions of the trigonometric functions $\cot \theta = \frac{\cos \theta}{\sin \theta}$ and $\csc \theta = \frac{1}{\sin \theta}$, we get the third Pythagorean identity:

$$1^2 + \cot^2 \theta = \csc^2 \theta ,$$

and its variation, $\cot^2 \theta = \csc^2 \theta - 1$.

None of the Pythagorean identities is on the Praxis formula sheet, but you really need to know only the first ($\sin^2 \theta + \cos^2 \theta = 1$), the most important one, because it is used in many contexts. The other two Pythagorean identities are easily found by dividing the first one by $\cos^2 \theta$ and $\sin^2 \theta$, as above.

5.13.9a Other Trig Identities

Two other basic identities that will help in finding the other trig identities are the sum and difference identities, all three of which are given on the Praxis reference sheet.

$$\sin(a \pm b) = \sin a \cos b \pm \cos a \sin b$$

$$\cos (a \pm b) = \cos a \cos b \mp \sin a \sin b$$

$$\tan(a \pm b) = \frac{\tan a \tan b}{1 \mp \tan a \tan b}$$

The shorthand symbols $\pm$ and $\mp$ are written that way to indicate that the top symbols, + or –, match, and the bottom symbols also match. For example, $\cos (a + b) = \cos a \cos b - \sin a \sin b$. Again, remember that any trigonometric function can be treated as an unknown in an algebraic equation, as shown in Section 5.13.5.

From the two sum identities, we can get several other identities, such as the double angle identities for $\sin(2a)$ and $\cos (2a)$. Although the double angle identities are not on the Praxis formula sheet, they can be derived by substituting $b = a$ in the sum identities, which are on the sheet:

$$\sin(a + a) = \sin(2a) = \sin a \cos a + \cos a \sin a = 2\sin a \cos a,$$

$$\cos(a + a) = \cos(2a) = \cos a \cos a - \sin a \sin a = \cos^2 a - \sin^2 a,$$

but we aren't done yet. The variations of the fundamental Pythagorean identity, $\sin^2 a = 1 - \cos^2 a$ and $\cos^2 a = 1 - \sin^2 a$, yield the following double angle identity for $\cos(2a)$:

$$\cos(2a) = \cos^2 a - (1 - \cos^2 a) = 2\cos^2 a - 1.$$

or

$$\cos(2a) = (1 - \sin^2 a) - \sin^2 a = 1 - 2\sin^2 a.$$

The last set of identities is the half-angle identities, which are on the Praxis formula sheet and are included here for completeness:

$$\sin\frac{\theta}{2} = \pm\sqrt{\frac{1 - \cos\theta}{2}} \text{ and } \cos\frac{\theta}{2} = \pm\sqrt{\frac{1 - \cos\theta}{2}}$$

The $\pm$ signs are used here because the values depend on the quadrant of $\frac{\theta}{2}$.

5.13.9b Using Trigonometry

All we need to prove many of the trig identities, to simplify a trigonometric expression, or to solve a trigonometric equation are:

1. The basic equations for the sum of two angles, $\sin(a + b) = \sin a \cos b + \cos a \sin b$ and $\cos(a + b) = \cos a \cos b - \sin a \sin b$.

2. The fundamental Pythagorean identity, $\sin^2 a + \cos^2 a = 1$.

3. The relationships (definitions) of the trigonometric functions sin, cos, tan, cot, sec, and csc.

5.13.10 Polar Coordinates

Polar coordinates are just another coordinate system to describe a point at a distance r and an angle θ from the origin.

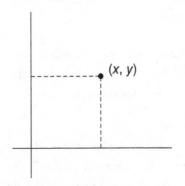
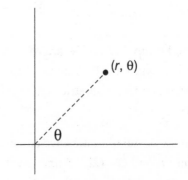

Cartesian coordinates (x, y) Polar coordinates (r, θ)

In Cartesian (also called rectangular) coordinates, a point is designated by (x, y). In polar coordinates, the same point is designated by (r, θ). Since $\cos\theta = \frac{x}{r}$ and $\sin\theta = \frac{y}{r}$, we have $x = r\cos\theta$ and $y = r\sin\theta$. If this reminds you of the unit circle, it's because that's just what it is with $r = 1$.

Sometimes the Cartesian coordinate system is better suited to solving a problem, and sometimes it's the polar coordinate system. Therefore, it is important to know how to convert from one system to another.

The rectangular coordinates of any point can be expressed as polar coordinates. Four conversion identities will help you through the process, and the good news is that you already know them.

Rectangular to Polar System	Polar to Rectangular System
$x^2 + y^2 = r^2$	$r = \sqrt{x^2 + y^2}$
$y = r \sin \theta$	$\sin \theta = \dfrac{y}{r}$
$x = r \cos \theta$	$\cos \theta = \dfrac{x}{r}$
$\dfrac{y}{x} = \tan \theta$	$\theta = \arctan\left(\dfrac{y}{x}\right)$

The conversion from one coordinate system to the other is best understood by looking at examples. An equation in terms of x and y is rectangular; an equation in terms of r and θ is polar. The final equation should not be a "hybrid" of the two systems.

EXAMPLE 5.48

Convert $r = 4 \sin \theta$ to a rectangular equation.

SOLUTION 5.48

$r = 4 \sin \theta$

$r = 4\left(\dfrac{y}{r}\right)$

$r^2 = 4y$

$x^2 + y^2 = 4y$

EXAMPLE 5.49

Convert $x^2 + y^2 = 16\left(\dfrac{y}{x}\right)^2$ to a polar equation.

SOLUTION 5.49

$$x^2 + y^2 = 16\left(\frac{y}{x}\right)^2$$

$$r^2 = 16(\tan\theta)^2$$

$$r = \pm 4\tan\theta$$

EXAMPLE 5.50

Convert $r = \sin\theta + \cos\theta$ to a rectangular equation.

SOLUTION 5.50

$$r = \sin\theta + \cos\theta$$

$$r = \frac{y}{r} + \frac{x}{r}$$

$$r^2 = y + x$$

$$x^2 + y^2 = y + x$$

Practice Exercises

1. Which of the following properties is not true for the diagonals of square *PQRS*?

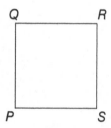

    (A) $SQ = PR$

    (B) *QS* is perpendicular to *RP*

    (C) *SQ* is parallel to *RP*

    (D) *SQ* bisects *RP*

2.   A regular polygon is composed of equilateral triangles. What kind of regular polygon can it be?

(A) Square

(B) Trapezoid

(C) Hexagon

(D) 13-sided polygon

3.   Multiply: $\dfrac{1 + \sin A}{\sin A} \cdot \dfrac{\sin^2 A}{1 - \sin^2 A} =$

(A) 1

(B) $\dfrac{\sin A}{1 - \sin A}$

(C) $\sin A$

(D) $\dfrac{\sin^2 A}{1 - \sin A}$

4.   Calculate the solution(s) to the equation $\tan^2 \theta - \tan \theta = 0$ in the first quadrant.

(A) 0°

(B) 45°

(C) 0° and 45°

(D) The solution isn't in Quadrant I.

5.   Three angles in a triangle are in the ratio 2 : 3 : 4. What is the smallest angle?

(A) 20°

(B) 40°

(C) 60°

(D) 80°

6.   Jaime has a piece of leather with dimensions 14 inches by 30 inches. He wants to cut out a square 6 inches on a side and a circle as shown in the sketch. How much waste, in square inches, will he have? (Round to the nearest whole number and use $\pi = 3.14$.)

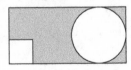

(A) 36

(B) 154

(C) 230

(D) 420

7. Tan $A = \cot(A + 30°)$ for acute angles A and $A + 30°$. What is the value of A? Fill in the blank.

_____

8. The acute angle between the line $x - y - 4 = 0$ and the x-axis is $\left\{ \begin{array}{c} 30° \\ 45° \\ 60° \end{array} \right\}$.

9. In which quadrant must an angle lie if its cosine is negative and its tangent is positive?

   (A) Quadrant I

   (B) Quadrant II

   (C) Quadrant III

   (D) Quadrant IV

10. How does the graph of $y = \sin 2x + \pi$ differ from the $y = \sin x$ graph?

   (A) The period of the graph is doubled and the graph is shifted π units to the right.

   (B) The period of the graph is halved and the graph is shifted π units to the right.

   (C) The period of the graph is halved and the graph is shifted up by π units.

   (D) The period of the graph is doubled and the graph is shifted up by π units.

Topic not done till now

Solutions

1. (C) SQ is parallel to RP. The diagonals intersect, so they cannot be parallel to each other. All of the other properties listed are true.

2. (C) Hexagon. This answer is best derived by elimination. If you draw the diagonal of a square, the triangles formed are right triangles, so answer choice (A) is incorrect. Answer choice (B) isn't a regular polygon. Answer choice (C) does, in fact, contain six equilateral triangles, as seen in the figure in Section 5.6.2. Answer choice (D) is incorrect because a sketch will show that the greater the number of sides, the more "pointy" the top angle is for each triangle.

Good Expl

3. (B) $\dfrac{\sin A}{1 - \sin A}$. Treat $\sin A$ as you would a variable and do the algebra. For simplicity, we can use the substitution $y = \sin A$. Then the original problem is $\dfrac{1 + y}{y} \cdot \dfrac{y^2}{1 - y^2} = \dfrac{(1 + y)y^2}{y(1 + y)(1 - y)}$. With cancellations, this becomes $\dfrac{y}{1 - y} = \dfrac{\sin A}{1 - \sin A}$.

4. (C) $0°$ and $45°$. Factor the equation as an algebra equation: $\tan\theta(\tan\theta - 1) = 0$. Set each factor equal to 0 to get $\theta = \arctan 0$ and $\arctan 1 = 0°$ and $45°$.

5. (B) 40°. The total angle measure in a triangle is 180°, so the equation for three angles with a ratio of 2 : 3 : 4 is $2x + 3x + 4x = 180°$. Solving for x yields $x = 20°$ but the question asks for the smallest angle, which is $2x = 40°$.

6. (C) 230. The area of the leather rectangle is $A = lw = 14 \times 30 = 420$ square inches. The area of the square is $A^2 = s^2 = 6^2 = 36$ square inches, and the area of the circle is $A = \pi r^2 = (3.14)(7)^2 = 3.14 \times 49 = 153.86$ square inches. Therefore, the amount of waste is the original size minus the square and circle, or $420 - (36 + 153.86) = 230.14$, or 230 square inches to the nearest whole number.

7. 30°. If a function of an acute angle equals the cofunction of another acute angle, the two angles are complementary. Therefore, $A + (A + 30°) = 90°$, or $2A = 60°$ and thus $A = 30°$.

8. 45°. First, find the slope of the line. Write the equation in slope-intercept form: $y = x - 4$. The slope is the coefficient of x, or 1, which means the change in y is the same as the change in x, so the angle must be 45°.

9. (C) Quadrant III. If the cosine is negative, then x on the unit circle is negative, which is true for Quadrants II and III. If the tangent is positive, then the sine and cosine must have the same sign, which is true for Quadrants I and III. Both of these conditions are true only in Quadrant III.

10. (C) The period of the graph is halved and the graph is shifted up by π units. The basic graph of a sine curve is $y = A \sin B(x - C) + D$. Each of the variables A, B, C, and D has an effect on the basic curve. Specifically, B, the coefficient of x, changes the period by a factor of $\frac{1}{B}$, and D is a vertical shift that raises the graph by D units if $D > 0$. Here, B is 2 so the period is halved, and D equals π, even though it is an unusual value for the y-axis. Without parentheses, π is not a phase shift, as it would have been if the graph were $y = \sin(2x + \pi)$.

Functions

6.1 DEFINITIONS AND CRITERIA

6.1.1 Function Definitions

A **function** is a special kind of **relation**, which is a set (collection) of ordered pairs. Each ordered pair in the relation is called an **element**. The order within each element makes a difference—for example, the element (2, 3) is not the same as (3, 2).

For each ordered pair of a relation, the first part is called the **domain**; and the second part is called the **range**, which is the same definition that is used, for example, in graphing a linear equation, in which each coordinate is given in (x, y), or (domain, range), order (see Chapter 4, Section 4.2.4).

The elements in a relation can be written in set notation, indicated by braces. For example, relation A can be defined as $A = \{(5, 7), (5, 1), (a, b), (\text{bee, hive})\}$. Notice that the elements can consist of numbers, letters, or even "things." There are no repetition of elements in a relation, so if we want to add another element to set A, it can't be the same as the four elements already in the set. Set A is a relation, but it's not a function. Let's see why.

In a **function**, the domain of each different element has exactly one range assigned to it. That means ranges can be repeated in the elements of a function, but domains cannot. So set A shown above is not a function because domain 5 is repeated and it has two values for the range. Set $B = \{(5, 7), (7, 5), (a, b), (\text{bee, hive})\}$ and set $C = \{(5, 7), (6, 7), (7, 7), (8, 7)\}$ are functions. No two elements have the same domain in either set, and that's all that matters.

Many functions are equations for which all of the solutions are ordered pairs (x, y). For example, for the equation $y = x + 2$, if we restrict the set of elements for the domain to be

$y = \{x + 2 : -2 \le x \le 1, x \in \mathbb{Z}\}$ (the colon is read as "such that") then the set of elements for the solution is $\{(-2, 0), (-1, 1), (0, 2), (1, 3)\}$. Since this equation is clearly a function (because for every x, there is only one y), we use the notation $f(x)$ for y. $f(x) = \{x + 2 : -2 \le x \le 1, x \in \mathbb{Z}\}$ has the same meaning as $y = \{x + 2 : -2 \le x \le 1, x \in \mathbb{Z}\}$ but emphasizes that $x + 2$ is a function of x. The notation $f(x)$ is generally read as "f of x." It does not mean to multiply $f \times x$, even though it looks the same. Also, the letter f doesn't have to be used; we could just as well have written $g(x) = \{x + 2 : -2 \le x \le 1, x \in \mathbb{Z}\}$.

Sometimes functions are written in set notation as $f = \{(x, y) : y = 2x + 1\}$, where the notation says "f is the set of all (x, y) such that $y = 2x + 1$."

Likewise, x is just a placeholder that shows where the input goes and what happens to it. Any thing, usually letters, can be used for the input. So $f(x) = x^2 + x + 1$ is the same as $f(q) = q^2 + q + 1$ or even $f(\text{pig}) = (\text{pig})^2 + (\text{pig}) + 1$, which doesn't make much sense. The variable (x, q, pig) just tells where to put the values, so if we substitute $x = 2$ into $f(x) = x^2 + x + 1$, we get $f(2) = 2^2 + 2 + 1 = 7$.

For a relation to be a function, it doesn't have to be in the $f(x)$ format—it just has to have only one output for each input. An example of a function is buying cookies at a price of 50 cents each. Two cookies, cost $1.00, 4 cost $2.00, and so on. The cost is a *function* of the number of cookies bought because for every number of cookies there is only one cost. In function notation, this would be cost × (number of cookies) = $0.50 × (number of cookies), or $C = .50n$, where C is the cost in dollars and n is the number of cookies.

6.1.2 Vertical Line Test

Many equations are functions, which can easily be seen when they are graphed. This is not to be interpreted as saying that graphing many functions is easy because some are indeed difficult. Here we concentrate on the graphs of relations that can easily be seen as functions (or nonfunctions). Remember that the criterion is that for every input there is one and only one output. Some common graphs can be seen as functions:

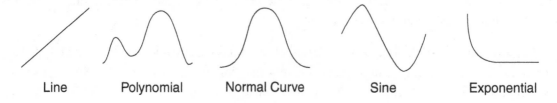

Line   Polynomial   Normal Curve   Sine   Exponential

1. It means you can draw many vertical lines for the graph of a function if it must ∩ ≤ the graph only at one pt.

FUNCTIONS

CHAPTER 6

2. Quad. function funcs are always parabolic

Other graphs are certainly not functions:

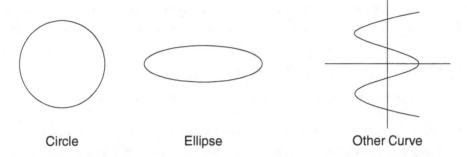

Circle   Ellipse   Other Curve

The easy part is that if you have the graph of a relation, there is an easy test, called the **vertical line test**, to determine whether it is a function. If every vertical line that can be drawn through the graph has only one point of intersection with the graph, it is a function. If there are two or more points of intersection, it isn't a function. That's all there is to it. To illustrate, imagine a series of vertical lines (parallel to the y-axis) through all of the graphs shown above.

6.2 TYPES OF FUNCTIONS

6.2.1 Linear Functions

For a linear equation, for every x, there is one and only one value of $f(x)$, so a linear equation is always a function, except the line $x =$ constant, which is a vertical line. The graph of a linear equation is a line. It is not difficult to see on the graph that a linear equation is a function because it certainly passes the vertical line test.

6.2.2 Quadratic Functions

The second-degree functions called **quadratic functions** graph as **parabolas**. All parabolas are basically U-shaped, opening up or down, and have one lowest (or highest) point called the **vertex** (see Chapter 5, Section 5.8.1a), which helps determine the **range**. Parabolas may or may not have x-intercepts, but they will always have a single y-intercept. The **domain** of a quadratic equation is all real numbers.

The general form of a parabola, $f(x) = ax^2 + bx + c$, gives information about the shape of the parabola. The sign of a determines whether the parabola opens up (positive a) or down (negative a). For any quadratic function $f(x)$, the domain of the vertex is the value $x = -\dfrac{b}{2a}$, and the range is the corresponding value $f\left(-\dfrac{b}{2a}\right)$. Thus, the vertex is the point

$$\text{vertex} = \left(-\frac{b}{2a}, f\left(-\frac{b}{2a}\right)\right)$$

The axis of symmetry of a parabola is a vertical line that divides the parabola into two congruent halves. The axis of symmetry always passes through the vertex of the parabola. In other words, to sketch the graph of a parabola, put it in the general form $f(x) = ax^2 + bx + c$, determine whether the parabola will open up ($\cup$) or down ($\cap$), and draw the parabola through the following points.

1. The vertex is point $\left(-\dfrac{b}{2a}, f\left(-\dfrac{b}{2a}\right)\right)$.

2. The y-intercept is always the point $(0, c)$, since $f(0) = a(0)^2 + b(0) + c = c$.

3. The x-intercept(s), if there are any, are the solutions to $f(x) = 0$, or $ax^2 + bx + c = 0$. These are also called the **zeros** of the function. They are the real solutions to the quadratic formula (see Chapter 4, Section 4.5.2).

4. The line $x = -\dfrac{b}{2a}$ is the axis of symmetry. Since a parabola is symmetric around this axis, any point that is found on one side of the axis of the parabola has a mirror image on the other side.

6.2.3 Polynomial Functions

A **polynomial function** of degree n is of the form

$$f(x) = a_n x^n + a_{n-1} x^{n-1} + \ldots a_1 x + a_0,$$

where all a_i are real numbers and $a_n \neq 0$. The **domain** of polynomial functions is all real numbers $(-\infty, \infty)$, but the range and the roots of a polynomial depend on the equation $a_n x^n + a_{n-1} x^{n-1} + \ldots a_1 x + a_0 = 0$. The graph crosses the y-axis when $x = 0$, so the y-intercept is $y = a_0$. Chapter 4, Section 4.6.1 presents the method for finding the real roots of a polynomial. The following chart shows the general shape of the graph of a polynomial, but the graph within the dotted line portions may increase, decrease, or both, depending on the equation.

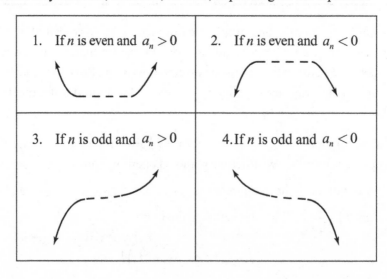

1. If n is even and $a_n > 0$

2. If n is even and $a_n < 0$

3. If n is odd and $a_n > 0$

4. If n is odd and $a_n < 0$

Therefore, the only general statements that can be made for a polynomial are:

- The domain is all real numbers $(-\infty, \infty)$.

- The y-intercept is $y = a_0$.

- Depending on the values of n and a_n, the general shape is as shown in the above chart.

- Any real roots (values for which $x = 0$) can be described by using Descartes' Rule of Signs. Any complex roots come in pairs, $c + di$ and $c - di$. Finding the actual roots is not easy (see Chapter 4, Section 4.6.1).

6.2.4 Rational Functions

As emphasized in this book, the operations and properties described in Chapter 3, Section 3.4, for real numbers hold for several other relationships. Rational functions have rules that are similar to those for rational numbers.

A **rational function** is the quotient of two polynomials. Rational numbers, which can be written as fractions, include all numbers, since integers can be written with a denominator of 1. In addition, the denominator cannot equal 0. The same is true for rational functions, for which the numerator and denominator are usually, but not exclusively, polynomials of degree 2 or more. The following discussion involves only these types of rational functions, which take the form of

$$f(x) = \frac{a(x)}{b(x)} = \frac{a_m x^m + a_{m-1} x^{m-1} + \ldots + a_1 x + a_0}{b_n x^n + b_{n-1} x^{n-1} + \ldots + b_1 x + b_0}$$

A distinguishing factor of rational functions is that they may have asymptotes. **Asymptotes** are lines that a curve gets closer and closer to but never crosses. On the graph of a curve that has asymptotes, the asymptotes are not part of the curve but they may be drawn in as dashed lines to show that the curve gets close to that particular line. A rational function may have several **vertical asymptotes** (values for which the denominator equals zero, since division by zero is not possible) and either one **horizontal asymptote** (values that the function approaches as the variable in the function approaches $+\infty$ or $-\infty$) or one **slant asymptote** (an oblique, or slanted, line similar to the horizontal asymptote).

Vertical asymptotes of a rational function, if any exist, occur wherever the denominator equals zero and the numerator does not equal zero. To find the vertical asymptote(s), solve the equation formed when the denominator equals zero. However, if both denominator and numerator equal zero at some point, there is a hole in the graph. When graphing, remember that vertical asymptotes stand for x-values that are not allowed.

There can be one or zero horizontal asymptotes. To determine whether the rational function has a horizontal asymptote, look at the degrees of the numerator and denominator:

- If the degree of the numerator is lower than the degree of the denominator, the horizontal asymptote is the line $y = 0$ (the x-axis).

- If the degree of the numerator is the same as the degree of the denominator, the horizontal asymptote is the line $y = \dfrac{a_m}{b_n}$, where a_m is the coefficient of the highest power variable in the numerator and b_n is the coefficient of the highest power of that same variable in the denominator.

- If the degree of the numerator is higher than the degree of the denominator, there is no horizontal asymptote but there is a slant asymptote.

A slant asymptote is any asymptote that is neither vertical nor horizontal. A rational function in which the degree of the numerator is one greater than the degree of the denominator has a slant asymptote, which is found by using polynomial long division, ignoring any remainder.

Rational functions can have only one horizontal *or* one slant asymptote, independent of whether the function has any vertical asymptotes. Note that the horizontal or slant asymptote indicates how the curve behaves as the variable in the function approaches $+\infty$ or $-\infty$. It is possible for the curve to cross the asymptote at other locations, as shown in the figures below, in which $g(x)$ crosses a horizontal asymptote (left figure) and a slant asymptote (right figure).

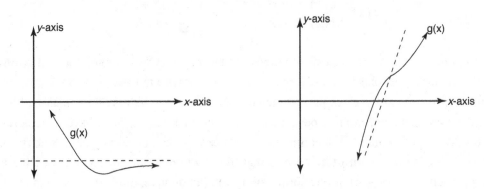

6.2.5 Piecewise Functions

Just as the name implies, **piecewise functions** are pieces of different functions defined for a particular scenario. They are graphed all on one graph. The value of the piecewise function $f(x)$ can be obtained by following the "directions" for a particular x value, without necessarily graphing the function. An example of a piecewise function is:

$$f(x) = \begin{cases} 2x + 8 & \text{if } x \le -2 \\ x^2 & \text{if } x > -2 \end{cases}$$

The conditions for this function are to determine whether $x \le -2$ or $x > -2$ for any given x and to evaluate it accordingly. For $x = -4$, $f(-4) = 2(-4) + 8 = 0$, and for $x = 4$, $f(4) = 4^2 = 16$. When finding $f(x)$ for $x = -4$, just look at the function $2x + 8$, and don't even think about the function for the other interval. That's all there is to it.

To tell whether a piecewise graph is continuous (no gaps), look at the boundary points (here, it is -2), and evaluate $f(-2)$ at all functions. If these two values are the same, the graph is continuous at that point, if the values are different, there's a "jump" in the graph at that point. Here, $f(-2) = 2(-2) + 8 = 4$ for the end of the first "piece" and $f(-2) = (-2)^2 = 4$ for the beginning of the second "piece," so this function is continuous at $x = -2$, and therefore is a continuous function. Note that $f(x) = (x)^2$ is not part of the function at $x = -2$. It is just being evaluated to check for continuity.

6.2.6 Absolute Value Function

When we speak of an absolute value function, it is important to know whether we mean the absolute value of the function itself or the function that contains an absolute value. Mostly, it is the function that contains an absolute value, such as $f(x) = |2x| + 3$, which is commonly called an absolute value function.

The shape of an absolute value function is a V which is symmetric around the vertex. The general form of an absolute value function is $f(x) = |x - h| + k$, where (h, k) is the vertex. Therefore, for $f(x) = |2x| + 3$, the vertex is at $(0, 3)$ and we can construct a table of values around that point by choosing x values 1 and 2 units above it and below it. Put the vertex in the middle of the five values and fill in the others to get:

x	y
2	7
1	5
0	3
-1	5
-2	7

The symmetric shape is becoming evident. The graph looks like

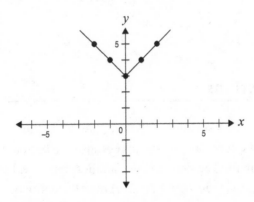

The absolute value function is actually a well-known example of a piecewise function. Remember that absolute value changes the value of the expression inside the absolute value signs to a positive value. Therefore, consider that $f(x) = |2x| + 3$ has two conditions, one for $2x \geq 0$ and one for $2x < 0$. Note that in the interval $2x < 0$, since x is negative, the function is $f(x) = -2x + 3$ since a negative (x) times a positive (2) makes a negative ($-2x$). If $2x \geq 0$, $f(x) = 2x + 3$. Therefore, in piecewise function notation,

$$f(x) = |2x| + 3 = \begin{cases} 2x + 3 & \text{if } x \geq 0 \\ -2x + 3 & \text{if } x < 0 \end{cases}$$

The graph will be the same as we found above. In fact, graphing the function of any absolute value of x ($f(|x|)$) reflects the points to the left of the axis of symmetry of the original function $f(x)$ across the y-axis, so they coincide with the points of the original function $f(x)$, which are retained. The **axis of symmetry** of an absolute value function is the vertical line through the vertex (similar to that of parabolas, see Chapter 5, Section 5.8.2c). If there was a y-intercept of $f(x)$, it is also the y-intercept of $f(|x|)$.

NOTE If the absolute value is preceded by a minus sign, such as in $f(x) = -|x + 1|$ the graph is in the shape of an upside-down V since now the y values of all the points of $f(x) = |x + 1|$ are negatives.

In contrast, the absolute value an entire function, $|f(x)|$, retains the points of the original function that were above the x-axis, but flips the points that were below the x-axis to above the x-axis so they become a mirror reflection across the x-axis. ($f(x) \rightarrow |f(x)|$). This produces graphs such as those shown below.

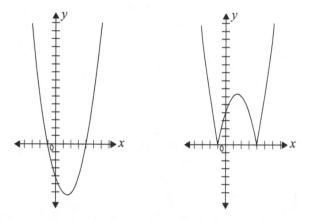

6.2.7 Periodic Functions

Periodic functions repeat on a set interval. All trigonometric functions are periodic (see Chapter 5, Section 5.13.7). Periodic functions are useful because the period determines the value of the function anywhere in the domain. The period is the smallest repeat value for the function. In other words, if a function has period n, then $f(x) = f(x + n)$ over the entire domain of the function.

6.2.8 Symmetric Functions

Symmetric functions can be reflected around a specific location. They can be of three different types, even, odd, or neither, which are determined by the following rules.

- Even: $f(-x) = f(x)$ for all x. The name "even" comes from the fact that for x to any even power it is true that $f(-x) = f(x)$. But watch out—an even exponent does not always make an even function. For example, $(x + a)^2$ is not an even function because $f(x) = x^2 + 2ax + a^2$ but $f(-x) = x^2 - 2ax + a^2$. The graphs of even functions are symmetric about the y-axis (like a reflection).

- Odd: $f(-x) = -f(x)$ for all x. The name "odd" comes from the fact that for x to any odd power it is true that $f(-x) = -f(x)$. But watch out again—an odd exponent does not always make an odd function. For example, $(x + a)^3$ is not an odd function because $f(-x) = -x^3 + 3x^2a - 3xa^2 + a^3$ but $-f(x) = -x^3 - 3x^2a - 3xa^2 - a^3$. Odd functions are symmetrical with respect to the origin.

- Neither odd nor even. A function does not have to be even or odd, and in fact most functions are neither. For example, $f(x) = x^3 - x + 1$ is neither because $f(-x) = -x^3 + x + 1$, which equals neither $f(x)$ nor $-f(x) = -x^3 + x - 1$.

EXAMPLE 6.1

Is the function $f(x) = \dfrac{3x}{(x^2 - 2)}$ even or odd?

SOLUTION 6.1

Odd. $f(-x) = \dfrac{-3x}{(x^2 - 2)} = -f(x)$, so it is odd.

Unlike the case for adding odd and even numbers, the sum of two even functions is even, the sum of two odd functions is odd, and the sum of an even function and an odd function is neither unless one function is 0. The products also are different than for numbers: the product of two even functions or two odd functions is always even, and the product of an even and an odd function is always odd.

6.2.9 Exponential Functions

Whereas linear functions grow by equal differences over equal intervals, **exponential functions** grow or decay by equal *factors* over equal intervals. Therefore, exponential functions grow or decay much faster than linear functions. You can recognize an exponential function from several points by noticing that as one unknown varies by a constant term, the other variable varies by a constant factor. In other words, the general form is $y_n = a^{nx}$, where the constant ratio a can be any positive number except 1, and n is the number of the term.

For example, compare the first few values for the domain $\{x = 2, 3, 4, 5\}$ of the linear function $f(2x) = \{4, 6, 8, 10\}$ and the exponential function $g(2^x) = \{4, 8, 16, 32\}$, or the linear function $t\left(\left(\frac{1}{2}\right)^x\right) = \left\{\frac{1}{4}, \frac{1}{8}, \frac{1}{16}, \frac{1}{3}\right\}$ and the exponential function $t\left(\left(\frac{1}{2}\right)^x\right) = \left\{\frac{1}{4}, \frac{1}{8}, \frac{1}{16}, \frac{1}{32}\right\}$.

The graphs below are decreasing exponentially (dashed curve) and increasing exponentially (solid curve). Notice that they both cross the y-axis at $(0, 1)$ because $y = a^x$ always equals 1 at $x = 0$. Also because a^0 always equals 1, the graph of any exponential function $y = a^x$ passes through the point $(1, a)$. It has a horizontal asymptote of $y = 0$ because $y = a^x$ doesn't equal 0 for any x value. If a is a real number greater than 1, the domain of $f(x) = a^x$ is $(-\infty, \infty)$, and the range is $(0, \infty)$.

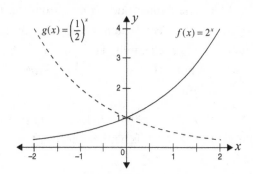

Exponential functions always follow the properties of exponents shown in Chapter 3, Section 3.8.2, except now the exponent, or power, is x. Therefore, using positive numbers a and b as the base, we have

- $b^{x+c} = b^x b^c$ To multiply two quantities with the same base, add their exponents.

- $(b^c)^x = (b^x)^c = b^{cx}$ To find a power of a power, multiply the exponents.

- $(ab)^x = a^x b^x$ To raise a product to a power, raise each factor to that power.

- $\dfrac{a^{cx}}{a^{dx}} = a^{cx-dx}$ To divide two quantities with the same base, subtract the exponents.

- $\left(\dfrac{a}{b}\right)^x = \dfrac{a^x}{b^x}$ To raise a quotient to a power, raise each factor to that power.

- $b^{-cx} = \dfrac{1}{b^{cx}}$ Negative exponents are the reciprocals of positive exponents.

- $b^x = 1$ if $x = 0$.

EXAMPLE 6.2

A chain letter is sent out to 10 people telling everyone to make 10 copies of the letter and to send them to 10 new people. Assume that everyone who receives the letter actually sends it to 10 new people and that it takes a week for each cycle. How many letters are sent out on the ninth week?

Cycle: 1 Phase → 2 phase

PART II

*for 9 weeks, each member
completed / distrib. 10 letters
10 9. Also,
beginning 10
selected*

SOLUTION 6.2

10^{10}. At the beginning, call it week 0, 10 letters are sent out, and if everyone the directions, at the beginning of week 1, $10 \times 10 = 10^2$ letters are sent so on through 9 weeks. The exponential formula would be $y = 10^{x+1}$ where y is the number of letters sent out in week x. Therefore, in week 9, the number of letters sent is $10^{10} = 10,000,000,000$, which is more than the world's population! The catch in this that makes it near impossible is the instruction to send the letter to 10 *new* people, or people who haven't already received the letter.

6.2.10 Radical Functions

When working with radical equations we have to consider the domain of the equation because we cannot have a negative value inside an even root sign. In addition to keeping track of the domain, we also need to graph very neatly, or the graph can be at least partially wrong.

EXAMPLE 6.3

Rev: What is the domain of the radical function $\sqrt{4-x}$?

SOLUTION 6.3

$x \leq 4$. The domain doesn't include any points for the values for which $4 - x < 0$, since that would be the square root of a negative number, which isn't real. So we must set $4 - x \geq 0$ and solve that inequality, which is $x \leq 4$. Therefore, the graph would all be to the left of the line $x = 4$, including that line.

6.2.11 Logarithmic Functions

Exponents and logarithms (logs) are inverse functions (see Section 6.5), so the **logarithm** (or log) is defined as

$$\log_a x = b \text{ means } a^b = x,$$

where $a > 0$ and $a \neq 1$. If a is not specified, it is assumed to be 10, and the log is known as the **common log**.

Because exponents and logs are inverse functions, they cancel each other out. So $\log_3 3^5 = 5$ because it is asking "**3** raised to what power equals 3^5?" If translated from logs to exponents, it would look like: $\mathbf{3}^x = 3^5$. (The boldface type distinguishes that the 3 is the log index here.) Likewise, $4^{\log_4 x} = x$. In other words, exponential and logarithmic functions with the same base (e.g., $y = a^x$ and $y = \log_a x$) are inverses of each other.

EXAMPLE 6.4

Simplify the expression $\log_4 4^3$.

SOLUTION 6.4

3. If we rewrite this expression equal to an unknown b, the problem is asking for b. Using the definition of logarithms, $\log_a x = b$ means $a^b = x$, $\log_4 4^3 = b$ means $4^b = 4^3$, which means $b = 3$. So $\log_4 4^3 = 3$.

Example 6.4 underscores a fundamental logarithmic fact:

$$\log_a a^n = n$$

Therefore, to solve simple logarithmic functions, we can rewrite them as exponentials: To find $\log_5 x = 3$, solve $5^3 = x = 125$, and $\log_{10} x = -2$ becomes $10^{-2} = x = \dfrac{1}{10^2} = \dfrac{1}{100}$. If the solution gives more than one value for x, use only the positive value. For example, $\log_x 4 = 2$ becomes $x^2 = 4$, or $x = \sqrt{4} = 2$. Discard the -2.

Rem

The domain of a logarithmic function is the range of its inverse exponential function, and the range of a logarithmic function is the domain of its inverse exponential function. Thus, for $f(x) = \log_a x$, the domain is $(0, \infty)$ and the range is $(-\infty, \infty)$.

6.2.11a Graphing Logarithmic Functions

The basic curve of a log function looks like the exponential curve (see Section 6.2.9), with the vertical side asymptotic to the y-axis. Graphing a log function involves three main steps:

1. Write the equivalent equation in exponential form using the definition $\log_a x = b$ means $a^b = x$.

2. Make a table of points (assign values to y in this case and solve for x).

3. Plot the points and connect them with a curve.

EXAMPLE 6.5

Graph the function $y = f(x) = \log_4 x$.

SOLUTION 6.5

$\log_4 x$ is $4^y = x$ in exponential form. Make a table of points (assign values to y in this case and solve for x) and connect them with a curve.

y	−1	0	1	2
x	$\frac{1}{4}$	1	4	16

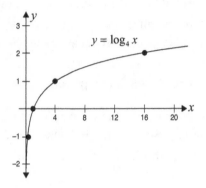

$y = \log_4 x$

6.2.11b Characteristic and Mantissa

Logarithms do not have to be whole numbers. From the definition of logarithms as the inverse of exponents, logarithms clearly can be any number. It is important to know what the numbers stand for. For example, $\log 8 = 0.903$ (according to the calculator), which means $10^{0.903} = 8$. If we examine 0.903, we see that the number before the decimal point (called the **characteristic** of the log) is between 0 and 1, which means the value of the number is between $10^0 = 1$ and $10^1 = 10$, which is correct (it is 8). The characteristic merely tells the limits of the power, so if $\log 8 = 0.903$, then $\log 80 = 1.903$, which says the numerical value has an 8 in it, but now it is between 10 and 100 (between 10^1 and 10^2), so it is 80. The numbers after the decimal point (.903), called the **mantissa**, identify the exact number between 1 and 10. In summary, the log has two parts that identify its value: the mantissa identifies the numerical value (8, here) and the characteristic identifies the placement of the decimal point.

EXAMPLE 6.6

If $\log (728.2) = 2.862$, what is $\log 7.282$?

SOLUTION 6.6

Look at the mantissa of the log, which is .862; this number will be the mantissa of all numbers with the digits 7282, and the characteristic just tells us whether it is 7.282, or 72.82, or 7,282, etc. Here the characteristic should be 0, since the number 7 is between 1 (or 10^0) and 10 (or 10^1) , and the answer is 0.862. Check it out on your calculator.

Watch out! If you type "l-o-g 7.282" on your computer (not calculator) during the test, you will get the message "Unknown variable" because you must use the "log" button on the calculator to enter the value for which you want the log to base 10.

Instead of 10, the base of a **natural logarithm** (ln) is the irrational number e, or Euler's number, which is equal to 2.71828 . . . In other words, $\ln a = \log_e a$. The value of e is programmed into the calculator. **Exponential growth** and **exponential decay** are given in terms of e as e^x, and use natural logs. For example, a typical function that uses natural logs involves compounded interest, where the amount accrued is $A = Pe^{rt}$, where P is the initial principal amount, r is the rate, and t is the time.

Logarithms to base e are treated the same as logs to any other base with $\log_e$ denoted by the abbreviation ln. Again, do not type "l-n" on your computer during the test—you must use the "ln" button on the calculator to enter the value for which you want the natural log.

EXAMPLE 6.7

Solve the equation $\ln(e^3 \cdot e^{5x}) = 13$ for x.

SOLUTION 6.7

2. Rewrite the problem as $\ln(e^3 \cdot e^{5x}) = \ln(e^{5x+3}) = 13$. From the fact that natural logs and the exponential e are inverse functions, this becomes $5x + 3 = 13$, so $x = 2$.

EXAMPLE 6.8

Simplify $\ln\left(\dfrac{1}{e^x}\right)$.

SOLUTION 6.8

$-x$. $\ln\left(\dfrac{1}{e^x}\right) = \ln e^{-x}$, and ln and e are inverse functions, so $\ln e^{-x} = -x$.

EXAMPLE 6.9

Express the logarithmic equation $\log_5 125 = 3$ exponentially.

SOLUTION 6.9

$5^3 = 125$. Use the definition $y = \log_b x$ if and only if $b^y = x$. Then $\log_5 125 = 3$ means $5^3 = 125$.

EXAMPLE 6.10

Express the equation $5^{-2} = \dfrac{1}{25}$ as a logarithm.

SOLUTION 6.10

$\log_5\left(\dfrac{1}{25}\right) = -2$. Again, use the definition $y = \log_b x$ if and only if $b^y = x$. So just determine what x, y, and b are from the given equation: $x = \dfrac{1}{25}$, $y = -2$, and $b = 5$. Thus, $-2 = \log_5\left(\dfrac{1}{25}\right)$.

EXAMPLE 6.11

Evaluate $\log_8 \sqrt{8}$.

SOLUTION 6.11

$\dfrac{1}{2}$. From the definition of log as an exponent, we are looking for the power we would need to raise 8 to get $\sqrt{8}$. Thus, $\log_8 \sqrt{8} = x$, which is asking to find x for $8^x = \sqrt{8}$. $x = \dfrac{1}{2}$.

Any problems that use exponential or logarithmic formulas, whether they are common, natural, or otherwise, will indicate the formula within the problem on the Praxis test. However, you are expected to know the relationship that is the definition for logs: $\log_a x = b$ means $a^b = x$ and $\ln x = c$ means $e^c = x$.

6.2.11c Change of Base Formula

The on-screen calculator doesn't compute logs to bases other than 10 and e. However, the **change of base formula** allows you to change a log with any other base to an expression that involves the common log to base 10 (or e, the natural log). That formula is

$$\log_a b = \frac{\log b}{\log a} \text{ or } \ln_a b = \frac{\ln b}{\ln a},$$

which can be found by using the online calculator.

Remember that the log of the base goes in the denominator of the change of base formula. However, if you suddenly cannot remember which goes on the top, you can always derive this formula just from the definition of logs and basic algebra:

Set $\log_a b = c$, which is equivalent to	$a^c = b$
Take the log of both sides of this equation	$\log a^c = \log b$
which is equivalent to	$c \log a = \log b$
Divide both sides of the equation by $\log a$	$c = \dfrac{\log b}{\log a} = \log_a b$ the definition of c

EXAMPLE 6.12

Given the equation $\log_5 625 = x$, what is the value of x?

SOLUTION 6.12

4. Use the change of base formula. Rewrite $\log_5 625 = x$ as $\dfrac{\log 625}{\log 5} = x$. Use the online calculator to find the answer. Remember that the online calculator works only with common and natural logs.

When evaluating $\dfrac{\log b}{\log a}$, enter it on the calculator as $\log b \div \log a$ all in one command because it's quicker and more accurate. Using the numerical value for $\log b$ and then dividing it by the numerical value for $\log a$ often involves rounding because these are irrational numbers, and using rounded numbers in a calculation such as division often causes rounding errors.

EXAMPLE 6.13

Evaluate $\log_4(8)$.

SOLUTION 6.13

1.5. Here the argument is 8 and the base is 4. We can use log or ln and the change of base formula to get the answer. Let's do it both ways to show it doesn't make a difference when using the change of base formula.

Using common log: $\log_4(8) = \dfrac{\log(8)}{\log(4)} = 1.5$. Using natural log: $\ln_4(8) = \dfrac{\ln(8)}{\ln(4)} = 1.5$.

When using the calculator and keeping in mind the previous note, remember to get out of the log function before you enter the division sign; otherwise, you would get $\log(8/\log(4)) = 1.12345$, which is a completely different (and wrong) answer.

6.2.11d Properties of Logarithms

- The sum of logarithms with equal bases is equal to the logarithm of the product. Since logarithms are inverses of exponents, just as $2^3 \cdot 2^2 \cdot 2 = 2^{3+2+1} = 2^6$, the sum of logarithms with equal bases is equal to the logarithm of the product. For example, $\log_a b + \log_a c = \log_a(bc)$. The reverse is also true; that is, the logarithm of a product is equal to the sum of the logarithms with the same base, or $\ln xy = \ln x + \ln y$.

- The difference of logarithms with equal bases is equal to the logarithm of the quotient. Therefore, $\ln a - \ln b = \ln\left(\dfrac{a}{b}\right)$. The reverse is also true; that is, the logarithm of a quotient is equal to the difference of the logarithms with the same base. Therefore, $\log\left(\dfrac{a}{b}\right) = \log a - \log b$.

- Thus, $n \log_a x = \log_a x^n$ and the reverse $\log x^a = a \log x$. This fact follows from the fact that a times a logarithm is equal to the logarithm added to itself n times (e.g., $3 \log x = \log x + \log x + \log x$), and the sum of n logarithms with the same base becomes ($\log x + \log x + \ldots \log x = \log [(x)(x) \ldots (x)] = \log x^n) = n \log x$. The reverse is also true.

EXAMPLE 6.14

Rewrite as a single logarithm: $\log_2 x + \log_2 7 + \log_2 y$.

SOLUTION 6.14

$\log_2 7xy$. Since the sum of logs equals the log of the product,
$\log_2 x + \log_2 7 + \log_2 y = \log_2 7xy$.

 Hint: You probably can do log base 2 in your head since you should know at least the first five powers of 2, because $\log_2 x = n$ means $2^n = x$.

EXAMPLE 6.15

Simplify $\log_4 5 - (\log_4 8 + \log_4 2)$.

SOLUTION 6.15

$\log_4 5 - 2$. $\log_4 5 - (\log_4 8 + \log_4 2) = \log_4 \left(\dfrac{5}{8 \times 2}\right) = \log_4 \left(\dfrac{5}{16}\right) = \log_4 5 - \log_4 16 = \log_4 5 - 2$.

EXAMPLE 6.16

Expand the logarithmic expression $\ln x^2 y^3$.

SOLUTION 6.16

$2 \ln x + 3 \ln y$. Use the rule that $\ln x^2 = a \ln x$ and the logarithm of a product is the sum of the logarithms.

6.2.11.e Logarithms of Trigonometric Functions

Since the trigonometric functions of an angle are numbers, we can find the logarithms of these functions. To find $\log(\sin 20°)$, first find $\sin 20°$, and then find the log of this answer. On the calculator, enter $\log(\sin(20))$ and press the Enter button. The answer is -0.466. Again, be sure to use the log button (in math mode) and the sin button (in trig mode) and that deg shows rather than rad, unless you are using radian measure.

EXAMPLE 6.17

What is the log of cos 0?

SOLUTION 6.18

0. Cos 0 = 1, and log (1) = 0 since $10^0 = 1$.

6.3 TRANSFORMATIONS OF FUNCTIONS

A **transformation** of a function is a change of variables or coordinates in which a function of new variables or coordinates is substituted for each original variable or coordinate. In the following discussion of these transformations, the symbol → means "transforms to," and the function is a curve in the xy-plane. Transformations of geometric shapes are done similarly, as shown in Chapter 5, Section 5.9. Transformation is the general term for four specific ways to manipulate the shape of a point, a line, or shape.

- Translation

- Dilation

- Reflection

- Rotation

 If a change is made to the variable, be sure to make that change for every appearance of that variable in $f(x)$. For example, if $f(x) = x^2 + 3x + 5$, then $f(Fx) = (Fx)^2 + 3(Fx) + 5$ and $f(x + C) = (x + C)^2 + 3(x + C) + 5$.

6.3.1 Translation

The operation of addition or subtraction **translates** the graph of a function $f(x)$ up or down but does not change its shape. Adding (or subtracting) a constant to (or from) a function $f(x)$ shifts the graph vertically. Adding a constant A $(f(x) \rightarrow f(x) + A)$ shifts every point up A points; subtracting a constant B $(f(x) \rightarrow f(x) - B)$ shifts it down B points. Do not confuse this with adding (or subtracting) a constant to (or from) the variable in a function $f(x)$, which shifts the graph horizontally. Adding a constant to the variable $(f(x) \rightarrow f(x + C))$ moves the function to the left (contrary to what instinct might tell you because it shifts –C units); subtracting a constant from the variable $(f(x) \rightarrow f(x - D))$ moves the function to the right because it shifts $-(-D) = +D$ units.

 An easy way to remember what happens to the graph when we add a constant is the poem (well, it *almost* rhymes):

Add to y, go high
Add to x, go left

6.3.2 Dilation and Compression

Dilation of a function means it has been stretched away from an axis. All the distances on the coordinate plane are lengthened by multiplying either all x-coordinates (horizontal dilation) or all y-coordinates (vertical dilation) by a factor $E > 1$.

Compression of a function means it has been squeezed toward an axis. All the distances on the coordinate plane are shortened by multiplying either all x-coordinates (horizontal compression) or all y-coordinates (vertical compression) by a factor $F < 1$.

This is a little more difficult to envision than translation because the shape is being changed, as shown in the graphs below. If the left graph is the original graph, vertical dilation will change it to look like the right graph. Alternatively, if the right graph is the original graph, vertical compression will change it to look like the left graph.

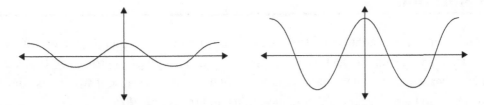

In summary, multiplying a function $f(x)$ by a constant E ($f(x) \rightarrow E f(x)$) compresses the graph (makes it squatter) if $0 < E < 1$, or stretches the graph (makes it taller) if $E > 1$, but the x-values are unchanged. This is shown in the graphs below, in which the middle curve is the original curve, and it is multiplied by 3 to get the top curve and multiplied by 0.5 to get the bottom curve. Note that the x values don't change in a vertical dilation or compression; only the y values do.

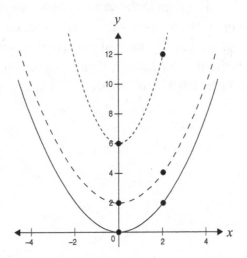

Likewise, multiplying x by a constant F ($(f(x) \rightarrow f(Fx))$) compresses the graph (makes it narrower) if $F > 1$, or stretches the graph (makes it wider) if $0 < F < 1$, but the y-values are unchanged.

Note that for the y-direction, larger values of the constant cause more compression in the x-direction. In the x-direction, larger values of the constant cause more compression in the y-direction.

6.3.3 Reflection

Reflection of a function actually reflects the function across an axis or the line $f(x) = x$ to form a mirror image. Multiplying a function $f(x)$ by -1 reflects its graph across the x-axis ($f(x) \rightarrow -f(x)$). However, multiplying x by -1 reflects the graph across the y-axis ($f(x) \rightarrow f(-x)$). Switching x and $f(x)$ for a function (which is the same as finding the inverse) reflects the graph of the function across the line $f(x) = x$. This type of reflection is discussed below in Section 6.5.

6.3.4 Rotation

Rotation of a function that results in a another function requires rotating the original function by $180°$. This is achieved by changing x to $-x$ as well as changing $f(x)$ to $-f(x)$. If a function is rotated by other than $180°$, the resulting graph is not a function because it won't pass the vertical line test. This can be seen easily if the rotation of a parabola is only $90°$.

6.3.5 Transformation Combinations

Two transformations can be carried out on one function by doing one transformation and then performing the other transformation on the result. The graph on the left below shows the result of a triple transformation from the solid graph to the dashed graph consisting of a reflection over the x-axis (vertical multiplication of $f(x)$ by a minus sign), a vertical dilation (by 2), and then a vertical translation (by $+1$). For the graph on the right, the dashed curve is $y = \log_3 x$, and the solid curve is $g(x) = -\log_3(x + 4)$, which is two transformations: flipping the graph over the x-axis (because of the minus sign) and moving it to the left 4 units (because 4 is added to x).

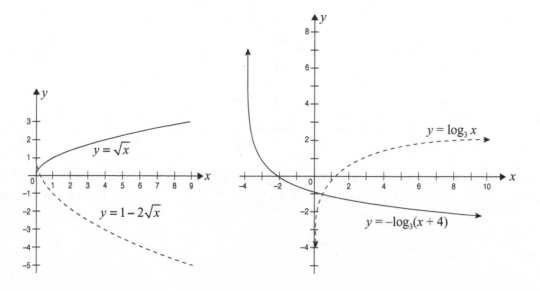

PART II

Multiplying by −2 will flip a graph upside down *and* stretch it in

EXAMPLE 6.18

What happens in the transformation of $f(x) = (x)^2$ to $g(x) = (-x)^2$?

SOLUTION 6.18

Nothing. Changing x to $-x$ flips $f(x)$ left and right, but it can't be seen because x^2 is an even function—it is symmetrical about the y-axis.

Summary Table of Transformations of $f(x)$

Translation	$f(x) \to f(x) + C$	$C > 0$ moves $f(x)$ up
		$C < 0$ moves $f(x)$ down
	$f(x) \to f(x + C)$	$C > 0$ moves $f(x)$ left
		$C < 0$ moves $f(x)$ right
Dilation	$f(x) \to Cf(x)$	$C > 1$ stretches $f(x)$ in the y-direction
		$0 < C < 1$ compresses $f(x)$
	$f(x) \to f(Cx)$	$C > 1$ compresses $f(x)$ in the x-direction
		$0 < C < 1$ stretches $f(x)$
Reflection	$f(x) \to -f(x)$	Reflects $f(x)$ about x-axis
	$f(x) \to f(-x)$	Reflects $f(x)$ about y-axis

6.4 COMPOSITION OF FUNCTIONS

Simply put, the **composition of functions** is applying one function, let's call it $f(x)$, to the results of another function, let's call that one $g(x)$. The symbol for the composite function would then be $f(g(x))$ or sometimes $f(x) \circ g(x)$. In other words, a **composite function**, also called a **function of a function**, is one in which the output of one function, $g(x)$, becomes the input for another, $f(x)$.

Key to understanding the composition of functions is remembering that x is just a placeholder for the input, as mentioned in Section 6.1.1. That leads to statements such as "If $f(x) = 2x$, what is $f(3x - 1)$?" We simply replace the x in $f(x) = 2x$ with $3x - 1$ to get $f(3x - 1) = 2(3x - 1) = 6x - 2$. Composition of functions is precisely this, with $g(x) = 3x - 1$.

So to evaluate the composition $f(g(x))$, it is obvious that you cannot evaluate $f(x)$ without knowing $g(x)$. So first find what $g(x)$ is and then replace the x in the $f(x)$ expression with the expression for $g(x)$, then simplify the result.

For the inputs given above, $f(x) = 2x$ and $g(x) = 3x - 1$, let's now find $g(f(x))$. This time we have to know $f(x)$ first so we can replace the x in $g(x)$ with that expression. Since $f(x) = 2x$, $g(x)$ now becomes equal to $g(f(x)) = g(2x) = 3(2x) - 1 = 6x - 1$.

$f(g(x))$ usually gives a different answer than $g(f(x))$, so don't get mixed up.

Values for the expressions in a composite function can also come from a table of the functions. For example, given the table below, let's find $f(g(x))$ and then find $f(g(h(x)))$ for $x = 6$, using values from the table. Again, we should keep track of what we should be looking for in each step. Working from the "inside" out, first we have to find a value for $h(6)$ from the table. $h(6)$ is the value of h for $x = 6$, which is $h(6) = 8$. Now we have to find $g(h(x))$, which is $g(8)$, and substitute that (4) into the final equation $f(g(h(x)))$, which now reads $f(4) = 6$. So the answer is that for $x = 6$, given the table below, $f(g(h(x))) = 6$.

x	f(x)	g(x)	h(x)
0	2	0	5
2	4	1	6
4	6	2	7
6	8	3	8
8	10	4	9

The other symbol that means the same as $f(g(h(x)))$ is $(f \circ g \circ h)(x)$. Both are read as "f of g of h of x." For $x = 6$ from the table above, $(f \circ g \circ h)(6) = 6$, which agrees with the result found above. (When $x = 6$, $h(6) = 8$, and then $g(8) = 4$, and $f(4) = 6$.)

EXAMPLE 6.19

For $g(x) = x + 1$, what is the value of $(g \circ g)(x)$ when $x = 1$?

SOLUTION 6.19

3. If $g(x) = x + 1$, $g(1) = 1 + 1 = 2$. Then $g(2) = 2 + 1 = 3$. So $(g \circ g)(1) = 3$.

The **domain of any function**, including composites, is the set of all possible values of the independent variable that will make the function real. The domain of a composite function is a combination of the domain of the composite, $f(g(x))$, and the domain of the second function, $g(x)$.

Rev: **EXAMPLE 6.20**

If $f(x) = \dfrac{x}{x+1}$ and $g(x) = \dfrac{4}{x}$, what is the domain of $f(g(x))$?

Rem. You have to look # pts. where $g(x)$ is also not defined

SOLUTION 6.20

All real x except $x = -4$ and 0. $f(g(x)) = \dfrac{\frac{4}{x}}{\frac{4}{x}+1} = \dfrac{4}{4+x}$. The domain of $f(g(x)) = \dfrac{4}{4+x}$, is all real x except $x = 4$, which would make the denominator equal zero. The domain of $g(x) = \dfrac{4}{x}$ is all real x except $x = 0$. Therefore, the domain of the composite function is all real x except $x = -4$ and 0, which has the **interval notation** $\{(-\infty, -4) \cup (-4, 0) \cup (0, \infty)\}$.

EXAMPLE 6.21

If $f(x) = x^2$ and $g(x) = \sqrt{x}$, what is the domain of their composite, $f(g(x))$?

SOLUTION 6.21

All nonnegative real numbers. The composite is $f(g(x)) = (\sqrt{x})^2 = x$. Usually the domain of x is all real numbers, but the domain of $g(x) = \sqrt{x}$ is all real numbers $x \geq 0$ since square roots of negative numbers aren't real. The domain of the composite $f(g(x))$ has to be a combination of these two domains, so it is all nonnegative real numbers, or $x \geq 0$.

6.5 THE INVERSE OF A FUNCTION

The **inverse of a function** behaves the same way as other inverses: The inverse of a function undoes the action of the function. The inverse of a function $f(x)$ is denoted $f^{-1}(x)$. In other words, if $f(x)$ is a function that maps x to y, then the inverse function $f^{-1}(x)$ maps y back to x. Thus, for any function and its inverse, $f(f^{-1}(x)) = f^{-1}(f(x)) = x$.

Imp: The graph of $f^{-1}(x)$ is a reflection of $f(x)$ across the line $y = x$. Not all functions are **invertible**, the adjective used when the function and its inverse exist and are both functions. Sometimes the inverse of a function is not a function itself. A function $f(x)$ has an inverse *function* only if for every y in its range there is only one value of x in its domain for which $f(x) = y$. Any function whose inverse is also a function is termed a **one-to-one function**.

If you look at a graph of a function and it fails the "**horizontal line test,**" its inverse will not be a function because it will fail the vertical line test that determines functions. Similar to the vertical line test, the horizontal line test says that any *horizontal* line can cross the graph at only one point. Note that the horizontal line test is done on the original function and is used only to determine whether that function is invertible.

To generate the inverse of a function $f(x) = y$,

1. Solve $f(x) = y$ for x.

2. Name the new function; for example, $g(y) = x$.

3. Switch the variables x and y in $g(x) = y$.

EXAMPLE 6.22

Does the inverse of $y = 5x - 2$ exist? If so, what is it?

SOLUTION 6.22

Yes; $g(x) = \dfrac{x+2}{5}$. The original function passes the horizontal line test, so the inverse exists. To find the inverse, follow the steps:

1. Solve for x: $5x = y + 2$, or $x = \dfrac{y+2}{5}$.

2. The new function is $g(y) = x = \dfrac{y+2}{5}$. → *Rem this step.*

3. Form $g(x) = y = \dfrac{x+2}{5}$ by switching x and y. It is definitely also a function.

EXAMPLE 6.23

Find the inverse function of $f(x) = y = x^2 + 2$.

SOLUTION 6.23

It doesn't exist. This graph doesn't pass the horizontal line test (this is true for all parabolas), so the inverse is not a function and $f(x)$ does not have an inverse. If you tried to find the inverse algebraically (which you shouldn't bother doing if you already know it doesn't exist), it would look like this:

1. Solve $y = x^2 + 2$ for x. $x^2 = y - 2$ or $x = \pm\sqrt{y-2}$

2. Every x will have two y values, as shown by the $\pm$ sign, so the inverse is not a function. It is important to understand that even though the inverse is not a function, it still exists.

EXAMPLE 6.24

Find the inverse function of $y = x^2 + 2$, $x \le 0$.

SOLUTION 6.24

Compare this example and the previous one. The difference between them is that the domain has been restricted to $x \leq 0$. This restriction makes the graph look like the following:

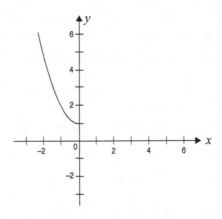

The inverse of this function is also a function because this graph passes the horizontal line test. Here's how the algebra looks:

1. Solve $y = x^2 + 2$, $x \leq 0$ for x: $x^2 = y - 2$ or $x = -\sqrt{y - 2}$

2. The domain is limited to negative numbers since the sign before the square root is only negative.

3. Switch x and y to get $y = -\sqrt{x - 2}$, $x \geq 2$, so every x value will have only one y value, and the inverse exists and is a function. Note that the restriction $x \geq 2$ must be included to avoid a negative square root.

Here is the graph for this function and its inverse (dashed line).

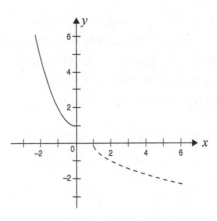

6.6 FUNCTIONS OF TWO VARIABLES

A **function of two variables**, let's call them x and y, assigns to each ordered pair (x, y) a unique value $f(x, y)$, or z. This is a function that is adding another dimension to $f(x)$, the two-dimensional function we have considered so far. Thus, the function of two input variables, x and y, is a three-dimensional function with a unique output $z = f(x, y)$ defined in a specified set of points called the **domain** D. $f(x, y)$ graphs as a surface in three-dimensional space.

The operations performed with one-variable functions can also be performed with functions of two variables. Also similar to functions of one variable, you cannot take the square root of a negative number or divide by zero. Therefore, if $f(x, y) = \sqrt{x + 2y}$, then $x + 2y \geq 0$, and if $f(x, y) = \dfrac{2x}{3y + 6}$, then $3y + 6 \neq 0$, or $y \neq -2$. In addition, since logarithms exist only for values greater than zero, if $f(x, y) = \ln(x^2 - 2y)$, then $x^2 - 2y > 0$.

A common three-dimensional surface is a plane, which has length, width, and depth. If we represent these three dimensions by x, y, and z, we can write the general equation of a plane as $Ax + By + Cz = D$, where D is some constant, and such functions are usually solved for z as a function of x and y:

$$z = f(x, y) = Ax + By + D$$

Recall that in two dimensions a line is defined by two points, and the two points often used to graph the line are intersections of the line with the two axes, or the x- and y-intercepts. Likewise, to graph a three-dimensional plane we will generally find the intersection points with the three axes and then graph the triangle that connects those three points. This triangle will be a portion of the plane of interest, and it will give us a fairly decent idea on what the plane itself looks like.

For example, to graph a given plane, we use a coordinate system with three axes, which are perpendicular to each other. An excellent visual of the x-y-z axes is the corner of a room, where the intersection of the ceiling with the two walls can be thought of as the x- and y-axes, and the intersection of the two walls is the z-axis. Notice that each axis is perpendicular to the other two axes. When three dimensions are drawn on a two-dimensional surface, as is done here, it looks like

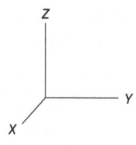

As an example, let's find the plane defined by

$$f(x, y) = z = 12 - 3x - 4y.$$

We simply find the three intersection points with the axes and then graph the triangle that connects those three points. Each of the intersection points with the three main coordinate axes is defined by the fact that two of the coordinates are zero. For example, the intersection with the z-axis is defined by $x = y = 0$, and the other intersection points are defined similarly. So the three intersection points are found by substituting 0 for the other two values, or the intersection with

the x-axis is $(4, 0, 0)$

the y-axis is $(0, 3, 0)$

the z-axis is $(0, 0, 12)$

Imp.

The graph of the triangle formed by these three points is shown below. This is just a portion of the whole plane, which extends the surface in all directions.

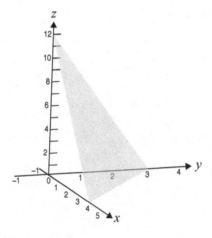

Three-dimensional figures do not have to be flat surfaces. If $f(x, y)$ involves x and/or y to the second power, the graph will involve curved surfaces. Common examples are a cone or a sphere, but can even include something as interesting as a football.

Imp.

Finding the points for such a complicated figure as well as many other problems like this are made simpler by using calculus, the topic of Chapter 7.

Practice Exercises

1. Is $f(x) = \dfrac{x}{x^2 - 1}$ even, odd, or neither?

2. The transformation of $f(x) = x^2$ called $g(x) = 2(x+3)^2 + 4$. This transformation (choose *all* that apply):

   A stretches $f(x) = x^2$ by 2 units in the y-direction

   B shifts $f(x) = x^2$ to the left 3 units

   C shifts $f(x) = x^2$ to the right 3 units

   D shifts $f(x) = x^2$ down 4 units

Rev.

3. The characteristic of log .001 is   *Also find its mantissa*

   (A) 10^{-3}

   (B) -1

   (C) -3

   (D) 3

4. If log $x^2 = 0.6522$, then log $10x$ is

   (A) 1.3261

   (B) 3.2610

   (C) 2.3044

   (D) 1.3044

5. If $T = 10x^2$, then log T equals

   (A) $1 + 2 \log x$

   (B) $1 + 2x$

   (C) $10 + 2 \log x$

   (D) $20 \log x$

6. Which type of graph describes the following set of points?

$$\left\{(1, 9), (2, 3), (3, 1), \left(4, \frac{1}{3}\right), \left(5, \frac{1}{9}\right), \left(6, \frac{1}{27}\right)\right\}$$

   (A) Linear

   (B) Exponential

   (C) Quadratic

   (D) Cannot tell

7. Log tan x =

   (A) $\dfrac{\log \sin x}{\log \cos x}$

   (B) $\log \sin x - \log \cos x$

   (C) $\log \cos x - \log \sin x$

   (D) $\dfrac{\log \cos x}{\log \sin x}$

8. If one of the roots is 0, the value of c in the equation $ax^2 + bx + c = 0$ must be

   (A) 0

   (B) ∞

   (C) negative

   (D) positive

9. For the function $y = f(x) = \log_4(x + 1)$, what is the asymptote of the graph?

   $\mathcal{R}ev$.

   (A) $x = 0$

   (B) $y = 0$

   (C) $x = -1$

   (D) $y = -1$

10. Simplify $10^{\log(5x^2)}$.

   (A) $10(5x^2)$

   (B) $\log(5x^2)$

   (C) $5x^2$

   (D) 10^{5x^2}

Solutions

1. Odd. $f(-x) = \dfrac{-x}{x^2 - 1}$, so it isn't even. $-f(x) = -\dfrac{x}{x^2 - 1} = f(-x)$, so it is odd.

2. $\boxed{A}$ and $\boxed{B}$ only. The stretch is caused by the coefficient 2 and the shift is caused by adding 3 to x^2, and it is to the left because 3 is positive. If -3 were added to x, then the shift would be to the right. The shift is up, not down, 4 units because 4 is added to the function.

3. (C) -3. The characteristic is the value of the log before the decimal point. Rewrite log .001 as $\log 10^{-3}$, so log .001 $= -3$, with characteristic -3.

4. (A) 1.3261. Use the rules for logs: Log of a power: $\log x^2 = 2(\log x) = 0.6522$, so $\log x = \dfrac{0.6522}{2} = 0.3261$. Log of a product: $\log 10x = \log 10 + \log x = 1 + .3261 = 1.3261$.

5. (A) $1 + 2 \log x$. Take the log of both sides: $\log T = \log(10x^2) = \log(10) + 2 \log x = 1 + 2 \log x$ by using the laws of logs.

6. (B) Exponential. You can recognize an exponential function from several points by noticing that as one unknown varies by a constant term, the other variable varies by a constant factor. Here, as the values of x increase by a constant term 1, the values of y decrease by a constant *factor* of $\dfrac{1}{3}$. That eliminates a linear model, in which the variables will increase or decrease by constant terms, not factors. A quadratic is eliminated because the change in x for a modest change in y is dramatic.

7. (B) log sin x – log cos x. The logarithm of the quotient of two numbers is equal to the logarithm of the dividend minus the logarithm of the divisor. Since $\tan x = \dfrac{\sin x}{\cos x}$, $\log \tan x = \log \sin x - \log \cos x$.

8. (A) 0. Substitute the value 0 of the root into the quadratic equation $ax^2 + bx + c = 0$ to get $c = 0$. This is true no matter what the values of a and b are.

9. (C) $x = -1$. There are several ways to find the answer to this question.

    •   Graphs of the $\log_b x$ format always have an x asymptote at $x = 0$. Since x is increased by 1 in $\log(x + 1)$, the graph is moved one unit to the left, so the new asymptote is $x = -1$.

    •   Make a table of values by writing the function in exponential form: $\log_4(x+1)$ is $4^y = x + 1$, or $x = 4^y - 1$. Assign values to y in this case and solve for x. It is obvious that as y goes toward $-\infty$, x gets close to -1 but never crosses it (definition of an asymptote).

y	2	1	0	−1	−3	−5
x	15	3	0	$-\dfrac{3}{4}$	$-\dfrac{63}{64}$	$-\dfrac{1023}{1024}$

Graph the function or use the graphing calculator to see the asymptote.

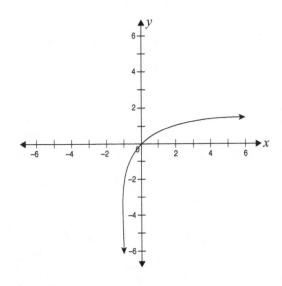

10. (C) $5x^2$. Since log has a base of 10, this is the same as asking the log of what number is $\log(5x^2)$, which, of course, is $5x^2$.

Calculus

7.1 LIMITS

7.1.1 Definitions and Notations for Limits

Limits are fundamental to understanding calculus. A **limit** is the value that a function is closing in on. The function doesn't have to actually equal the limit, but it clearly must *intend* to do so. The notation for limits is $\lim_{x \to c} f(x)$, which is read as "the limit of $f(x)$ as x approaches c. If x is approaching c from the left (or negative side), c is usually denoted as c^-, and if x is approaching c from the right (or positive side), c is usually denoted as c^+. The notation $\lim_{x \to \infty}$ means x is getting really, really large; likewise, $\lim_{x \to -\infty}$ means x is getting really, really small.

Asymptotic functions involve limits, as discussed in Chapter 6, Section 6.2.4. In limit notation,

- • If $\lim_{x \to c^-} f(x) = \infty$ and $\lim_{x \to c^+} f(x) = -\infty$ or $\lim_{x \to c^-} f(x) = -\infty$ and $\lim_{x \to c^+} f(x) = \infty$, the line $x = c$ is a vertical asymptote of $f(x)$.

- If $\lim_{x \to c} f(x) = \infty$ or $\lim_{x \to c} f(x) = -\infty$, the line $x = c$ is a vertical asymptote of $f(x)$.

- If $\lim_{x \to \infty} f(x) = c$ or $\lim_{x \to -\infty} f(x) = c$, then $y = c$ is a horizontal asymptote of $f(x)$.

- If the degree of the denominator of a rational function $f(x)$ is greater than the degree of the numerator, the function has a horizontal asymptote at $y = 0$, and $\lim_{x \to \pm\infty} f(x) = 0$.

- If the highest powers in the numerator and denominator of a rational function are the same, their coefficients become the limit as $x \to \pm\infty$. So for $f(x) = \dfrac{3x^2 - x + 4}{5x^2 + 2x - 3}$, $\lim_{x \to \infty} f(x) = \dfrac{3}{5}$ and $\lim_{x \to -\infty} f(x) = \dfrac{3}{5}$.

- If the limit of a rational function is $\lim\limits_{x \to c} f(x) = \infty$ or $-\infty$, there is a vertical asymptote where the denominator equals 0. But check to see whether the numerator also equals 0 at this point because if so, it's a hole, not an asymptote. In both cases, the limit still exists.

EXAMPLE 7.1

Find $\lim\limits_{x \to \infty} \dfrac{c}{x^2}$.

SOLUTION 7.1

$\lim\limits_{x \to \infty} \dfrac{c}{x^2} = 0$ because the degree of the numerator is 0 (since $c = c \cdot 1 = cx^0$).

If for any function $f(x)$, $\lim\limits_{x \to c^+} f(x) \neq \lim\limits_{x \to c^-} f(x)$,

- the limit of $f(x)$ at c, $(\lim\limits_{x \to c} f(x))$, does not exist,

- the graph of $f(x)$ has a hole, asymptote, or break at c.

But if those two limits are equal, $\lim\limits_{x \to c^+} f(x) = \lim\limits_{x \to c^-} f(x)$ and $\lim\limits_{x \to c} f(x) = f(c)$, the graph of $f(x)$ has no break at c.

Two special limits that are important to know are

- $\lim\limits_{x \to 0} \left(\dfrac{\sin x}{x} \right) = 1$, which means, for example, that $\lim\limits_{x \to 0} \dfrac{\sin 5\theta}{5\theta} = 1$.

- $\lim\limits_{x \to 0} \left(\dfrac{\cos x - 1}{x} \right) = 0$, which means, for example, that $\lim\limits_{x \to 0} \left(\dfrac{\cos \pi - 1}{\pi} \right) = 0$.

EXAMPLE 7.2

Find the value of $\lim\limits_{x \to 0} \dfrac{\sin 5\theta}{\theta}$.

SOLUTION 7.2

5. We want the denominator to be the same as the argument of the sine function, so multiply the limit by $\dfrac{5}{5}$, which equals 1 and doesn't change the value. Then we have $\lim\limits_{x \to 0} \dfrac{\sin 5\theta}{\theta} = \lim\limits_{x \to 0} \left(\dfrac{5}{5} \right) \left(\dfrac{\sin 5\theta}{\theta} \right) = 5 \lim\limits_{x \to 0} \dfrac{\sin 5\theta}{5\theta} = 5(1) = 5$.

EXAMPLE 7.3

Find the value of $\lim\limits_{x \to 0} \dfrac{\cos 3x - 1}{x}$.

SOLUTION 7.3

0. We want the denominator to be the same as the argument of the cosine function, so multiply the limit by $\dfrac{3}{3}$, which equals 1 and doesn't change the value. Then we have $\lim\limits_{x \to 0} \dfrac{\cos 3x - 1}{x} = \lim\limits_{x \to 0} \left(\dfrac{3}{3} \right) \left(\dfrac{\cos 3x - 1}{x} \right) = 3 \lim\limits_{x \to 0} \left(\dfrac{\cos 3x - 1}{3x} \right) = 3(0) = 0$.

7.1.2 Continuity

If a function is everywhere **continuous**, there are no holes, asymptotes, or breaks. Part of a function can be called continuous if the endpoints of that part are defined.

A function is continuous at a point $x = c$ if $\lim\limits_{x \to c} f(x)$ exists; $f(c)$ exists, and $\lim\limits_{x \to c} f(x) = f(c)$. If any of these requirements is unfulfilled, c is a point of discontinuity.

Hint: A graph is continuous if you can draw it without lifting your pen from the paper.

7.1.3 Operations on Limits

- The limit of a sum (or difference) equals the sum (or difference) of the individual limits.

- The limit of a product (quotient) is equal to the product (quotient) of the limits.

7.1.4 Methods for Finding Limits

7.1.4a Intermediate Value Theorem

To find the limit by **substitution**, just plug in the limit for the unknown. This works only if the function is continuous in the vicinity of the limit. The **Intermediate Value Theorem** states:

> If $f(x)$ is continuous on the interval $[a, b]$ and $f(a)$ and $f(b)$ exist, then direct substitution will find the value of $f(c)$ for any c for which $a < c < b$.

In other words, if $f(x)$ is continuous on the interval (a, b), then $\lim\limits_{x \to c} = f(c)$ for any c such that $a < c < b$ can be found by direct substitution of $x = c$ into $f(x)$. So substitution works for all continuous functions, but it fails for some values if the function is not continuous.

EXAMPLE 7.4

Evaluate $\lim_{x \to 3} = (x^2 - 2x + 3)$.

SOLUTION 7.4

6. $\lim_{x \to 3} = (x^2 - 2x + 3) = 3^2 - 2(3) + 3 = 9 - 6 + 3 = 6$ because $x^2 - 2x + 3$ is a continuous function.

Rev.

EXAMPLE 7.5

Evaluate $\lim_{x \to 6} = \frac{2x}{x - 6}$.

SOLUTION 7.5

$\lim_{x \to 6} = \frac{2x}{x - 6}$ does not exist because at the limit, the denominator $x - 6 = 6 - 6 = 0$, the numerator $2x = 2(6) \neq 0$, and division by 0 is undefined. Therefore, there is a vertical asymptote at $x = 6$.

EXAMPLE 7.6

Evaluate $\lim_{x \to -1} 3^x$.

SOLUTION 7.6

$\frac{1}{3}$. Substitute $x = -1$ into the expression to get: $\lim_{x \to -1} 3^x = 3^{-1} = \frac{1}{3}$.

*arc tan = Rev.
inverse of tan
= $\tan^{-1}$*

EXAMPLE 7.7

Evaluate $\lim_{x \to e} \arctan(\ln x)$.

SOLUTION 7.7

$\frac{\pi}{2}$. $\lim_{x \to e} \arctan(\ln x) = \lim_{x \to e} \arctan(\ln e)$ (since $e^x = x$). But $\ln e = 1$ since $\ln$ and e are inverse functions, so we now have $\lim_{x \to e} \arctan(\ln x) = \arctan 1 = \frac{\pi}{4}$.

7.1.4b Factoring

If substitution doesn't work, try **factoring**. If the function is a fraction (as in Example 7.3), eliminate any factors that make the denominator equal zero because there will be a hole in the graph and it will be discontinuous at that point.

EXAMPLE 7.8

Evaluate $\lim\limits_{x \to 4} \dfrac{x^2 + 2x - 24}{x - 4}$.

SOLUTION 7.8

10. Factor the function $\lim\limits_{x \to 4} \dfrac{x^2 + 2x - 24}{x - 4} = \lim\limits_{x \to 4} \dfrac{(x-4)(x+6)}{(x-4)} = \lim\limits_{x \to 4} \dfrac{x+6}{1} = 10$ but keep in mind that the original function, with $x - 4$ in the denominator, has a hole at $x = 4$. The graph is the same as $f(x) = x + 6$ except for the hole at (4, 10), but the limit exists because the limit of the function *approaches* 10 from either side of 4.

 Remember that for the limit, the function doesn't have to actually equal the limit, it just must clearly *intend* to do so.

 Hint: If the function is a quadratic divided by a binomial, try factoring it by using the opposite of F-O-I-L with the binomial as one factor. It will usually work.

Sometimes, the limit will result in $\dfrac{0}{0}$, which is called **indeterminate**, such as happens with direct substitution into $\lim\limits_{x \to -2} \dfrac{3x^2 - 3x - 18}{x + 2}$. But $\lim\limits_{x \to -2} \dfrac{3x^2 - 3x - 18}{x + 2} = \lim\limits_{x \to -2} \dfrac{(x+2)(3x-9)}{(x+2)} = \lim\limits_{x \to -2}(3x - 9) = -15$. So the limit exists, even though the graph has a hole at $x = 2$ (which makes both the numerator and denominator of the original expression zero).

EXAMPLE 7.9

Evaluate $\lim\limits_{x \to 2} \dfrac{4x^2 - 5x - 6}{x - 2}$.

SOLUTION 7.9

11. Since the function is a fraction, try to factor the numerator to reduce the fraction. It is a good idea, if the numerator isn't readily factored, to try the denominator as one of the factors. Sure enough, we find that $4x^2 - 5x - 6 = (x - 2)(4x + 3)$ by either the opposite of F-O-I-L or by division (long or synthetic) of the numerator by the denominator. Therefore, $\lim\limits_{x \to 2} \dfrac{4x^2 - 5x - 6}{x - 2} = \lim\limits_{x \to 2} \dfrac{(x-2)(4x+3)}{(x-2)}$, and we can cancel out the $(x - 2)$ factors to get the equivalent limit of $\lim\limits_{x \to 2}(4x - 3) = 4(2) + 3 = 11$. So $\lim\limits_{x \to 2} \dfrac{4x^2 - 5x - 6}{x - 2} = 11$.

7.1.4c Conjugate Method

Often, if the function contains a radical and nothing else works readily, you can use the **conjugate method** with radicals. For example, for $\lim\limits_{x \to 4} \dfrac{x-4}{\sqrt{x}-2}$, just substituting $x = 4$ right away gives the indeterminate answer $\dfrac{0}{0}$. The conjugate method says to multiply the numerator and denominator of a radical fraction by the conjugate of the radical. Remember that conjugate just means changing the sign in the middle of the two terms. Thus, the conjugate of $\sqrt{x} - 2$ is $\sqrt{x} + 2$.

EXAMPLE 7.10

Find $\lim\limits_{x \to 4} \dfrac{x-4}{\sqrt{x}-2}$.

SOLUTION 7.10

4. $\lim\limits_{x \to 4} \dfrac{x-4}{\sqrt{x}-2} = \lim\limits_{x \to 4} \dfrac{x-4}{\sqrt{x}-2} \cdot \dfrac{\sqrt{x}+2}{\sqrt{x}+2} = \lim\limits_{x \to 4} \dfrac{(x-4)(\sqrt{x}+2)}{(x-4)} = \lim\limits_{x \to 4}(\sqrt{x}+2) =$

$\sqrt{4} + 2 = 4$. Therefore, $\lim\limits_{x \to 4} \dfrac{x-4}{\sqrt{x}-2} = 4$.

7.2 DERIVATIVES AND DIFFERENTIATION

One of the defining characteristics of the graph of a linear equation is its **slope** $= \dfrac{\text{change in } y}{\text{change in } x}$ (see Section 4.2.5a), which is easy to see if $f(x)$ is a linear equation. If $f(x)$ is a curve, however, that slope changes as x changes, and every point on the curved line has a different slope. A tangent line to a curve is a line that touches the curve at one point, similar to the tangent to a circle (Section 5.7.1). At the tangent point, the curve and the tangent line have the same slope. The figure below shows tangent lines to various points on a curve.

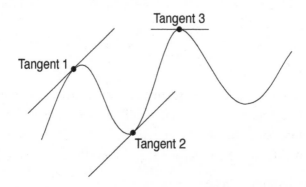

7.2.1 Average Rate of Change

For a linear equation, the slope is the rate of change, or $\dfrac{\text{change in } y}{\text{change in } x}$. But if the graph isn't a straight line, the slope keeps changing, so there isn't one slope for the whole graph. However, an average rate of change will give information about the slope in a small interval of the curve. The method to find the **average rate of change** is to find the slope at a point on a curve by basically choosing two x values, one below and one above the point in question, and to calculate the value of y at each of those values and then use the slope of the interval between the two points to approximate the slope at the point, or $\dfrac{\Delta f(x)}{\Delta x}$ or $\dfrac{\Delta y}{\Delta x}$, where Δ means "change." In other words, it is the average of all the rates of change between the designated two points on the curve. It isn't exact for every point, but as long as the curve is continuous (has no holes), it is a good approximation.

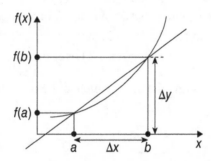

EXAMPLE 7.11

What is the average rate of change of $x^2 - 6x - 7 = 0$ on the interval between $x = 2$ and $x = 3$?

SOLUTION 7.11

–1. We know the change in x is $2 - 3 = -1$, but we have to calculate the change of y in that interval. At $x = 2$, $y = (2)^2 - 6(2) - 7 = -15$, and at $x = 3$, $y = (3)^2 - 6(3) - 7 = -16$. Therefore, the average rate of change between $x = 2$ and $x = 3$ is $\dfrac{(15) - (-16)}{2 - 3} = \dfrac{1}{-1} = -1$.

EXAMPLE 7.12

What is the average rate of change of $x^2 - 6x - 7 = 0$ on the interval between $x = 3$ and $x = 4$? (This is the same curve as in Example 7.11.)

SOLUTION 7.12

1. Again, the change in x is $3 - 4 = -1$, but we have to calculate the change of y in that interval. At $x = 3$, we already know from Example 7.11 that $y = -16$, and

at $x = 4$, $y = (4)^2 - 6(4) - 7 = -15$. Therefore, the average rate of change between $x = 3$ and $x = 4$ is $\dfrac{(-16)-(-15)}{3-4} = \dfrac{-1}{-1} = 1$.

Since the curve in Examples 7.11 and 7.12 is a parabola, the vertex of this parabola is at $x = -\dfrac{-6}{2(1)} = 3$ (see Section 6.2.2). The parabola becomes a mirror image at the vertex, so the values of y on the left side of $x = 3$ are a reflection of the values of y on the right side.

7.2.2 Mean Value Theorem

Related to the idea of the average rate of change is the **Mean Value Theorem**. Using a continuous function $f(x)$ on a closed interval $[a, b]$, this theorem states:

> There is at least one value c, between a and b in the open interval (a, b)
> for which the instantaneous rate of change (slope of the tangent line)
> equals the average rate of change of $f(x)$ over the closed interval $[a, b]$.

The figure shown below illustrates this theorem, which is the basis for derivatives discussed in the next section.

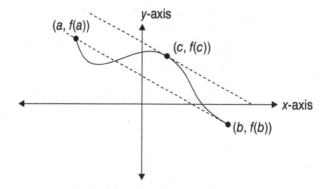

7.2.3 Limit Definition of Derivatives

The average rate of change method works if an approximation is all that is needed, but to get a precise value for the slope at any point on a curve, we need the concept of the **limit definition of derivatives**, which give the **instantaneous rate of change**. The limit definition of derivatives essentially says to use the basic idea behind the average rate of change (Section 7.2.1), but to make the interval $\Delta f(x)$ around the point in question small—infinitesimally small—in fact, to make the distance between $f(x + \Delta x)$ and $f(x)$ approach zero.

So derivatives are limits of the difference quotient, $\dfrac{\Delta f(x)}{\Delta x}$. The most common formula for calculating the general derivative $f'(x)$ of a function $f(x)$ is

$$f'(x) = \lim_{\Delta x \to 0} \frac{f(x + \Delta x) - f(x)}{\Delta x}$$

The three common ways in which derivatives are indicated are $f'(x)$, y', and $\dfrac{dy}{dx}$.

So $f'(x)$ can evaluate that slope at any point along the curve. For example, to find the slope of the curve $f(x) = x^2 + 4x - 7$ at the point $x = 2$, we first use this equation, but for illustration purposes only because there is an easier "shortcut" that doesn't involve going through this lengthy calculation.

$$f'(x) = \lim_{\Delta x \to 0} \frac{f(x + \Delta x) - f(x)}{\Delta x}$$

$$= \lim_{\Delta x \to 0} \frac{[(x + \Delta x)^2 + 4(x + \Delta x) - 7] - (x^2 + 4x - 7)}{\Delta x}$$

$$= \lim_{\Delta x \to 0} \frac{[x^2 + 2x\Delta x + (\Delta x)^2 + 4x + 4\Delta x - 7] - (x^2 + 4x - 7)}{\Delta x}$$

which, after canceling like terms with opposite signs, becomes

$$f'(x) = \lim_{\Delta x \to 0} \frac{2x\Delta x + (\Delta x)^2 + 4\Delta x}{\Delta x}$$

$$= \lim_{\Delta x \to 0} 2x + \Delta x + 4$$

$$= 2x + 4$$

Then we can say that at the point $x = 2$, the derivative, or the slope of the curve, is 8, or

$$f'(2) = 2(2) + 4 = 8.$$

The time spent in all of this calculation is eliminated by the use of the power rule, as shown in the next section.

7.2.4 Power Rule

Differentiation, or the method to find the derivative, of $f(x) = x^2 + 4x - 7$ shown in Section 7.2.3 is not overly complicated, but imagine if the curve were $g(x) = 3x^4 - 2x^3 + x^2 - 6$. Wow!! That would take a lot of time, even just to expand $3(x + \Delta x)^4$, let alone all of the other terms. Fortunately, the **power rule** is a shortcut for differentiating functions that involves only simple powers of the variable given in the form ax^n:

$$f'(ax^n) = \frac{d}{dx}(ax^n) = (n \cdot a)x^{n-1}.$$

Even though that doesn't look so simple, it really is. First, you must realize that $\dfrac{d}{dx}f(x)$ is just another way to write $\dfrac{df(x)}{dx}$ —they both mean the derivative of $f(x)$ with respect to x.

So the power rule is saying that for every term in $f(x)$, multiply the exponent by the coefficient and then subtract 1 from the existing exponent. Therefore, $\frac{d}{dy}(2x^3) = (3 \cdot 2)x^{3-1} = 6x^2$ and likewise, $\frac{d}{dy}(5x^4 - 2x^2 + 6x - 7) = 20x^3 - 4x + 6$. Note two important things in this last differentiation:

- The differentiation of an "x" term results in just the coefficient of x because when you subtract 1 from the exponent of $x = x^1$ you get $x^0 = 1$

- Constant terms just drop out because the x term for a constant is x^0 and zero times anything is zero.

So now let's go back to the equation that we differentiated the "hard" way in Section 7.2.3: $f(x) = x^2 + 4x - 7$. Using the power rule, right away we can say that $\frac{d}{dx}(x^2 + 4x - 7) = 2x + 4$.

This also works for negative exponents and radicals. Note that a function that has the variable in the denominator can be rewritten with a negative exponent to do the differentiation quickly. If $f(x)$ contains a radical, replace it by its equivalent fractional exponent.

EXAMPLE 7.13

Differentiate $s = \dfrac{6}{\sqrt{t}}$ with respect to t.

SOLUTION 7.13

$-3t^{-\frac{3}{2}}$. First, we rewrite $\dfrac{6}{\sqrt{t}}$ as $6t^{-\frac{1}{2}}$ so we can use the power rule. Then $\dfrac{d}{dt}\left(6t^{-\frac{1}{2}}\right) = -\dfrac{1}{2}(6)t^{\left(-\frac{1}{2}-1\right)} = -3t^{-\frac{3}{2}}$. The two steps in the middle of that calculation can easily be done mentally.

Note in this calculation that s took the place of the usual x and t took the place of the usual y since the names of variables are arbitrary.

EXAMPLE 7.14

Differentiate $g(x) = ax^{a+2}$, where a is a real number.

SOLUTION 7.14

$(a^2 + 2a)x^{a+1}$. Using the power rule, $g'(x) = (a + 2)(ax^{a+2-1}) = (a^2 + 2a)x^{a+1}$.

EXAMPLE 7.15

Differentiate $y = \sqrt[3]{x^2}$ with respect to x.

SOLUTION 7.15

$\dfrac{2}{3x^{\frac{1}{3}}}$. First, we rewrite the variable in exponent notation (Sections 3.8.2 and 3.9) so we can use the power rule: $y = x^{\frac{2}{3}}$. Then $\dfrac{dy}{dx} = \dfrac{2}{3}x^{\frac{2}{3}-1} = \dfrac{2}{3}x^{-\frac{1}{3}} = \dfrac{2}{3x^{\frac{1}{3}}}$. But since

we usually rationalize fractions that have a radical in the denominator (see Section

4.4.2), we change $\dfrac{2}{3\sqrt[3]{x}}$ to its rationalized form: $\dfrac{2}{3\sqrt[3]{x}} \cdot \dfrac{\sqrt[3]{x^2}}{\sqrt[3]{x^2}} = \dfrac{2\sqrt[3]{x^2}}{3x}$.

 When we rationalize a root in the denominator other than a square root, we must make sure the radicand will get rid of the radical sign. In Example 7.15, we want to end up with $\sqrt[3]{x^3} = x$ in the denominator, so we rationalize with $\sqrt[3]{x^2}$.

7.2.5 Product and Quotient Rules

Not all functions are plain polynomials, though. To take the derivative of a functions that are products or quotients of functions, we must use the following specific rules. Luckily, for the Praxis test, these rules are included in the drop-down formula sheet on the computer, so you don't have to memorize them. Instead, use those brain cells to remember how to use them, as shown in Examples 7.16 and 7.17.

- Derivative of a product of functions: $\quad (f(x)g(x))' = f'(x)g(x) + f(x)g'(x)$

  In other words, multiply the derivative of the first function by the second function, and then add the first function multiplied by the derivative of the second function.

- Derivative of a quotient of functions: $\quad \left(\dfrac{f(x)}{g(x)}\right)' = \dfrac{f'(x)g(x) - f(x)g'(x)}{(g(x))^2}$, if $g(x) \neq 0$.

  Notice that the numerator is the same as the derivative of a product with the plus sign replaced by a minus sign, and the denominator is just the original denominator squared.

EXAMPLE 7.16

If $y = (x^2 - 2x + 9)(6x + 3)$, what is $\dfrac{dy}{dx}$ at $x = 2$?

SOLUTION 7.16

84. Here, and in most functions that are of the form (polynomial) × (polynomial), we can just multiply them out and use the power rule, or we can use the formula

for the derivative of a product of functions. Either way, we end up with the same polynomial.

- Using the power rule: $y = (x^2 - 2x + 9)(6x + 3) = 6x^3 - 9x^2 + 48x + 27$ after combining like terms, so $\dfrac{dy}{dx} = 3(6)x^2 - 2(9)x + 48 = 18x^2 - 18x + 48$. Then at $x = 2$, $\dfrac{dy}{dx} = 18(2^2) - 18(2) + 48 = 84$.

- Using the derivative of a product, $f(x) = x^2 - 2x + 9$ so $f' = 2x - 2$ and $g(x) = 6x + 3$ so $g'(x) = 6$. Therefore, after a lot of multiplying and combining terms, $\dfrac{dy}{dx} = (6x + 3)(2x - 2) + (x^2 - 2x + 9)(6) = 18x^2 - 18x + 48$.

  Again, at $x = 2$, $\dfrac{dy}{dx} = (18)(2^2) - (18)(2) + 48 = 84$.

The choice of which method to use depends on the complexity of the problem. They both take a lot of math.

EXAMPLE 7.17

Use the quotient rule to differentiate $s = \dfrac{6}{\sqrt{t}}$ with respect to t. (This is the same function as in Example 7.13, but we'll do it by quotients here rather than powers.)

SOLUTION 7.17

For this problem, $f(t) = 6$, $f'(t) = 0$, $g(t) = t^{\frac{1}{2}}$, $g'(t) = \dfrac{1}{2}t^{\frac{1}{2}}$, so the quotient rule

gives us $s'(t) = \dfrac{(t^{\frac{1}{2}})0 - 6\left(\dfrac{1}{2}t^{-\frac{1}{2}}\right)}{(t^{\frac{1}{2}})^2} = -3\dfrac{t^{-\frac{1}{2}}}{t} = -3t^{-\frac{3}{2}}$, the same result as we had for

Solution 7.13.

7.2.6 The Chain Rule

The chain rule is used for differentiating composite functions, such as $f(g(x))$. Both $f(x)$ and $g(x)$ must be differentiable to use the chain rule. This rule is also on the formula sheet on the Praxis pull-down formula menu, but you should know how to use it.

$$(f(g(x)))' = f'(g(x))g'(x)$$

EXAMPLE 7.18

Use the chain rule to differentiate $y = (3x - 2)^2$.

SOLUTION 7.18

$18x - 12$. In this problem, use $f(g(x))$ with $g(x) = 3x - 2$ and $f(x) = x^2$. Then $g'(x) = 3$ and $f'(x) = 2x$. Plug these values into the chain rule formula to get

$$\frac{d}{dx}(3x-1)^2 = 2(g(x)) \cdot g'(x) = 2(3x-2) \cdot 3 = (6x-4) \cdot 3 = 18x-12 \ .$$

If we were to just use algebra on the original function for Example 7.18, we would get $(3x - 2)^2 = 9x^2 - 12x + 4$, which differentiates as $\frac{d}{dx}(9x^2 - 12x + 4) = 18x - 12$. This method seems perhaps easier than the chain rule here, but it wouldn't be easier if the original function was $y = (2x^3 + 4x^2 - 3x + 5)^4$.

7.2.7 Derivatives of Trigonometric and Logarithmic Functions

In addition to the power rules and other rules for differentiation of functions, the derivatives of the basic trigonometric and logarithmic functions are useful. The following table shows the rules you are expected to know.

Function	Derivative
$f(x) = \sin x$	$f'(x) = \cos x$
$f(x) = \cos x$	$f'(x) = -\sin x$
$f(x) = e^x$	$f'(x) = e^x$
$f(x) = a^x$	$f'(x) = (\ln a)a^x$
$f(x) = \ln x$	$f'(x) = \frac{1}{x}$
$f(x) = \log_a x$	$f'(x) = \frac{1}{x(\ln a)}$

The derivatives of other trigonometric functions can be found from those for sine and cosine by using trig identities and the quotient rule.

EXAMPLE 7.19

If $y = \dfrac{1}{\ln x}$, what is $\dfrac{dy}{dx}$?

SOLUTION 7.19

$-\dfrac{1}{x(\ln x)^2}$. Here, $f(x) = 1$ and $g(x) = \ln x$, so $f'(x) = 0$ and $g'(x) = \dfrac{1}{x}$. Then

$$\frac{dy}{dx} = \frac{\ln x \cdot (0) - 1 \cdot \frac{1}{x}}{(\ln x)^2} = -\frac{1}{x(\ln x)^2} \ .$$

EXAMPLE 7.20

If $f(x) = \sin^3 5x$, find $f'(x)$.

SOLUTION 7.20

$15 \sin^2 5x \cos 5x$. Rewrite this problem as $f(x) = (\sin 5x)^3$ and use the chain rule twice: $(f(g(x)))' = f'(g(x))(g'(x)) = f'[g(h(x))][g'(h(x))(h'(x))]$, where $f(x) = g(x)^3$, $g(x) = \sin h(x)$, and $h(x) = 5x$. Then $f'(x) = 3(\sin(5x))^2 (\cos(5x))(5) = 15 \sin^2 5x \cos 5x$.

7.2.8 Differentiability

Since derivatives mean slopes, the derivative of a function at a point implies a smooth curve so the slope at that point exists. The slope at either side of that point must be the same, which is another way of saying the derivative at that point as approached from the left and from the right are the same. If this isn't true, the function is not differentiable at that point.

If a function is differentiable at a point, it is continuous there as well. Keep in mind here that we are talking about a specific region of a function, such as the region in the vicinity of point a. We aren't talking about the entire function because we frankly don't care what happens outside of the region right around our point.

Let's review here the definition of **continuity**: A function $f(x)$ is continuous at point a if $\lim_{x \to a} f(x)$ exists (which means it exists from the left and from the right) and is equal to $f(a)$. The simple way to think of continuity is that if you were to trace the graph of a continuous function, you would never have to lift your pencil. So it is easy to see that all smooth functions (no gaps, no asymptotes, no cusps) are continuous. But what about those exceptions? Obviously, a gap or an asymptote would cause you to lift your pencil, so the function is discontinuous at that point. A corner or cusp, on the other hand, can be traced without lifting your pencil, so the function is continuous at a corner or cusp. But they are sharp points in the graph, and the function is not differentiable at that point, which can be seen in the graphs of functions with a cusp and a corner shown below.

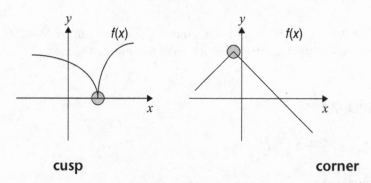

cusp   corner

The important conclusion here is that

- all differentiable functions are continuous,

but

- not all continuous functions are differentiable.

7.2.9 Meaning of Derivatives

The derivatives discussed in the sections above are **first derivatives** (thus, only one "prime" in $f'(x)$). What about a **second derivative**? Of course there is a second derivative, and it is denoted as $f''(x)$. It is obtained by taking the derivative of the first derivative. Therefore, the derivatives of $f(x) = 3x^2 + 2x + 1$ are $f'(x) = 6x + 2$ and $f''(x) = 6$. But what do these derivatives mean?

7.2.9a First Derivative

We saw that for any function, the first derivative gives us the instantaneous rate of change of the function, which is the slope of the tangent line to any point on the graph of the function, or essentially the slope of the function at a specific point.

Essentially, it tells whether the graph of $f(x)$ is increasing at that point and by how much. In summary,

- If $f'(a) > 0$, the graph is increasing at $x = a$.

- If $f'(a) < 0$, the graph is decreasing at $x = a$.

- If $f'(a) = 0$, the graph is parallel to the x-axis at a or the slope of the graph is changing sign at a, which means there is a smooth critical point (maximum or minimum) at a.

- If f is continuous at a and $f'(a)$ is indeterminate (e.g., the denominator is 0), the graph has a cusp at a, which can also be a critical point.

Critical points are points on the graph of the function where the curve changes direction and an extremum (a maximum or a minimum) could possibly occur, as shown in the figure below.

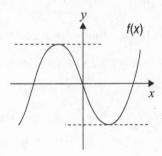

7.2.9b Second Derivative

1. The second derivative, denoted by $f''(x)$ or $\dfrac{d^2}{dx^2} f(x)$, then, should give us the slope of the slope. Right? Technically, that is true, but the slope of the slope actually tells the shape of the curve, whether it is curving upward or curving downward. In other words, the first derivative tells us whether the function is increasing or decreasing, and the second derivative tells us whether the slope is increasing or decreasing, which tells whether the shape of the curve at that point is concave up (like a parabola open upward) or concave down (like a parabola open downward), or maybe (if $f''(a) = 0$), the graph has a point of inflection. A point of inflection is a point at which the curvature of the graph changes from positive to negative or negative to positive, as shown in the figure below. Another way to look at it is as the point where a curve changes from concave up to concave down or vice versa.

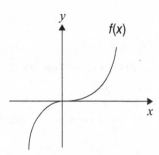

- If $f''(x) > 0$ at $x = a$, then $f(x)$ is concave up at $x = a$. If, in addition, $f'(a) = 0$, then $f(a)$ is a local minimum value.

- If $f''(x) < 0$ at $x = a$, then $f(x)$ is concave down at $x = a$. If, in addition, $f'(a) = 0$, then $f(a)$ is a local maximum value.

- If $f''(x) = 0$ at $x = a$, then we possibly have a point of inflection of $f(x)$ at a.

Let's consider $f(x) = 3x$, which is simply the graph of a line with a slope of 3. We find that $f'(x) = 3$, which just confirms that the instantaneous rate of change at any point is 3. Now let's look at $f''(x) = 0$, which means that there is no change in the first derivative. This is no surprise because the slope of any line is constant.

Now suppose that $g(x) = x^2 - x$. If we want to determine the values of x for which the tangent line has a positive slope, we only need to solve $g'(x) = 2x - 1 > 0$. This leads to $x > \dfrac{1}{2}$, which means that the tangent line has a positive slope for all x values greater than $\dfrac{1}{2}$. With a similar argument, we can show that the tangent line has a negative slope for $x < \dfrac{1}{2}$. Also, since $g'\left(\dfrac{1}{2}\right) = 2\left(\dfrac{1}{2}\right) - 1 = 0$, we know that a critical point exists for $x = \dfrac{1}{2}$, as seen in the following graph.

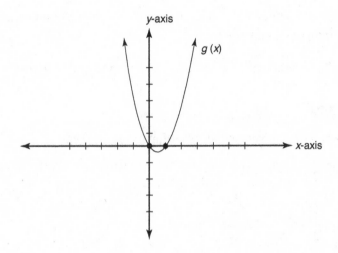

This graph immediately tells us that if we were to choose a point whose x value is less than $\frac{1}{2}$, the slope of the tangent line would be negative. By choosing a value of x greater than $\frac{1}{2}$, the tangent line has a positive slope.

To understand the second derivative, $g''(x)$, let's consider any two values of x. For $x = -3$, $g'(-3) = (2)(-3) - 1 = -7$; for $x = 0$, $g'(0) = -1$. Bearing in mind that the second derivative measures the change in the first derivative, we can see that $g'(0)$ is actually greater than $g'(-3)$. So, as x increases by three units, from -3 to 0, $g'(x)$ increases by six units, from -7 to -1. This implies that for $x = -3$, $g''(x)$ is actually positive. In fact, since $g'(x) = 2x - 1$, it follows that $g''(x) = 2$. This statement tells us that for $g(x) = x^2 - x$, the second derivative is always the positive number 2.

EXAMPLE 7.21

If $f(x) = 2x^3 + x^2 - 4x + 2$, find $f'(x)$ and $f''(x)$.

SOLUTION 7.21

Using the power rule, we get

$$f(x) = 2x^3 + x^2 - 4x + 2$$

$$f'(x) = 6x^2 + 2x - 4$$

$$f''(x) = 12x + 2$$

7.2.10 Graphing the Derivative Function

The graph of $f'(x)$ provides information about the original function $f(x)$. Consider the following two basic facts about the first derivative of a function $f(x)$:

1. The value of $f'(x)$ at $x = a$, $f'(a)$, is the slope of the tangent to the graph of the function at point a.

2. $f'(x)$ is also a function of x, which means the slope at a point on the graph depends on the x-coordinate of that point.

Example 7.22 shows how to sketch the graph of $f'(x)$ from the graph of $f(x)$.

EXAMPLE 7.22

Sketch the graph of $f'(x)$ given the following graph of $f(x)$.

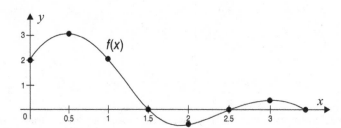

SOLUTION 7.22

Let's get as much information about $f'(x)$ as we can from the slope of $f(x)$. We set up a table to keep track of the information. We are interested here in the intervals where the slope changes.

$f(x)$	Interval	$f'(x)$
increasing	$x = (0, 0.5)$	positive
maximum	$x = 0.5$	0
decreasing	$x = (0.5, 2)$	negative
minimum	$x = 2$	0
increasing	$x = (2, 3)$	positive

So a rough sketch of $f'(x)$ will have the following summary: It is positive from $x = 0$ to 0.5, equal to 0 at $x = 0.5$, is negative from $x = 0.5$ to 2, equal to 0 at $x = 2$, and positive from $x = 2$ to 3. Here, where we are talking about positive and negative for $f'(x)$, this means above or below the x-axis, respectively, in a graph of $f'(x)$ versus x. Since we don't have the actual function for $f(x)$, we can just give it an educated guess as to what the values of the slope $f'(x)$ can be from the graph of $f(x)$. We know that the graph of $f'(x)$ changes direction somewhere between $x = 0$ and $x = 0.5$, between $x = 0.5$ and $x = 2$, and between $x = 2$ and $x = 3$. So a first sketch of $f'(x)$ would look like the following graph. The actual "turning points" for this graph would be found at the points for which $f'(x) = 0$, which indicate where the slope $f'(x)$ changes direction and will give more definition to the graph of the function.

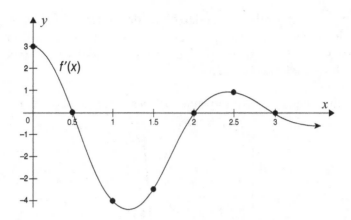

 The critical points in the graph of $f(x)$ correspond to $x = 0$ in the graph of $f'(x)$.

$\rightarrow$ Imp.

7.2.11 Using Derivatives to Solve Problems

On a position-time graph (also called a displacement-time graph):

- Positive slope implies motion in the positive direction.

- Negative slope implies motion in the negative direction.

- Zero slope implies a state of rest.

Rev.

- Average velocity is the slope of the straight line connecting the endpoints of the position-time curve.

- Instantaneous velocity is the slope of the line tangent to the position-time curve at any point.

- Acceleration is the slope of the velocity-time curve.

7.2.11a Position, Velocity, and Acceleration Problems

Let's look at an equation for the position of a particle as a function of time,

$$s(t) = t^3 - 8t^2 + 10t.$$

The equation for the velocity is given by the first derivative of the position function:

$$v(t) = s'(t) = 3t^2 - 16t + 10$$

and the equation for acceleration is given by the second derivative of the position function:

$$a(t) = s''(t) = 6t - 16.$$

Speed is velocity without regard to direction. The speedometer in a car shows speed, not velocity, as it says "50 mph," but not "50 mph northward." Movement backwards at 10 mph involves a speed of 10 mph but a velocity of –10 mph. Here the sign of the velocity indicates its direction.

The graphs of these three equations are shown below as a screen shot of the online calculator.

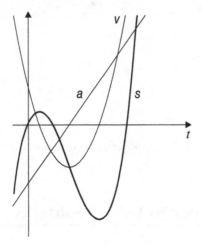

Let's assume the position is in centimeters (cm) and time is in seconds (sec). Note that we are looking at a small part of a large graph. At $t = 0$ sec (along the vertical axis), the position of the particle is $s(0) = 0$ cm, the velocity of the particle is $(v) = 10$ cm/sec, and the acceleration of the particle is $(a) = -16$ cm/sec^2.

Note the following attributes of these curves:

- *Position function* (thick solid curve): The curve for the position function crosses the *x*-axis at three points, which is to be expected since the highest power in the equation is t^3. The graph of $s(t)$ goes to ∞ as $t \to ∞$. If $s(t)$ is positive the particle is situated toward the direction that is designated as positive; here, of course, that is anything above the horizontal (*t*)-axis. Negative values of $s(t)$ indicate the opposite direction.

Hint: In dealing with position, it is important to make a distinction between position and distance (which is difference in position). This is easily visualized by this simple scenario: Let's say you leave your house to go to the gym, which is 2 miles away, and then you return home. When you return home, what distance did you travel? Easy, 4 miles. But what is your position compared to when you started? Also easy, 0 miles.

- *Velocity function* (thin solid curve): This curve is a parabola. In the part of the graph we are concerned with ($t \geq 0$), the particle is already slowing down and eventually it will reach a minimum negative velocity at its vertex, at about $t = -2.6$ sec and then speed up again. A positive velocity indicates the particle is traveling in the positive direction and a negative velocity indicates that the particle is traveling in the opposite direction. Note that when the velocity is zero, the position curve changes direction.

 Although velocity is a parabola and acceleration is a line in this situation, that is not always the case for other situations.

- *Acceleration function* (straight line): For this example, the acceleration is a straight line, which means the velocity changes with time at a constant rate. When acceleration is zero, the velocity changes direction. The positive slope of the acceleration line indicates that acceleration is increasing with time.

 Positive acceleration is called acceleration, and "negative acceleration" is actually called deceleration, such as when you put your foot on a brake.

In general, we can imply the following information when looking at a position-time graph (without velocity or acceleration graphed):

- If the position function is a straight line the velocity is constant (neither increasing nor decreasing) and the acceleration is zero. This makes sense because a straight line has a constant slope, and if the velocity is constant, there is no acceleration to change it.

- If the position function is a portion of a parabola, then the velocity is a straight line whose slope tells whether the velocity is constantly increasing (positive slope) or decreasing (negative slope). A velocity with a constant slope implies constant acceleration.

- If the position function is a curved line other than a parabola, the velocity will change direction, which implies varying acceleration.

EXAMPLE 7.23

If a position function is given as $s(t) = 4t^2 - 3t + 5$, what are the position, velocity, and acceleration at time $t = 2$ seconds?

SOLUTION 7.23

$s = 15$, $v = 13$, and $a = 8$. To find the answer for position, just plug $t = 2$ into the position equation:

$$s(2) = 4(2)^2 - 3(2) + 5 = 16 - 6 + 5 = 15$$

To find the velocity, differentiate the position function and plug $t = 2$ into the resulting velocity equation:

$$v(t) = s'(t) = 8t - 3, \text{ so } v(2) = 8(2) - 3 = 16 - 3 = 13$$

To find the acceleration, take the second derivative of the position function or the first derivative of the velocity function and plug $t = 2$ into the resulting acceleration equation:

$$a(t) = v'(t) = 8$$

The acceleration in Example 7.23 is constant, as it is for any parabolic position function.

EXAMPLE 7.24

What is the velocity of a particle whose position function is $s(t) = 2t^3 - 12t^2 + 20t$ when the acceleration is zero?

SOLUTION 7.24

–4. This is a little more involved than Example 7.23. When acceleration is zero, $s''(t) = 0$. From the position function, find $s'(t) = 6t^2 - 24t + 20$ and $s''(t) = 12t - 24$. If acceleration is zero, then $12t - 24 = 0$ and $t = 2$. Then find the velocity at $t = 2$:

$$s'(2) = 6(4) - 24(2) + 20 = -4.$$

As another example of distance, let's look at the general physics equation for the position s of an object in free fall, such as dropping a ball from a height, such as a window:

$$s = \frac{1}{2}at^2 + v_0 t + s_0,$$

which has a lot of unknowns, but they all get simplified once we know what they mean. First, we will look at this scenario from a logical viewpoint. An object in free fall means only gravity is acting on the object—no friction, no air resistance, just free fall. The acceleration a in free fall is the acceleration due to gravity, which isn't an unknown here, it is constant at -32 ft/sec^2 (or -9.8 m/s^2). Time is represented by t, v_0 is the initial velocity (0 when you drop a ball with no force on it), and s_0 is the initial vertical position of the object (that is, height above the distance you want to measure). So the equation reduces to

$$s = -16t^2 + s_0$$

and we can see that if a ball is dropped from a 30-foot building, 1 second later it is at a height of 14 feet from the ground. The math is $s = -16 \cdot (1)^2 + 30 = 14$ feet from the ground at 1 second.

Acceleration with a negative sign indicates a downward direction in free fall.

Now let's look at this free-fall problem from a calculus point of view, using derivatives to calculate instantaneous rates of change. Velocity is the instantaneous rate of change of position with respect to time (first derivative of the displacement equation), and acceleration is the instantaneous rate of change of velocity with respect to time (first derivative of the velocity equation, which is the same as the second derivative of the displacement equation). Using these ideas, we can analyze one-dimensional particle movement given position as a function of time. The original displacement equation is:

$$s = \frac{1}{2}at^2 + v_0 t + s_0,$$

where a is again the acceleration due to gravity, -32 ft/sec^2 or -9.8 m/s^2. The velocity at any time is

$$\frac{ds}{dt} = at + v_0.$$

The acceleration at any time is

$$\frac{d^2 s}{dt^2} = \frac{dv}{dt} = a$$

So at 1 second after letting go, the object has a velocity of $\frac{ds}{dt} = at + v_0 = -32(1) + 0 = -32$ ft/sec^2, at an acceleration of -32 ft/sec^2.

Imp.

The important lesson here is that no matter what the equation for the distance traveled, the velocity and acceleration at any time t can be calculated from the first and second derivatives of the displacement equation. So given an equation of $s = t^3 + 2t + 6$, we know the equation for the velocity at any time t is $v = \frac{ds}{dt} = 3t^2 + 2$, and the acceleration at any time t is $a = \frac{dv}{dt} = 6t$.

7.2.11b Optimization Problems

Imp.

Optimization focuses on maximizing or minimizing a particular quantity. Since this relates to maxima and minima, we use the first derivative of the appropriate function. Write the equation of interest as a function of one variable by using the given information, take the first derivative, and find the critical points by setting the first derivative equal to zero. Then take the second derivative (derivative of the first derivative), and if it is positive, the curve is concave up (basically ∪) so the point is a minimum; if it is negative, the curve is concave down (basically ∩) so the point is a maximum.

EXAMPLE 7.25

Find the smallest possible sum of the squares of two numbers if their product is -9.

SOLUTION 7.25

18. The given information is that we want the smallest value of $(x^2 + y^2)$ when we know that $xy = -9$. Solve this last equation for y and substitute it into the first equation and then take the first derivative of that equation:

$$y = \frac{-9}{x}$$

$$S = x^2 + \left(\frac{-9}{x}\right)^2 = x^2 + 81x^{-2}$$

$$S' = 2x - 162x^{-3}$$

Now set $S' = 0$ to get $2x = 162x^{-3} = 0$. Although $x = 0$ is a solution to this equation, it is not possible, given the problem (for example, the product must equal -9). To find other possible solutions, multiply both sides by x^3 and solve for x:

$$2x^4 = 162$$

$$x^4 = 81$$

$$x = \pm 3$$

Substitute $x = 3$ into the second derivative of S to check whether it is a maximum or minimum. Since $S' = 2x - 162x^{-3}$, the second derivative is $S'' = 2 + 3(162x^{-4})$, which is always positive, so it is concave up, and $x = 3$ is a minimum. The other number is $3y = -9$, $y = -3$, and the answer to the problem is $3^2 + (-3)^2 = 9 + 9 = 18$.

7.2.11c Related Rates Problems

As a general rule, **related rates** mean if z is related to y and y is related to x, then z is related to x by using the following first derivatives:

$$\frac{dz}{dx} = \left(\frac{dz}{dy}\right)\left(\frac{dy}{dx}\right)$$

In this sort of problem, the rate of change of one variable is given and you need to find the rate of change of another variable at a certain point in time. Before you start a related rates problem, determine which information is general and which is particular to the problem. **General information** is information that is always true and is usually contained in the text of the problem, and **particular information** is true only at the instant of the problem, usually contained in the final question. Particular information must be set aside and not be used until the very last step of solving the problem.

A frequently made mistake is to use the particular information too early, which invariably leads to incorrect answers. Wait until the last step of the problem to insert this information.

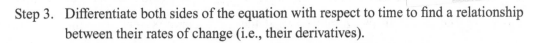

Use the following steps in related rates problems:

Step 1. Identify the known rate of change and the desired rate o
        problem.

Step 2. Use known values to relate the variable with the known rate
        able with the unknown rate of change.

Step 3. Differentiate both sides of the equation with respect to time to find a relationship
        between their rates of change (i.e., their derivatives).

Step 4. Use known geometric formulas or whatever pertains to the problem, and then use
        the chain rule, since we are taking derivatives with respect to t.

Step 5. Plug in the particular information to solve for the desired rate.

EXAMPLE 7.26

The radius of a spherical balloon is increasing at a rate of 4 inches per minute. At
what rate is the volume increasing when the radius is equal to 12 inches?

SOLUTION 7.26

The general information is that the radius is growing at the rate of 4 inches per
minute, or $\frac{dr}{dt} = \frac{4}{1}$. The particular information is "when the radius is equal to
12 inches," or $r = 12$. The known rate is $\frac{dr}{dt}$, and we want to find $\frac{dV}{dt}$, the rate of

change of the volume. The chain rule for this problem is $\frac{dV}{dt} = \left(\frac{dV}{dr}\right)\left(\frac{dr}{dt}\right)$. Since
this is a sphere, then $V = \frac{4}{3}\pi r^3$ (see Section 5.12.5b; this formula is also given on
the Praxis formula sheet), and thus $\frac{dV}{dr} = 4\pi r^2$. This is when we use the particular
information, that the radius is equal to 12 inches.

$$\frac{dV}{dr} = \left(\frac{dV}{dr}\right)\left(\frac{dr}{dt}\right) = (4\pi(12)^2)(4) = 2304\pi$$

So when the radius of the balloon is 12 inches, the volume is increasing at a rate of
2304π cubic inches per second.

7.3 INTEGRALS

An **antiderivative**, as the name implies, is a general function $F(x)$ of $f(x)$ if $F' = f(x)$. Determining an antiderivative (or **integral**, which is the more popular name for antiderivative) is the
reverse process of finding a derivative. In fact, integration and differentiation are inverse functions.

The symbol for an integral is $\int dx$, where the usual letter x can be replaced by any other letter, depending on the function. For example, if $s = f(t) = 16t^2 + 3t - 10$, the integral would be $\int f(t)\,dt$. It is important that the part of the function in question be continuous (see Section 7.1.2).

There are two types of integrals: indefinite integrals and definite integrals. Indefinite integrals have an algebraic interpretation, and definite integrals have a geometric application, which is the area under a curve. We define the definite integral $\int_{a}^{b} f(x)\,dx$ as the area between the function $f(x)$ and $x = a$ and $x = b$. In the graph below, if the given curve is $f(x)$, then the shaded region is $\int_{-1}^{4} f(x)\,dx$.

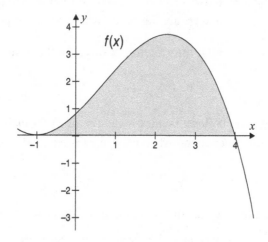

7.3.1 Mean Value Theorem for Integration

The **Mean Value Theorem for Integration** states:

For any continuous function $f(x)$ over the interval $[a, b]$,

there exists a c, $a \le c \le b$, for which $\int_{a}^{b} f(x)\,dx = f(c)(b - a)$.

This guarantees that there will be a value $x = c$ between a and b such that the area of the rectangle from a to b with height c equals the area between $f(x)$ and the x-axis between a and b. This theorem is the basis for approximation of integrals, the topic of Section 7.3.2.

As a consequence of the Mean Value Theorem, we can say the average, or mean, value of an integral of a function in a closed interval is $\dfrac{1}{b - a}\int_{a}^{b} f(x)\,dx$.

7.3.2 Approximation of Integrals

7.3.2a Riemann Sums and Accumulation

Among many other uses, integration can be used to find areas and volumes. Let's start with finding the **area under a curve** of a function such as the one shown below.

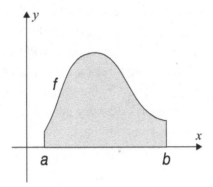

To find this area, one method, known as **Riemann sums**, divides that space into rectangles, finds the area of each rectangle by multiplying the value of width of each rectangle (Δx), by the height of the rectangle (using the value of x at the left side of Δx), and adds up all those rectangular areas. This method, which results in a rough estimate of the area under the curve, is sometimes referred to as an **accumulation**, and looks like the figure below.

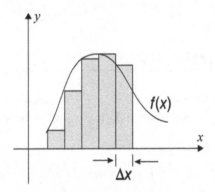

The accuracy of this accumulation could be improved by making the widths smaller, similar to what we did with derivatives when we calculated the limit as $\Delta x \to 0$. As the slices of area get smaller, the area gets closer to the true area, as shown by the figure below.

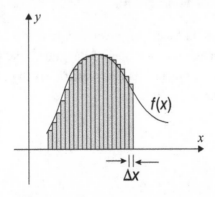

Integration is a method of adding these slices together because as the slices get narrower, the area approaches the true area under the curve. In other words, dx is the limit of each $\Delta x \to 0$.

7.3.2b Midpoint Rule and Trapezoid Rule

Similar to Riemann sums, the **midpoint rule** uses the midpoint of each rectangle rather than the left height when measuring the area of the rectangles under the curve. The result is very much like the figure above, especially as $\Delta x \to 0$. The **trapezoid rule** actually uses trapezoids rather than rectangles, but the idea is the same. On each subinterval of width Δx, a line is drawn between the places where the curve crosses the interval on the left and the right side, and this line forms a trapezoid. The area under the curve is approximated by the sum of the areas of these trapezoids. As can be seen in the figure below, some trapezoids do a very good job of approximating the actual area under the curve but others don't (see the area between x_5 and x_6).

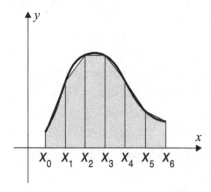

7.3.3 Indefinite Integrals

Finding the antiderivative is the same as asking, "Given the derivative of a function, what is the function?" Or said another way, "If we take the derivative of an antiderivative of a function, we get the function back again," or

$$\frac{d}{dx}\left[\int f(x)\,dx\right] = f(x).$$

Indefinite integrals are in the form $\int f(x)\,dx$ and do not have limits of integration.

7.3.3a Rules for Rational Functions

Luckily, the work to find certain functions, given the derivative, has been done by mathematicians and is available for everyone's use in tables of integrals. Five of the rules for rational functions, for example, are as follows, where k is a constant, e is the constant related to the natural logarithm ln, and n is an exponent.

Table 7.1. Differentiation and Integration Rules for Rational Functions

Function	Differentiation of the Function	Integration of the Function
kx^n	$\dfrac{d}{dx}kx^n = knx^{n-1}$	$\int kx^n \, dx = \dfrac{k}{n+1}x^{n+1} + C,$ provided that $n \neq -1$
ke^x	$\dfrac{d}{dx}ke^x = ke^x$	$\int ke^x \, dx = ke^2 + C$
$[f(x) \pm g(x)]$	$\dfrac{d}{dx}f(x) \pm \dfrac{d}{dx}g(x)$	$\int f(x)\,dx \pm \int g(x)\,dx + C$
$\sin x$	$\dfrac{d}{dx}\sin x = \cos x$	$\int \sin x \, dx = -\cos x + C$
$\cos x$	$\dfrac{d}{dx}\cos x = -\sin x$	$\int \cos x \, dx = \sin x + C$

All derivatives of trigonometric cofunctions are negative (e.g., $\dfrac{d}{dx}\cos x = -\sin x$) and all integrals of trigonometric non-cofunctions are negative (e.g., $\int \sin x \, dx = -\cos x + C$).

The constant C must be used in each of these indefinite integrals. For example, if $f'(x) = 6x$, which of the following functions could be $f(x)$? $f(x) = 3x^2$, $f(x) = 3x^2 - 10$, or $f(x) = 3x^2 + 4$? The answer is it could be any of the three choices because if we take the first derivative of any of them, we get $f'(x) = 6x$. So there could actually have been an infinite number of answers to finding the function for which $f'(x) = 6x$, and they would each differ from the others by the constant term in each. This constant is known as the **constant of integration**.

Likewise, when we find the integral $\int 6x\,dx$, we are looking for a function for which $f'(x) = 6x$. For an integral of this type, we use the integration rule $\int kx^n\,dx = \dfrac{k}{n+1}x^{n+1} + C$ (from Table 7.1) with $k = 6$ and $n = 1$, so $\int 6x\,dx = \dfrac{6}{1+1}x^{1+1}$ plus a constant, or $\int 6x\,dx = 3x^2 + C$. The value of C is determined by the context of the problem. These integrals are called **indefinite integrals** for that very reason—we cannot pin down a definite answer for what the function $f(x)$ is because the values of C might differ. An indefinite integral has no upper or lower limit. It gives a general result with a C term.

7.3.3b Integration by Parts

Integration by parts is the antiderivative of the product rule for differentiation $(f(x)g(x))' = f'(x)g(x) + f(x)g'(x)$, generally written using the notation for functions $u = f(x)$ and $v = g(x)$. The product rule for differentiation can be rewritten with u and v as

$$(uv)' = u'v + uv' = uv' + uv'$$

Integration by parts is a technique for expressing an integral in the form $\int d(uv)$ in terms of a known integral $\int v\,du$ by expanding the differential of a product of functions $d(uv)$. Integration by parts starts with a rewrite of the product rule above as

$$d(uv) = udv + vdu.$$

Integrating both sides, and remembering that $\int d(uv) = uv$,

$$\int d(uv) = uv = \int u\,dv + \int v\,du,$$

which can be rearranged to give the rule for integration by parts (which is on the formula sheet of the Praxis exam):

$$\int u\,dv = uv - \int v\,du$$

But we are still left with figuring out what type of integral has "parts" and how to determine which part is u and which part is dv. First of all, the integral has to have two functions multiplied together and the variable of integration has to be the variable in each function.

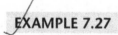

EXAMPLE 7.27

Find $\int x\cos x\,dx$.

SOLUTION 7.27

$x \sin x + \cos x + C$. Use integration by parts with $u = x$ and $dv = \cos x dx$. Now find du, the derivative of u, which is dx, and find v by integrating dv. Here, $v = \int dv = \int \cos x\,dx = \sin x$. Finally, substitute the equivalents $u\,(= x)$, $v\,(= \sin x)$, and $du\,(= dx)$ into the formula for integration by parts:

$$\int u\,dv = uv - \int v\,du = x\sin x - \int \sin x\,dx = x\sin x + \cos x + C$$

The most difficult part of integration by parts is determining what u and dv should be. The formula for integration by parts is on the sheet in the Praxis exam, so the rest is substitution and a bit of simple integration.

Integration by parts does not always succeed because some choices of u may lead to more complicated integrals than the original. If u and v aren't simple functions, don't use integration by parts.

7.3.4 Definite Integrals

A **definite integral** has an upper and lower limit and graphically represents the area between a function curve and the x-axis between the upper and lower limit in two dimensions. Evaluating definite integrals usually requires a little bit more work than just finding the general antiderivative (or indefinite integral) of a function. It also involves evaluating the integral at the upper limit and subtracting the value at the lower limit.

One part of the **Fundamental Theorem of Calculus** states:

If $F(x)$ is any antiderivative of $f(x)$, where $f(x)$ is continuous on the closed interval $[a, b]$,

then $\displaystyle\int_a^b f(x)\,dx = F(b) - F(a)$.

This is the definition of the definite integral.

 The evaluation of the definite integral is the same as for indefinite integrals, and when the subtracting is done, the C values disappear.

The first two of the following properties of definite integrals come from the corresponding properties for indefinite integrals. Functions f and g are continuous on $[a, c]$, point b is any point within $[a, c]$, and k is a constant. The last three properties come from the Fundamental Theorem of Calculus.

1. The definite integral of a function multiplied by a constant equals the constant multiplied by the definite integral of the function:

$$\int_a^b kf(x)\,dx = k\int_a^b f(x)\,dx$$

2. The definite integral of the sum or difference of functions equals the sum or difference of the definite integrals of the functions:

$$\int_a^b [f(x) \pm g(x)]\,dx = \int_a^b f(x)\,dx \pm \int_a^b g(x)\,dx$$

3. The definite integral in the interval $[a, a]$ is zero because there is no change in x:

$$\int_a^a f(x)\,dx = 0$$

4. If the limits of integration are switched, the value of the definite integral changes sign:

$$\int_{b}^{a} f(x)\,dx = -\int_{a}^{b} f(x)\,dx$$

5. The definite integral between two points on an interval $[a, c]$ can be calculated as the sum of the definite integrals on the intervals $[a, b]$ and $[b, c]$:

$$\int_{a}^{c} f(x)\,dx = \int_{a}^{b} f(x)\,dx + \int_{b}^{c} f(x)\,dx$$

7.3.5 The Definite Integral as the Area under a Curve

As stated previously, the definite integral represents the area between a function curve and the x-axis between an upper and lower limit. A simple example of this fact for a "curve" that is actually a straight line is shown in Example 7.28.

EXAMPLE 7.28

Find the area under line $y = 2x$ between $x = 1$ and $x = 3$.

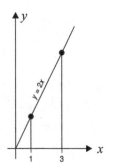

SOLUTION 7.28

The definite integral for this problem is $\int_{1}^{3} 2x\,dx$. The area is found by evaluating the definite integral $\int 2x\,dx = x^2$ at $x = 3$ and at $x = 1$ and subtracting: $F(3) = 3^2 = 9$, and $F(1) = 1^2 = 1$, so

$$\int_{1}^{3} 2x\,dx = x^2 \Big|_{1}^{3} = 9 - 1 = 8.$$

The notation $F(x)\Big|_{a}^{b}$ is shorthand that indicates evaluating $F(x)$ at the endpoints a and b.

Rev. V. Imp.

EXAMPLE 7.29

Find the total area between the function $f(x) = \sin x$ and the x-axis bounded by $x = \dfrac{\pi}{2}$ and $x = 2\pi$.

SOLUTION 7.29

3. Sketch the associated diagram as shown below.

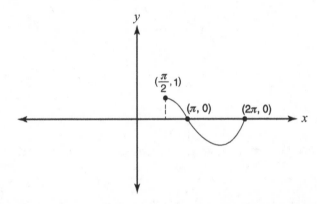

Evaluate the areas above the axis and below the axis separately. Since we are evaluating the areas, and areas are positive, we are evaluating the absolute values and adding them.

$$\text{Area} = \left| \int_{\frac{\pi}{2}}^{\pi} \sin x \, dx \right| + \left| \int_{\pi}^{2\pi} \sin x \, dx \right| = \left| \cos \pi - \cos \frac{\pi}{2} \right| + \left| \cos 2\pi - \cos \pi \right|$$

$$= \left| -1 - 0 \right| + \left| 1 - (-1) \right| = 1 + 2 = 3.$$

Finding the area is different from finding the "value" of a definite integral. The value of the definite integral of a function that crosses the x-axis is the net value of the areas above and below the x-axis, where a minus sign for the area just tells us that the area is below the x-axis.

Imp.

For Example 7.29, although the area is 3, the *value* is

$$\text{Value} = \int_{\frac{\pi}{2}}^{2\pi} \sin x \, dx = -\cos x \Big|_{\frac{\pi}{2}}^{2\pi} = -\cos 2\pi - \left(-\cos \frac{\pi}{2} \right) = 0 - 1 = -1.$$

The minus sign in the value of the definite integral tells us that there is more area below the x-axis than above it.

EXAMPLE 7.30

Find the area of the cosine curve between $\dfrac{\pi}{2}$ and π.

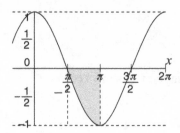

SOLUTION 7.30

The definite integral for this area is

$$A = \int_{\frac{\pi}{2}}^{\pi} \cos(x)\,dx = \sin x \Big|_{\frac{\pi}{2}}^{\pi} = \sin \pi - \sin \frac{\pi}{2} = 0 - 1 = -1.$$

The value of the definite integral is -1, but the area is actually $|-1| = 1$ square unit.

In summary, the value of the definite integral is positive if the curve is above the x-axis (for positive values of $f(x)$, or y), and the value of the definite integral is negative if the curve is below the x-axis (for negative values of $f(x)$, or y), so we must find the value(s) of x at which the function $f(x) = 0$, which determines the value(s) at which $f(x)$ changes sign. Then add the absolute values of the definite integrals for each part of the curve.

NOTE

Draw a sketch of the curve for the required range of x-values to see how many separate calculations will be needed. Then calculate the area between the curve and the x-axis, by calculating the parts of the curve above the axis separately from the parts of the curve below the axis. The integral for any part of a curve below the axis gives minus the area for that part.

The same concept would be used to find total distance.

V. V. Imp.

In summary, to find the area between a function and the x-axis between two x-values, follow these steps:

1. Make a sketch of the function between the two values of x, which is very helpful.

2. Find the zeros of the function (where $f(x) = 0$) to see where the function changes from positive (above the x-axis) to negative (below the x-axis) or vice versa. This will create distinct sections of the graph, each totally above or below the x-axis.

3. Find the area of any section by calculating the definite integral of the absolute value of the function between the two boundary points. Your answer will be positive.

4. Sum these areas.

Rev **EXAMPLE 7.31** → *Check the word &
its~~the~~ meaning in the context.*

Find the value of the graph of $f(x) = -x^2 + 4$ between $x = -5$ and $x = +2$.

SOLUTION 7.31

27. First, sketch the function. Set the function equal to 0 to find where the function crosses the x-axis: $-x^2 + 4 = 0$, so $x = \pm 2$. The critical values of the function are the points where the derivative (or slope) equals 0, or $-2x = 0$, which occurs at $x = 0$. The value of y at that point is (putting $x = 0$), $f(x) = -(0)^2 + 4 = 4$. So the sketch of the function is:

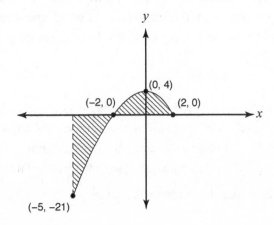

This sketch shows two areas: the area between $x = -5$ and $x = -2$, and the area between $x = -2$ and $x = +2$. According to the fifth property of definite integrals, which says $\left| \int_a^c f(x)\,dx \right| = \left| \int_a^b f(x)\,dx \right| + \left| \int_b^c f(x)\,dx \right|$, we have

$$\left| \int_{-5}^{2} (-x^2 + 4)\,dx \right| = \left| \int_{-5}^{-2} (-x^2 + 4)\,dx \right| + \left| \int_{-2}^{2} (-x^2 + 4)\,dx \right| = \left| -\frac{1}{3}x^3 + 4x \right|_{-5}^{-2} + \left| -\frac{1}{3}x^3 + 4x \right|_{-2}^{2}$$

$$= \left| \left(\frac{8}{3} - 8 \right) - \left(\frac{125}{3} - 20 \right) \right| + \left| \left(-\frac{8}{3} + 8 \right) - \left(\frac{8}{3} - 8 \right) \right| = \left| -\frac{117}{3} + 12 \right| + \left| -\frac{16}{3} + 16 \right|$$

$$= |-27| + \left| \frac{-32}{3} \right| = 27 + \frac{32}{3} = \frac{113}{3}$$

So the combined area of the function $f(x) = -x^2 + 4$ between $x = -5$ and $x = +2$ is $\frac{113}{3}$.

Note, however, that the value of the definite integral is

$$\int_{-5}^{2} (-x^2 + 4)\,dx = \int_{-5}^{-2} (-x^2 + 4)\,dx + \int_{-2}^{2} (-x^2 + 4)\,dx = \left[-\frac{1}{3}x^3 + 4x \right]_{-5}^{-2} + \left[-\frac{1}{3}x^3 + 4x \right]_{-2}^{2}$$

$$= \left[\left(\frac{8}{3} - 8 \right) - \left(\frac{125}{3} - 20 \right) \right] + \left[\left(-\frac{8}{3} + 8 \right) - \left(\frac{8}{3} - 8 \right) \right] = -\frac{81}{3} + \frac{32}{3} = -\frac{49}{3} = -16\frac{1}{3}$$

7.3.6 Position, Velocity, and Acceleration

Section 7.2, which discussed differentiation, showed that when the equation for position as a function of time is $s(t)$, the equation for the velocity is given by the first derivative, $v(t) = s'(t)$, and the equation for acceleration is given by the second derivative, $a(t) = s''(t)$. Acceleration is therefore also the first derivative of velocity, $a(t) = v'(t)$. Now let's look at this scenario from the viewpoint of integration.

Let's look at the position formula $s(t) = 2t^3 - 6t^2 + 6t$. Every point on the graph of this function gives a position at a particular time. We can differentiate to get velocity and acceleration, but what if all we are given is acceleration, can we get velocity? Yes, we can use the antiderivative, or integral, and work the other way around: The integral of the acceleration function gives the velocity function, and the integral of the velocity function gives the position function.

EXAMPLE 7.32

A police officer arrives on the scene of a one-vehicle auto accident. The only information that she has is the 200-foot skid marks on the road before the car hit the barricade. Weather doesn't seem to be a factor. Can she figure out how fast the car was going before the driver hit the brakes? If so, what was it if the standard braking deceleration used by police departments is $-16\dfrac{\text{ft}}{\text{sec}^2}$?

SOLUTION 7.32

80 mph. Let's let the time be $t = 0$ at the time of braking, and $t = n$ seconds at the point of impact. We know that $v(n) = 0$ at the point of impact because the car certainly was stopped, and we know that $s(n) = 200$ feet. Now, working backward from the acceleration of -16, we can write the velocity function as the antiderivative of acceleration, and we use the indefinite integral because we don't know what n, the time of impact, is yet.

$$v(t) = \int a(t)\,dt = \int (-16\,dt) = -16t + C$$

There were two forces on the car at the moment of impact: the velocity due to the deceleration of the brakes and the velocity due to the forward motion of the car, so C is a constant due to the speed of the car.

Now, let's write the position function as the antiderivative of the velocity,

$$s(t) = \int v(t)\,dt = \int (-16 + C)\,dt = -\frac{16t^2}{2} + Ct + D = 8t^2 + Ct + D$$

At this point, we have two constants of integration, C from the velocity integration and D from the position integration. However, our starting point has $s(0) = 0$ at $t(0) = 0$, so we can substitute those values into the equation for position, and we have $s(0) = 8(0)^2 + C(0) + D$, which gives us $D = 0$.

Now let's evaluate the functions at the point of impact, $t = n$. We know that $v(n) = 0$, so let's substitute these values into $v(t) = -16n + C$ to get

$$v(n) = -16n + C = 0, \text{ or } C = 16n.$$

Likewise, using $s(t) = 8t^2 + Ct$ at $t = n$, $s(n) = 200$, we get

$$s(n) = -8n^2 + (16n)n = 200, \text{ or}$$

$$-8n^2 + 16n^2 = 8n^2 = 200$$

$$n^2 = 25$$

$$n = 5.$$

So it took 5 seconds for the car to stop, and since $C = 16n$, the car was traveling at 80 mph.

Police departments have a simple table that uses the industry standard of -16 ft/sec^2 as deceleration due to braking to tell car speed versus skid mark length. Therefore, police officers don't have to use a càlculator to find whether the driver was speeding.

7.3.7 Using Integrals for Volume

7.3.7a Cross-Section Method

One of the methods of using integrals to find volume simply extends the method of using integrals to find area by adding a third dimension (depth). This can be done by using a cross-section along one of the axes (usually the z-axis) or by rotating the area around the x-axis or y-axis. So we are extending the accumulation process to three dimensions.

This approach is similar to the one used to find the area under a curve by combining areas of small widths Δx over the interval of interest (see Section 7.3.2). As $\Delta x \to 0$ the sum of all these areas approaches the area under a smooth curve.

For the cross-section method, the solid is a three-dimensional solid that has a two-dimensional area as the base, a three-dimensional surface above it, and the cross-sections of the solid are perpendicular to the base. In the next figure, the base is the quadrilateral and the distance from the base to the surface above it varies with distance from the axes. The volume of such a solid requires a double integral—one to find the area under the curve at any "slice" and another to find the volume of these slices by multiplying each slice by the infinitesimal width of the slice, similar to the accumulation method used in two dimensions.

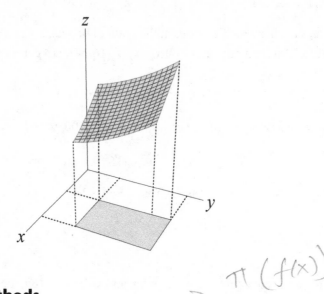

$\pi \left(f(x)\right)^2$

7.3.7b Rotation Methods

Here base is of the new fig. obtained

Other methods to find volume, such as the disk or washer method, use rotation of an area about a line, which can be an axis or, in fact, any straight line in the x-y plane. Since volume is basically the area of the base times the height, we can approximate the volume of the solid by adding the small volumes of disks that are the products of each small slice times the circular area bounded by the curve of the solid at that point, with $A = \pi r^2$, and r determined by the figure.

Imp.

If the rotation is around a horizontal line, the integral will use dx, the limits of integration are x values, and all variables are changed to x; if the rotation is around a vertical line, the integral will use dy, the limits of integration are y values, and all variables are changed to y.

Let's look at a few examples to show how this works.

EXAMPLE 7.33

What is the volume of the figure produced by a rectangular region in the first quadrant bounded by $x = 0$, $x = 4$, $y = 0$, and $y = 6$?

SOLUTION 7.33

The area of the rectangle of width 4 and height 6 is 24 square units. If we will rotate this rectangle around the y-axis, the resulting volume is a right circular cylinder of radius 4 (because the center is the y-axis) and height 6.

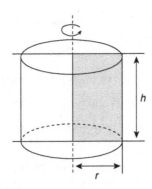

By integration, since the area of the base is the area of the circle formed by the rotation of the rectangle of side 4, or $A = \pi r^2 = 16\pi$,

$$V = \int_{y=0}^{y=6} 16\pi y \, dy = 16\pi y \Big|_{y=0}^{y=6} = 16\pi(6) - 16\pi(0) = 96\pi$$

Let's compare the volume by integration to the volume using the equation for the volume of a right rectangular cylinder given in Section 5.12.2b as $V = \pi r^2 h = \pi(4)^2(6) = 96\pi$. True, in this case go right to the volume found by the formula, but not all shapes will be as regular as a rectangle. Or even a triangle—can you envision that the rotation around the y-axis of a right triangle with one leg along the y-axis would form a cone?

Let's look now at a not-so-simple shape rotated around the x-axis.

EXAMPLE 7.34

What is the shape and volume of the solid formed by rotating the curve $y = e^x$ around the x-axis between $x = -1$ and $x = 1$?

SOLUTION 7.34

$\dfrac{\pi(e^4 - 1)}{2e^2}$. The y value of each "slice" for integration is $r(x) = e^x$, as seen in the figure below.

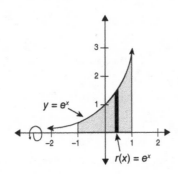

Since the cross-sectional area is the area formed by rotating $y = e^x$ around the x-axis between $x = -1$, and $x = 1$, the integral of rotation is $\pi \int_{-1}^{1} (e^x)^2 \, dx = \pi \int_{-1}^{1} e^{2x} \, dx$. We don't know right away what $\int e^{2x} \, dx$ is, but we do know that $\int e^u \, du = e^u$, so let's just make $u = 2x$ (in which case $du = 2dx$) and plug these back into the first integral to get $\pi \int_{-1}^{1} e^{2x} \, dx = \frac{\pi}{2} \pi \int_{-2}^{2} e^u \, du = \frac{\pi}{2} e^u \Big|_{-2}^{2}$. (Notice that the limits of integration also change to $u = 2x$.) The answer is thus $\frac{\pi}{2} e^u \Big|_{-2}^{2} = \frac{\pi}{2}(e^2 - e^{-2}) = \frac{\pi}{2}\left(e^2 - \frac{1}{e^2}\right) = \frac{\pi(e^4 - 1)}{2e^2}$.

The rotation of the curve for $y = e^x$ looks like the figure below.

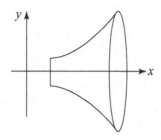

Practice Exercises

1. If $f(x)$ and $g(x)$ are continuous functions for all real numbers and some of their values are defined by the following table, evaluate $\lim_{x \to -1}(f(x) + 2g(x))$.

x	$f(x)$	$g(x)$
-1	5	-7
0	-3	1
1	-1	3
2	0	-4

(A) -2

(B) -3

(C) -9

(D) 19

2. Evaluate $\lim_{x \to 2} f(x)$ for the piecewise function

$$f(x) = \begin{cases} 8, & x \le 1 \\ 4 - x^3, & -1 < x < 2 \\ 6 - 5x, & x \ge 2 \end{cases}$$

(A) -4

(B) 4

(C) 2

(D) The limit doesn't exist for this piecewise function.

3. Evaluate $\lim_{x \to 4} \left(\dfrac{2x^2 + 7x + 6}{x + 2} + \dfrac{2x + 7}{x - 2} \right)$.

(A) $16\dfrac{1}{2}$

(B) $18\dfrac{1}{2}$

(C) 11

(D) $\dfrac{15}{2}$

Rav

4. If $y = \dfrac{1}{\sqrt[3]{t}}$, what is $\dfrac{dy}{dt}$ in rational form?

(A) It cannot be rationalized

(B) $t^{-\frac{1}{3}}$

(C) $-\dfrac{1}{3} t^{-\frac{4}{3}}$

(D) $\dfrac{\sqrt[3]{t^2}}{3t^2}$

5. Find $\dfrac{dy}{dx}$ for the equation $xy = x^2 y^2 + \cos y$.

(A) $\dfrac{2xy^2 - y}{x - 2x^2 y + \sin y}$

(B) $\dfrac{2xy^2 + y}{x - 2x^2 y + \sin y}$

(C) $2xy^2 - y$

(D) $2xy^2 + y$

6. Let $s = t^3 - 6t^2$ be the position function of a particle, where t is in seconds and s is in feet. What are the particle's velocity and acceleration at 1 second?

    (A) $v(t) = -6$ ft/sec and $a(t) = -9$ ft/sec²

    (B) $v(t) = 9$ ft/sec and $a(t) = -6$ ft/sec²

    (C) $v(t) = -9$ ft/sec and $a(t) = -6$ ft/sec²

    (D) $v(t) = -9$ ft/sec and $a(t) = 6$ ft/sec²

7. What is the average value of $f(x) = x^2$ between $x = 0$ and $x = 4$?   — *Not under.*

    (A) 4

    (B) $\dfrac{8}{3}$

    (C) 16

    (D) $\dfrac{16}{3}$

8. What is the volume of a solid formed by rotating a right triangle around the y-axis with a 4-unit leg along the x-axis and a 3-unit leg along the y-axis?

    (A) 16π

    (B) $\dfrac{16}{3}$

    (C) $\dfrac{4}{9}\pi$

    (D) 9π

9. Is the piecewise function $g(x) = \begin{cases} 3x - x^2, & x < -1 \\ 6x + 2, & x > -1 \end{cases}$ continuous at $x = -1$?

    (A) Yes, since $\lim\limits_{x \to 1^+} g(x) = \lim\limits_{x \to 1^-} g(x)$

    (B) Yes, since $g(-1) = -4$ for both functions

    (C) No, since $g(-1)$ doesn't exist

    (D) Yes, since we can replace $<$ with $\le$ or $>$ with $\ge$ in the original equation.

10. Integrate the expression $\int (5 - \sin x)\, dx$.

    (A) $5x + \cos x + C$

    (B) $5x - \cos x + C$

    (C) $\cos 5x + C$

    (D) $5\cos x + C$

Solutions

1. (C) –9. Since the limit of a sum equals the sum of the limits, and the limit of a product equals the product of the limits,

$$\lim_{x \to -1}(f(x) + 2g(x)) = \lim_{x \to -1}(f(x)) + \lim_{x \to -1}(2g(x)) = \lim_{x \to -1}(f(x)) + 2\lim_{x \to -1}(g(x))$$

(since $\lim_{x \to -1} 2 = 2$). Now find $f(x)$ and $g(x)$ for $x = -1$ from the given table to get

$$\lim_{x \to -1}(f(x)) + 2\lim_{x \to -1}(g(x)) = f(-1) + 2g(-1) = 5 + 2(-7) = -9.$$

2. (A) –4. The rule in the piecewise function changes at $x = 2$, so the limit coming from the left and the right of $x = 2$ must be evaluated and compared. The left-hand limit is $\lim_{x \to 2^-} f(x) = 4 - (2)^3 = 4 - 8 = -4$, and the right-hand limit is $\lim_{x \to 2^+} f(x) = 6 - 5(2) = 6 - 10 = -4$. Since the two limits are equal, the general limit exists and is $\lim_{x \to 2} = -4$.

3. (B) $18\frac{1}{2}$. Resist the urge to combine the two fractions $\left(\dfrac{2x^2 + 7x + 6}{x + 2} + \dfrac{2x + 7}{x - 2}\right)$ into one with a common denominator of $(x - 4)$, which would give a 0 denominator at the limit of 4. Since one of the fractions has a quadratic, perhaps it can be factored to simplify the problem. The quadratic is divisible by $(x + 2)$—no surprise here—so the equation is simplified to $\lim_{x \to 4}\left(\dfrac{(2x + 3)(x + 2)}{(x + 2)} + \dfrac{2x + 7}{x - 2}\right) = \lim_{x \to 4}\left((2x + 3) + \dfrac{2x + 7}{x - 2}\right) = 11 + \dfrac{15}{2} = 18\frac{1}{2}$.

4. (D) $\dfrac{\sqrt[3]{t^2}}{3t^2}$. Rewrite $y = \dfrac{1}{\sqrt[3]{t}} = t^{-\frac{1}{3}}$ to be able to use the power rule. Then $y' = -\dfrac{1}{3}t^{-\frac{1}{3}-1} = -\dfrac{1}{3}t^{-\frac{4}{3}} = -\dfrac{1}{3t\sqrt[3]{t}} \cdot \dfrac{\sqrt[3]{t^2}}{\sqrt[3]{t^2}} - \dfrac{\sqrt[3]{t^2}}{3t^2}$. Even though answer choices (B) and (C) are equivalent to the given expression, they are not in rational form.

5. (A) $\dfrac{2xy^2 - y}{x - 2x^2 y + \sin y}$. The solution uses both the product rule and the chain rule. By using the chain rule and then the product rule, we get

$$y + x\frac{dy}{dx} = \left[\frac{d(x^2 y^2)}{dx}\right] + \frac{d(\cos y)}{dy} \times \frac{dy}{dx} = 2xy^2 + 2x^2 y\frac{dy}{dx} - \sin y\frac{dy}{dx}$$

Rearranging terms, we get $x\dfrac{dy}{dx} - 2x^2 y\dfrac{dy}{dx} + \sin y\dfrac{dy}{dx} = 2xy^2 - y$, which becomes $\dfrac{dy}{dx} = \dfrac{2xy^2 - y}{x - 2x^2 y + \sin y}$.

6.　(C)　$v(t) = -9$ ft/sec and $a(t) = -6$ ft/sec². If $s = t^3 - 6t^2$, then $v(t) = \dfrac{ds}{dt} = 3t^2 - 12t$ and $a(t) = \dfrac{dv}{dt} = 6t - 12$. At $t = 1$, $v(t) = -9$ ft/sec and $a(t) = -6$ ft/sec², which means the particle is moving in the opposite direction (negative velocity, with "opposite" not necessarily down—it could be a car backing up) but speeding up since the signs of the velocity and acceleration are both negative. Indeed, we see in the next second ($t = 2$), the velocity is -12 ft/sec.

7.　(D)　$\dfrac{16}{3}$. Use the Mean Value Theorem:

$$\frac{1}{b-a}\int_a^b f(x)\,dx = \frac{1}{4-0}\int_0^4 x^2\,dx = \frac{1}{4}\left(\frac{x^3}{3}\right)\Big|_0^4 = \frac{1}{4}\left[\frac{64}{3} - 0\right] = \frac{16}{3}.$$

8.　(A)　16π. Sketch the triangle as shown.

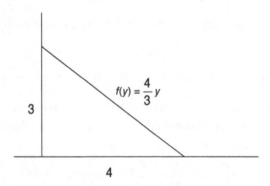

If it is rotated around the y-axis, it will have the shape of a cone with radius $r = 4$ and height $h = 3$. Using integrals, find the volume by rotating the line $f(y) = \dfrac{r}{h}y = \dfrac{4}{3}y$ around the y-axis (everything needs to be in terms of y when rotating about the vertical axis). The volume is then given by the integral $\displaystyle\int_a^b \pi(f(y))^2\,dy = \int_0^h \pi\left(\frac{4}{3}\right)^2\left(\frac{y^3}{3}\right)\Big|_0^3 = \pi\left(\frac{4^2}{3^2}\right)\left(\frac{3^3}{3}\right) - 0 = 16\pi$, which is the same as found by using the equation for the volume of a cone (see Section 5.12.4b) with radius 4 and height 3, or $V_{\text{cone}} = \dfrac{1}{3}\pi r^2 h = \dfrac{1}{3}\pi(4)^2(3) = 16\pi$.

9.　(C)　No, since $g(-1)$ doesn't exist. For a function to be continuous at a point, the limits from the left and right must be equal (they are), and the point must be in the domain of the functions (it isn't). Although changing one of the inequality signs would make a continuous function, it would be a different function than $g(x)$.

10.　(A)　$5x + \cos x + C$. The given integral can be written as the difference of two integrals. So it is equal to $\int 5\,dx - \int \sin x\,dx = 5x - (-\cos x) + C = 5x + \cos x + C$.

CHAPTER 8

Probability and Statistics

8.1 PROBABILITY

Probability is simply the chance that something will occur. The probability of something happening is calculated as

$$\text{Pr(something happening)} = \frac{\text{number of ways something can happen}}{\text{total number of ways something can and cannot happen}},$$

Probability is therefore a fraction (or its equivalent ratio or percentage) between 0 and 1.

At one end, a probability of 0 means that something cannot happen. Period. Since in this case, the number of ways something can happen is 0, we don't even have to worry about the number of ways it can and cannot happen (the denominator, which is also called the **sample space**) because 0 divided by anything (except another 0) is 0. An example is pigs flying. Pigs cannot fly (at least not on their own), so the probability of a pig flying is 0.

At the other end, a probability of 1 means that something always happens. It cannot "not happen" and we have the same number at the top and bottom of the fraction, so it equals 1. Do you have to know how many ways something can happen if it always happens? No, what you have to know is that it cannot not happen, so the probability is 1, or 100% certain. A simple example is the probability that your birthday will be on the month and day you were born. It's a sure thing—there is no wiggle room. The probability is 1. Period.

All other types of probability always fall between 0 and 1. There are no negative probabilities. Here and in the rest of the discussion on probability, we are talking about **theoretical probability**, or the number of ways that an event can occur divided by the total number of possible outcomes.

This is somewhat different from empirical, or experimental, probability, which will be discussed in Section 8.1.3.

Since the probability of something not happening plus the probability of it happening equals 100%, we can say Pr(something not happening) = 1 – Pr(something happening) or,

$$Pr(\text{not } A) = 1 - Pr(A),$$

in which Pr(not A) and Pr(A) are **complementary events**. One or the other must occur. An example is the probability it will snow in the next hour and the probability it will *not* snow in the next hour. It's one or the other, but certainly not both.

Let's look at some examples and follow them to their logical conclusions. We will introduce more complicated situations as we go, but the idea is the same for all. Notice in these examples that everything must be fair. **Fair** means, for instance, that a coin must not be weighted to favor one side, or a die also must not be weighted to favor a particular side to be the top number. Therefore, the probability of tossing heads on one flip of a fair coin is $\frac{1}{2}$, and the probability of tossing a 3 on a fair die is $\frac{1}{6}$.

EXAMPLE 8.1

What is the probability of tossing a number less than 7 on the toss of a die?

SOLUTION 8.1

1. The numbers on a die are 1 through 6, so you always can toss a number less than 7. Pr(<7) = 1.

8.1.1 Compound Events

What if we are considering something that has more than one part, for example, two parts that we'll call A and B. What is the probability that A *or* B will occur? Or what is the probability that A *and* B will occur? The following general rules will help:

Addition Rule of Probability	"or" means add
Multiplication Rule of Probability	"and" means multiply

To remember that "and" means *multiply*, think of a jar of only yellow marbles. Of course, the probability of picking a yellow marble from the jar is 1 since they all are yellow. The probability of picking two yellow marbles is likewise 1. But if we used addition for "and," we would have gotten Pr(yellow and yellow) = 1 + 1 = 2, which is impossible since all probabilities are between 0 and 1. So Pr(yellow *and* yellow) = 1 × 1 = 1.

EXAMPLE 8.2

What is the probability of tossing a 1 or a 2 or a 3 or a 4 or a 5 or a 6 on a die?

SOLUTION 8.2

1. The probability of tossing any particular number on a die (as long as the number is 1 through 6) is $\frac{1}{6}$. Each number has a probability of $\frac{1}{6}$, and this is an "or" situation, so we add the probabilities: Pr(1 or 2 or 3 or 4 or 5 or 6) = Pr(1) + Pr(2) + Pr(3) + Pr(4) + Pr(5) + Pr(6) = $\frac{1}{6} + \frac{1}{6} + \frac{1}{6} + \frac{1}{6} + \frac{1}{6} + \frac{1}{6} = 1$.

Example 8.2 is included here to help remember that "or means add" works.

EXAMPLE 8.3

What is the probability of tossing a number greater than 4 on a die?

SOLUTION 8.3

$\frac{1}{3}$. A number greater than 4 would be a 5 or a 6, which means 2 of the possible tosses, so Pr(5 or 6) = $\frac{2}{6} = \frac{1}{3}$. Another way to think of this problem is Pr(5 or 6) = Pr(5) + Pr(6) = $\frac{1}{6} + \frac{1}{6} = \frac{2}{6} = \frac{1}{3}$.

This is all well and good because we are talking about one toss of one die. What if we now talk about tossing two dice, or even one die twice? We must decide whether the problems involving more than one event are **independent** (the outcome of one doesn't influence the outcome of the other), **mutually exclusive** (both outcomes cannot happen at the same time), or **overlapping** (there are outcomes in common). They are treated differently, as shown in Sections 8.1.1a–c, respectively.

8.1.1a Independent Events

Any string of events that each don't influence the others are called **independent events**. These types of events don't have any effect on the probability of any other event. So, for example, if you throw two dice, what shows up on die 1 is independent of what shows up on die 2.

EXAMPLE 8.4

What is the probability of getting two 1's on the two tosses of one die or on one toss of two dice (called "snake eyes")?

SOLUTION 8.4

$\frac{1}{36}$. This is an "and" situation, so we multiply the probabilities:

$\Pr(1 \text{ and } 1) = \Pr(1) \times \Pr(1) = \frac{1}{6} \times \frac{1}{6} = \frac{1}{36}$.

EXAMPLE 8.5

What is the probability of getting a 1 and a 6, in that order, on two tosses of one die or on one toss of two dice?

SOLUTION 8.5

$\frac{1}{36}$. $\Pr(1 \text{ and } 6) = \Pr(1) \times \Pr(6) = \frac{1}{6} \times \frac{1}{6} = \frac{1}{36}$.

Several tosses of a fair coin or one toss of several fair coins give the same result.

EXAMPLE 8.6

Assume the probability of rain on any day is independent of the probability of rain the day before or after (a bold assumption). The probability of rain on each of the next three days is as shown in the following table.

Day	Tuesday	Wednesday	Thursday
Probability of Rain	30%	45%	50%

Based on the table, what is the lowest probability (in percent) that it will rain all three days?

SOLUTION 8.6

6.75%. Assuming independence, the probability that it will rain all three days is the product of the three probabilities, or 6.75%. Thus, the question asks for the lowest percent rather than the actual percent because, as we all know, rain isn't an independent event.

EXAMPLE 8.7

What is the probability of tossing a fair coin four times and getting four heads?

SOLUTION 8.7

$\frac{1}{16}$. This is an "and" situation, so the probability of getting a head (H), and another H, and another H, and another H is $\Pr(HHHH) = \Pr(H) \times \Pr(H) \times \Pr(H) \times \Pr(H) = \frac{1}{2} \times \frac{1}{2} \times \frac{1}{2} \times \frac{1}{2} = \frac{1}{16}$.

Can you see that the answer to Example 8.7 would be the same if we asked for Pr(HTTH) or Pr(HHTT), where T is "tails"? Why is this so? In each toss, whether it is four successive tosses of the same coin, or a toss of four coins, the probability of landing heads or tails doesn't have any effect on the probability of any other coin or other toss. Therefore, if you tossed a fair coin seven times and it came up heads each time, the probability of the eighth toss being a head is still only $\frac{1}{2}$.

However, the probability of the exact string of eight heads, $\Pr(HHHHHHHH) = \left(\frac{1}{2}\right)^8 = \frac{1}{2^8} = \frac{1}{256}$, or 1 in 256.

Let's look at some more examples.

EXAMPLE 8.8

What is the probability of tossing snake eyes (two 1's) on four successive tosses of two dice?

SOLUTION 8.8

$\left(\frac{1}{36}\right)^4$. The probability of one toss of snake eyes is $\frac{1}{36}$. If we rolled snake eyes once, does it influence the next toss? No, they are totally independent events. So the probability here is an "and" situation: Pr(snake eyes on first toss *and* snake eyes on second toss *and* snake eyes on third toss *and* snake eyes on fourth toss) = $\left(\frac{1}{36}\right) \times \left(\frac{1}{36}\right) \times \left(\frac{1}{36}\right) \times \left(\frac{1}{36}\right) = \left(\frac{1}{36}\right)^4$, which is the same as 1 in 36^4 or 1 in 1,679,616.

Now let's look at a combination "or" and "and" situation. Notice that each independent situation presented so far has just involved logic and multiplication or division. So does the next example, but it needs some more thinking.

EXAMPLE 8.9

What is the probability of getting a *total* of 4 with a toss of two dice?

SOLUTION 8.9

$\frac{1}{12}$. Watch out here. We have to first figure out how many ways we can get a total of four with two dice: (1, 3), (3, 1), and (2, 2), or three ways. So the probability is

$$\text{Pr}(1 \text{ and } 3 \text{ } or \text{ } 3 \text{ and } 1 \text{ } or \text{ } 2 \text{ and } 2) =$$

$$\text{Pr}(1 \text{ and } 3) + \text{Pr}(3 \text{ and } 1) + \text{Pr}(2 \text{ and } 2) =$$

$$[\text{Pr}(1) \times \text{Pr}(3)] + [\text{Pr}(3) \times \text{Pr}(1)] + [\text{Pr}(2) \times \text{Pr}(2)] =$$

$$\frac{1}{36} + \frac{1}{36} + \frac{1}{36} = \frac{3}{36} = \frac{1}{12}.$$

The challenge in the solution to Example 8.9 is figuring out all of the parts, but they are the same as the calculations in all of the preceding independent examples.

The reason we don't count another (2, 2) as a possibility is that (2, 2) is the same whether the first or second die comes up a 2. To see how (2, 2) counts as only one possibility, whereas the combination of 1 and 3 counts as two possibilities, look at the following chart of the 36 tosses of two dice, where the horizontal column is the first die and the vertical column is the second die.

	1	2	3	4	5	6
1	(1, 1)	(1, 2)	(1, 3)	(1, 4)	(1, 5)	(1, 6)
2	(2, 1)	(2, 2)	(2, 3)	(2, 4)	(2, 5)	(2, 6)
3	(3, 1)	(3, 2)	(3, 3)	(3, 4)	(3, 5)	(3, 6)
4	(4, 1)	(4, 2)	(4, 3)	(4, 4)	(4, 5)	(4, 6)
5	(5, 1)	(5, 2)	(5, 3)	(5, 4)	(5, 5)	(5, 6)
6	(6, 1)	(6, 2)	(6, 3)	(6, 4)	(6, 5)	(6, 6)

All of the double tosses (1,1), (2,2), and so on appear only once (the main diagonal), whereas (3,1) is considered a different toss than (1,3).

There are 36 possibilities on a toss of two dice, 6 possible numbers on the second die (or second toss of a single die) for each of the 6 numbers on the first die (or second toss of the same die).

This is a good time to talk about the term **probability distribution**, or **experimental probability distribution**, which is a table or an equation that links each outcome of a statistical experiment with its probability of occurrence. Consider the probability of tossing a coin four times and counting the number of heads.

The following probability distribution table associates each outcome with its probability. Note that the probability table concerns only the population of interest: getting x heads in four tosses of a fair coin, and that the probabilities total 1.

Configuration	Probability
0 heads TTTT	$\dfrac{1}{16}$
1 head HTTT TTHT THTT TTTH	$\dfrac{4}{16}$
2 heads HHTT TTHH HTHT THTH HTTH THHT	$\dfrac{6}{16}$
3 heads THHH HHHT HTHH HHTH	$\dfrac{4}{16}$
4 heads HHHH	$\dfrac{1}{16}$

The graph of this distribution is

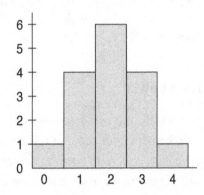

Both of these presentations are examples of probability distributions. The graph is roughly a normal distribution, which is the subject of Section 8.6 later in this chapter and is fundamental to statistical analysis.

Now, let's consider a situation that is similar to using a fair coin or a fair die. This is a favorite scenario in problems on most tests: selecting socks in a drawer. This involves two assumptions. First, the socks are chosen randomly without looking. (Besides, if the person selecting the socks looks, then the probability would be 100% that the socks selected are the ones that are wanted.) Second, the socks are in color-matched pairs, not just tossed into the drawer when they come from the dryer, which is usually the case.

EXAMPLE 8.10

Jim has 9 pairs of socks in a drawer, 2 tan, 3 brown, and 4 black, and he selects a pair without looking.

    a. What is the probability that he picks a pair of brown socks?

    b. What is the probability that he picks a pair of brown or tan socks?

    c. What is the probability that he doesn't pick a pair of black socks?

SOLUTION 8.10

a. $\frac{1}{3}$. Jim has 9 pairs of socks and 3 are brown, so the probability of picking a brown pair is $\frac{3}{9} = \frac{1}{3}$.

b. $\frac{5}{9}$. This is $\text{Pr}(\text{brown or tan}) = \text{Pr}(\text{brown}) + \text{Pr}(\text{tan}) = \frac{2}{9} + \frac{3}{9} = \frac{5}{9}$.

c. $\frac{5}{9}$. This question asks for the probability of something *not* happening. The "something" is choosing a pair of black socks. So $\text{Pr}(\text{not black}) = 1 - \text{Pr}(\text{black}) = 1 - \frac{4}{9} = \frac{5}{9}$.

The answer to Example 8.10 part (c) is the same as that for part (b), the probability of picking brown or tan socks, which makes sense. If Jim doesn't pick black socks, he must pick brown or tan socks.

8.1.1b Mutually Exclusive Events

Mutually exclusive events are not the same as independent events. Whereas independent events don't influence each other, and therefore can both occur at the same time with some probability, as shown above, mutually exclusive events cannot both occur at the same time. The probability of both occurring is 0. The "or" type of probability of mutually exclusive events can be calculated, but the "and" type of probability for mutually exclusive events is always 0.

EXAMPLE 8.11

Let's say we have a special type of die. In addition to having the usual six numbers, the even numbers are red and the odd numbers are blue.

    a. What is the probability of tossing the die and getting a red number or a 5?

    b. What is the probability of tossing the die and getting a red number and a 5?

SOLUTION 8.11

a. $\frac{2}{3}$. This is an "or" situation, so the probabilities are added.

$$\text{Pr}(\text{red or } 5) = \text{Pr}(\text{red}) + \text{Pr}(5) = \frac{1}{2} + \frac{1}{6} = \frac{3}{6} + \frac{1}{6} = \frac{4}{6} = \frac{2}{3}.$$

b. 0. It is impossible to get both a red side and a 5 since the 5 is only blue. So $\text{Pr}(\text{red and } 5) = 0$.

Hint: The distinction between mutually exclusive and independent events is sometimes difficult to grasp. It is a little easier if you realize that the distinction involves "and" situations, since for mutually exclusive events, "and" *cannot happen*, whereas for independent events, "and" is possible.

8.1.1c Overlapping Events

Overlapping events have outcomes in common, or one or more outcomes occur at the same time. An example is the probability of rolling an odd number or a number greater than 4 in a roll of a die. These events overlap because it is possible for both to occur at the same time, such as rolling a 5. Let's look at these events individually to see how they differ from mutually exclusive events.

- The probability of rolling a number greater than 4, or $\text{Pr}(5 \text{ or } 6) = \frac{2}{6} = \frac{1}{3}$.

- The probability of rolling an odd number is $\text{Pr}(1 \text{ or } 3 \text{ or } 5) = \frac{3}{6} = \frac{1}{2}$.

If these events were independent, the "or" rule (addition rule) gives

$$\text{Pr}(\text{number is} > 4 \text{ or odd}) = \frac{1}{3} + \frac{1}{2} = \frac{5}{6}.$$

And the complementary event in this scenario is $\text{Pr}(2 \text{ or } 4) = \frac{2}{6} = \frac{1}{3}$.

Certainly $\frac{5}{6} + \frac{1}{3} \neq 1$. What happened is that we included 5 in the first probability we considered $(5 > 4)$ and then we included it again in the second probability (5 is an odd number). How this translates into probability is that with an "or" situation, if any of the events overlap, we must be careful not to count the overlap twice.

Formally, the **addition rule for probability** of overlapping cases is given by

$$\text{Pr}(A \text{ or } B) = \text{Pr}(A) + \text{Pr}(B) - \text{Pr}(A \text{ and } B)$$

In fact, this calculation works for all cases, but if the two situations are mutually exclusive, meaning they do not overlap, the $\text{Pr}(A \text{ and } B)$ part equals 0.

EXAMPLE 8.12

There are an even number of boys and girls at a school, and the eighth-graders are one-third of the student population of 600. What is the formula for the probability that a student chosen at random is in the eighth-grade or is a girl?

SOLUTION 8.12

$\frac{1}{3} + \frac{1}{2} - \frac{1}{6}$. $\text{Pr}(\text{8th grade or girl}) = \text{Pr}(\text{8th grade}) + \text{Pr}(\text{girl}) - \text{Pr}(\text{8th-grade girl}) =$

$\frac{200}{600} + \frac{300}{600} - \frac{100}{600} = \frac{1}{3} + \frac{1}{2} - \frac{1}{6} = \frac{2}{3}$.

EXAMPLE 8.13

In a class of 30 students, 20 students have dogs or cats. Thirteen have a dog, and 10 have a cat. If a student is chosen at random from the class, what is the probability that the student has a dog or cat?

SOLUTION 8.13

$\frac{20}{30}$. If we don't take into consideration that some students might have both pets, we might incorrectly calculate $\text{Pr}(\text{dog or cat}) = \text{Pr}(\text{dog}) + \text{Pr}(\text{cat}) = \frac{13}{30} + \frac{10}{30} = \frac{23}{30}$, when in fact only 20 of the 30 students have a dog or cat, as stated in the first sentence of the problem. This means 3 of the students must have both pets.

$$\text{Pr}(\text{dog or cat}) = \text{Pr}(\text{dog}) + \text{Pr}(\text{cat}) - \text{Pr}(\text{dog and cat})$$

$$= \frac{13}{30} + \frac{10}{30} - \frac{3}{30} = \frac{20}{30}$$

Situations that involve events that overlap are often shown by using **Venn diagrams,** discussed in Section 8.1.1d.

8.1.1d Venn Diagrams

All of the space within the borders of a **Venn diagram** represent the **universe**, U, which simply means the population of interest. In the space within the borders are two or more circles, each representing a specific part of the universe. For mutually exclusive events, the circles don't intersect, but we are now going to consider cases in which they do intersect.

The Venn diagram below consists of two overlapping circles, one labeled A and one labeled B. The intersection of the two circles is labeled A & B. Each section of the Venn diagram represents the items that belong to A, to B, or to both. The items can be anything that sometimes "overlaps."

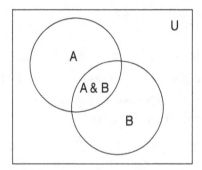

Let's look at the Venn diagram for the situation considered in Section 8.1.1c about the students who have a dog or a cat.

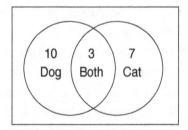

In this Venn diagram, we can see that 13 students do have dogs (the whole left circle for dogs and both) and 10 students do have cats (the whole right circle for cats and both). But we have counted the students who have both pets twice, once for dogs and once for cats. We have to subtract one of the duplicate "both" cases, which is 3 students.

Now let's consider two different scenarios for students' language classes. Suppose students at School A can study only one foreign language, so students who have Spanish classes cannot also have French classes. School B also offers Spanish and French, but allows students to take two languages at the same time.

In the Venn diagrams shown next, School A is shown on the left, with all the students at the school being the universe. There is no overlap between the circles because no student is in both Spanish and French class. School B is shown on the right, with the universe again being all the students in the school. The two circles represent students who are taking at least one language. The portion shared by the two circles represents those students who are taking both Spanish and French. The space outside of the circles in both diagrams represents all the students who aren't taking Spanish or French at all.

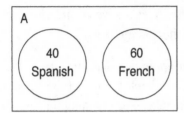

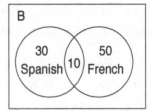

EXAMPLE 8.14

In the diagram above, school A shows 40 students in Spanish class and 60 in French class. Likewise, school B also shows 40 students in Spanish class and 60 in French class. However, at school B, 10 students take both classes. How many students in each school are taking at least one language?

SOLUTION 8.14

School A = 100 students; School B = 90 students. For school A, it is easy to see that there is no overlap because students are allowed to take only one language, so 40 + 60 = 100 students in school A take a French or Spanish class. In this case, the "or" question is simply the sum of the students in each language class. For school B, however, the Venn diagram shows that only 90 students take French or Spanish. Ten of these students take both languages. We cannot count those students twice in the total, which is 30 Spanish only + 50 French only + 10 both Spanish and French = 90. If we had just totaled the students in Spanish class (30 + 10) and the students in French class (50 + 10), we would have gotten 40 + 60 = 100, which is incorrect, as we can see in the Venn diagram. We cannot count students who take both classes twice, so we must subtract from the total the extra 10 for those who take both classes.

8.1.2 Conditional Probability

Conditional probability is the probability of an event happening dependent on another event already occurring. This ratchets up the probability a little more, but the logic is similar. This is another favorite type of problem on many tests. The symbol for conditional probability is Pr(A|B), read as "the probability of A occurring when B has already occurred." This is obviously a dependent type of probability.

A popular form of conditional probability is similar to the socks-in-a-drawer problem. It involves whether there is **replacement**.

EXAMPLE 8.15

Let's say we have a jar that contains 20 marbles: 3 red, 4 yellow, 6 green, and 7 blue. Further, we randomly pick one or more marbles from the jar, meaning we don't look.

    a. What is the probability of picking a yellow marble from the jar, putting it back in the jar, and then picking a blue marble?

    b. What is the probability of picking a yellow marble from the jar, not putting it back in the jar, and then picking a blue marble?

SOLUTION 8.15

a. $\dfrac{7}{100}$. The probability is the same as the standard independent event probability.

$$\text{Pr(yellow and blue, with replacement)} = \text{Pr(yellow)} \times \text{Pr(blue)} = \frac{4}{20} \times \frac{7}{20} = \frac{28}{400} = \frac{7}{100}.$$

b. $\dfrac{28}{380}$. This scenario is different because in the second pick, there aren't 20 marbles anymore. The yellow one is missing. The method is similar—only the numbers change.

$$\text{Pr(yellow and blue, without replacement)} = \text{Pr(yellow)} \times \text{Pr(blue)} =$$
$$\frac{4}{20} \times \frac{7}{19} = \frac{28}{380}.$$

The difference between the situations in the two parts of Example 8.15 is replacement. In part (a), with replacement, the two picks were independent. But in part (b), without replacement, the probability of picking a blue marble depends on the fact that once the yellow marble was taken out, there was a greater chance of picking a blue marble.

EXAMPLE 8.16

Jerrod turns up the top card of a deck of playing cards and it is an ace.

    a. What is the probability that Jerrod would pick the ace in the first place?

    b. What is the probability that Jerrod will pick another ace from the rest of the cards?

SOLUTION 8.16

a. $\dfrac{1}{13}$. There are four aces in a deck of 52 cards, so the probability is $\dfrac{4}{52} = \dfrac{1}{13}$.

b. $\frac{1}{17}$. For the second pick, without replacement, there are only three aces and only 51 cards, so the probability is $\frac{3}{51} = \frac{1}{17}$.

The following table summarizes how to find probabilities.

Summary of Probability Types

Description	Example	Formula	Type of Probability
One event	Flip of a fair coin	$Pr(A) = \dfrac{\text{number of ways A can happen}}{\text{number of ways A can and cannot happen}}$	Simple probability
Event A or event B	Tossing a 5 or 6 on a die	$Pr(A \text{ or } B) = Pr(A) + Pr(B)$	Independent events
Event A and event B	Getting THHT in 4 tosses of a coin (or a toss of 4 coins)	$Pr(T \text{ and } H \text{ and } H \text{ and } T) =$ $Pr(T) \times Pr(H) \times Pr(H) \times Pr(T)$ where T = tails and H = heads	Independent events
Events (A and B) or (C and D)	Getting a total of 4 with a toss of 2 dice	$Pr(A \text{ and } B \text{ } or \text{ } C \text{ and } D)$ $= Pr(A \text{ and } B) + Pr(C \text{ and } D)$ $= [Pr(A) \times Pr(B)] + [Pr(C) \times Pr(D)]$	Independent events
Pr(not A)	Probability of event A not happening	$Pr(\text{not } A) = 1 - Pr(A)$	Simple probability
Pr(A and not A at same time)	Probability of a 2 and an odd number in 1 pick	$Pr(A \text{ and not } A \text{ at same time}) = 0$	Mutually exclusive
Pr(A and B) in two events with replacement	Picking a blue marble and then a yellow marble	$Pr(A \text{ and } B) = Pr(A) \times Pr(B)$	Independent events
Pr(A and B) in two events, with no replacement	Picking a blue marble and then a yellow marble	$Pr(A \text{ and } B) = Pr(A) \times Pr(B|A)$, where the denominator for event B depends on event A	Dependent events, or conditional probability
Pr(A or B) with Pr(A and B) $\neq 0$	Dealing with non-mutually exclusive events	$Pr(A \text{ or } B) = Pr(A) + Pr(B) - Pr(A \text{ and } B)$	Overlapping events

EXAMPLE 8.17

Match each scenario with the type of probability.

a. Not choosing an ace from a deck of cards.

b. Being the third of three people chosen one at a time for a committee out of a group of fifty.

c. Choosing a "1" from a standard deck of cards when aces don't count as 1's.

d. Choosing a student who takes French from a group of 50 students, when 20 take French, 30 take Spanish, and 10 take German.

I.   Independent

II. Dependent

III. Overlapping

IV. Impossible

SOLUTION 8.17

a. II. Independent. This is the same as choosing a 2, 3, 4, 5, 6, 7, 8, 9, 10, J, Q, or K.

b. I. Dependent. The probability changes once the first and second people are chosen.

c. IV. Impossible. There are no 1's in a deck of cards if aces don't count as 1's.

d. III. Overlapping. The Venn diagram will have some overlap but it won't change the fact that 20 students out of 50 take French.

8.1.3 Theoretical and Empirical Probability

When we discussed coin flips and dice tosses in the introduction to Section 8.1, the type of probability described was **theoretical probability**: theoretically we know that a fair flip of a coin should result in heads-up half the time, or a toss of a fair die should show a 5 one-sixth of the time. When discussing an experiment from which we want to come to a conclusion as to the probability of an event happening, such as DNA sampling (discussed in Section 8.6), we are talking about **empirical probability**, or probability resulting from experiment or observation.

 "Success" in probability, and therefore also in statistics, doesn't necessarily mean a good thing, as one would think "success" suggests. **Success** simply means the occurrence of what we are looking for. It could be the number of abnormal babies due to a mosquito bite while the mother was pregnant—not good at all, but if that is the focus of the study, that occurrence is considered as a "success" in discussing probabilities and statistics.

The **Law of Large Numbers** theorem states that as the number of trials of a probability experiment increases, the observed number of "successful" outcomes will get increasingly closer to the theoretical number of "successful" outcomes. Another way to state this concept is that the *empirical probability* will approach the *theoretical probability*. For example, if a fair coin is flipped, and we identify the number of tails as the number of "successful" outcomes, on any one flip, the theoretical probability of getting tails is 0.5. If this coin is flipped 10,000 times, the expected number of tails is $(0.5)(10,000) = 5,000$. The Law of Large Numbers theorem states that we should observe that the actual number of tails is very close to 5,000. If we decide to flip this coin 100,000 times, we should observe that the number of tails is extremely close to 50,000.

8.2 EXPECTED VALUE

Expected value deals with the different outcomes associated with a specific event. It provides a method of determining the potential value or the likelihood of each particular outcome of that event. In short, expected value is the average of all possible outcomes, adjusted (or "weighted") for the likelihood that each outcome will occur.

A raffle is an excellent example of the usefulness of expected value. Suppose you are thinking of buying a $10 ticket to a fundraising raffle in which the grand prize is $20,000. If you bought the only ticket, your chance of winning are 100%; otherwise, your chance of winning depends on how many people buy tickets. If the number of tickets is limited to 10,000, then your chance of winning becomes 1 in 10,000, or $\frac{1}{10,000}$. The expected value of winning $20,000 is now $\frac{1}{10,000} \times \$20,000 = \$2$. What does this mean? It means on average, you would win $2, but remember that the ticket cost you $10, so your expected value is down to a loss of $8.

Expected value usually involves more than one outcome, however, and its value is what you should expect, *on average*. Let's amend the raffle to not only have one $20,000 prize, but also 20 prizes of $500 each with an expected value of $\frac{20}{10,000} \times \$500 = \$1$. To complete the scenario, we must also include the expected value of losing, which is –$10, reflecting that you paid out $10. If we add up the values of all the possible outcomes, you will realize that your expected value is $\$2 + \$1 + (-\$10) = -\$7$. The chance of winning any of the top prizes is very, very small, and in fact your expected value is –$7.00, or for every ticket sold, the ticket holder is losing $7.00 on average.

Another way to look at the above scenario is to suppose you bought all 10,000 raffle tickets. Then you would be guaranteed to win $20,000 plus 20 prizes of $500 each, or $20,000 + $10,000 = $30,000. But you would have paid $10 × 10,000 = $100,000 for the tickets, so the expected value would be $30,000 – $100,000 = –$70,000, or –$7 per ticket.

In plain terms, the general formula for expected value (EV) is

$$EV = \Pr(A) \times (\text{value of } A) + \Pr(B) \times (\text{value of } B) + \ldots + \Pr(n) \times (\text{value of } n) - (\text{cost of event}).$$

If EV is positive, that means on average you will win *something*, if it is negative, on average you will lose *something*. Is it evident, then, that if the EV equals zero, on average you will just break even, and so will the organization that sponsored the raffle.

Let's look at a few examples for expected value.

EXAMPLE 8.18

A local club plans to invest $10,000 to host an outdoor concert. They expect to sell tickets worth $25,000. But the forecast for the day of concert is 20% severe thunderstorms, in which case the club will have to refund the money collected and in addition lose all the money it invested. Is this a good investment? (Note that in reality, the concert would probably go on anyway or be postponed, so there wouldn't be a refund, but let's look at this specific scenario and assume that if the concert was canceled the club would still have its expenses.)

SOLUTION 8.18

Yes. The expected value is that they will double the $10,000 they invested. In this scenario, the club has an expected value of

$$EV = \left(\frac{8}{10} \times (+\$25,000)\right) + \left(\frac{2}{10} \times 0\right) - \$10,000 = \$20,000 + 0 - \$10,000 = \$10,000$$

Note that the $10,000 is what the club would expect to gain if there were no thunderstorms (with a probability of $\frac{8}{10}$). Note also that if there were no thunderstorms forecast, the equation would have been $EV = \left(\frac{10}{10} \times (+\$25,000)\right) - \$10,000 = \$25,000 - \$10,000 = \$15,000$.

EXAMPLE 8.19

A lawyer figures that he has one chance in eight of winning a case. His expenses for the case are $8,000. If he is paid only if he wins the case, what should he charge the client in order to break even?

SOLUTION 8.19

$64,000. The lawyer must determine the fee so the expected value will be 0 to break even. Let x be the lawyer's fee. Then the expected value is determined by the income of the lawyer if he gets paid ($x - \$8,000$) or doesn't get paid at all ($-\$8,000$). The expected value equation is thus $(x - \$8,000)\left(\frac{1}{8}\right) - \$8000\left(\frac{7}{8}\right) = 0$. Therefore, $x - \$8,000 - \$56,000 = 0$ to break even. Solving for x, the lawyer must charge at least $64,000. Notice in this equation that the amount he can expect if he gets paid is his fee *minus his expenses*, or $x - \$8,000$.

8.3 COUNTING PRINCIPLE

Probability and statistics have a lot to do with counting, and thus with the **counting principle**. The counting principle states:

> If there are m ways to do one thing, and n ways to do another,
> then there are $m \times n$ ways of doing both.

The counting principle works with any number of inputs.

For example, if there are 2 ways for one activity to happen and 3 ways for a second activity to happen, then there are $2 \times 3 = 6$ ways for both to happen. A tree diagram shows how this works. Suppose a soft-serve shop has two ice cream flavors and three toppings. How many choices are there? The tree diagram shows there are 6.

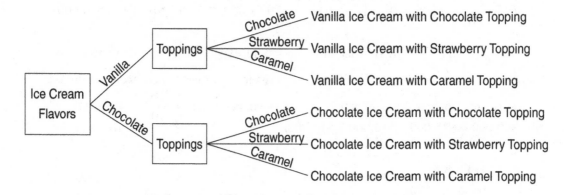

Even though a tree diagram for the following would be too big to show here, the principle is the same: If a restaurant offers 3 types of meat, 2 types of potato, 4 types of vegetable, and 5 different desserts, how many choices does a customer have, picking only one from each category? The answer is $3 \times 2 \times 4 \times 5 = 120$ choices. Notice that if, in addition, one of the choices was to not have a vegetable or dessert, thus adding 1 (none) to each of those choices, the customer would have $3 \times 2 \times 5 \times 6 = 180$ choices.

We can compute the probability that someone picked a specific type of meat, potato, vegetable, and dessert (assuming "no thank you" isn't allowed). That would be $1 \times 1 \times 1 \times 1 = 1$ choice out of 120, $\frac{1}{120}$, or .0083.

EXAMPLE 8.20

If a sandwich menu offers 6 types of meat, 4 types of cheese, and 2 types of bread (rye or white), what is the probability that someone chooses a sandwich on rye bread?

SOLUTION 8.20

$\frac{1}{2}$. The total number of choices are $6 \times 4 \times 2 = 48$. The number of choices of a sandwich on rye would be $6 \times 4 \times 1 = 24$. So the probability is 24 out of 48, $\frac{1}{2}$, or .50. Actually, this solution is much simpler if only the bread choices are considered, since that is all that is asked. There are two bread choices, and rye is one of them: 1 out of 2, $\frac{1}{2}$.

8.4 STATISTICS

Probability is closely related to **statistics**, which in general involves four steps:

- collecting data

- analyzing data

- presenting data

- interpreting data

In the menu selection shown in Example 8.20, we performed all of these functions, but we were dealing with a relatively small amount of data. What if the possibilities are humongous? What if we wanted to represent responses from the whole population of the United States? The answer lies in taking statistics from a sample of the population (population here means the population of interest, even though here the statistical population is actually the population of the whole United States), as shown in the following sections.

8.4.1 Collecting Data

Statistics presents data from a sample taken from a specific population and states the probability of a statement about the whole population based on the fact that the sample results are representative of that whole population. Statistics can present data on elections as well as on money, age, and brand names, among myriad other populations.

How we pick the sample from the population is most important. The sample must be representative of the population of interest and unbiased. As a simple example, if we wanted to gather information on egg sizes from chicken farms in New Jersey, the population would be all the chicken farms in New Jersey. The sample therefore would not include any chicken farms in any other state. It would not include farms in New Jersey that didn't have egg-producing chickens. It would include only egg-producing chicken farms in New Jersey, which would take care of the representative part of sampling.

In addition, the sample would not include farms in just one county in New Jersey because that would introduce a bias. Suppose the farms in the southern part of the state used a breed of chicken that produced larger eggs than the breed used in the northern part of the state? Suppose the water in the western part of the state was remarkably different from that in the eastern part, and that contributed to the size of eggs produced? To be unbiased, the sample must be drawn from the whole population with every member of the population having an equal chance of being picked for the sample. Random sampling—for example, every tenth name on a list of the entire population—is one way to take bias out of a sample.

You could question why not just use every member of the population in the first place. If we are talking about a small population, it is possible to do that, but for a large population, the costs and time involved in querying every member quickly become prohibitive. If the constraints on statistics (such as representative and unbiased samples) are strictly followed, the results from a sample mimic the results of the whole population rather well.

It is important, however, that the sample be large enough to be truly representative of the whole population. If a machine can package 5-ounce bags of potato chips at the rate of 100 per minute, and the foreman of the factory wants to be sure, allowing slight variation, that the bags contain close to 5 ounces of chips, a sample of 3 bags won't give as much assurance as a sample of, say, 100 bags taken at random throughout the production day.

There are four methods of data collection with which you should be familiar: census, sample survey, experiment, and observational study.

- A **census** is a study that observes, or attempts to observe, every individual in a population. The **population** is the collection of all individuals under consideration in the study.

- A **sample survey** is a study that collects information from a sample of a population in order to determine one or more characteristics of the population. A **sample** is a selected subset of a population from which data are gathered.

- An **experiment** is a study in which the researcher deliberately influences individuals by imposing conditions and determining the individuals' responses to those conditions.

- An **observational study** attempts to determine relationships between variables, but the researcher imposes no conditions such as done in an experiment. Surveys are a form of observational study.

Suppose we want to know how satisfied customers are with a new checkout procedure in a supermarket. Let's look at four groups to see which would be the best sample to use for such a survey.

1. Choose every 50th name in the phonebook for the city in which the supermarket is located. This sampling method is wrong on several counts. It is biased toward only

people who have telephones and are listed in the phonebook, so it excludes a whole lot of people who no longer have landlines or choose not to be listed in the phonebook. In addition, it includes many more people than those who shop at that particular store.

2. Go door-to-door in the neighborhood within five blocks of the supermarket. This method is biased and not inclusive because not everyone who lives within five blocks of the store is necessarily a customer, and such a sample excludes all the people who are customers but live farther away.

3. Wait in the parking lot and ask every customer who returns a cart in a given period of time. This method excludes customers who didn't drive to the store (and likely includes only the considerate ones who returned their carts).

4. Choose every 20th customer leaving the store throughout a day. This method is the best, especially if the day is chosen at random, because it is representative of the population—people who actually shop at that supermarket and use the checkout. The choice of every 20th customer makes the sample random, and the choice to do the sampling throughout the day doesn't incidentally exclude any part of the population. For example, possible biases due to time of day include senior citizens who are less likely to shop late at night, and certainly people who have a daytime job and probably don't shop during the hours of 8 a.m. to 5 p.m.

8.4.2 Analyzing Data

Once the data are collected, they must be analyzed so the results can be interpreted statistically. For raw data (the actual data points that are collected), we must first determine whether they are **categorical** (answers are categories, such as yes/no—sometimes called **qualitative**), or **quantitative** (answers are numbers—therefore, these are sometimes called **numerical**).

8.4.2a Categorical Data

Categorical data are best represented pictorially, such as on a pie chart or bar chart (see Section 8.4.3a). Descriptive comparisons can be made among categories, but there can be no "average" as such. For example, if the categories are Democrat, Republican, and Other, what is the average political party? There is no meaningful answer to that question—what we can see, however, is which category had the most respondents.

The categories in this type of data can also be ordered choices, such as "poor," "fair," "average," "good," "excellent," but the idea is still the same—the data are categories, not numerical values. We can see the tally of each category, but not the average.

8.4.2b Quantitative Data

Quantitative data can be analyzed by standard statistical methods. Three measures, the mean, median, and mode, give a sense of **central tendency**, or how the group of data tends to look, whether the data points represent age, height, hours, or another numerical value.

- The **mean**, also called the **average**, is the most familiar measure of central tendency. It is calculated by totaling all of the data points and dividing by the number of points. For example, a student who scored 45, 65, 80, and 90 on four tests would have an average of $\frac{45+65+80+90}{4} = 70$ on the four tests. The good grades on the last two tests are offset by the poor performance on the first two tests. Notice that the mean doesn't have to be a member of the data set. It is just the average so that the differences of the data points from the mean cancel each other out, giving it the quality of being representative of the whole data set. In this case, the four differences from 70 are 25, 5, –10, and –20, which total 0.

- The **median** is the middle data point. To find the median, the data have to be arranged in order. It makes no difference if it is lowest to highest or highest to lowest. The exact middle point, which has as many data points above it as below it, is the median. For a data set with an odd number of points, it is easy to count over to find the median. For an even number of data points, two are in the middle, so the median is the average of the middle two. For example, for the data set 1, 2, 4, 5, 6, 9, 10, the median is 5, with three data points above it and three below it. If the data set didn't have the 10, the median would be the average of the two middle points, 4 and 5, and it would be 4.5. So the median need not be a member of the data set if the number of data points is even. Notice that the mean of the 7-number set is not 5 but $5.3 = \left(\frac{1+2+4+5+6+9+10}{7}\right)$. The mean and median are often close but usually not the same value.

- The **mode** is the data point with the highest frequency. This has meaning if the data points repeat, such as in 3, 4, 5, 5, 5, 6, 7, 7, 8, 9, 9, 9, 9. The mode here is 9, with a frequency of 4 (the frequency of 5 is 3, and the frequency of 7 is 2). This value (remember to use the value, not its frequency) is *always* a member of the data set. It is less precise in describing the data set, as we can see in this data set, where 9 is not very representative of the rest of the numbers.

Another measure of quantitative data is called the **range**, which is simply the highest value minus the lowest value. The range gives information on the spread of the data. For example, for the data set {2, 2, 15, 16, 45}, the range is 43 (= 45 – 2), which is very large for a set of only five data points. This measure isn't a measure of central tendency, since it doesn't tell us anything about the data values, not even what the highest and lowest points are. It just tells how spread out they are.

Usually, the mean is used as the measure of central tendency for quantitative data, and it works fine unless the data are skewed. **Skew** means one or a few high (or low) points pull the mean too far in one direction or the other. To illustrate how skew affects data, consider the salaries of nine bank employees, in thousands of dollars:

25   25   27   28   30   35   35   40   200

Let's look at the mode: There are two, $25,000 and $35,000, and both are fairly representative of most of the salaries. How about the median? It is $30,000, also fairly representative of the salaries. However, the mean (average) is $49,444, which is far from being representative of the salaries of the employees because included in the data set is the $200,000 salary of the CEO of the bank. If the CEO's salary is excluded from the data set, the mode and median don't change much (the median becomes $29,000), but the mean now becomes a more representative $30,625.

EXAMPLE 8.21

A children's baseball team played a 14-game season. The number of runs scored in each game, respectively, is shown below:

Runs scored:

6   2   0   17   4   5   3   8   1   13   4   7   2   4

What was the average number of runs scored per game in the season, rounded to the nearest whole number?

SOLUTION 8.21

5. Add the 14 numbers and divide by 14 to get the average = 5.42857 (use the calculator), which rounds to 5 runs per game.

8.4.2c Distinguishing Types of Data

Let's look at some examples and determine what type of data are presented.

EXAMPLE 8.22

The freshman class at a local college is required to take a test in their first week of classes. Anyone who fails the test must take a remedial course to continue taking classes in the school. Four versions of the same test were given, with the following numbers of students passing and failing:

Version of Test	Pass	Fail
A	200	50
B	225	25
C	210	40
D	220	30

The data presented in this table are what kind of data?

SOLUTION 8.22

(B) Categorical. They involve two categories. The data fall within the two categories of "pass" and "fail." The numbers are the data points, but they can be presented only as a bar graph or a pie chart (see Section 8.4.3a).

EXAMPLE 8.23

This question is similar to Example 8.22, except that it includes the criteria for pass/fail, which is a score of 70. So the table becomes:

Version of Test	≥ 70 points	< 70 points
A	200	50
B	225	25
C	210	40
D	220	30

The data presented in this table are what kind of data?

SOLUTION 8.23

Categorical. The answer doesn't change. The data still involve two categories. Even though these categories have numbers in them (≥ 70 points and < 70 points), they are still categories, just different ways of stating pass and fail.

Example 8.23 shows that categories may include numbers, but that doesn't make the data numerical. It is the data, not how they are sorted, that determines whether a data set is numerical or categorical. Here we don't have the individual data points, just the categories into which they fall.

EXAMPLE 8.24

This example is similar to Example 8.23, except that now the data are for 20 students taking a particular test. Their scores are:

45, 95, 69, 99, 86, 71, 68, 79, 69, 68, 87, 94, 85, 68, 91, 83, 88, 87, 88, 99

These data represent what kind of data?

SOLUTION 8.24

Quantitative. These are quantitative, or numerical, data. Of course, we can categorize these into scores that are 70 and above (pass), and below 70 (fail), as we did for Example 8.23, but now that we have the individual scores, we can say a lot more about the data by presenting and analyzing the data points as shown in Sections 8.4.3 and 8.4.4.

Notice that of the scores that indicate "failing," only one (45) is far from passing, but five of them, the 68s and 69s, are close to passing scores. That could be useful information for the college, but it isn't shown when the data are just put into categories. For example, what if, instead of the 68s and 69s, the scores were 38s and 39s. Then the college should consider that the test is perhaps biased or that their admission standards should be revised.

8.4.3 Presenting Data

Data can be presented in many forms. The table format of the data can guide which further visual presentation to use.

8.4.3a Categorical Data

The table for categorical data points usually consists of two columns, and it may be sufficient for most of these data sets. The left column lists the categories and the right column lists the number of responses for that category or the percentage of all responses for that category. An example of such a table would show the education levels of the chief executive officers (CEOs) of the 500 top U.S. companies:

Education Level	Number of CEOs
No college	15
Bachelor's degree	165
MBA	190
Law degree	50
Other higher education degree	80

Bar graph. The data in this table also can be presented by a **bar graph**, or **bar chart**, which makes comparison of the numbers of CEOs in each different education level easier to visualize.

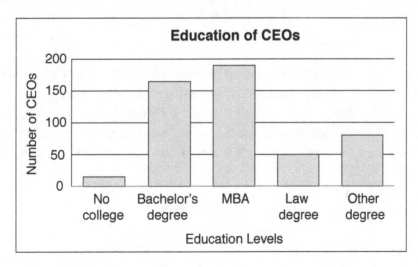

Pie chart. The following table revises the same data so that the number of respondents is reported as a percentage of the 500 respondents, which makes comparison even easier to see.

Education Level	Number of CEOs	Percentages
No college	15	3%
Bachelor's degree	165	33%
MBA	190	38%
Law degree	50	10%
Other higher education degree	80	16%

From percentage data such as shown in the above table, we can construct another clear comparison of the education levels of the CEOs, namely, the **pie chart** (sometimes called a **circle graph**). Pie charts are constructed from percentages, even though they may report actual numbers. The pie chart shown below reports both actual numbers and percentages.

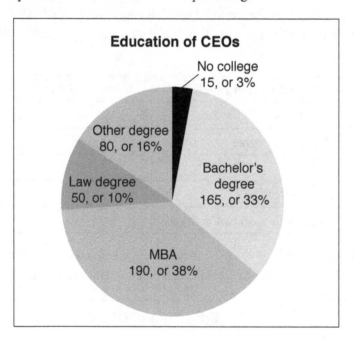

In a pie chart, the percentages must add up to 100%. This means a pie chart is not appropriate for a survey in which people are asked to "select all that apply" from the choices, since multiple answers to a question will add up to more than 100%. For example, if a survey asks what type of vacation people prefer, person A may choose mountains, beaches, and international; person B may choose only mountains; and person C may choose mountains and cities. The tally for this would be as follows:

Mountains	3
Beaches	1
International	1
Cities	1

This tally implies that there were six inputs, and half of them chose the mountains, when in fact there were three inputs, and they all chose the mountains.

Multiple-response data cannot be shown on a pie chart.

EXAMPLE 8.25

From the following pie chart, what would be the missing numerical value if the total number of students is 500?

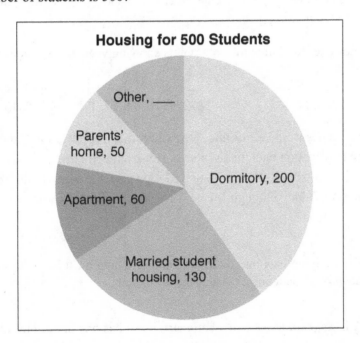

Housing for 500 Students

Other, ___

Parents' home, 50

Apartment, 60

Dormitory, 200

Married student housing, 130

SOLUTION

60. The total of all of the sectors must equal 500, so $200 + 130 + 60 + 50 + x = 500$, or $440 + x = 500$; thus, $x = 60$.

EXAMPLE 8.26

For the data given in the pie chart for Example 8.25, what percentage of students live in college housing (dormitories and married student housing)?

SOLUTION 8.26

66%. The number of students who live in dormitories (200) and married student housing (130) totals 330, so the percentage is $\frac{330}{500} = 66\%$.

8.4.3b Quantitative Data

The choice of how to present quantitative data depends partly on the size of the data set. For example, if there are just a few (perhaps fewer than 12) numerical data points, each individual data point can be presented clearly. But if there are many numerical data points, it is best to group them. If we were to start with a table for individual data points, let's say 20 points, that could get very unwieldy. But even though we may group data for ease of handling them, these are still quantitative data because they deal with numerical data.

For example, consider the following data points showing years of experience of 20 teachers in a particular school:

$$2, 2, 5, 11, 9, 7, 3, 2, 34, 18, 2, 4, 16, 14, 27, 12, 17, 21, 8, 15$$

A table of these values would be 17 lines long (the value 2 appears four times), but it wouldn't give us much more information than the list above. However, if we group the data in intervals, let's say, 1–5, 6–10, 11–15, 16–20, 21–25, 26–30, and 31–35 years, the table would be only 7 lines long, which is much more readable, although it is still not ideal. A better choice for readability in this case would be a histogram.

When grouping data into intervals, each grouping must have the same span, even if some have no data points associated with them.

Histogram. A **histogram** looks like a bar chart, but it has one important difference. It is continuous because each equal interval is numerical and there are no gaps between the bars. All of the bars touch each other. The histogram for the data above, grouped in five-year intervals is shown below. This histogram readily shows that the majority of the teachers at that school have 15 or fewer years of experience.

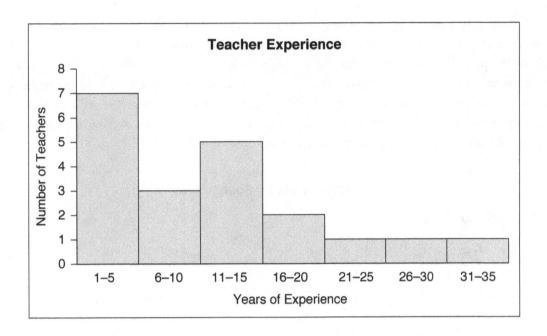

EXAMPLE 8.27

Based on the histogram shown below, how many sophomores had a course load of more than 16 credits?

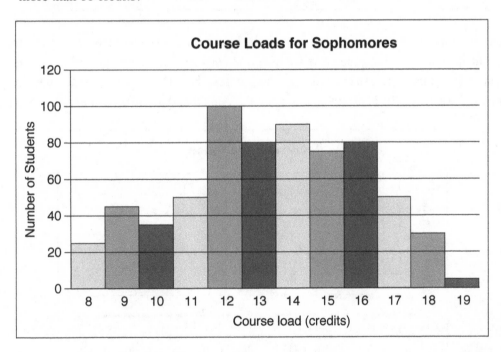

SOLUTION

85. More than 16 credits means 17, 18, and 19, credits, but not 16. Add up the number of students in each of these groups: $50 + 30 + 5 = 85$. Be careful in reading histograms precisely though. Without having the actual data, we cannot be sure, for example, whether 4 or 5 sophomores are taking 19 credits.

Line graph. This same group of data can also be shown in a **line graph** by connecting the midpoints of each bar of a histogram with a line. The straight line graph shown below was obtained by joining the midpoints of each column for the grouped data for course loads for sophomores from the previous example. This plot gives an idea of the data distribution. For very large numbers of data or small intervals, this line can be smoothed out to a **frequency curve**, in which the vertical axis can be frequency or percentage of the total and the horizontal axis shows the values of the data. This curve can aid in interpreting data, as discussed in Section 8.4.4.

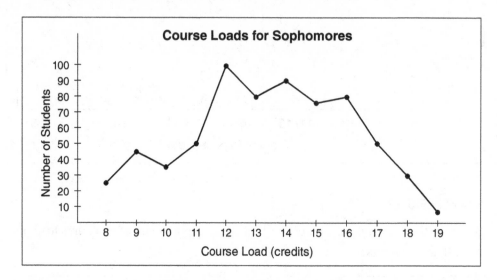

The next line graph comes from the data on the histogram for years of teacher experience. Note that for the data shown below, the years were reported as whole numbers. Quantitative data can be reported as fractions or decimals as well. In those cases, the intervals for the data above might be stated as 1–5.99, 6–10.99, 11–15.99, etc., or any intervals that don't overlap and are of equal size.

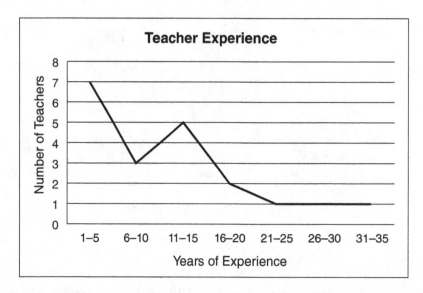

Dot plots. Another way to present data is by using **dot plots**, which is like tallying, also shown in the following figure. A tally for the above data is shown on the left, and the corresponding dot plot is shown on the right. Note that the dot plot is like a tally viewed from the side.

Years of Experience

1–5	///// //
6–10	///
11–15	/////
16–20	//
21–25	/
26–30	/
31–35	/

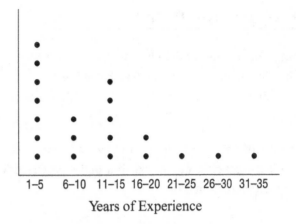

The mean and median can be calculated from a dot plot that has quantitative data, and the mode can be seen right away. If, instead of the intervals in the dot plot above, we used the middles of the intervals as their values (so we have the years labeled as 3, 8, 13, 18, 23, 28, and 33 years), we would use **weighted means** to calculate the mean of the data. To find the weighted means, we multiply each data point (here they are the midpoints of the intervals) by the frequency of the interval, sum them, and then divide by the total number of data points.

$$\text{mean} = \frac{3(7) + 8(3) + 13(5) + 18(2) + 23(1) + 28(1) + 33(1)}{20} =$$

$$\frac{230}{20} = 11.5 \text{ as the average number of years of experience.}$$

In contrast, for these data the median, since there are two middle values, 8 and 13, is their average, or 10.5. The mode is clearly the interval 1–5 years of experience.

Pictographs. An eye-catching way to display data is the use of pictographs. These are related to dot plots, but use icons instead of dots; in addition, each icon can represent multiples of the data. An example is shown below. Note that each ice cream icon represents not one but 100 ice cream cones, and the half-icons represent 50 ice cream cones.

Cafeteria Ice Cream Sales			
Sept.	🍦🍦🍦	Feb.	🍦
Oct.	🍦🍦	Mar.	🍦🍦
Nov.	🍦🍦	Apr.	🍦🍦
Dec.	🍦	May	🍦🍦🍦
Jan.	🍦	June	🍦🍦🍦🍦
🍦 = 100 Ice Cream Cones			

8.4.4 Interpreting Data

For *categorical* data, as already stated, there is no mean or median. However, the data can be interpreted by using the mode to say which category had the highest count. A pie chart or bar graph of the data visually indicates the distribution of the categories by comparing the areas for the categories.

For *numerical* data, the **frequency curve** is a smoothed-out line that more or less connects all points. An ideal frequency curve, called a **bell-shaped curve** for obvious reasons, is the **normal curve** discussed in Section 8.6.

8.5 COMPARING DATA SETS

8.5.1 Correlations

The **correlation** of two or more variables is an indication of the extent to which the variables fluctuate together. The values of one variable are plotted against the values of the other value (see Section 8.5.1b). By using a scatter plot, we may determine the best linear relationship between two given quantities. Correlation is the measure of the corresponding mathematical relationship. If there are two variables being considered, this is termed **bivariate data**. The discussion and examples in this section consider bivariate data.

8.5.1a Correlation Coefficient

Correlation between the variables is measured by a **correlation coefficient**, usually designated as r, which works quite well if the relationship between the variables is somewhat linear. The value of r can vary between $+1$ and -1. Correlation coefficients measure the strength of the linear association between the variables. The formula to determine the correlation coefficient looks more complicated than it is, but most calculators have a program to do the computation once the data points are entered. For now, what is important is that you know what the correlation coefficient indicates.

- A positive linear correlation indicates the extent to which both variables increase or decrease in parallel. A value of $r = 1$ indicates a perfect fit.

- A negative linear correlation indicates the extent to which one variable increases as the other decreases. A value of $r = -1$ indicates a perfect fit but in a reverse pattern.

- A correlation of 0 indicates that there is no linear relationship between the variables.

- The closer the correlation coefficient is to ± 1, the stronger the linear association.

8.5.1b Scatter Plots

To determine whether there is a **correlation** (or association) between two variable quantities, we use **scatter plots**. These look similar to line graphs in that they use Cartesian coordinates. Scatter plots are created by plotting the pairs of points, where the horizontal axis represents the independent variable and the vertical axis represents the dependent variable.

Examples of scatter plots of the three types of correlation are shown below.

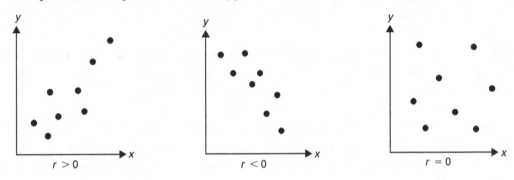

8.5.1c Regression Line

Determining linear regression consists of finding the best-fitting straight line through the data points. The line that approximates the correlation relationship is called the **regression line** or **line of best fit**. Do the data points line up exactly in a straight line? No, but the distances of the data points above the regression line are offset by the distances of the data points below the line.

If two variables are perfectly correlated, the plot is a straight line. The more the line deviates from a straight line, the less the two variables are correlated. A common example of very good correlation is hours of study time and grades—as the hours of study time increase, so do grades.

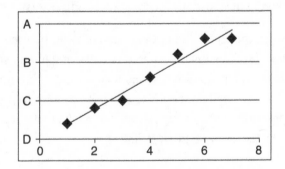

The data shown in the graph above have a correlation of about 0.9. The data in the graphs on the next page have correlations of about 0.5 (left) and 0 (right).

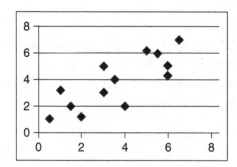
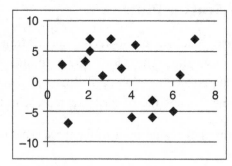

 The value of the correlation coefficient does not show how steep the regression line is. It shows only how good the correlation is and whether it is positive or negative. Linear regression is limited to predicting numeric output.

For linear regression, be sure the relationship can be approximated by a straight line. Linear regression is often inappropriately used to model nonlinear relationships, such as when one of the variables is squared. Sometimes, the "best fit" is in the form of a curve, such as for an exponential function, a quadratic equation, or even a circle—these may show up with a 0 correlation coefficient if they are tested by using linear regression criteria.

Since the regression line is a straight line, it can be written in the familiar slope-intercept form, $y = mx + b$, where m and b are the slope and y-intercept, respectively.

8.5.1d Trend

Many organizations use statistical analysis to interpret data or to predict future **trends**. Trend estimation is used to make and justify statements about the data; it is a statistical technique that helps to describe and analyze data. A trend can be seen in the regression line, or line of best fit, of the data. A trend is more likely the closer the correlation coefficient is to ±1.

If one of the variables in the data is time, trend analysis can be used to predict future events, known as **trend estimation**. Trend estimation is used to make and justify statements about the data; it is a statistical technique that helps to describe and analyze data. **Extrapolation** is an estimation of a value outside of the known data based on extending the data by continuing the regression line at the same slope. **Interpolation** is like extrapolation but, as the name implies, it involves figuring values *within* the data set by using the regression line.

8.5.1e Correlation versus Causation

 Correlation is NOT Causation.

Correlation does not mean that the change in one variable *causes* a change in the other variable. The two can be correlated through the regression line, but there can be other reasons for the data to have a good correlation. **Causation** is defined as one event being the result of the occurrence of another event. For example, when the weather gets warmer in the summer, more sunglasses and more ice cream are sold than in the cooler weather. There is probably a good correlation between temperature rise and sunglass sales, and another good correlation between temperature rise and ice cream sales, but even though the sales of the two items seem to correlate, it is with temperature, not with each other. There is no causal relationship between sunglasses and ice cream, even though there is a correlation. In other words, sunglasses do not make people crave ice cream, nor the other way around.

Causation can be extremely difficult to prove. Essentially it is trying to prove 100 percent correlation, which rarely happens. A popular example is the relation between smoking and lung cancer. It is indisputable that smoking *can* cause lung cancer and that historical data have shown a strong correlation between smoking and lung cancer. However, is smoking the cause of lung cancer in all cases? No. Can someone smoke and never get lung cancer? Of course. Can someone smoke but get lung cancer for a reason other than smoking? Also possible. So even though there is a correlation between the two, it is not 100 percent. And there is no causal relationship, which would imply that every single person who smoked even just one cigarette would get lung cancer.

Some Internet viral facts are humorous because they state a true and strong correlation between totally disparate events, implying that there is a cause and effect. One, for example, is the near perfect 99.79% correlation between U.S. spending on science, space, and technology versus the number of suicides by hanging, strangulation, and suffocation. Thousands of these absurd correlations exist—even though they are statistically correlated, they are not correlated in reality. When finding correlations, engage your brain.

8.5.2 Two-Way Frequency Tables

Similar to the one-way tables, which are familiar (examples are the tables in this chapter that were used to construct bar graphs, pie charts, and other categorical data), **two-way frequency tables** represent the possible relationships between *two* sets of categorical data whose values have been paired in some way. These tables are also called **contingency tables**.

Two-way tables visually represent the possible relationships between two sets of categorical data. Let's look at the simple two-way table shown below, in which the two sets of data are the ages of students (indicated by their grade in school) and whether they eat or skip breakfast.

	Eat breakfast	Skip breakfast	Totals
Middle school students	50	32	82
High school students	42	48	90
Totals	92	80	172

The categories are labeled along the top (whether a student eats breakfast) and the left side (the school grade of the student) of the table, with the counts appearing in the interior cells of the table.

From these data, we can fill out the totals for the rows, columns, and the whole table. For example, we see that there were 172 students in the data set. We can also state that 32 of the middle school students skip breakfast and 42 of the high school students eat breakfast.

In a two-way table, the total of the rows equals the total of the columns.

The numbers in the table are frequency counts, but we cannot make any *relative* comparisons because we would have to compare their relative frequencies to see whether there really is a difference. **Relative frequencies** compare the frequencies *in relation to* the rest of the data (thus the term "relative" frequencies).

Even though this table contains numbers, it is still a categorical table because the numbers are just how many of each category, or a **frequency count**, like a tally. Remember that for categorical data, there is no average, and that is true here.

The data presented as relative frequencies make comparisons easier. A similar two-way table converts each count to a **relative frequency**, which is the ratio of the value of the count to the value of the total count. Frequencies that appear within the table are called **joint frequencies**, and those in the margins are called **marginal frequencies**. The frequencies are stated in fractions, in decimals rounded to the nearest hundredth, or in percentages.

We can construct a table that gives relative frequencies based on the total (here, 172) or conditional frequencies, which are ratios of a joint relative frequency and the related marginal frequency. The choice depends on which question we want to answer. Let's look at each situation.

This first table is based on the total number of students, 172, and that percentage tells how the data compare to the whole total of inputs.

	Eat breakfast	Skip breakfast	Totals
Middle school students	$\frac{50}{172} = .29$	$\frac{32}{172} = .19$	$\frac{82}{172} = .48$
High school students	$\frac{42}{172} = .24$	$\frac{48}{172} = .28$	$\frac{90}{172} = .52$
Totals	$\frac{92}{172} = .53$	$\frac{80}{172} = .47$	1.00

From this table, we can answer questions, such as how does the proportion of middle school students who eat breakfast compare with high school students who skip breakfast. Our answer would be that they are comparable, with a slightly higher percentage in the first category (29% versus 28%). We can also, from the marginal frequencies tell what percentage of students in the group were middle school students (48%) by following the middle school row to its total. Likewise, we see that 53% of the students in the group eat breakfast.

If instead, however, we wanted to compare *within* a category, we would construct the relative frequency table differently, so the emphasis is on that particular category. Each entry in the table is relative to the total for that category, not the grand total of 172. Consider the frequencies by student class, from which we can answer questions comparing the percentage of *middle school students* who eat breakfast versus those who skip breakfast. Since we are considering the proportion just among middle school students, each original joint frequency is divided by the total of the middle school students, as seen in the table below. The difference is that 22% (or 61% – 39%) more of the middle school students eat breakfast than skip it. We would do likewise for the second row if high school students was the group of interest.

In relative frequency problems, concentrate only on the row or column that is "given" in the wording. In the above problem, the words "comparing the percentage of *middle school students* who eat breakfast versus those who skip breakfast" are essentially saying, "*given* that a student is a middle school student, compare the percentage who eat breakfast versus skip it."

	Eat breakfast	Skip breakfast	Total
Middle school students	$\frac{50}{82} = .61$	$\frac{32}{82} = .39$	1.00
High school students	$\frac{42}{90} = .47$	$\frac{48}{90} = .53$	1.00
Total	$\frac{92}{172} = .53$	$\frac{80}{172} = .47$	1.00

If we were interested in comparing students who eat breakfast, we would construct a relative frequency table by column, as shown below. Then we could compare whether high school students were more likely than middle school students to skip breakfast, and we would see that the difference is 20% (60% – 40%) or 20% more high school students skip breakfast compared to middle school students. Here, the question can be construed as asking "*given* that the student skips breakfast, what is the difference between high school and middle school students?"

	Middle school students	High school students	Total
Eat breakfast	$\frac{50}{82} = .61$	$\frac{42}{90} = .47$	$\frac{92}{172} = .53$
Skip breakfast	$\frac{32}{82} = .39$	$\frac{48}{90} = .53$	$\frac{80}{172} = .47$
Total	1.00	1.00	1.00

EXAMPLE 8.28

The following frequency counts show how many of a group of 34 high-school students work at an after-school job and how many have a car. What is the relative frequency of those students who work and have a car to those who have a car?

	Have a Car	Do Not Have a Car
Work	12	4
Do Not Work	8	10

SOLUTION 8.28

.60. The question is the same as asking, "Given that the student has a car, what is the relative frequency (probability) that the student also works?" That means the conditional relative frequency is the ratio of the number of students who have both a car and a job to the number of students who have a car, or $\dfrac{12}{12+8} = \dfrac{12}{20} = .60$.

8.6 NORMAL DISTRIBUTIONS

The most widely used distribution of data is the **normal distribution**. Some examples of this type of distribution are (a) the heights of all adult women, (b) the weights of all adult men, (c) the highest daily temperatures in a given city over a period of time, and (d) the diameters of cylinders manufactured in a factory.

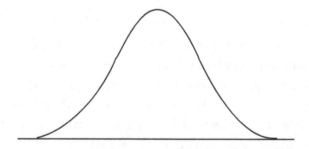

In the typical bell-shaped curve, as shown above, the horizontal axis shows the data (often but not necessarily in intervals), with the center point being the mean of the data. The vertical axis is the frequency of the data points, with the maximum corresponding to the mean. The normal curve forms the basis of statistics; how actual data points vary from it allow statisticians to make their analyses.

An example of a situation that would have close to a normal curve is the toss of a fair coin, where the horizontal axis would be the number of heads. (Again, the term "fair coin" simply means it is equally weighted, so there is no bias for heads or tails.) The vertical axis would be the frequency of getting a specific number of heads in a number of trials.

For example, let's say we flip a coin 32 times, and write down the possible number of heads (1 through 32) on the horizontal axis and the frequency of each number on the vertical axis. If we then repeat the experiment a thousand times, a graph of the number of 32-flip sets that resulted in a given number of heads would look very much like a bell-shaped curve. The high point would be for exactly 16 heads, occurring (in this ideal case) in 500 of the 1,000 times.

Most of the data will appear near the middle of a bell curve, and the farther from the middle a data point is, the less likely it is to have happened by chance. That is what statistics is all about—basically, if a verifiable data point (one not due to error) is very far from the mean of the data, which is the middle of the bell curve, then the chances that it occurred due to chance are very slim, so that data point must be due to something, or in statistics-speak, it must be "significant." For the coin experiment above, if two of the 32-flip sets had heads 31 times, we would suspect that there is something "unfair" about the coin because the chances of this happening due to pure chance is very, very low (with a probability way less than .003).

As a practical example, DNA sampling uses statistics by comparing certain parameters to what would be expected in a random sample of the population. When the conclusion in court is that there is a 1 in 400 million chance that the DNA found at a crime scene isn't that of the defendant, it means that the DNA match for that defendant is so extremely far from the middle of the bell curve, determined by statistical analysis, that it cannot be due to chance, and the conclusion is that the defendant was at the crime scene.

8.6.1 Properties of the Normal Curve

When graphed, a group of data that is normally distributed will resemble a symmetric histogram. The normal curve has these general properties.

- The mean, median, and mode are equal.

- The curve is symmetric about the mean.

- The y-coordinate of the mean is the maximum point on the curve.

- The curve never touches the x-axis and all y-values are positive.

- The curve is continuous and assumes all values of x.

8.6.2 Variance and Standard Deviation

To measure how spread the data are and to assess whether any data point is significant, we calculate the variance and its square root, called the standard deviation. First, it is important to recognize that "significance" as used here is a statistical term that says there is an actual difference (not just due to chance) between a data point and what is to be expected, and in addition there is a measure of significance that tells whether this relationship is strong, moderate, or weak. Often the strength of significance depends on how much data were used to determine significance. Statistical significance plays the primary role in statistics, as is shown in the rest of this chapter.

This becomes evident when we look at the formula for **variance**, which tells how much variability exists in a distribution. Without going into the derivation of the formula, it is enough to know that variance, designated as s^2, is the average of the squared differences between the data values and the mean.

$$s^2 = \frac{1}{n-1}\sum_{i=1}^{n}\left(x_i - \bar{x}\right)^2,$$

where i is an index to identify the different data points, from $i = 1$ to n, $\bar{x}$ is the mean of the population, and n is the number of data points. The reason the division is by $n - 1$ rather than n has to do with eliminating bias. But variance, although it is a measure of the variability of the data distribution, is not as important in statistical analysis as is its square root, called the **standard deviation**, s, which can be thought of as the typical distance of each data point from the mean.

 Remember that the square root of a sum is not the sum of the square roots. Write the squares of 1, 2, and 3 to show that $\sqrt{1 + 4 + 9} \neq \left(\sqrt{1} + \sqrt{4} + \sqrt{9}\right)$ because $\sqrt{14} \neq 6$. (In fact, using these numbers is an easy way to remember this rule—it's equal only for multiplication, not addition of the terms.)

$$s = \sqrt{\frac{1}{n-1}\sum_{i=1}^{n}\left(x_i - \bar{x}\right)^2}$$

The question arises as to why we square the distances in the variance and then have to take the square roots to find the standard deviation, which tells how spread out the data points are. The answer is simple: If we just summed the differences of the data points from the mean, by the very definition of the mean, the sum would always be 0. Not any information about the spread there. We square the sum of the differences and then take the square root to get a value that has meaning.

For example, the mean of {1, 2, 3, 4, 5} is 3. The sum of the distances from the mean are $(1 - 3) + (2 - 3) + (3 - 3) + (4 - 3) + (5 - 3) = (-2) + (-1) + 0 + 1 + 2 = 0$, and when divided by 5 it is still 0, and the standard deviation of $\sqrt{0} = 0$. The sum of the *squares* of the distances from the mean are $(1 - 3)^2 + (2 - 3)^2 + (3 - 3)^2 + (4 - 3)^2 + (5 - 3)^2 = (-2)^2 + (-1)^2 + 0^2 + 1^2 + 2^2 = 10$, which when divided by 5 is 2, and $\sqrt{2} = 1.414$. Sure enough, for our sample of five numbers, the average distance from the mean is $\frac{2 + 1 + 0 + 1 + 2}{5} = 1.2$, a better indicator than 0.

Why did we divide here by $n = 5$ and not $n - 1 = 4$? This is an important distinction: When we are finding the standard deviation of a sample from a population, the $n - 1$ takes care of bias; when we have the whole population, which in this example is the five numbers {1, 2, 3, 4, 5}, there is no bias—it is the whole population, so we take the average the usual way, by dividing by the number of items, $n = 5$.

For a sample population to find information for a larger population, use $n - 1$ to eliminate bias; for a total population, use n because there is no sample to introduce bias.

$$s = \sqrt{\frac{1}{n-1}\sum_{i=1}^{n}\left(x_i - \bar{x}\right)^2}$$ for a sample, where the mean is measured to be $\bar{x}$.

$$\sigma = \sqrt{\frac{1}{n}\sum_{i=1}^{n}\left(x_i - \mu\right)^2}$$ for the whole population, where is mean is estimated to be μ.

Note that the symbols used for mean and standard deviation are different based on whether the data represents a sample or a population, which use Greek letters.

	Sample	Population
Mean	$\bar{x}$	μ
Standard deviation	s	σ

8.6.3 Normal Distribution Percentages

So how do we use standard deviation—what does it mean? Let's look at the normal distribution, the force behind statistics, to see how standard deviation plays an important role. The area percentages between the mean and plus or minus 1, 2, or 3 standard deviations are important for solving normal distribution problems.

- Approximately 68.3% of the data are within one standard deviation of the mean ($\mu \pm \sigma$).

- Approximately 95.4% of the data are within two standard deviations of the mean ($\mu \pm 2\sigma$).

- Approximately 99.7% of the data are within three standard deviations of the mean ($\mu \pm 3\sigma$).

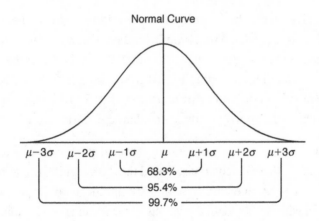

Normal Curve

EXAMPLE 8.29

Given the following data that represent the average amount of rainfall for each month in Birmingham, England, in a random sample of 20 years, what general conclusion can we state about the average monthly rainfall and standard deviation?

Average Monthly Rainfall (inches)

January	February	March	April	May	June
2.3	1.9	2.1	1.8	2.2	2.2

July	August	September	October	November	December
2.0	2.8	2.2	2.1	2.5	2.6

SOLUTION 8.29

$\bar{x} = 2.225$ inches, $s = 0.290$ inches. To compute the standard deviation, we must first compute the mean. In this data set, $\bar{x} = \dfrac{26.7}{12} = 2.225$. To compute the standard deviation, find the variance and take the square root:

$$s^2 = \frac{1}{n-1} \sum_{i=1}^{12} (x_i - x)^2$$

$$= \frac{1}{12-1}(2.3 - 2.225)^2 + (1.9 - 2.225)^2 + \ldots + (2.6 - 2.225)^2$$

$$= \frac{1}{11}(0.9225) \approx 0.084$$

So the standard deviation, s, is $\sqrt{0.084} = 0.290$.

We can state a conclusion that the monthly mean rainfall in Birmingham is 2.225 inches, and it varies by about ±0.290 inches 68.3% of the time. Said another way, about 68.3% of the time, the monthly rainfall in Birmingham is between 1.935 and 2.515 inches. Similarly, the data show that about 95.4% of the time, the monthly rainfall in Birmingham is 1.645 to 2.805 inches, and about 99.7% of the time, the monthly rainfall in Birmingham is 1.355 to 3.095 inches. These last calculations were for two standard deviations and three standard deviations from the mean.

To give a simple idea of what this means, let's say it rained an average of 3.05 inches in one month the following year. Based on these calculations, would that be a significant rainfall (meaning *statistically* significant, since we can assume it was emotionally significant to the people in Birmingham)? If we decided that anything within 3 standard deviations of the mean is not significant (in other words, it can be expected), then no, it is not statistically significant. What if it rained only 1 inch the year after that—is that statistically significant? Yes, in this case it is because that is outside of −3 standard deviations, which suggests that so little rain is not due to chance and may be due to another reason, such as "global warming," which is a common explanation for a lot of weather anomalies.

8.6.4 Standard Normal Distribution: Z-Scores

A **standard normal distribution** is a special case of the normal distribution above, in which the mean is normalized to 0, one standard deviation is 1, and the area under the whole curve above the x-axis is 1. This is just a neater way to write the normal distribution, and it is easier to calculate and understand. Compare the curve on the left with the actual numbers to the curve on the right with the standardized numbers.

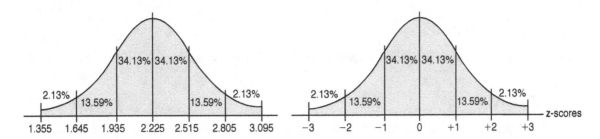

The values of x of a normal distribution (the curve on the left, 1.355, 1.645, etc.) are called **raw scores**. For a *standard* normal distribution, the independent values become **z-scores**, or **standard scores**. Z-scores are used to determine how many standard deviations from the mean a data value lies. Just as x-scores can assume any value, z-scores can also assume any value, but since they represent the number of standard deviations above or below the mean, they usually lie between –3 and +3. A negative z-score indicates how many standard deviations below the mean, and a z-score of 0 indicates a raw score that is equal to the mean.

Raw scores (x-scores) are converted to z-scores by the simple formula

$$z = \frac{x - \mu}{\sigma}$$

where x is the raw score. Since z-scores are normalized, each z-score is associated with a percentage of the area under the curve above (or below) the mean. Therefore, the z-score of 1 is associated with 34.13% of the data above the mean or 84.13% of the data, since from $z = 0$ to the left end of the curve is 50% of the area. Similarly, $z = 2$ means (34.12 + 13.59 =) 47.72% of the data above the mean, or 97.72% of the data.

The formula $z = \frac{x - \mu}{\sigma}$ applies to *any* distribution of data, not just those that belong to a normal distribution.

Due to the symmetry of the standard normal distribution, the area under the graph from $z = 0$ to either "end" of the distribution (positive or negative) is 50%. "End" is written with quote marks because the graph goes on to infinity in either direction. In addition, the area between $z = 0$ and a given positive z value is equivalent to the area between $z = 0$ and the corresponding negative z value. That is, the area between $z = 0$ and $z = 1.5$ is the same as the area between $z = 0$ and $z = -1.5$.

A z-score of 0 means 50% of the data are below and 50% of the data are above that point.

EXAMPLE 8.30

What is the area between $z = 0$ and $z = 1$?

SOLUTION 8.30

From the graph of the standardized normal distribution, this area is 34.13%.

EXAMPLE 8.31

What percentage of the data are below $z = -1$?

SOLUTION 8.31

There are two ways to look at this problem. One is to add $13.59\% + 2.13\% = 15.72\%$. However, beyond the z-scores of ± 3 is a tiny percentage of data that isn't being counted. A more accurate way to calculate this is to compute the area to the right of $z = -1$ and subtract it from 100%. In that case, use the fact that everything from z to either end of the curve is 50% of the area, so the answer is $(1 - (.50 + 34.13) = 15.87\%$, the correct answer.

8.6.5 Applications of the Normal Distribution

The steps used to solve the preceding examples can be applied to any normal distributions, provided that the mean and standard deviation are known. In some cases, the word "probability" will be used in place of "area" or "percentage." The procedure for finding a probability is identical to that of finding a percentage or area under the normal curve.

The overwhelming advantage of z-scores is that they allow comparison of two different sets of data.

EXAMPLE 8.32

A mathematics test was given to a class that met in the morning and to a class that met in the afternoon. For the morning class, the mean was 84 and the standard deviation was 3.4. For the afternoon class, the mean was 82 and the standard deviation was 3.6. Both distributions were normal. For which class would a raw score of 90 correspond to a higher z-score?

SOLUTION 8.32

Calculate the *z*-scores separately. For the morning class, a raw score of 90 corresponds to a *z*-score of $z = \dfrac{90 - 84}{3.4} = \dfrac{6}{3.4} \approx 1.76$. For the afternoon class, $z = \dfrac{90 - 82}{3.6} = \dfrac{8}{3.6} \approx 2.22$. Thus, the grade of 90 corresponded to a higher *z*-score in the afternoon class than in the morning class, indicating a *relatively* better score, even though both scores were 90.

EXAMPLE 8.33

A watch company makes watches with a mean lifetime of 38 months, and a standard deviation of 5 months. What percentage of this company's watches is expected to last longer than 4 years, assuming the company's watches wear out according to a normal distribution?

SOLUTION 8.33

2.28%. Before starting this solution, recognize that the question is asking about 48 months. Then recognize that 48 months is the mean (38) plus two standard deviations (2×5). So this example translates to "What is the percentage of a normal curve above 2 standard deviations?" The percentage below 2 standard deviations is $50 + (34.13 + 13.59) = 97.72\%$, so the percentage above 2 standard deviations is $100 - 97.72 = 2.28\%$. (Note that this differs from the percentage of 2.13% shown on the graph of the standard normal distribution because 2.13% is the percentage between 2 and 3 standard deviations not including the small percentage above 3 standard deviations.)

8.6.6 Sampling

Statistics draw conclusions concerning a sample taken from a population of normally distributed data. Section 8.4.1 emphasized that all samples should be unbiased and representative of the population. Here we talk about the usefulness of sampling and how statistics drawn from samples relate to the population.

An important factor in choosing a sample from a normal population is the size of the sample. As an indication of the possible number of samples from a population, let's consider a population of only 10,000 items and a sample size of 40 from this population. At first glance, we might assume that means a possible $\dfrac{10,000}{.40} = 250$ samples from which we would choose one. But in actuality, since this is a combination of 10,000 items taken 40 at a time, or $_{10,000}C_{40} = \dfrac{10,000!}{.40!(10,000 - 40)!}$, there are much more than a billion different samples! This is because any one item has a chance to be chosen for more than one sample.

Interestingly, if we were to take the means of each of these samples, which themselves form a normal distribution, the mean of that distribution of sample means, designated as $\mu_{\overline{x}}$, equals the mean of the population, μ. Now, if we look at the standard deviations of each of the samples, it turns out that the standard deviation of this same distribution of sample means, designated as $\sigma_{\overline{X}}$ equals the standard deviation of the whole population σ, divided by the square root of the size of each sample $\sqrt{n}$, which we can regard as a correction factor. In summary, the mean and standard deviation of the whole population can be obtained from the mean and standard deviation of the sample (also called the **sampling error**), or

$$\mu_{\overline{X}} = \mu \text{ and } \sigma_{\overline{X}} = \frac{\sigma}{\sqrt{n}}.$$

So to get an idea of the distribution of the 10,000 items in our example, we don't have to mess with all 10,000, but instead just a sample of the 10,000, which will give us our population parameters.

This opens up a bunch of questions:

- *Does the original population have to be normally distributed?* No, but it should be much larger than 30. The **Central Limit Theorem**, states that as sample size increases, the distribution of the sample means of *any* population with mean μ and standard deviation σ will approach a normal distribution related to the mean and standard deviation by the relationships noted above.

- *How big does the sample have to be?* For the Central Limit Theorem to hold, the sample size should be 30 or more. It is for this reason that the *population* should be much larger than 30.

- *Where does the $\sqrt{n}$ come from?* There is some variation in the standard deviations of the distribution of all the sample means in a population, and statisticians have determined that a correction factor of $\frac{1}{\sqrt{n}}$ will take care of that variability. We'll trust them on this.

- *What kind of error is the sampling error?* The sampling error, another name for the standard deviation of the distribution of sample means, is not an error at all. It just reflects the variability in the data. The sampling error is a way to acknowledge that the whole population isn't being measured but instead a sample that may vary from the general population in some way. However, these samples are unbiased and representative of the population, so the variability shouldn't be too large.

Some examples will help to understand the use of samples to describe a population.

EXAMPLE 8.34

A random sample of 300 students was found to have a mean height of 64 inches with a standard deviation of 2.3 inches. What is the standard error of the mean?

SOLUTION 8.34

0.13. First, we must assume that the whole student population is much larger than 300, the size of the sample. The question asks for the standard error of the mean, which is $\sigma_{\overline{X}} = \dfrac{\sigma}{\sqrt{n}} = \dfrac{2.3}{\sqrt{300}} \approx 0.13$.

EXAMPLE 8.35

A popular magazine surveyed its readers to indicate the number of hours of sleep needed per night. The results showed a mean of 6 hours, with a standard deviation of 1.5 hours. A random group of 100 surveys are selected. What is the probability that the sample mean will be less than 5.7 hours? (Assume that a very large number of readers responded.)

SOLUTION 8.35

2.3%. Since the value of n is greater than 30, the distribution of sample means must be normally distributed. For this distribution of sample means,

$$\mu_{\overline{X}} = \mu = 6 \text{ and } \sigma_{\overline{X}} = \frac{\sigma}{\sqrt{n}} = \frac{1.5}{\sqrt{100}} = 0.15.$$

We want to find the probability that a value of this distribution is less than 5.7. For a normal distribution with mean 6 and standard deviation of 0.15, this is the same as asking for the area under the normal curve to the left of two standard deviations below the mean. We can find this by calculating $1 - (0.50 + 0.341 + 0.136) = 1 - 0.977 = 0.023$, where 0.50 represents everything above the mean, and $0.341 + 0.136$ is the sum of the areas between the mean and two standard deviations below the mean. An area of 0.023 corresponds to a probability of 2.3%.

EXAMPLE 8.36

The town of Whispering Winds has been keeping statistics on its highest temperature each day for more than 200 years. For that period of time, its mean high temperature has been 47.3 degrees with a standard deviation of 4.8 degrees. A random sample of 64 days is chosen. What is the probability that the sample mean will exceed 47.9 degrees?

SOLUTION 8.36

15.87%. We are not told whether the population of temperatures is normally distributed, but since the sample size is $64 > 30$, the distribution of means can be treated as a normal distribution. We first determine that $\mu_{\overline{X}} = \mu = 47.3$ and $\sigma_{\overline{X}} = \dfrac{\sigma}{\sqrt{n}} = \dfrac{4.8}{\sqrt{64}} = 0.6$. Since 47.9 = the mean (47.3) plus one standard deviation (0.6), we just have to find the area under the normal curve to the right of $+1\sigma_{\overline{X}}$. This is $50 - .3413 = .1587$, or a probability of 15.87%.

EXAMPLE 8.37

The mean score of the first two tests in a math class is 80, and the standard deviation is 10.5. Assume a normal distribution and that the score on the third test will have the same distribution. What is the probability that the mean score for the third test will be higher than 59 (passing)?

SOLUTION 8.37

First, compute the z-score for the passing grade of 59: $z = \dfrac{x - \bar{x}}{s} = \dfrac{59 - 80}{10.5} = -2$.

So a score of 59 is 2 standard deviations below the mean. This is a one-tailed test because we are interested only in scores above 59; we can ignore scores below 59. So the requested probability includes the scores from 59 to 80 plus the scores greater than 80. We just calculated that the scores from 59 to 80 include 2 standard deviations below the mean, which is half of 95.5%, or 47.75%. To that we have to add the probability of getting above 80, which is 50%. Therefore, the requested probability is 47.75% + 50% = 97.75%.

8.6.7 Confidence Intervals

Often, the information that is known is about sample data and this information is used to draw conclusions about the population data. For example, the value of a sample mean, $\bar{x}$, is usually easy to find. This value can provide a good estimate of the mean of the population, μ, from which this sample was extracted. The **confidence interval** for the mean of a population indicates the accuracy of estimating the population mean from the sample mean.

A confidence interval for the mean of a population is a two-sided open interval that corresponds to the percentage of samples whose mean is within the range specified. A common percentage is a 95% confidence interval, which says that there is a 95% chance that the calculated confidence interval contains the true population mean. (Alternatively, it is saying that 5% of the time, the true population mean may lie outside that interval.) This is not the same as finding a range that contains 95% of the values.

For the following discussion, at least one of the following two conditions must hold:

- the sample size n is at least 30.

- the population standard deviation, σ, is known and the population is normally distributed. (If we do not know the value of σ but the sample size is greater than 30, then we may substitute the sample standard deviation, s, for the population standard deviation.)

So the confidence interval for the case where the population standard deviation σ is known is given by the expression

$$\bar{x} \pm (z_c)\left(\frac{\sigma}{\sqrt{n}}\right).$$

When σ is not known, the sample size must be at least 30, and the expression changes to

$$\bar{x} \pm (z_c)\left(\frac{s}{\sqrt{n}}\right).$$

where s is the sample standard deviation.

8.6.7a Critical Values

The z value is the same as before, the number of standard deviations from the mean, except we are looking at it slightly differently here. Previously, the values of z that we were interested in corresponded to the percentage of the data within an interval of standard deviations above and below the mean:

- $z = \pm 1$, corresponds to 68.3% of the data

- $z = \pm 2$ corresponds to 95.5% of the data

- $z = \pm 3$ corresponds to 99.7% of the data

Now, with confidence intervals, z has the same role, but the percentages relate to 90%, 95%, and 99% confidence. The value of z_c, which is the critical z value of the standard normal distribution designated as $(z_c)\left(\frac{\sigma}{\sqrt{n}}\right)$ or $(z_c)\left(\frac{s}{\sqrt{n}}\right)$, is known as the **maximum error of estimate**. Again, the word "error" is not a mistake, it just reflects the variability in the data.

The z_c, or **critical values** of these standard percentages fall right where we would assume, given the values for z above. In other words, $z = \pm 2$ corresponds to 95.5%, and here for 95% confidence, $z_c = 1.960$—it makes sense.

- $z_c = 1.645$ for 90% confidence

- $z_c = 1.960$ for 95% confidence

- $z_c = 2.576$ for 99% confidence

These are termed "critical" values because they determine the cutoff values (upper and lower limits) for the confidence intervals, or statistical significance at the designated degree of confidence. Confidence intervals can be computed for any desired degree of confidence, but they are traditionally expressed with 95% confidence. They correspond to making the statement that "There is a 95% probability that the calculated confidence interval encompasses the true value of the population parameter."

To get a sense of what all of these percentages mean, the following graph shows the 95% interval on a normal curve. The tails of this curve take up the remaining 5%, divided into two equal areas. The upper and lower limits correspond to $z_c = \pm 1.96$.

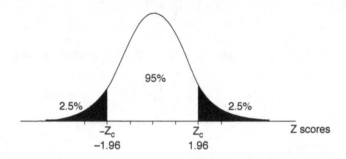

Similar graphs pertain to the 90% and 99% confidence intervals. Would you expect the 99% confidence interval to be wider or narrower? The answer is wider, because for more confidence that an interval contains the true parameter, the intervals should contain more points, and thus be wider. At the extreme case of 100% confidence that the interval contains the true population, the curve has to encompass every data point, so it would be infinitely wide. In contrast, if you are willing to be only 50% sure that an interval contains the true value, the interval can be much narrower (and much less meaningful).

8.6.7b Alpha Values

Alpha values, or **significance levels**, are the rest of the probability after the confidence percentage is determined. So for a 95% confidence interval, the alpha value is 5%. As seen in the normal curve above, this 5% is divided evenly between the tails of the distribution. Alpha values can express the cutoffs for statistical significance just as confidence intervals did.

For a **two-tailed distribution**—one in which the values of the maximum error of estimate both above and below the mean are considered—the difference between 100% and the confidence percentages must be divided evenly between the two tails, values that are half the alpha value. A two-tailed test would be used to answer whether there is a statistically significant difference (either positive or negative) between values obtained from different samples or in different (but equal) circumstances for a particular sample.

A **one-tailed distribution** considers the alpha to be on one or the other side of the mean but not both. In those cases, all of the alpha percentage is on one of the tails, dependent on the problem. In contrast to the two-tailed distribution, a one-tailed test would be used to answer whether there is a statistically significant *increase* in values obtained from different samples or perhaps a *decrease* in different (but equal) circumstances for a particular sample. By limiting the problem to only one direction (increase, more, or words such as these), the attention is on one side of the normal distribution, and thus a one-tailed focus.

EXAMPLE 8.38

A survey of 64 homeowners in Maryland discovered that the average age of their homes was 25 years, with a sample standard deviation of 4 years. What is the 95% confidence interval for the age of all homes in Maryland?

SOLUTION 8.38

This problem calls for a confidence interval for which the probability is 95% that this range of values includes the true mean of the population (μ). Since the sample size is 64, we know that the distribution of all samples of size 64, from the population of Maryland homes, is normally distributed. Here are the known quantities thus far: $\bar{x} = 25$, $s = 4$, and $n = 64$. Essentially, we want include the middle 95% of a normal distribution, or $z_c = 1.96$. Thus, the required interval becomes $25 \pm (1.96)\left(\dfrac{4}{\sqrt{64}}\right) = 25 \pm (0.98)$, or written another way, $24.02 < \mu < 25.98$. This means we are 95% confident that the average age of the homes is between 24.02 and 25.98 years.

EXAMPLE 8.39

The heights of a particular type of plant are normally distributed. The heights of 400 plants were measured with a mean of 26 inches and a standard deviation of 4.8 inches. To the nearest hundredth, what is the 90% confidence interval for the mean height of all these plants?

SOLUTION 8.39

Using the values $\bar{x} = 26$, $s = 4.8$, and $n = 400$, the required interval for the population mean is $26 \pm (1.645)\left(\dfrac{4.8}{\sqrt{400}}\right) \approx 26 \pm 0.39$. The interval may also be written as $25.61 < \mu < 26.39$.

Practice Exercises

1. The wheel of fortune at the county fair has a grand prize of $1,000, 5 prizes of $500, 10 prizes of $100, and the rest of the 100 "prizes" are worth nothing. What should the vendor charge to make at least $1,000 in a day in which 500 people play? (Round to the nearest dollar.)

   (A) $1.00

   (B) $2.00

   (C) $5.00

   (D) $10.00

2. The principal of a new school wants to know what mascot the incoming students would prefer. She summons every student into her office and asks what the new mascot should be. What type of study is this?

    (A) census

    (B) sample survey

    (C) experiment

    (D) observational study

3. An example of categorical data is

    (A) The heights of the students in the class

    (B) All the whole numbers between 1 and 2

    (C) All the numbers between 1 and 2

    (D) Strongly agree, agree, no opinion, disagree, strongly disagree

4. On a standardized normal curve, what percentage of the area under the curve is between $z = -1$ and $z = 1$?

    (A) 1.0%

    (B) 34.1%

    (C) 50.0%

    (D) 68.3%

5. Suppose the mean age of school principals in the United States is 54 years old, with a standard deviation of 7 years. What percentage of these principals are younger than 47 years old, assuming their ages are normally distributed?

    (A) 15.87%

    (B) 34.13%

    (C) 50%

    (D) 84.13%

6. Eighteen books are purchased at an average cost of $40 each, and 54 other books are purchased at an average cost of $50 each. What is the average cost of all the books?

    (A) $45.00

    (B) $47.50

    (C) $63.33

    (D) $190.00

7. Quintin tells Nick to draw one card from a standard deck of playing cards. If Nick picks a spade, Quintin will give him $10. If Nick picks a face card that isn't a spade, he will get $8. If Nick picks any other card, he will have to pay Quintin $6. Should Nick play?

    (A) Yes, Nick should expect to win.

    (B) No, the odds are that Nick will lose.

    (C) No, chances are that Nick will just break even.

    (D) It depends on how many times Nick draws a card.

8. Q: A sample of U.S. adults was asked how many days per week each read a daily newspaper (defined as reading not just the comics and at least one article besides sports). What is the average number of days per week these adults read the newspaper, rounded to the nearest whole number?

    Days read paper:

    5 3 0 7 4 0 7 6 1 0 1 3 2 3 2 0 5

    (A) 2.88

    (B) 3

    (C) 3.5

    (D) 4

9. If a die is weighted so that the probability of throwing an even number is twice the probability of throwing an odd number, what is the probability of throwing a 4?

    (A) $\dfrac{1}{6}$

    (B) $\dfrac{1}{2}$

    (C) $\dfrac{1}{3}$

    (D) $\dfrac{2}{3}$

10. In a group of 25 students, 12 were studying French, 15 were studying German, and 8 were studying neither. What is the universal set?

    (A) 35 students

    (B) 27 students

    (C) 25 students

    (D) 18 students

Solutions

1. (D) $10.00. The vendor wants the expected value per spin to be $\left(\dfrac{\$1000}{500} = \$2 \right)$. The expected value per spin from the vendor's point of view (where money coming in is positive and money paid out is negative) is

$$(-\$100)\left(\frac{1}{100}\right) + (-\$50)\left(\frac{5}{100}\right) + (-\$25)\left(\frac{10}{100}\right) + \left(\frac{84}{100}\right)x = \$2.$$

This reduces to $-1 - 2.5 - 2.5 + .84x = 2$, or $84x = 8$, so each chance has to cost more than $x = \$9.52$.

2. (A) census. The principal has collected data from every individual in the population, in this case, the population of all school students. If the principal had asked only some of the students, chosen randomly, this would have been a sample survey.

3. (D) Strongly agree, agree, no opinion, disagree, strongly disagree. This is a ranking of categorical data.

4. (D) 68.3%. This is the area under the graph one standard deviation below to one standard deviation above the mean. It is $2 \times (34.13\%) = 68.26\%$ (see the graph in Section 8.6.4).

5. (A) 15.87%. The phrase "younger than 47" translates to "is less than 1 standard deviation below the mean" (or $z = -1$), since the mean (54) minus one standard deviation (7) equals 47. So this problem is asking for the area under the curve to the left of -1 standard deviation. Use the fact that the area under the normal curve from the mean to 1 standard deviation = 34.13% and from the mean to either end of the curve is 50% of the total area, so subtract them from 100% and the answer is $(1.00 - (.50 + 34.13)) = 15.87\%$. Alternatively, sketch the distribution and look at the answer choices and eliminate anything more than $(.50 - 34.13) \approx 16\%$ as being too high.

6. (B) $47.50. The average cost equals $\dfrac{\text{Total cost}}{\text{Total number of books}} = \dfrac{(18 \times \$40) + (54 \times \$50)}{(18 + 54)}$. Use the calculator, or because every term is divisible by 18, the problem reduces to $\dfrac{\$40 + (3 \times \$50)}{1 + 3} = \dfrac{\$190}{4} = \$47.50$.

7.   (A) Yes, Nick should expect to win. The expected values are the values of the winnings, $10 for a spade, $8 for a non-spade face card, and –$6 for all the other cards. The weighted probabilities are thus $10\left(\dfrac{13}{52}\right)$, $+8\left(\dfrac{9}{52}\right)$, and $-6\left(\dfrac{30}{52}\right)$, respectively. This calculates to $\dfrac{130}{52}+\dfrac{72}{52}-\dfrac{180}{52}=\dfrac{22}{52}=\$.42$. Since the expected value of the game is positive although small (approximately 42 cents), it is to Nick's advantage to play the game.

8.   (B) 3. Add the 17 numbers and divide by 17 to get 2.88, which rounds to 3 days. Even though some of the numbers were 0, they still get included in the count of 17.

9 .   (D) $\dfrac{2}{3}$. The probability of throwing any number on the die is no longer one-sixth, as it was for a fair die. Now the probability of throwing an odd number is $\dfrac{1}{3}$ and the probability of throwing an even number is $\dfrac{2}{3}$ (twice the probability of an odd number).

10.   (C) 25 students. The universe is given in the first sentence. Since the numbers total more than 25, some students must be studying both languages, but that doesn't change the universe.

Discrete Mathematics

Discrete mathematics, in contrast to continuous mathematics, deals with distinct items. A good way to think of discrete items is the integers marked on a number line that goes from -10 to $+10$. The integers are discrete—they are separate and countable, and they differ by some finite amount. Discrete numbers don't have to be whole numbers or positive numbers—they just have to be separate. If we connect the points in a line, we no longer can count all of the real numbers (decimals) between the integers—there are an infinite number between them and they are continuous, and not discrete.

9.1 SEQUENCES AND SERIES

Sequences are of various types: arithmetic (pronounced as "arith-MA-tic"), geometric, recursive, and patterns, among other sequences. A **sequence** is a set of things that have some rule for their order. A **series** is the sum of a finite sequence.

9.1.1 Arithmetic Sequence

An **arithmetic sequence** is a sequence of numbers in which a fixed number is added from each term to the next. The terms are usually designated as $a_1, a_2, a_3, \ldots$, and the **constant difference** between successive terms is usually designated as d, such that $d = a_n - a_{n-1}$, where n is any positive integer greater than 1. An arithmetic sequence is also known as an **arithmetic progression**.

Examples of arithmetic sequences include increasing terms, such as 2, 4, 6, 8, 10, . . . in which $d = 2$. Or the terms can decrease, such as in the sequence 21, 18, 15, 12, 9, . . ., in which $d = -3$.

It is easy to calculate the nth term of an arithmetic sequence, since it is the original term with d added n times. Thus, the nth term of an arithmetic sequence is given by

$$a_n = a_1 + (n-1)d.$$

What this formula is saying is that if we take the first number in the sequence, we can find any other term in the sequence by multiplying the common difference by one less than the position of the term we are finding. The -1 comes in because we already are adding the first term by including a_1 in the formula. So to find the tenth term of the sequence 10, 12, 14, 16, 18, ..., $a_{10} + 9(2) = 28$. This checks out by counting ten terms of the sequence starting with the number 10 and counting by twos, but for other sequences and higher terms, we'd better just rely on the formula.

Since the terms of an arithmetic sequence increase steadily, if we plot the placement of a term versus the value of the term, we get a straight line with a positive slope for $d > 0$ and a negative slope for $d < 0$.

EXAMPLE 9.1

Find b_{15} in the arithmetic sequence in which $b_3 = -4$ and $b_6 = -13$.

SOLUTION 9.1

-40. To find the value of any term in an arithmetic sequence, we use the formula $a_n = a_1 + (n-1)d$. Here the a's are replaced by b's, but any letter can be used to name the terms. To find b_{15}, we need to find d. Rather than try to find b_1, let's just say b_3 is the first term and adjust the formula accordingly, so we now have $b_6 = b_3 + (4-1)d$, or $-13 = -4 + 3d$, or $d = -3$. So to find b_{15}, we have to adjust its position in the series if the first term is $b_3 = -4$ as well. Thus, b_{15} is the 13th term (just subtract 2 from each subscript to find its new position), so we have

$$a_{15} = a_1 + (13-1)(d)$$
$$b_{15} = b_3 + (13-1)(-3) = -4 + (12)(-3) = -40$$

To find n, subtract the first term index from the last term index (in the example above, that would be $15 - 3 = 12$), but add 1 to include the first term in the count. As a reminder that you should add the 1, keep in mind the number of terms from a_1 to a_3—it's 3, not 2.

When solving for n, be sure your answer is a positive integer. There is no such thing as a fractional or negative number of terms in a sequence!

An application of an arithmetic sequence in the world of finance is *simple interest*. Suppose P = the original principal, r = annual interest rate, t = time in years, and A = amount. Then $A = P + Prt$. The corresponding values of the amount for 1 year, 2 years, 3 years, and 4 years, are $P + Pr$, $P + 2Pr$, $P + 3Pr$, and $P + 4Pr$, which is an arithmetic sequence in which the first term is $P + Pr$ and the common difference is Pr.

EXAMPLE 9.2

If $200 is deposited into a bank in which the annual simple interest rate is 4.5%, what is the amount after 9 years?

SOLUTION 9.2

$A = \$200 + (\$200)(0.045)(9) = \$281$.

EXAMPLE 9.3

Insert the three terms of the arithmetic sequence from 5 to 21.

SOLUTION 9.3

9, 13, 17. In an arithmetic sequence, this would be the three terms that complete the sequence 5, ___, ___, ___, 21. The first term is $a_1 = 5$ and the 5th term is $a_5 = 21$. We have to find the common difference, d, to find the missing terms. Using the formula $a_n = a_1 + (n - 1)d$ for the five terms, we have $21 = 5 + (5 - 1)d$, or $d = \dfrac{21 - 5}{5 - 1} = \dfrac{16}{4} = 4$, so the missing terms are 9, 13, and 17.

9.1.2 Arithmetic Series

An **arithmetic series** is just the sum of a certain number of terms of an arithmetic sequence, usually designated as S_n. The formula is based on the average value between the first and nth term multiplied by n, or

$$S_n = \left(\frac{a_1 + a_n}{2}\right)(n) = \frac{n(a_1 + a_n)}{2}.$$

It looks like we don't even have to know d to use this formula, but if we aren't given the value for a_n, we'll need to know d to find a_n. For example, to answer the question, "What is the sum of the sequence of five numbers 11, 13, 15, 17, 19?" you would just substitute the numbers into $S_n = \dfrac{n(a_1 + a_n)}{2}$ to get $\dfrac{5(11 + 19)}{2} = 75$.

EXAMPLE 9.4

Find the sum of 10 terms of an arithmetic progression when the first term is 5 and the tenth term is –13.

SOLUTION 9.4

–40. Use the formula $S_n = \dfrac{n(a_1 + a_n)}{2} = \dfrac{10(5 + (-13))}{2} = -40$.

EXAMPLE 9.5

Find the sum of the first seven even integers greater than 10.

SOLUTION 9.5

126. This is the same as asking for the sum of the first seven integers of the sequence 12, 14, 16, ... So what is the seventh integer in this series? (Yes, we can count to find it here, but not every problem would be that simple.) We have to use the $a_n = a_1 + (n-1)d$ formula for that, where a_n is what we are finding, $a_1 = 12$, $n = 7$, and $d = 2$. So we do have to know d to find an arithmetic sequence sometimes, even though it isn't in the formula for the series. Then we have $a_7 = a_1 + (n-1)d = 12 + 6(2) = 24$ and the sum is $S_n = \dfrac{n(a_1 + a_n)}{2} = \dfrac{7(12 + 24)}{2} = 126$.

9.1.3 Geometric Sequence

A **geometric sequence** is a sequence with a constant ratio between any two consecutive terms. This ratio is called the **common ratio**. The terms are usually designated as $a_1, a_2, a_3, \ldots$, and the constant ratio between successive terms is usually designated as r, such that $r = \dfrac{a_n}{a_{n-1}}$, where n is any positive integer greater than 1. A geometric sequence is also known as a **geometric progression**.

The common ratio r can never be 0 or 1. If r is a fraction, the geometric sequence gets smaller. If r is negative, any two successive terms have opposite signs.

No term in a geometric sequence can ever be 0 because we cannot divide by 0.

Examples of geometric sequences include increasing terms, such as 2, 4, 8, 16, 32, . . . in which $r = 2$. Or decreasing terms, such as in the sequence 243, 81, 27, 9, 3, . . ., in which $r = \dfrac{1}{3}$.

To calculate the nth term of a geometric sequence, multiply the original term by r to the $(n-1)$st power. The value of n is diminished by 1 because the first term is already in the equation. Thus, the nth term of a geometric sequence is given by

$$a_n = a_1 r^{n-1}.$$

EXAMPLE 9.6

Which of the following is a geometric sequence?

       (A) 2, 4, 8, 16, 30, 32, . . .

       (B) 2, 4, 6, 8, 10, 12, . . .

       (C) 2, 4, 8, 16, 32, 64, . . .

       (D) 2, 4, 8, 10, 20, 40, . . .

SOLUTION 9.6

(C) 2, 4, 8, 16, 32, 64, . . . Remember that every term has to be multiplied by a common ratio (here, 2) to get the next term. That is true in answer choice (A) for only the first four terms. Answer choice (B) is an arithmetic sequence. Answer choice (D) has a common ratio of 2, except for from the third to the fourth term.

EXAMPLE 9.7

Find the 5th term of the geometric sequence $\frac{1}{4}$, 1, 4, 16, . . .

SOLUTION 9.7

64. First, find the common ratio by dividing any term by the one before it. Here it is $r = \frac{1}{\frac{1}{4}} = \frac{4}{1} = \frac{16}{4}$, etc. If you know the sequence is geometric, you need to do only one of these calculations, they will all equal r. So $r = 4$ here, and the 5th term is

$$a_n = a_1 r^{n-1} = a_5 = \frac{1}{4}(4)^4 = 4^3 = 64.$$

EXAMPLE 9.8

The fourth term of a geometric sequence is $\frac{1}{2}$ and the seventh term is $\frac{1}{16}$. What is the first term?

SOLUTION 9.8

4. The sequence is ___, ___, ___, $\frac{1}{2}$, ___, ___, $\frac{1}{16}$. We can work backward to find the first term if we know the value of r. To find r, we use the equation $a_n = a_1 r^{n-1}$ but we make the first term of the sequence $\frac{1}{2}$. Then $a_1 = \frac{1}{2}$, $n = 4$, and $a_4 = \frac{1}{16}$. Note that $n = 4$ because we are momentarily shifting over to making $\frac{1}{2}$ the first term, so $\frac{1}{16}$ becomes the fourth term. Once we find r, it will be the r for the original sequence and we can go back to the original sequence. Thus, $a_n = a_1 r^{n-1} = \frac{1}{16} = \frac{1}{2} r^3$, so $r^3 = \frac{1}{8}$ and $r = \frac{1}{2}$. Now, we just work backward multiplying by 2 (or dividing by $\frac{1}{2}$) to find the actual first term. The sequence is 4, 2, 1, $\frac{1}{2}$ . . .

9.1.4 Geometric Series

A **geometric series**, usually designated as S_n, is the sum of the first n terms of a geometric sequence. For a finite geometric series, this sum is given by

$$S_n = \frac{a_1(1 - r^n)}{1 - r}$$

An **infinite geometric series** is one for which $n \to \infty$. Its value depends on the value of r. Remember that r can never be 0, or 1.

- $S_\infty = \frac{a_1}{1 - r}$ for an infinite geometric series with $-1 < r < 1$ (i.e., r is a fraction).

- $S_\infty = \infty$ for an infinite geometric series with $r > 1$.

- S_∞ doesn't exist if $r \leq -1$.

EXAMPLE 9.9

Find the sum of the terms in the sequence 256, –64, 16, –4, . . . $-\frac{1}{64}$.

SOLUTION 9.9

$204\frac{51}{64}$. First, we must find the number of terms in this sequence. We can easily find that $r = \frac{-4}{16} = -\frac{1}{4}$, so the missing numbers are 1, $-\frac{1}{4}$, and $\frac{1}{16}$, which makes 8 terms. Then $S_n = \frac{a_1(1 - r^n)}{1 - r}$ since this is a finite sequence. The equation to use is

$$S_n = \frac{a_1(1 - r^n)}{1 - r} = \frac{256\left(1 - \left(-\frac{1}{4}\right)^8\right)}{1 - \left(-\frac{1}{4}\right)} = \frac{256 - \frac{1}{256}}{\frac{5}{4}} = 204\frac{51}{64}.$$

Just as the arithmetic sequence is useful for *simple interest* problems, the geometric sequence is useful for **compound interest** problems. The equation for $P(t)$, the compounded amount after t years, is given by

$$P(t) = P_0\left(1 + \frac{r}{n}\right)^{nt}$$

where P_0 = original principal, r = annual interest rate, n = number of compounding periods per year, and t = total number of years.

The corresponding values of the amount for 1 year, 2 years, 3 years, 4 years, ... are given by $P_0\left(1+\frac{r}{n}\right)^{n}$, $P_0\left(1+\frac{r}{n}\right)^{2n}$, $P_0\left(1+\frac{r}{n}\right)^{3n}$, $P_0\left(1+\frac{r}{n}\right)^{4n}$ .... This is a geometric sequence in which the first term is $P_0\left(1+\frac{r}{n}\right)^{n}$ and the common ratio is $\left(1+\frac{r}{n}\right)^{n}$.

EXAMPLE 9.10

If $600 is deposited into a bank in which the interest rate is 8% compounded quarterly, what is the amount after five years?

SOLUTION 9.10

$891.57. Quarterly compounding means there are four compounding periods per year and a total of (5)(4) = 20 compounding periods in five years. Thus $P(5) = (\$600)\left(1 + \frac{0.08}{4}\right)^{20} \approx \$891.57.$

EXAMPLE 9.11

A person will need $5000 in 3 years to help pay off a car loan. To the nearest dollar, how much money should be deposited into a bank in which the interest rate is 2% compounded monthly?

SOLUTION 9.11

$4,709. Monthly means there are twelve compounding periods per year, so there are a total of (12)(3) = 36 compounding periods in three years. Then $\$5000 = P_0\left(1 + \frac{0.02}{12}\right)^{36} \approx 1.0618P_0$, and thus $P_0 \approx \$4,709.$

9.1.5 Repeating Decimals

A **repeating decimal** (sometimes called a **recurring decimal**) is a decimal that has a digit, or a block of digits, that repeat over and over again without ever ending; for example, $\frac{1}{3} = .333333... = .\overline{3}$, where the bar over the 3 means it repeats forever. The repeat can be one, two, or more digits, so the bar goes over the first occurrence of the repeating digits. As an example of a decimal that has a six-digit repeat, $\frac{1}{7} = 0.142857142857\ldots = 0.\overline{142857}$. The repeats do not have to start right after the decimal point; for example, $\frac{77}{600} = 0.128\overline{3}$.

Decimals do not have to be either terminating, such as .5, or repeating; they can also go on forever and never repeat, such as the decimals for $\sqrt{2}$ and π, both of which are usually rounded to a certain decimal place. These nonterminating, nonrepeating decimals are *irrational numbers*, as we saw in Chapter 3, Section 3.2.1. Repeating and terminating decimals are *rational numbers*.

Repeating decimals can be changed to equivalent fractions by considering them as geometric series. For example, to find the value of the repeating decimal $0.\overline{53} = 0.535353\ldots$, consider it to be the series in which the first term is .53 and the common ratio is $r = 0.01$. Thus, $0.535353\ldots = .53 + .0053 + .000053 + \ldots$ Since r is a positive number less than 1, the sum is given by $S_\infty = \frac{a_1}{1-r} = \frac{.53}{1-.01} = \frac{.53}{.99} = \frac{53}{99}$.

EXAMPLE 9.12

What is the fraction equivalent of $0.\overline{423}$?

SOLUTION 9.12

$\frac{47}{111}$. Here the common ratio is $r = 0.001$, and the sum is $S_\infty = \frac{a_1}{1-r} = \frac{.423}{1-.001} = \frac{.423}{.999} = \frac{423}{999} = \frac{47}{111}$.

(Hint:) A fact that may come in handy when finding fraction equivalents is that any number whose digits add up to 9 (or a multiple of 9) is divisible by 9. When changing repeating decimals to fractions, the first denominator is a series of 9's, but since the sum of the digits of 423 in the above example are divisible by 9 (because $4 + 2 + 3 = 9$), division of the numerator and denominator by 9 is indicated to simplify the resulting fraction.

When the repeat is not the first digit in the decimal, conversion to a fraction is done similarly. In fact, the following method works for all repeating decimals, no matter where the repeat starts. Let's look at the decimal .326363 . . ., which we can write as $.32\overline{63}$. Since there are two digits that repeat, multiply both sides of the equation by $10^2 = 100$. Let's call the original decimal $D = .32\overline{63}$. Then we get

$$100D = 32.\overline{63} = 32.63\overline{63}$$

so we now have the repeating decimals starting right after the decimal point. Now subtract $D = .32\overline{63}$ from both sides of the equation, to get

$$100D = 32.63\overline{63}$$
$$-\quad D = 00.32\overline{63}$$
$$99D = 32.31$$

All of the repeating 63's cancel out, so the subtraction on the right-hand side is simply $32.63 - 0.32 = 32.31$. Then $D = \dfrac{32.31}{99} = \dfrac{3231}{9900} = \dfrac{359}{1100}$. Notice here that the numerator 3231 is divisible by 9, so we can reduce the fraction according to the hint above. Thus, $D = .32\overline{63} = \dfrac{359}{1100}$.

NOTE

ALL repeating decimals can be converted to fractions. That's what makes repeating decimals rational.

9.1.6 Recursive Sequences

A **recursive sequence** is a list of numbers in which each number depends on the values of previous numbers. In this type of sequence, the value of the first term is given. A formula is given for each successive term that depends on the value of the previous term. A recursive sequence may consist of only two equations—the value of the first (or first and second) term and the formula for finding succeeding terms.

An example of a recursive sequence is given by the first term $a_1 = 2$, and the formula for the rest of the terms, $a_n = (a_{n-1})^2 + 1$. Using the formula, $a_2 = (a_1)^2 + 1 = 4 + 1 = 5$. Then for the next term, $a_3 = (a_2)^2 + 1 = 25 + 1 = 26$, and so on. It is often easier to compute the sequence than to be presented with a sequence and have to figure out the formula. This sequence is 2, 5, 26, 677, . . ., so the formula is not so obvious, but once the "code is cracked," it's easy to see. This sequence is neither arithmetic nor geometric. It does, however, have a pattern of development based upon each previous term, which is what makes it a recursive sequence.

EXAMPLE 9.13

What are the first four terms of the recursive sequence in which $a_1 = -12$ and $a_n = \dfrac{1}{2} a_{n-1} + 1$?

SOLUTION 9.13

$-12, -5, -\dfrac{3}{2}, \dfrac{1}{4}. \; a_1 = -12; \; a_2 = \dfrac{1}{2}(-12) + 1 = -5; \; a_3 = \dfrac{1}{2}(-5) + 1 = -\dfrac{3}{2};$

$a_4 = \dfrac{1}{2}\left(-\dfrac{3}{2}\right) + 1 = \dfrac{1}{4}.$

In some cases, the values of the first two terms are given, and a formula is given for each successive term that depends on the values of the two previous terms.

EXAMPLE 9.14

What are the first four terms of the recursive sequence in which $a_1 = 0.6$; $a_2 = 2$; $a_3 = 3a_{n-1} - 5a_{n-2}$ for $n > 2$?

SOLUTION 9.14

$0.6, 2, 3, -1$. $a_1 = 0.6$; $a_2 = 2$; $a_3 = 3a_2 - 5a_1 = 3(2) - 5(0.6) = 3$; $a_4 = 3(3) - 5(2) = -1$.
This surely would be a difficult one for which to find the formula!

A well-known recursive sequence is 1, 1, 2, 3, 5, 8, 13, 21, 34, . . . This is known as the **Fibonacci sequence**. Even though it was published in the year 1202, has been featured in numerous modern-day books, movies, and television shows (mainly in mysteries in the context of a code breaker). The Fibonacci sequence also has been found to be the basis of applications in nature and fractals (e.g., the spiral of galaxies, nautilus shell, arrangement of a pine cone, structure of crystals, branching of trees, and arrangement of leaves on a stem).

The formula for this sequence is that every number after the first two is just the sum of the two numbers before it, or $a_1 = 1$, $a_2 = 1$, $a_n = a_{n-2} + a_{n-1}$. Some mathematicians write the first two numbers as $a_1 = 0$ and $a_2 = 1$ but the resulting sequence is the same, just starting with 0.

9.1.7 Pattern Sequences

Still other sequences aren't arithmetic or geometric or recursive, but they are sequences nonetheless—these are called **pattern sequences**. For example, can you fill in the blank in the sequence 1, 4, 9, 16, __, 49, 64? Of course, this is a sequence of integer squares, and the missing number is $5^2 = 25$. What about the sequence 1, 4, __, 256? The pattern for this is n^n where n is the place in the sequence, so the missing number is $3^3 = 27$. Many pattern sequences are mathematical, and some are artistic or have some other basis. Can you fill in the missing letter: J F M A M __ J A . . .? The missing letter is J—these are the first letters of the names of the months.

9.2 SET THEORY

9.2.1 Set Definitions

Sets occur in many contexts. Considering sets of numbers, examples include the set of even numbers : {. . . , −4, −2, 0, 2, 4, . . .}; the set of prime numbers: {2, 3, 5, 7, 11, 13, 17, . . .}, or the set of positive multiples of 3 that are less than 10: {3, 6, 9}. A **set** is simply any collection of objects restricted only by the definition of the set. Sets can be anything: points, numbers, people, cities, and so on. The individual objects in a set are called the **members** or **elements** of the set. Thus, the mathematical meaning of the word *set* is the same as the regular, nontechnical meaning of the word.

Sets are usually denoted by capital letters such as A, B, S, etc. and the elements within them by lower case letters, sometimes with subscripts that designate their position in the set: $A = \{a, b, c, \ldots\}$ or $B = \{b_1, b_2, b_3, \ldots\}$, where the letters stand for specific elements.

Finite sets (those with a countable number of elements) can be defined by explicitly listing each of the elements of the set; this is called the **roster method**. Thus,

- $A = \{3, 6, 9, 12\}$ is the set of all numbers from 3 to 12 that are divisible by 3.

- $B = \{-2, 3\}$ is the set of all solutions of the equation $x^2 - x - 6 = 0$.

- $C = \{$all rivers of Mexico$\}$ can be a very large set, but it is possible to list them explicitly as members of set C.

Sets also can be defined by describing the properties that define it because it is not possible or feasible to list all of the elements, such as these **infinite sets**:

- $D = \{$all points in a given line segment$\}$

- $E = \{$all lines through a given point in space$\}$

- $F = \{$the set of all rational numbers$\}$

A **universal set**, usually designated as U, is a set that contains everything that is relevant to the things we are considering. For the three example sets mentioned in the first paragraph of this section, the universal set would be all numbers or could even be all integers.

A **subset** of a set is itself a set in which all of its members are members of the set, so integers are a subset of numbers, but this is not true the other way around. A **proper subset** means all the elements of set S are elements of set T, but set $S \neq T$. Note that $T \supset S$ means the same thing, and is read as "S is a **superset** of T."

 Any set is a subset of itself.

All items in the universe that aren't included in a set I are called the **complement** of set I, denoted with a bar, written as $\overline{I}$.

9.2.2 Set Notation

Set builder notation looks like $\{x : x \text{ has property } P\}$, which indicates a set of objects x having property P. The colon in $\{x :\}$ is read as "such that." Therefore, set $S = \{x : x \text{ is an even integer}\}$ is the set of all even integers. Sometimes instead of a colon, a vertical bar (|) is used, so this could also be written as $\{x \mid x \text{ has property } P\}$.

The following standard set notation can be accessed on the computer screen during the actual test. Most of these appear under "Notations" on the list of Notations, Definitions, and Formulas on the pull-down sheet on the Praxis test.

$x \in S$ means that x is an element of S.

$x \notin S$ means x is not an element of S.

$S \subset T$ means set S is a proper subset of set T.

$S \subseteq T$ means set S is either a proper subset of set T or $S = T$.

$S = T$ means the two sets S and T consist of the same elements. The order in which set elements are listed is immaterial, and repetition of an element of a set does not change the set. Thus, $\{1, 2, 3, 4\} = \{1, 4, 3, 2\} = \{1, 1, 2, 3, 3, 4\}$.

$S \cup T$ means the union of sets S and T, or all the elements of set S and elements of set T together. Sometimes this is written as $S + T$, which does not mean adding the elements of S to the elements of T.

$S \cap T$ means the intersection of sets S and T, or all the elements of set S that are also elements of set T.

$\overline{S}$ is the complement of set S; the set of all elements not in set S.

$\emptyset$ means the **null set**, or the **empty set**, or the set with no elements. The null set $\emptyset$ is considered to be a subset of every set.

$T \setminus S$ is the relative complement of set S in set T. This is the same as the **difference** $T - S$, or the set of all elements of set T that are not elements of set S.

The notation $T - S$ does not mean subtraction. If $T = \{1, 3, 6, 8, 10\}$ and $S = \{3, 6, 9\}$, $T - S = \{1, 8, 10\}$, or all the elements in set T that are not in set S, or $T - S = \{1, \cancel{3}, \cancel{6}, 8, 10\} = \{1, 8, 10\}$.

The symbol for u̲nion, $\cup$, is in the shape of a U. The symbol for "is an e̲lement of," $\in$, is in the shape of an e.

EXAMPLE 9.15

If $A = \{a, b, c, d\}$ and $B = \{a, e, c, f\}$, then $A \cup B =$

(A) $\{a, b, b, c, d, e, f\}$

(B) $\{a, b, c, d, e, f\}$

(C) $\{a, c\}$

(D) $\{a, e, f\}$

SOLUTION 9.15

(B) {*a*, *b*, *c*, *d*, *e*, *f*}. For a union, the position of the elements doesn't matter, nor do duplicates. Union simply means a list of all the elements in the two sets. Answer choice (C) is the intersection, not the union.

9.2.3 Venn Diagrams

Venn diagrams were discussed in Section 8.1.1d of Chapter 8. The union, intersection, difference and complement of sets can be depicted graphically by means of Venn diagrams. In a Venn diagram, the universe *U* is represented by points within a rectangle and sets are represented by points inside circles within the rectangle. The Venn diagram of sets of real numbers shown below makes clear the following number facts that were discussed in Chapter 3.

- All real numbers are either **rational** or **irrational**; there are no numbers that are both.

- The set of **whole numbers** includes all the **natural numbers** plus 0.

- The set of **integers** includes all the whole numbers plus negative whole numbers.

- The set of rational numbers includes all the integers plus numbers that can be expressed as fractions (positive or negative), repeating decimals, and terminating decimals.

- Said another way, the set of natural numbers is a proper subset of the set of whole numbers, which is a proper subset of the set of integers, which is a proper subset of the set of rational numbers.

- If the universal set *U* is all numbers, the complement of the universal set, $\overline{U}$, is the set of all imaginary numbers.

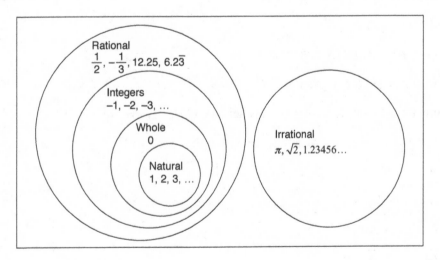

9.2.4 Set Laws and Properties

The usual laws and properties that hold for numbers also hold for sets.

- **Closure law**: For any two sets A and B, $A \cup B$ is a unique set, and $A \cap B$ is a unique set. **Unique** just means that there is only one set that is the answer for the union of two sets. Likewise for the intersection of two sets.

- **Commutative law**: For any two sets A and B, $A \cup B = B \cup A$ and $A \cap B = B \cap A$.

- **Associative law**: For any three sets A, B, and C, $(A \cup B) \cup C = A \cup (B \cup C)$ and $(A \cap B) \cap C = A \cap (B \cap C)$.

- **Distributive law**: For any three sets A, B, and C, $A \cup (B \cap C) = (A \cup B) \cap (A \cup C)$ and $A \cap (B \cup C) = (A \cap B) \cup (A \cap C)$.

- **Idempotent law**: A set doesn't change value with the operations of union or intersection by itself. Symbolically, $A \cup A = A$ and $A \cap A = A$.

- **Identity laws**

  ▶ For any set with the universe U, $A \cup U = U$ and $A \cap U = A$.

  ▶ For any set with the null set $\emptyset$, $A \cup \emptyset = A$ and $A \cap \emptyset = \emptyset$.

- **Properties of subsets**: For any sets A, B, and C,

  ▶ $A \subset U$

  ▶ $\emptyset \subset A$

  ▶ If $B \subset A$, then $A \cup B = B$ and $A \cap B = A$

  ▶ $A \subset (A \cup B)$

  ▶ $(A \cap B) \subset A$ and $(A \cap B) \subset B$

  ▶ If $A \subset B$ and $B \subset C$, then $A \subset C$

- **Properties of complements**: For any sets A and B,

  ▶ For every A there exists a unique set $\overline{A}$ with respect to U

  ▶ $A \cup \overline{A} = U$

  ▶ $A \cap \overline{A} = \emptyset$

  ▶ $\overline{(A \cup B)} = \overline{A} \cap \overline{B}$

  ▶ $\overline{(A \cap B)} = \overline{A} \cup \overline{B}$

  ▶ $\overline{\emptyset} = U$

  ▶ $\overline{U} = \emptyset$

  ▶ $\overline{\overline{A}} = A$

- **Difference laws**: For any three sets A, B, and C, $A - (B \cup C) = (A - B) \cap (A - C)$ and $A - (B \cap C) = (A - B) \cup (A - C)$.

- **Absorption laws**: For any two sets A and B, $A \cup (A \cap B) = A$ and $A \cap (A \cup B) = A$.

9.3 BINARY RELATIONS

As the name implies, **binary relations** are relations between two objects. These are sometimes called **equivalence relations**. These "objects" may be sets, numbers, geometric figures, points on a graph, even people. Examples of relations are "A is a subset of B," "10 is greater than 5," "2 divides 8," "$\triangle ABC$ is congruent to $\triangle DEF$," "Kara is the mother of Amber," "$\angle 1$ is adjacent to $\angle 2$," and "line l is perpendicular to line m."

A binary relation relates elements of one set to elements of another set. The **Cartesian product** of two sets A and B is a set of ordered pairs $A \times B$ that contain elements from each set as an ordered pair. This is written mathematically as $A \times B = \{(a,b) : a \in A \text{ and } b \in B\}$, which says that the Cartesian product of sets A and B is the set of ordered pairs (a,b) such that a is an element of A and b is an element of B.

Properties of relations between the elements in one set to elements in the other set must be tested for **closure** on each ordered pair. A set is **closed** if for some operation on a set of elements, the result is also in the set. In other words, the binary relation from one set to another is always a subset of the Cartesian product.

The following four **properties** pertain to binary relations: reflexive, transitive, symmetric, and antisymmetric. Although individually these properties are similar to the properties of numbers (see Section 3.3 in Chapter 3), differences do exist, so be sure to not only understand what they mean, but also what they are called. The symbol for "relation" is $\Re$. In general, for any pair of objects, x and y, x is related to y by relation $\Re$, written as $x \, \Re \, y$, if and only if x and y both belong to $\Re$.

Counterexamples are a method of disproving something. For example, if you were told that prime numbers include 1, 3, 5, 7, and you concluded that all primes are odd, that assumption could be found incorrect by one counterexample: 2 is a prime number. Only one counterexample is needed to disprove a statement, proposition, or theorem.

Let's look at the properties, with an example of each.

9.3.1 Reflexive Property, $x \, \Re \, x$

The **reflexive property** of equivalence says that any value is equal to itself. Algebraically, for any real number a, $a = a$, or any quantity is equal to itself. Geometrically, for all angles A, $\angle A \cong \angle A$, or an angle is congruent to itself.

9.3.2 Symmetric Property, $x \, \Re \, y \Rightarrow y \, \Re \, x$

The **symmetric property** of equivalence says that both sides of an equal sign are equal no matter which side of the equal sign they are on, or $x \, \Re \, y \Rightarrow y \, \Re \, x$. Algebraically, if $2a = 3b$, then $3b = 2a$, or if one value is equal to another value, then the second value is also equal to the first value. Geometrically, for any angles A and B, if $\angle A \cong \angle B$, then $\angle B \cong \angle A$, or the order of congruence does not matter.

9.3.3 Transitive Property, $(x \, \Re \, y$ and $y \, \Re \, z) \Rightarrow x \, \Re \, z$

The **transitive property** of equivalence says that if one value is equal to another value, and that second value is equal to a third value, then the first value is also equal to the third value. Algebraically, if $a = b$ and $b = c$, then $a = c$. Geometrically, for any angles A, B, and C, if $\angle A \cong \angle B$ and $\angle B \cong \angle C$, then $\angle A \cong \angle C$.

The converse of the reflexive and symmetric properties are obviously true. The converse of the transitive property, if two values are both equal to a third value, then the first two values are also equal, or if $a = c$ and $b = c$, then $a = b$, is also true, just not so obviously.

9.3.4 Equivalence Relation

The symmetric, reflexive, and transitive properties together define an **equivalence relation**. In the preceding sections, the algebraic and geometric examples of equality and congruence were shown to symmetric, reflexive, and transitive, so the properties of equality and congruence are equivalence relations. An equivalence relation between x and y is generally denoted by $x \sim y$.

9.3.5 Substitution Property

If $x = y$, then x may be replaced by y in any equation or expression, as we saw in Chapter 4.

9.3.6 Antisymmetric Property, $(x \, \Re \, y$ and $y \, \Re \, x) \Rightarrow x = y$

The **antisymmetric property** states that if for any relation $\Re$ for all values of a and b, if $a \, \Re \, b$ and $b \, \Re \, a$, then $a = b$. For example, if $x \geq y$, and $y \geq x$, then $x = y$ (and, by symmetry, $y = x$).

Antisymmetric is not the same as "not symmetric."

9.3.7 Other Relations

Relations other than equality and congruence may or may not have all of the properties defined above. Let's look at the relations from the beginning of this section on Binary Relations. "A is a subset of B," "10 is greater than 5," "2 divides 8," "$\triangle ABC$ is congruent to $\triangle DEF$," "Kara is the mother of Amber," "$\angle 1$ is adjacent to $\angle 2$," and "line l is perpendicular to line m."

EXAMPLE 9.16

Rev.

Answer "Yes" if the following properties (reflexive, symmetric, and transitive) are true for each relation and "No" if not. Remember that one counterexample will make the property false.

Relation	Reflexive	Symmetric	Transitive
A is a subset of B: $A \subset B$			
10 is greater than 5: $10 > 5$			
2 divides 8 (meaning 2 is a factor of 8)			
$\triangle ABC$ is congruent to $\triangle DEF$: $\triangle ABC \cong \triangle DEF$			
Kara is the mother of Amber			
$\angle 1$ is adjacent to $\angle 2$			
line l is perpendicular to line m (all on same plane)			

...TION 9.16

Relation	Reflexive	Symmetric	Transitive
A is a subset of B: $A \subset B$	Yes. Any set A is a subset of itself.	No. Not if B = {all animals}, A = {zebras}	Yes, for proper subsets.
10 is greater than 5: $10 > 5$	No. Would be "yes" for $\geq$.	No. $5 > 10$ is false.	Yes.
2 divides 8 (meaning 2 is a factor of 8)	Yes. Any number is a factor of itself.	No. $8 \div 2 = 4$, but 8 doesn't divide 2.	Yes. A factor of a factor of a value is a factor of that value.
$\triangle ABC$ is congruent to $\triangle DEF$: $\triangle ABC \cong \triangle DEF$	Yes. Any triangle is congruent to itself (all corresponding angles and sides are equal)	Yes. All corresponding angles and sides are equal, and equality is an equivalence relation.	Yes. All corresponding angles and sides are equal.
Kara is the mother of Amber	No. No one is their own mother.	No. Amber is not the mother of Kara.	No. Kara would be the grandmother of Amber's child.
$\angle 1$ is adjacent to $\angle 2$	No. An angle is not adjacent to itself.	Yes. Adjacency is mutual.	No. The first of three adjacent angles that share a vertex won't share a common side with the third angle.
line l is perpendicular to line m (all on same plane)	No. A line is not perpendicular to itself.	Yes. If they intersect at 90°, they both do, $l \perp m$ means $m \perp l$.	No. Line m can be perpendicular to a third line n, which is parallel to line l.

9.4 LOGIC

9.4.1 Terminology

Simply put, **logic** is the study of argument. In logic, an **argument** is an example of reasoning in which one or more **statements** are offered as **support** for another statement. This support can take the form of justification, grounds, reasons, or evidence. The statement being supported is the **conclusion** of the argument, and the statements that support it are the **premises** of the argument.

Two aspects of the argument need be considered in assessing an argument: the **truth** of the premises and the **validity** of the reasoning from the premises to the conclusion. Of these, logicians study only the reasoning.

An argument is considered valid for several somewhat equivalent reasons:

- The truth of its premises guarantees the truth of its conclusion.

- The conclusion would necessarily be true if it is assumed that all the premises were true.

- It is impossible for the conclusion to be false and all the premises true at the same time.

- The conclusion can be deduced from the premises in accordance with certain valid rules.

If an argument is not valid, it is **invalid**.

The first fundamental principle of logic is the independence of truth and validity:

Truth pertains only to statements; validity pertains only to arguments.

A further distinction is that validity pertains to reasoning, not propositions, whereas truth pertains to propositions, not reasoning.

Arguments can be deductive or inductive.

- In a **deductive** argument, the premises claim to give conclusive grounds for the truth of the conclusion, or the premises claim to necessarily support the conclusion. The categories of validity and invalidity apply only to deductive arguments. If all of the premises are true, the conclusion is true and it is impossible for it to be false. The conclusion of a valid deduction never contains more information than was contained the premises.

- An **inductive** argument claims that its premises support but do not guarantee its conclusion. Inductive arguments are strong or weak. In a strong inductive argument, if all of the premises are true, the truth of the conclusion is merely probable and its falsehood merely improbable; inductions are always uncertain to some degree. The conclusion of an induction always contains more information than was contained the premises.

An example of a typical deductive argument would have the premises

(1)   all As are Bs, and

(2)   all Bs are Cs,

which support the conclusion that

(3)   all As are Cs.

If (1) and (2) are true, then it must be the case that (3) is also true.

An example of a typical inductive argument would have as its premises:

(1)   I have seen a hundred tigers, and

(2)   they have all been orange.

If (1) and (2) are true, then inductively the conclusion is

> (3)   all tigers are orange.

Here, if (1) and (2) are true, the conclusion (3) is merely probable. One counterargument (e.g., white tigers) can prove the conclusion false.

 The difference between deduction and induction is not the difference between good and bad reasoning, but between two ways to support the truth of conclusions.

A **fallacy** is a bad method of argument, whether deductive or inductive, meaning one of the following may have occurred:

- One or more of the premises may be false (or irrelevant).

- The reasoning from the premises may be invalid.

- The language expressing the premises may be ambiguous or vague.

The term "fallacy" is usually used for faults in arguments that nevertheless are persuasive. An example of a fallacy is

> (1)   I saw a black cat and

> (2)   ten minutes later, I crashed my car.

Premises (1) and (2) are true, but the conclusion

> (3)   therefore, black cats are bad luck

is a fallacy because the reasoning from the premises is invalid.

9.4.2 Symbols and Truth Tables

A statement in logic may be built from simple statements using the logical connectives $\sim$, $\wedge$, $\vee$, $\rightarrow$, and $\leftrightarrow$. The truth or falsity of a statement with each of these five connectives depends on the truth or falsity of its components, as shown in **truth tables**.

- **Negation ($\sim$):**

P	~P
T	F
F	T

The negation table is easy to understand. If P is *true*, its negation $\sim P$ is *false*, and conversely, if P is *false*, its negation $\sim P$ is *true*. Note that **double negation** reverses the table; that is $\sim(\sim P) = P$.

- And (∧):

P	Q	P ∧ Q
T	T	T
T	F	F
F	T	F
F	F	F

$P \wedge Q$ should be *true* when both P and Q are *true*, and *false* otherwise. Therefore ∧ is a **logical conjunction**.

- Or (∨):

P	Q	P ∨ Q
T	T	T
T	F	T
F	T	T
F	F	F

$P \vee Q$ is *true* if either P is *true* or Q is *true* (or both). $P \vee Q$ is *false* only if both P and Q are *false*. Therefore ∨ is a **logical (inclusive) disjunction**.

- **Conditional (→):**

P	Q	P → Q
T	T	T
T	F	F
F	T	T
F	F	T

$P \rightarrow Q$ relates to an "if-then" statement: "if P then Q." An "if-then" statement is also known as an **implication,** and is *true* for all instances except when P is *true* and Q is *false*. To understand this logic, consider the following statement: "If you wash the car [P], then I'll give you five dollars [Q]."

▶ Suppose you wash the car (P is *true*) and I give you five dollars (Q is *true*). Since I kept my promise, the implication is *true*. This corresponds to the first line in the table.

▶ Suppose you wash the car (P is *true*) but I don't give you five dollars (Q is *false*). Since I didn't kept my promise, the implication is *false*. This corresponds to the second line in the table.

▶ Suppose you don't wash the car (*P* is *false*). Then whether I give you five dollars because I am just nice (*Q* is *true*) or don't give you five dollars because I want to teach you a lesson (*Q* is *false*), I haven't broken my promise. so the implication can't be false, and it must be *true*.

- **Equivalence (↔):**

P	Q	*P* ↔ Q
T	T	T
T	F	F
F	T	F
F	F	T

- *P* ↔ *Q* means that *P* and *Q* are **logically equivalent**. So the double implication is *true* if *P* and *Q* are both *true* or if *P* and *Q* are both *false*; otherwise, the double implication is false. ↔ means "if and only if." The implication is true whenever $(P \land Q) = (Q \land P)$ (see the table for "and (∧)" above).

In logic, the word "or" means either condition or both conditions are possible. (In everyday language, however, "or" means one or the other but not both.)

Logical analysis, helps to analyze whether the truth of the conclusion follows logically from the truth of the statements. Further, according to the Fundamental Principle of Argumentation, we can conclude that an argument is invalid if and only if it is logically possible for the conclusion to be false even though every premise is assumed to be true. Otherwise, truth tables don't say anything definitive about the merit of an argument.

It is possible to have truth tables with several statements, such as "If the teacher doesn't like me or thinks I am lazy then she will not give me a good grade and I won't get into my first-choice college." We won't get into these lengthy arguments here, but it is sufficient to know that they do exist, and that truth tables can have several columns. Basically the truth table has as many rows as the square of the number of statements, since each statement has two possibilities, true or false.

Even though we don't make truth tables in our everyday lives, we still use the logical reasoning that truth tables are built from to evaluate whether statements are true or false.

9.4.5 Inverses, Converses, Contrapositives

Inverses, converses and **contrapositives** exist for conditional $P \to Q$ (if-then) statements, which consist of two parts: the hypothesis (*P*, the "if" clause) and the conclusion (*Q*, the "then" clause).

- The inverse of $P \rightarrow Q$ is $\sim P \rightarrow \sim Q$.

- The converse of $P \rightarrow Q$ is $Q \rightarrow P$.

- The contrapositive of $P \rightarrow Q$ is $\sim Q \rightarrow \sim P$. It is the combination of the inverse and the converse.

The following table summarizes these statements

Statement	If P, then Q.
Converse	If Q, then P.
Inverse	If not P, then not Q.
Contrapositive	If not Q, then not P.

If the conditional statement is true, then the contrapositive is also logically true. If the converse is true, then the inverse is also logically true. But if the statement is false, there is no rule for the truth of the other related statements. Let's look at a couple of typical conditional statements and examine the truth of the related statements.

EXAMPLE 9.17

If it is raining, then the sky is cloudy. Assuming this statement is true, are the related statements true or false?

SOLUTION 9.17

Converse: If the sky is cloudy, it is raining (false). Inverse: If it is not raining, the sky is not cloudy (false). If the sky is not cloudy, then it is not raining (true).

EXAMPLE 9.18

If a quadrilateral is a square, then the diagonals are equal. Assuming this statement is true, are the related statements true or false?

SOLUTION 9.18

Converse: If the diagonals of a quadrilateral are equal, it is a square (false; it could be a rectangle). Inverse: If a quadrilateral is not a square, then the diagonals are not equal. (false; it could be a rectangle). If the diagonals of a quadrilateral are not equal, it is not a square (true).

9.5 COUNTING TECHNIQUES

9.5.1 Fundamental Principle of Counting

Chapter 8 discussed the **Fundamental Principle of Counting** (also known as the counting principle or multiplication principle; see Section 8.3). We will restate the principle here, as it is an important counting technique: If one event can occur in m ways and a second event can occur in n ways, the total ways both events can occur is $m \times n$. The counting principle works as well when there are more than two items being considered.

EXAMPLE 9.19

A golfer has four different golf shirts and three different pair of golf pants. How many outfits are possible?

SOLUTION 9.19

There are $4(3) = 12$ different outfits possible.

EXAMPLE 9.20

A pizza shop sells small, medium, and large pizzas. Each pizza can be ordered in thin or thick crust. And each pizza has a choice of five toppings—extra cheese, pepperoni, sausage, mushrooms, or anchovies. If a one-topping pizza is ordered, how many different pizzas choices are there?

SOLUTION 9.20

There are $3(2)(5) = 30$ different pizzas possible.

EXAMPLE 9.21

A lottery involves a number from 100 to 999. How many number choices are there?

SOLUTION 9.21

There are 9 possible first digits (1–9, since if 0 were allowed in the first position, it would be a two-digit number), 10 possible second digits, and 10 possible third digits. So there are $9(10)(10) = 900$ three-digit numbers. In this example, we can use a digit over again, so 444 could be one of the 900 three-digit numbers. Note that the answer isn't $999 - 100 = 899$ because both 100 and 999 are valid numbers.

9.5.2 Factorials

Similarly, using the counting principle, we can determine, for example, how many ways five people can line up: $5 \times 4 \times 3 \times 2 \times 1$. A special symbol for this calculation is !, called **factorial**. So n factorial is written as $n! = n \times (n-1) \times (n-2) \times \ldots \times 3 \times 2 \times 1$, or the product of n and every number less than n all the way down to 1. Note that 0! is defined as 1, or $0! = 1$. Five people can line up in $5! = 120$ ways because the first person has a choice of 5 places, the next has a choice of only 4, the next only 3, then 2, and the last one has only 1 choice because every other slot is taken.

EXAMPLE 9.22

Evaluate $\dfrac{n!}{(n+2)!}$.

SOLUTION 9.22

$\dfrac{n(n-1)(n-2)\ldots(2)(1)}{(n+2)(n+1)(n)(n-1)(n-2)\ldots(2)(1)} = \dfrac{1}{(n+2)(n+1)}$. Note that all the terms $n(n-1) \ldots (2)(1)$ in the numerator and denominator cancel each other out.

9.5.3 Permutations and Combinations

Factorials are handy when choosing r objects out of n objects, either when order makes a difference (called a **permutation** and denoted $_nP_r = \dfrac{n!}{(n-r)!}$) or when order doesn't make a difference (called a **combination** and denoted $_nC_r = \dfrac{n!}{r!(n-r)!}$). These formulas are not given on the Praxis formula sheet; however, the mechanics of working with these formulas is important. Fortunately, many factors cancel each other out in permutations and combinations, so the arithmetic is usually simple. For example,

$$_{12}P_2 = \frac{12!}{10!} = \frac{12 \times 11 \times 10 \times 9 \times 8 \times 7 \times 6 \times 5 \times 4 \times 3 \times 2 \times 1}{10 \times 9 \times 8 \times 7 \times 6 \times 5 \times 4 \times 3 \times 2 \times 1} = 12 \times 11 = 132.$$

Likewise, $_{12}C_2 = \dfrac{12!}{2!10!} = \dfrac{12 \times 11 \times 10 \times 9 \times 8 \times 7 \times 6 \times 5 \times 4 \times 3 \times 2 \times 1}{2 \times 1 \times 10 \times 9 \times 8 \times 7 \times 6 \times 5 \times 4 \times 3 \times 2 \times 1} = \dfrac{12 \times 11}{2 \times 1} = 66.$

Permutations and combinations are always whole numbers, which means every number in the denominator always cancels out. Let's try a few of these calculations.

EXAMPLE 9.23

Find the value of $\dfrac{10!}{8!}$.

SOLUTION 9.23

$$\frac{10!}{8!} = \frac{10 \times 9 \times 8 \times 7 \times \ldots \times 3 \times 2 \times 1}{8 \times 7 \times \ldots \times 3 \times 2 \times 1} = 10 \times 9 = 90.$$

Since this is multiplication and all the numbers from 8 down to 1 appear in the numerator and denominator, again we can cancel them all out. There is a pattern here.

EXAMPLE 9.24

Find the value of $\frac{8!}{3!5!}$.

SOLUTION 9.24

$\frac{8!}{3!5!} = \frac{8 \times 7 \times 6 \times 5 \times 4 \times 3 \times 2 \times 1}{3 \times 2 \times 1 \times 5 \times 4 \times 3 \times 2 \times 1}$. Since all of these numbers are multiplied, we can do a lot of cancellations, and the problem reduces to $\frac{8!}{3!5!} = \frac{8 \times 7 \times 6}{3 \times 2 \times 1} = 8 \times 7 = 56$.

Permutations are used when order makes a difference. The equation for a permutation of n things taken r at a time is $_nP_r = \frac{n!}{(n-r)!}$, which always reduces down to only the first $(n-r)$ factors of $n!$. Thus, as Example 9.23 showed, $\frac{10!}{8!} = 10 \times 9 = 90$. Since $(n-r) = 2$, only the first two factors of $n!$ are multiplied.

Combinations are used when order doesn't make a difference. The equation for a combination of n things taken r at a time is $_nC_r = \frac{n!}{r!(n-r)!}$, which always reduces down to only the first $(n-r)$ factors of $n!$ divided by $r!$. Thus, as Example 9.24 showed, $_8C_5 = \frac{8!}{3!5!} = \frac{8 \times 7 \times 6}{3 \times 2 \times 1} = 8 \times 7 = 56$. Since $(n-r) = 3$, only the first three factors of $n!$ are multiplied, and an equal number of factors (three) are in the denominator, which always cancel out with some of the three factors in the numerator.

Permutations and combinations are always integers.

EXAMPLE 9.25

The letters of the set $\{A, B, C, D, E, F, G\}$ can be arranged to form ordered codes of three letters in $_7P_3 = \frac{7!}{(7-3)!}$ ways. Evaluate $_7P_3$.

SOLUTION 9.25

$$_7P_3 = \frac{7!}{(7-3)!} = \frac{7!}{4!} = 7(6)(5) = 210.$$

EXAMPLE 9.26

An office has 16 workers. The boss decides to choose a manager and then an assistant from that group. This can be done in $_{16}P_2 = \dfrac{16!}{(16-2)!} = \dfrac{16!}{14!}$ ways. What is the value of $_{16}P_2$?

SOLUTION 9.26

This is a permutation of 16 things choosing 2 because order is important. John as the manager and Jane as the assistant is different from Jane as the manager and John as the assistant. $_{16}P_2 = \dfrac{16!}{(16-2)!} = \dfrac{16!}{14!} = 16(15) = 240$.

→ Why isn't he using FPC ?

EXAMPLE 9.27

An ice cream shop offers 20 flavors. Derek purchases a dish of 3 different flavors. He can choose the flavors in $_{20}C_3 = \dfrac{20!}{3!(20-3)!}$ ways. How many choices does Derek have?

SOLUTION 9.27

This is a combination because order is not important. A dish of chocolate, vanilla, and strawberry is the same as a dish of strawberry, vanilla, and chocolate. $_{20}C_3 = \dfrac{20!}{3!(20-3)!} = \dfrac{20!}{3!17!} = \dfrac{(20)(19)(18)}{(3)(2)(1)} = 1{,}140$.

EXAMPLE 9.28

An office has 16 workers. The boss decides to choose two managers from that group. This can this be done in $_{16}C_2 = \dfrac{16!}{2!(16-2)!}$ ways. How many ways can the boss choose two managers?

SOLUTION 9.28

Since both people chosen have the same rank (as opposed to manager and assistant in Example 9.26), order is not important. Choosing John and Jane as managers is the same as choosing Jane and John. $_{16}C_2 = \dfrac{16!}{2!(16-2)!} = \dfrac{16!}{2!14!} = \dfrac{(16)(15)}{2} = 120$.

A simple way to remember whether a problem should use permutations or combinations is that order makes a difference in a combination lock (9-2-3 will open the lock, whereas 3-9-2 will not) and that the combination formula is NOT the one that needs order. So the term "combination lock" is really a misnomer. It should be a "permutation lock."

9.5.4 Modulo

9.5.4a Definition and Mechanics of Modular Mathematics

In regular mathematics, when a number n is divided by another number (m), the result is a quotient (let's call it q) and a remainder (a), as in

$$\frac{n}{m} = q + \mathrm{R}a \text{, where R stands for "remainder."}$$

The mechanics behind **modular mathematics** involves **remainders**. It doesn't even matter what the value of q is. The interest is solely on the remainder a (also called the **residue**). The usefulness of modular mathematics will become apparent later in this section, but for now let's concentrate on the meaning and mechanics of modular mathematics.

The division problem above is stated in modular mathematics as

$$a = n(\bmod m), \text{ where } 0 \le a < m.$$

Sometimes the parentheses are left off of the modulus, as in $a \equiv n \bmod m$, but we will leave them on here so the modulus is obvious. This equation says that a is the remainder when a number n is divided by a modulus m. Notice that nothing is said about what the quotient is—the emphasis is on the value of the remainder a.

So working just with the mechanics of writing modular mathematics it should become apparent that, for example, $15(\bmod 7) = 1$ because 15 divided by 7 has a remainder of 1. Likewise, we can write $7(\bmod 6) = 1$, or $47(\bmod 5) = 2$. If n is a multiple of m, the remainder is $a = 0$, as in $8(\bmod 4) = 0$.

In modular mathematics, numbers restart when they reach m, the **modulus**. For example, the modulus for how we state time is 60 because at 60 minutes we state that as an hour and start counting minutes again from 1. We usually say, "1 hour and 15 minutes" rather than "75 minutes," and we do this mentally and quickly. Obviously, when a (the number of minutes) gets to m (60), it just bumps the quotient up 1 hour. So when we are dealing with time, we are still interested mainly in the residue, which is the number of minutes after the hour, but we do use the quotient because that tells the number of hours. However, we sometimes hear phrases for the time that just deal with the minutes, such as "15 minutes past the hour." A similar situation exists when talking about minutes and seconds.

A somewhat easier way to determine whether a modular statement is true involves the following simple subtraction method. Subtract the residue a from n, and the result must be a multiple of m. Thus the $2 = 50(\bmod 16)$ is true because $50 - 2 = 48$, which is a multiple of 16.

EXAMPLE 9.29

Which of the following statements in modular arithmetic is false?

(A) $1 = 45(\text{mod } 4)$

(B) $8 = 81(\text{mod } 12)$

(C) $1 = 43(\text{mod } 7)$

(D) $3 = 33(\text{mod } 10)$

SOLUTION 9.29

(B) $8 = 81(\text{mod } 12)$. Using only the definition, we see that $\frac{81}{12} = 6$ with a remainder of 9, so $81(\text{mod } 12) = 9$, not 8. Using the subtraction scheme, $81 - 8 = 73$, which is not a multiple of 12. The other answer choices are all true: (A) $\frac{45}{4} = 11R1$, so $1 = 45(\text{mod } 4)$; (C) $\frac{43}{7} = 6R1$, so $1 = 43(\text{mod } 7)$; and (D) $\frac{33}{10} = 3R3$, so $3 = 33(\text{mod } 10)$. Using the subtraction method instead, we see that they are true: (A) $45 - 1 = 44$, a multiple of 4; (C) $43 - 1 = 42$, a multiple of 7; and (D) $33 - 3 = 30$, a multiple of 10.

9.5.4b Modular Congruence

Modular congruence is different from geometric congruence. Geometric congruence ($\cong$, as in $\angle A \cong \angle B$) means exactly equal, whereas **modular congruence** ($\equiv$, also stated as an equivalence mod m) means "the same remainder as," or the same remainder (value of a) when two or more numbers (n's) are divided by the same modulus m.

 Watch the symbols! Modular equality ($=$), which defines a, the residual mod m, is different from modular congruence (or equivalence) ($\equiv$), which states that all remainders a, modulo m, are the same.

So 75 minutes of time given in modular terms is $15 = 75(\text{mod } 60)$, and it is understood that this means 75 minutes is equal to $\frac{n}{m} = \frac{75}{60} = q$ hours and a minutes (1 hour and 15 minutes). Similarly, 135 minutes would be stated as $15 = 135(\text{mod } 60)$, 195 minutes would be stated as $15 = 195(\text{mod } 60)$, and so on. Since all the modular terms for 15 minutes after the hour are the same, the following *congruence* can be stated:

$$195 \equiv 135 \ (\text{mod } 60)$$

But wait! Didn't we say that 195 minutes is $15 = 3(\text{mod } 60)$? The difference, again, is the $=$ sign versus the $\equiv$ sign. Whereas we can evaluate $15 = 3(\text{mod } 60)$ as $(60 \times 3) + 15 = 195$; the $\equiv$ sign just means the same value of a, the residual. So $195 \equiv 135 \ (\text{mod } 60)$ simply means 195 and 135 have the same values of a in modulus 60, and a must equal 15, since $a = 195(\text{mod } 60) = 135(\text{mod } 60)$.

So we see that the modulus is the number by which different numbers can be divided and produce the same remainder. Thus, in modular mathematics, when considering minutes, the following are congruent:

$$1(\text{mod } 60) \equiv 2(\text{mod } 60) \equiv 3(\text{mod } 60) \equiv \ldots \equiv n(\text{mod } 60)\ 60 \equiv 120 \equiv 180\ (\text{mod } 60),$$

and all multiples of 60, because they all mean 0 minutes after some value of n hours.

9.5.4c Recognizing Congruency

In general, two integers, c and d, are congruent modulo m when $c - d$ is a multiple of m. In other words, $c \equiv d\ (\text{mod } m)$ when $\dfrac{c - d}{m}$ is an integer. Otherwise, c and d are not congruent modulo m. Let's check the number of minutes for 15 past the hour from Section 9.5.4b: Is it true that $75 \equiv 135 \equiv 195\ (\text{mod } 60)$ using this test? Yes, the relevant numbers are $(135 - 75 = 60)$, $(195 - 135 = 60)$, and $(195 - 75 = 120)$, all of which are multiples of $m = 60$.

We can also know that all odd numbers are congruent to each other modulo 2, and all even numbers are congruent to each other modulo 2, but an odd number and an even number are not congruent modulo 2.

Odd numbers: $1 \equiv 3 \equiv 15 \equiv 99(\text{mod } 2)$ because they all equal 1.

Even numbers: $2 \equiv 4 \equiv 16 \equiv 88(\text{mod } 2)$ because they all equal 0.

But any odd number isn't congruent modulo 2 with any even number because $1 \neq 0$.

EXAMPLE 9.30

Which of the following potential *congruencies* is false?

 (A) $45 \equiv 9(\text{mod } 12)$

 (B) $81 \equiv 8(\text{mod } 12)$

 (C) $43 \equiv 22(\text{mod } 7)$

 (D) $33 \equiv 9(\text{mod } 12)$

SOLUTION 9.30

(B) $8 \equiv 81(\text{mod } 12)$. We see that if we subtract 8 from 81, we get 73, which is not a multiple of 12, so that modulus is false. For the other answer choices: (A), $45 - 9 = 36$, a multiple of 12; (C) $43 - 22 = 21$, a multiple of 7; and $33 - 9 = 24$, a multiple of 12. Note that the modular equivalents for (A) and (D) are congruent (so in modulo 12, $45 \equiv 33$).

9.5.4d Different Moduli

— *V. Imp.*

Mod 10 is the thinking behind carrying in standard arithmetic and borrowing in standard subtraction since standard arithmetic is based on the decimal (base 10) system. Other "special" moduli are 2, 3, and 5. These are special for the following reasons:

- If a number is even, we know 2 divides evenly into it, so any even number is the same as 0(mod 2). Also, since the remainder is always 1 if a number is divided by 2, any odd number is the same as 1(mod 2).

- If the sum of the digits in a number is divisible by 3 (e.g., 423 because $4 + 2 + 3 = 9$, which is a multiple of 3), the number that is divisible by 3 is the same as 0(mod 3). This also works for mod 9; for example, $4257 \equiv 0(\text{mod } 9)$ because $4 + 2 + 5 + 7 = 18$, a multiple of 9.

- If a number ends in 5 or 0, we know 5 divides evenly into it, so any number ending in 0 or 5 is the same as 0(mod 5). Not surprisingly, any number ending in 1 (or 6) is the same as 1(mod 5); ending in 2 (or 7) is the same as 2(mod 5); ending in 3 (or 8) is the same as 3(mod 5); and ending in 4 (or 9) is the same as 4(mod 5).

EXAMPLE 9.31

Find the modulo 4 residue of 102.

SOLUTION 9.31

2. The modulo 4 residue of 102 is the remainder when 102 is divided by 4. The equivalence is $102 \equiv 2(\text{mod } 4)$.

EXAMPLE 9.32

What is the modulo 5 residue of 48973?

SOLUTION 9.32

3. This refers to division by 5, and if the number ends in 3, the residue (mod 5) is 3. The equivalence is $48973 \equiv 3(\text{mod } 5)$. (The math, which should be unnecessary because mod 5 is special and should be recognize right away, is $48973 \div 5 = 9794 \text{ R } 3$.)

We can use the clock face analogy to place the m numbers equally spaced around a circle to visualize modulus m. This is just like taking a definite portion of the number line and putting it in a circle. When we have gone m units, the value of a starts all over again. For $m = 10$, this would look like

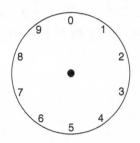

The 0 at the top could just as well be a 10, but making it a 0 just reminds us that for a positive number, when we make one clockwise revolution, the residue $a = 0$. And then a starts all over again with 1. If the number is negative, start at 0 and go counterclockwise.

Thus, modular mathematics is a descriptor for cyclical counting. Arithmetic modulo 2, in which the cycle is 2, is sometimes referred to a Boolean arithmetic, and it is the basis for the binary system that is at the heart of computer technology. Binary means there are just two elements, here 0 and 1, which stand for "off" and "on" in computer code. An even number is 0(mod 2) — that is, it has a remainder of 0 when divided by 2. An odd number is 1(mod 2) because it has a remainder of 1. Thus, 32 is 0(mod 2), 33 is 1(mod 2), 34 is 0(mod 2), etc., which is just stating the residue (or remainder) when, for example, a number is divided by 2. So, as shown above, we can say 32 and 34 are congruent modulo 2. So are 33 and 35, meaning they are the same, in modulo 2.

EXAMPLE 9.33

What is the modulo 12 residue of the standard negative number −18?

SOLUTION 9.33

6. Think of the common clock face, which is in mod 12. Starting at 0 (or 12) at the top, we go counterclockwise (because it is negative) 18 spaces. We end up at 6. We get the same answer if we add 12 to −18 twice: −18 + 12 + 12 = 6; although this always works, it gets unwieldy for large negative numbers.

An example in modulo 4 is the imaginary unit, $i = \sqrt{-1}$, which is manipulated just like any other number. Therefore,

$$i^0 = 1$$

$$i^{-1} = i$$

$$i^2 = -1$$

$$i^3 = -i$$

$$i^4 = i^{-0} = 1$$

Since each succeeding power of i is found by multiplying by i, we can see that $i^5 = i$, $i^6 = -1$, $i^7 = -i$, and $i^8 = 1$, and the powers of i cycle through these four values over and over. It's "clock face" would look like the following circle, where the exponents of i are in the inner part of the circle and their values are in the outer part of the circle. We can go around the circle in a clockwise fashion to see the values for i^5, i^6, i^7, and i^8 because they just go around the circle in a modular fashion.

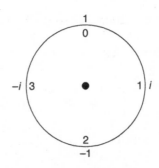

We can find the value of any power of i^n by dividing n by 4 and using the remainder to find the congruent power of i (which will be either 0, 1, 2, or 3). In modular language, $a = n \pmod 4$. If the remainder is 0, then 4 divides n evenly and the answer is $i^0 = 1$. For i^{29}, we find the remainder when 29 is divided by 4, which is 1. So we have the equivalence $29 \equiv 1 \pmod 4$, and similarly, $i^{29} \equiv i^1 = 1$. Notice the difference in meaning of the $\equiv$ and $=$ symbols. Following the same scheme for evaluating i^{242}, we find the remainder when 242 is divided by 4, which is 2. So $242 \equiv 2 \pmod 4$ so $i^{242} \equiv i^2 = -1$.

EXAMPLE 9.34

What is the value of i^{333}?

SOLUTION 9.34

-1. Divide the exponent 333 by 4 since the values of the powers of i are mod 4. The remainder is 3, so the value of i^{333} is i^3, which is $-i$. $\longrightarrow$ *wrong. Answer is It has to be i.*

Practice Exercises

1. An initial deposit of \$350 becomes \$402.50 after 2.5 years in the bank. What is the bank's annual simple interest rate?

   (A) 1.5%

   (B) 3.75%

   (C) 0.06%

   (D) 6%

2. Find the 8th term of the sequence 2, 6, 18, 54, . . .

   (A) 2187

   (B) 4,374

   (C) 6,561

   (D) 13,122

3. What are the first four terms of the recursive sequence in which $a_1 = 5$ and $a_n = 4a_{n-1} + 7$ for $n > 1$?

   (A) 27, 115, 467, 1875

   (B) 5, 27, 115, 467

   (C) 1, 5, 27, 115

   (D) Not enough information is given

4. The set of all even integers is a subset of which sets?

   (A) the set of all rational numbers

   (B) the set of all integers

   (C) the set of all real numbers

   (D) all of the above

5. If two angles are vertical angles, then they are equal. Assuming this statement is true, which of the related statements are false? Choose *all* that apply.

   A   The converse

   B   The inverse

   C   The contrapositive

   D   None of the above

6. Which of the following statements is equivalent to saying $a \equiv n \ (\mathrm{mod} \ m)$?

   (A) $a - n = km$ for some integer k.

   (B) $a = km + n$ for some integer k.

   (C) a divided by m has a remainder that equals the remainder of n divided by m.

   (D) All of the above.

7. In a group of 25 students, 12 were studying French, 15 were studying German, and 8 were studying neither, as shown in the Venn diagram to the right. How many students were studying both French and German?

   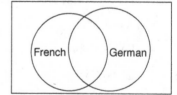

   (A) 27

   (B) 17

   (C) 10

   (D) 7

8. The repeating decimal $0.5\overline{6}$ is equivalent to what fraction in lowest terms?

(A) $\dfrac{5.1}{9}$

(B) $\dfrac{17}{30}$

(C) $\dfrac{57}{100}$

(D) $\dfrac{56}{100}$

9. Fill in the missing numbers in the first ten terms of the Fibonacci sequence, in which term $a_n = a_{n-1} + a_{n-2}$: 1, 1, 2, ___, 5, 8, ___, 21, 34, ___.

(A) 4, 13, 55

(B) 3, 13, 55

(C) 3, 13, 56

(D) 4, 13, 56

10. What is the numerical difference between 3 people chosen from a group of 8 when order is important and the same choice when order isn't important?

(A) 336

(B) 280

(C) 56

(D) 3!

Solutions

1. (D) 6%. $A = Pr + Prt$, so

$$\$402.50 = \$350 + (\$350)(r)(2.5)$$

$$\$402.50 = \$350 + \$875r$$

$$r = \frac{\$52.50}{\$875} = 0.06 \text{ or } 6\%$$

2. (B) 4,374. This is a geometric sequence in which r is the ratio of 6 to 2 (or 18 to 6 or 54 to 18), or $r = 3$. $n = 8$, and $a_1 = 2$. Substitution into the formula for the nth term gives $a_n = a_1 r^{n-1} = a_8 = 2 \times 3^7 = 2 \times 2,187 = 4,374$.

3. (B) 5, 27, 115, 467. $a_1 = 5$; $a_2 = 4(5) + 7$; $a_3 = 4(27) + 7$; $a_4 = 4(115) + 7 = 467$. The answer is also obvious because it is the only one that has 5 as the first number.

4. (D) All of the above. This exercise is a reminder to read all of the answer choices, and not just choose (A) because it is true.

5. $\boxed{A}$ and $\boxed{B}$. The converse is "If two angles are equal, they are vertical angles," which is false because they can be any two equal angles, even not in the same figure. The inverse, is "If two angles are not vertical angles, then they are not equal," which is false because they can, for example, be the base angles of an isosceles triangle. The contrapositive is "If two angles are not equal, they are not vertical angles," which is true.

6. (D) All of the above. All of the statements are definitions of modular arithmetic.

7. (C) 10. If there were 25 students of which 8 were studying neither language, then 17 students were studying only French, only German, or both. Therefore, the number studying only French is $F - (F \cap G)$, and likewise, the number studying only German is $G - (F \cap G)$. The number of students studying French or German is calculated as:

$$F \cup G = F + G - (F \cap G)$$

$$17 = 12 + 15 - (F \cap G)$$

$$F \cap G = 27 - 17 = 10$$

8. (B) $\dfrac{17}{30}$. Use the method of multiplying both sides by a power of 10 and then subtracting the original decimal. The power of 10 is just 10, since the repeating decimal part has only one digit. Call the original repeating decimal R. Then $10R = 5.6\overline{6}$ and subtracting $R = 0.5\overline{6}$ yields $10R - R = 5.6\overline{6} - 0.5\overline{6}$ or $9R = 5.1$, which means $R = \dfrac{5.1}{9} = \dfrac{51}{90} = \dfrac{17}{30}$ in lowest terms. Notice that answer choice (A) is not in lowest terms and it has a decimal in the fraction.

9. (B) 3, 13, 55. The formula for the general term of the Fibonacci sequence is given as $a_n = a_{n-1} + a_{n-2}$, which means each successive term is the sum of the two terms before it. Therefore, the fourth term is $2 + 1 = 3$, the seventh term is $8 + 5 = 13$, and the tenth term is $34 + 21 = 55$.

10. (B) 280. Three people chosen from a group of 8 if order is important is a permutation $_nP_r = \dfrac{8!}{5!} = 8 \times 7 \times 6 = 336$. If order isn't important, it is a combination $_nC_r = \dfrac{8!}{3!5!} = \dfrac{8 \times 7 \times 6}{3 \times 2 \times 1} = 56$. The question asks for the numerical difference, which is $336 - 56 = 280$.

PART III:
Praxis Math
Content Knowledge
Practice Tests

Praxis Math
Content Knowledge
Practice Test 1

Praxis Math Content Knowledge
Practice Test 1 Answer Sheet

1. (A) (B) (C) (D) (E)   21. (A) (B) (C) (D) (E)   41. (A) (B) (C) (D) (E)

2. (A) (B) (C) (D) (E)   22. (A) (B) (C) (D) (E)   42. (A) (B) (C) (D) (E)

3. (A) (B) (C) (D) (E)   23. (A) (B) (C) (D) (E)   43. [_____]

4. (A) (B) (C) (D) (E)   24. [_____]   44. (A) (B) (C) (D) (E)

5. [_____]   25. (A) (B) (C) (D) (E)   45. (A) (B) (C) (D) (E)

6. (A) (B) (C) (D) (E)   26. (A) (B) (C) (D) (E)   46. (A) (B) (C) (D) (E)

7. (A) (B) (C) (D) (E)   27. (A) (B) (C) (D) (E)   47. (A) (B) (C) (D) (E)

8. [A] [B] [C] [D] [E]   28. (A) (B) (C) (D) (E)   48. [A] [B] [C] [D] [E]

9. [_____]   29. (A) (B) (C) (D) (E)   49. (A) (B) (C) (D) (E)

10. [====]   30. (A) (B) (C) (D) (E)   50. (A) (B) (C) (D) (E)

11. (A) (B) (C) (D) (E)   31. (A) (B) (C) (D) (E)   51. (A) (B) (C) (D) (E)

12. (A) (B) (C) (D) (E)   32. [_____]   52. (A) (B) (C) (D) (E)

13. (A) (B) (C) (D) (E)   33. [_____]   53. (A) (B) (C) (D) (E)

14. [_____]   34. (A) (B) (C) (D) (E)   54. (A) (B) (C) (D) (E)

15. (A) (B) (C) (D) (E)   35. (A) (B) (C) (D) (E)   55. (A) (B) (C) (D) (E)

16. [_____]   36. (A) (B) (C) (D) (E)   56. (A) (B) (C) (D) (E)

17. (A) (B) (C) (D) (E)   37. (A) (B) (C) (D) (E)   57. (A) (B) (C) (D) (E)

18. (A) (B) (C) (D) (E)   38. (A) (B) (C) (D) (E)   58. (A) (B) (C) (D) (E)

19. (A) (B) (C) (D) (E)   39. (A) (B) (C) (D) (E)   59. (A) (B) (C) (D) (E)

20. (A) (B) (C) (D) (E)   40. (A) (B) (C) (D) (E)   60. (A) (B) (C) (D) (E)

Praxis Math Content Knowledge Practice Test 1

Time: 150 minutes for 60 items

> **Directions:** Answer each question by providing the correct response or responses. Most items on this test require you to provide the one best answer. However, some questions require you to select one or more answers, in which case you will be directed to respond with all answers that apply. Such response options are shown with squares around the letter choices to distinguish them from the questions with only one answer choice. Some questions are numeric-entry, requiring you to fill in a box or boxes with the correct answer.

To our readers: This printed practice test is designed to simulate as closely as possible the computerized Praxis Math test (5161). On test day, you will answer each question by either clicking on the correct response or inserting your answer into designated numeric-entry boxes. An on-screen calculator is available for the actual computerized Praxis Math test and at the REA Study Center.

1. If $y = e^{\frac{x^2}{4}}$, what is $\dfrac{dy}{dx}$?

   (A) $\dfrac{x^2}{4}$

   (B) $\ln \dfrac{x^2}{4}$

   (C) $\dfrac{x}{2} e^{\frac{x^2}{4}}$

   (D) $2xe^{\frac{x^2}{4}}$

2. In $y = \int_{-4}^{5} 2x^3\, dx$, which is the integrand?

   (A) -4

   (B) 5

   (C) $2x^3$

   (D) dx

3. Reduce to lowest terms: $\dfrac{6 - 2x}{x^2 - 9}$.

   (A) $\dfrac{2}{x + 3}$

   (B) $-\dfrac{2}{x + 3}$

   (C) $\dfrac{2}{x - 3}$

   (D) $-\dfrac{2}{x - 3}$

4. If the average of $x + 1$, $x + 3$, and $x + 5$ is 0, what is the value of x?

   (A) 0

   (B) -1

   (C) -2

   (D) -3

5. The formula for the nth term in an arithmetic sequence is $a_n = a_1 + (n - 1)d$, where a_1 is the first term, a_n is the nth term, and d is the common difference. Find the 12th term of the arithmetic progression 3, 8, 13, . . . The 12th term is _____.

6. When solving $\dfrac{7x - 4}{x^2 - x} = \dfrac{5}{x - 1}$, what step is used to get $7x - 4 = 5x$?

   (A) Switch numerators.

   (B) Divide both fractions by the LCD.

   (C) Multiply both fractions by the LCD.

   (D) This simplification isn't possible.

7. The percentage 0.7% is equal to

   (A) $\dfrac{7}{10}$

   (B) $\dfrac{7}{100}$

   (C) $\dfrac{7}{1000}$

   (D) $\dfrac{7}{10000}$

8. To find sin 60°, Sandy entered "sin (60)" on her calculator, and the result was −.30481 . . . Which of the following statement(s) are true? Choose *all* that apply.

   ☐A The answer for sin 60° is correct; calculators don't lie.

   ☐B Operator error; the calculator was set to radians, not degrees.

   ☐C A negative sign in the answer implies that the angle the calculator used is in the third or fourth quadrant.

   ☐D Sandy should have been expecting a rational number.

9. Solve the following radical equation for x: $\sqrt{x^2 + 9} - x = 0$. $x = $_____.

10. If $\tan\theta = \dfrac{4}{3}$ and $\sin\theta$ is negative, $\cos\theta = \left\{ \begin{array}{l} \dfrac{3}{5} \\ \dfrac{-3}{5} \\ \dfrac{-4}{3} \end{array} \right.$.

11. Solve $3x^2 = 9x$

    (A) 0, 3

    (B) 0, −3

    (C) 3, −3

    (D) 0, 0

12. If $\dfrac{2}{3}$ is a root of $3x^2 - bx + 4 = 0$, what is the value of b?

    (A) 8

    (B) −8

    (C) 2

    (D) −2

13. The graph of $(x - 2)^2 = 10 - y^2 - 4x$ is

    (A) a circle

    (B) an ellipse

    (C) a parabola

    (D) a square

14. When solving a pair of second-degree equations, the maximum number of solutions is _____.

15. The relation $x = y$ is reflexive, transitive, and symmetric. Is this also true for $x^2 = y^2$?

    (A) Yes, just square both sides.

    (B) Yes, no matter what x and y stand for, all values have the same properties as $x = y$.

    (C) No, It doesn't hold for negative values of x and y.

    (D) Cannot tell from the information that is given.

16. The perimeter of $\triangle ABC$ if $b = 10$, $c = 16$, and $\angle A = 60°$ is $\left\{ \begin{array}{c} 14 \\ 40 \\ 16 \end{array} \right\}$.

17. Rewrite as a single logarithm: $\log 6 + \log 4 - \log 12 - \log x + \log y$.

    (A) $\log 2 - \log xy$

    (B) $\log\left(\dfrac{2y}{x}\right)$

    (C) $\log\left(\dfrac{x}{2y}\right)$

    (D) $\log 2xy$

18. Find three positive numbers such that the second exceeds twice the first by 3 and the third is 1 less than 6 times the first. In addition, if 3 is added to each number, the result forms a geometric sequence.

    (A) 2, 7, 11

    (B) 2, 7, 17

    (C) 5, 13, 29

    (D) −2, −1, −13

19. If the measures of two of the angles of an isosceles triangle are 30° and 120°, which of the following must be the measure of the third angle?

    (A) 120°

    (B) 90°

    (C) 60°

    (D) 30°

20. Using the position function $s(t) = t - 3$, what is the total distance traveled from $t = 1$ to $t = 4$?

    (A) 1

    (B) 2

    (C) 3

    (D) 4

21. For the distance equation $d = rt$, which of the following statements is true:

    I. d varies directly as t if r is constant.

    II. d varies directly as r if t is constant.

    III. d varies inversely with r.

    (A) I only

    (B) II only

    (C) I, II, and III

    (D) I and II only

22. The equation of the axis of symmetry of the graph of the equation $y = 2x^2 + 6x - 5$ is

    (A) $x = -\dfrac{3}{2}$

    (B) $x = -3$

    (C) $y = -\dfrac{3}{2}$

    (D) $y = -3$

23. The BG Company manufactures plastic parts for a distributor. An internal audit determined that 1 out of every 50 of these parts is faulty, but the company doesn't know which ones are faulty until a customer complains to the distributor. BG makes a $3 profit on the sale of any working part, but suffers a loss of $50 for every faulty part due to the time spent in customer service and replacement of the part. Can the company expect a profit in the long term?

    (A) No, they lose almost $2 per faulty part.

    (B) Yes, the expected value is positive.

    (C) Yes, their profit is $1.06 per part.

    (D) No, their loss is $1.94 per part.

24. To reduce $\dfrac{x^3-1}{2x-2}$ to lowest terms, both the numerator and denominator should be divided by $\left\{\begin{array}{c} x+1 \\ x-1 \\ 2 \end{array}\right\}$.

25. Find the sum of the infinite geometric series $1+\dfrac{1}{2}+\dfrac{1}{4}+\dfrac{1}{8}\cdots$

    (A) $\dfrac{1}{2}$

    (B) 1

    (C) $1\dfrac{1}{2}$

    (D) 2

26. The number of terms in the expansion of $(a+b)^n$ is

    (A) n

    (B) $n+1$

    (C) $2n$

    (D) $n-1$

27. The numerator and denominator of a fraction are in the ratio of 3 : 4. If 1 is subtracted from the numerator and 2 is added to the denominator, the resulting fraction equals $\dfrac{2}{3}$. What is the original fraction?

    (A) $\dfrac{2}{3}$

    (B) $\dfrac{1}{5}$

    (C) $\dfrac{21}{28}$

    (D) $\dfrac{3}{4}$

28. An office uses paper drinking cups in the shape of a cone, with diameter 2.75 inches and height 4 inches. To the nearest tenth of a cubic inch, what is the volume of each drinking cup?

    (A) 2.5

    (B) 7.9

    (C) 23.7

    (D) 31.7

29. A farmer has enough grain on hand to feed 60 cattle for 20 weeks. How long in weeks would this amount of grain feed 40 cattle?

    (A) $13\dfrac{1}{3}$

    (B) 30

    (C) 60

    (D) 120

30. If you split any even number n into two parts, what split gives the maximum product of the parts?

    (A) 1 and $(n-1)$

    (B) $\left(\dfrac{n}{2}\right)$ and $\left(\dfrac{n}{2}\right)$

    (C) n^2

    (D) Depends on the value of n

31. To find the value of a function when the rate of change is constant, at a minimum we need:

    (A) arithmetic

    (B) differentiation

    (C) integration

    (D) all of the above

32. The graph of $ax^2 = 25 + ay^2$ is $\left\{\begin{array}{c} \text{always} \\ \text{sometimes} \\ \text{never} \end{array}\right\}$ a circle.

33. $\dfrac{1}{c}$ is $\left\{ \begin{array}{c} \text{always} \\ \text{sometimes} \\ \text{never} \end{array} \right\}$ less than 1.

34. Which of the following are not true?

    I. $54 \in \{\text{even integers}\}$

    II. $\{a, b, c\} \subset \{b, c, d, a\}$

    III. A set is not a subset of itself.

    IV. The null set is a subset of any set.

    (A) All are true.

    (B) II

    (C) III

    (D) IV

35. Completely factor $x^3 + 3x^2 - 6x - 8$ if it is known that $(x + 1)$ is a factor.

    (A) $(x + 1)(x + 4)(x - 2)$

    (B) $(x + 1)(x - 4)(x + 2)$

    (C) $(x + 1)(x + 4)(x + 2)$

    (D) $(x + 1)(x - 4)(x - 2)$

36. Which of the following choices is less than $\dfrac{1}{6}$?

    (A) 0.16666

    (B) 0.16667

    (C) 0.1667

    (D) $\dfrac{4}{24}$

37. If a ball falls from a height of 1,000 at a velocity of $32t$ feet per second. At any time t what equation would give the distance of the ball above the ground in feet?

    (A) $s = 32t + 1,000$

    (B) $s = -32t + 1,000$

    (C) $s = 16t^2 + 1,000$

    (D) $s = -16t^2 + 1,000$

38. What does the equation $y = ae^{-bx}$ represent when the independent variable x represents a long period of time?

    (A) Physical processes in which something is increasing rapidly.

    (B) Physical processes in which something is increasing gradually.

    (C) Physical processes in which something is rapidly dying away.

    (D) Physical processes in which something is gradually dying away.

39. Eighty crayons are laid out on the table in the following sequence: red, orange, yellow, green, blue, red, orange, yellow, green, blue, etc. What color is the 54th crayon?

    (A) orange

    (B) yellow

    (C) green

    (D) blue

40. Which of the following groups of fractions is in ascending order?

    (A) $\dfrac{9}{26}, \dfrac{1}{4}, \dfrac{3}{10}$

    (B) $\dfrac{9}{26}, \dfrac{3}{10}, \dfrac{1}{4}$

    (C) $\dfrac{1}{4}, \dfrac{3}{10}, \dfrac{9}{26}$

    (D) $\dfrac{3}{10}, \dfrac{1}{4}, \dfrac{9}{26}$

41. Jan bought n oranges for y cents. How much would x oranges cost?

    (A) $\dfrac{y}{n}$ cents

    (B) $\dfrac{y}{nx}$ cents

    (C) xy cents

    (D) $\dfrac{xy}{n}$ cents

42. If $\dfrac{1}{a} = \dfrac{1}{b} - \dfrac{1}{c}$, then b equals

    (A) $a + c$

    (B) $\dfrac{ac}{c - a}$

    (C) $\dfrac{a + c}{ac}$

    (D) $\dfrac{ac}{a + c}$

43. If a plane flies 750 miles in 4 hours, 10 minutes, what is its average speed in miles per hour?

    _____

44. Consider the inequality $\dfrac{x + 2}{2x - 1} \geq 0$. State the solution in interval notation.

    (A) $(-\infty, -2] \cup \left[-2, \dfrac{1}{2} \right) \cup \left(\dfrac{1}{2}, \infty \right)$

    (B) $(-\infty, -2] \cup \left(\dfrac{1}{2}, \infty \right)$

    (C) $\left(-\infty, \dfrac{1}{2} \right) \cup \left(\dfrac{1}{2}, \infty \right)$

    (D) $(-\infty, -2] \cup \left(-2, \dfrac{1}{2} \right) \right) \cup \left(\dfrac{1}{2}, \infty \right)$

45. Express $\dfrac{3}{5 - \sqrt{2}}$ as an equivalent fraction with a rational denominator.

    (A) $5 + \sqrt{2}$

    (B) $5 - \sqrt{2}$

    (C) $\dfrac{5 - \sqrt{2}}{9}$

    (D) $\dfrac{15 - 3\sqrt{2}}{23}$

46. If a rectangle is rotated around one of its edges, the resulting three-dimensional figure is a

    (A) circle

    (B) cone

    (C) rectangular solid

    (D) cylinder

47. Complete the following derivation of the standard form of the ellipse given the polar equations $x = 3 \cos \theta$ and $y = 4 \sin \theta$. Choose the best answer of the given choices.

    1. $x = 3 \cos \theta$ and $\qquad$ 1. Given
        $y = 4 \sin \theta$

    2. $\left(\dfrac{x}{3} \right) = \cos\theta$ and $\qquad$ 2. Division of
        $\left(\dfrac{y}{4} \right) = \sin\theta$ $\qquad\qquad\quad$ equalities

    3. $\left(\dfrac{x}{3} \right)^2 = (\cos\theta)^2$ and $\quad$ 3. Squaring both
        $\left(\dfrac{y}{4} \right)^2 = (\sin\theta)^2$ $\qquad\qquad$ sides of an
        $\qquad\qquad\qquad\qquad\qquad$ equation

    4. $(\cos\theta)^2 + (\sin\theta)^2 = 1$ $\quad$ 4. ?

    5. $\left(\dfrac{x}{3} \right)^2 + \left(\dfrac{y}{4} \right)^2 =$ $\qquad$ 5. Substitution
        $\dfrac{x^2}{9} + \dfrac{y^2}{16} = 1$

    (A) Pythagorean Theorem

    (B) Definition of sine and cosine

    (C) Pythagorean identity

    (D) Sum of the squares equals the square of the sums

48. Which of the following integral equations is always true? Choose *all* the apply.

$\boxed{A}$ $\int \cot \theta \, d\theta = \dfrac{\int \cos \theta \, d\theta}{\int \sin \theta \, d\theta}$

$\boxed{B}$ $\int_a^b f(x) \, dx = -\int_b^a f(x) \, dx$

$\boxed{C}$ $\int \sqrt{\cos^2 x + \sin^2 x} \, dx = x + C$

$\boxed{D}$ $\int 3 f(x) \, dx = 3 \int f(x) \, dx$

49. For the quadratic equation $ax^2 + bx + c = 0$, the value of $b^2 - 4ac < 0$. How many real roots does the equation have?

(A) 0

(B) 1

(C) 2

(D) Cannot tell if a, b, and c aren't known.

50. If $x = \log m$, then $x + 2$ equals

(A) $\log m^2$

(B) $\log 2m$

(C) $\log 100m$

(D) $\log (m + 2)$

51. When integrating $\int xe^x \, dx$ by parts and evaluating $\int u \, dv$, if we set $u = x$, what is the value of dv? (The formula for integration by parts is on the pull-down Formula Sheet for the Praxis test.)

(A) $e^x \, dx$

(B) e^x

(C) dx

(D) $xe^x \, dx$

52. Find the inverse of $y = x^2 + 3$, $x \geq 3$.

(A) $y = x^2 + 3$, $x \leq 3$

(B) $x = \pm\sqrt{y - 3}$

(C) $y = \sqrt{x - 3}$, $y \geq 3$, $x \geq 0$

(D) $y = \sqrt{x - 3}$, $x \geq 3$, $y \geq 0$

53. Find $\displaystyle\lim_{x \to \infty} \dfrac{7x^2 + 3x - 12}{4x^3 + 2}$.

(A) $\dfrac{7}{4}$

(B) 0

(C) ∞

(D) -6

54. What type of sequence is the following: 1, 1, 2, 3, 5, 8, 13, 21, 34, . . .?

(A) recursive

(B) repeating

(C) geometric

(D) arithmetic

55. If someone flips a coin 8 times, what is the probability that it lands heads up all 8 times?

(A) 2^8

(B) $\left(\dfrac{1}{8}\right)^2$

(C) $\left(\dfrac{1}{2}\right)^8$

(D) $\dfrac{1}{2}$

Praxis Math Content Knowledge
Practice Test 1 Answer Key

1. (C)

2. (C)

3. (B)

4. (D)

5. 58

6. (C)

7. (C)

8. B, C

9. 4

10. $-\dfrac{3}{5}$

11. (A)

12. (C)

13. (A)

14. 4

15. (B)

16. 40

17. (B)

18. (C)

19. (D)

20. (C)

21. (D)

22. (A)

23. (B)

24. $x - 1$

25. (D)

26. (B)

27. (C)

28. (B)

29. (B)

30. (B)

31. (A)

32. Never

33. Sometimes

34. (C)

35. (A)

36. (A)

37. (D)

38. (D)

39. (C)

40. (C)

41. (D)

42. (D)

43. 180

44. (B)

45. (D)

46. (D)

47. (C)

48. B, C, D

49. (A)

50. (C)

51. (A)

52. (D)

53. (B)

54. (A)

55. (C)

56. (B)

57. (A)

58. (A)

59. (B)

60. (B)

PRACTICE TEST 1: ANSWERS AND EXPLANATIONS

1. (C) $\dfrac{x}{2}e^{\frac{x^2}{4}}$

    The derivative of e^u is $e^u\dfrac{du}{dx}$. For $y=e^{\frac{x^2}{4}}$, $u=\dfrac{x^2}{4}$ and $\dfrac{du}{dx}=\dfrac{2x}{4}=\dfrac{x}{2}$. Therefore, $\dfrac{du}{dx}=\dfrac{x}{2}e^{\frac{x^2}{4}}$.

2. (C) $2x^3$

    The integrand is the expression to be integrated, appearing right after the integral sign.

3. (B) $-\dfrac{2}{x+3}$

    Rewrite the numerator so the first term is an x term and the common factors will more easily be seen. $\dfrac{6-2x}{x^2-9}=-\dfrac{2x-6}{x^2-9}=-\dfrac{2(x-3)}{(x+3)(x-3)}=-\dfrac{2}{x+3}$. Remember to carry the minus sign before the fraction through to the end.

4. (D) -3

    The average is $\dfrac{(x+1)+(x+3)+(x+5)}{3}=\dfrac{3x+9}{3}=x+3$, which is given as 0. So $x=-3$.

5. 58

    We are finding a_{12} with $a_1=3$ and $d=5$. Then the formula becomes $a_{12}=3+(11)(5)=58$.

6. (C)

    Multiply both fractions by the LCD. To clear the fractions from an equation, multiply both sides by the LCD, x^2-x. Here, $\dfrac{7x-4}{x^2-x}=\dfrac{5}{x-1}$ is the same as $(x^2-x)\dfrac{7x-4}{x^2-x}=\dfrac{5}{x-1}(x^2-x)$, where $x^2-x=x(x-1)$ is used on the right-hand side. Then $(x^2-x)\dfrac{7x-4}{x^2-x}=\dfrac{5}{x-1}x(x-1)$ becomes $7x-4=5x$ and $x=2$, but you are asked only for the method, not the value of x.

7. (C) $\dfrac{7}{1000}$

    To convert a percentage to a fraction, divide by 100%, so this would be $\dfrac{0.7\%}{100\%}=\dfrac{\frac{7}{10}}{100}=\dfrac{7}{10}\div100=\dfrac{7}{10}\times\dfrac{1}{100}=\dfrac{7}{1000}$. Most of this should be done mentally.

8. $\boxed{B}, \boxed{C}$

    The calculator answer is clearly incorrect for 60° because a negative cosine occurs only in the third or fourth quadrants and 60° is in the first quadrant. Answer choice $\boxed{A}$ is false—although we might say that calculators don't lie, the answer was for a different angle (60 radians). Answer choice $\boxed{D}$ is false because sin 60° is $\dfrac{\sqrt{3}}{2}$, an irrational number. Answer choices $\boxed{B}$ and $\boxed{C}$ are true.

9.   4

$$\sqrt{x^2 + 9} - x = 1$$

$$\sqrt{x^2 + 9} = 1 + x$$ Add $+x$ to both sides to isolate the radical on one side.

$$x^2 + 9 = x^2 + 2x + 1$$ Square both sides.

$$8 = 2x, \text{ or } x = 4$$ Combine like terms and solve for x.

10. $\dfrac{-3}{5}$

If the tangent is positive and the sine is negative, then the cosine must also be negative since $\tan\theta = \dfrac{\sin\theta}{\cos\theta}$. Thus, we have a right triangle in the third quadrant with a hypotenuse of 5 (a Pythagorean triple), $y = -4$, and $x = -3$. Then $\cos\theta = \dfrac{x}{r} = -\dfrac{3}{5}$.

11.   (A)   0, 3

$$3x^2 - 9x$$

$$3x^2 - 9x = 0$$

$$3x(x - 3) = 0$$

$$3x = 0 \text{ or } x - 3 = 0$$

$$x = 0, 3$$

12.   (C)   2

For the equation $3x^2 - bx + 4 = 0$, $a = 3$, $c = 4$, and one root is given as $\dfrac{2}{3}$. The product of the roots is $\dfrac{c}{a} = \dfrac{4}{3}$, so the other root must be $\dfrac{4}{3} \div \dfrac{2}{3} = \dfrac{4}{3} \times \dfrac{3}{2} = 2$.

13.   (A)   a circle

When we multiply out the original equation, $(x - 2)^2 = 10 - y^2 - 4x$, we get $x^2 - 4x + 4 = 10 - y^2 - 4x$, and combining like terms, this ends up as $x^2 + y^2 = 6$, the general equation of a circle with center at $(0, 0)$ and radius $\sqrt{6}$.

14.   4

Second-degree equations are conics (circle, ellipse, hyperbola, parabola), which are confined so there is no "wiggle" in their graphs, and they can intersect in no more than 4 points.

15.   (B)   Yes

No matter what x and y stand for, all values have the same properties as $x = y$. $x^2 = y^2$ is just a special case of equality, so all properties that apply to $x = y$ also apply to this case.

16.   40

Use the law of cosines to find the third side, $a^2 = b^2 + c^2 - 2bc \cos A$, or $a^2 = (10)^2 + (16)^2 - 2(10)(16)(\cos 60°)$. Therefore, $a^2 = 100 + 256 - 160 = 196$, and $a = 14$. Note that this answer can be obtained without these calculations because the choices 14 and 16 are too small for the perimeter given the lengths of b and c.

17. **(B)** $\log\left(\dfrac{2y}{x}\right)$

The sum of logs equals the log of the product, and the difference of logs equals the log of the quotient. Therefore, all of the positive logarithms are in the numerator and all of the negative logarithms are in the denominator of the final fraction. So $\log 6 + \log 4 - \log 12 - \log x + \log y =$ $\log(6 \times 4 \times y) = \log\left(\dfrac{24y}{12x}\right) = \log\left(\dfrac{2y}{x}\right)$.

18. **(C)** $5, 13, 29$

This is a complicated problem that can be solved by algebra, but rather than doing that, solve it by the process of elimination. First, eliminate answer choice (D) because the problem says these are positive numbers. The rest of the elimination can be done several ways. One is to first check out the second criterion (if 3 is added to each number, the result forms a geometric sequence) because it is easier. That eliminates answer choice (A). Then check the first criterion for (B) and (C), and it works only for (C).

19. **(D)** $30°$

Since it is an isosceles triangle, this angle must be the same as one of the given angles. But since a triangle can have only one obtuse angle, it must be 30°. Another way to look at this problem is that the angles of a triangle always total 180°, so $180 = 120 + 30 + x$, and $x = 30°$.

20. **(C)** 3

The position at $t = 1$ is -2, and the position at $t = 4$ is 1. The total distance is the absolute value of their difference, or $|1 - (-2)| = 3 = 3$ or $|(-2) - 1| = |-3| = 3$.

21. **(D)   I and II only**

If r or t are constant, d varies directly with the other variable because the formula for direct variation is $d = kt$ or $d = kr$. d doesn't vary inversely with r because that would be true only if distance decreased as the rate increased.

22. **(A)** $x = -\dfrac{3}{2}$

The parabola $y = 2x^2 + 6x - 5$ is a vertical parabola that opens upward. Since the general equation for a parabola is $y = ax^2 + bx + c$, $a = 2$ and $b = 6$. The axis of symmetry is given by the line $x = -\dfrac{b}{2a} = -\dfrac{6}{2(2)} = -\dfrac{3}{2}$.

23. **(B)   Yes, the expected value is positive.**

The expected value for this scenario is

$$EV = \$3\left(\dfrac{49}{50}\right) - \$50\left(\dfrac{1}{50}\right) = \dfrac{\$147}{50} - \dfrac{\$97}{50} = \$1.94.$$

Since the expected value is positive, the BG Company can expect to make a profit. On average, they make a profit of $1.94 per part produced, whether it is defective or not. Notice that to answer this problem you don't have to calculate the exact profit, you only need to determine whether the expected value is positive. But in this instance, you might want to calculate the expected value to be sure that choice (C)—"Yes, their profit is $1.06 per part"—isn't the correct answer.

24. $x - 1$

$(x - 1)$ is a common factor of the numerator and denominator.

25. **(D)** 2

First, find the common ratio by dividing the second term by the first term, or $r = \dfrac{1}{2} \div 1 = \dfrac{1}{2}$. Since r is positive and greater than -1, the limit as $n \to \infty$ is given by

$$S_\infty = \frac{a_1}{1-r} = \frac{1}{1-\frac{1}{2}} = 2 \,.$$

26. (B) $n+1$.

One way to answer this is by writing the rows of Pascal's triangle, and noticing that each row has one more term than the row number. Otherwise, notice that the exponent of the first term in the binomial is n in the first term of the expansion, and the exponent diminishes by 1 in each succeeding term all the way down to 0 in the last term, which gives $n+1$ (for the 0) terms.

27. (C) $\dfrac{21}{28}$

Represent the original fraction as $\dfrac{3x}{4x}$, which is in the ratio of $3:4$. The manipulations result in $\dfrac{3x-1}{4x+2} = \dfrac{2}{3}$. To solve for x, cross multiply and solve the equation:

$$3(3x-1) = 2(4x+2)$$
$$9x-3 = 8x+4$$
$$x = 7$$

so the original equation is $\dfrac{3x}{4x} = \dfrac{3(7)}{4(7)} = \dfrac{21}{28}$. Note that answer choice (D), although it is equivalent and I the ratio $3:4$, doesn't fulfill the rest of the problem because if 1 is subtracted from the numerator and 2 is added to the denominator, the resulting fraction equals $\dfrac{2}{6}$.

28. (B) 7.9

The volume of a cone is given by $V = \dfrac{1}{3}\pi r^2$. By substituting the given values, $V = \dfrac{1}{3}(3.14)(1.375)^2(4) = 7.9$ cubic inches. Be sure to use the radius, which is half the given diameter. This is not the same as squaring the diameter and then taking half of the result.

29. (B) 30

This is an inverse proportion. For a given amount of grain, you can feed more cattle for less time or fewer cattle for more time. So the amount of grain $= (60)(20) = (40)(t)$, and $t = 30$ weeks.

30. (B) $\left(\dfrac{n}{2}\right)$ and $\left(\dfrac{n}{2}\right)$

The two parts can be designated as a and $(n-a)$. Then their product is $a(n-a) = an - a^2$. Let's call y the product of the two parts, which we want to maximize. Then $y = an - a^2$ and the first derivative of the function must be zero for a maximum. So $\dfrac{dy}{da} = n - 2a = 0$, or $a = \dfrac{n}{2}$, so each part is half of the original number.

31. (A) arithmetic

If the rate of change is constant, or $\dfrac{dy}{dx} = k$, the function is $y = kx$, and all we need is arithmetic to find the value of y.

32. Never

The general equation for a circle is $ax^2 + ay^2 = r^2$, in which the coefficients of x^2 and y^2 are equal and positive. The given equation cannot be put in that form. In fact, this is a hyperbola, which has the general form $ax^2 - by^2 + dx + ey + f = 0$, where a and b can be equal, and e and f can be 0.

33. Sometimes

This is false if c is a positive fraction and true otherwise, except if $c = 0$.

34. (C) III

A set is not a subset of itself. Watch out for all the double negatives in this question. The question is asking which are false. Since a set is always a subset of itself, statement III is false, or not true. All of the other statements are true.

35. (A) $(x + 1)(x + 4)(x - 2)$

Use synthetic division to find the quotient:

$$
\begin{array}{r|rrrr}
-1 & 1 & +3 & -6 & -8 \\
   &   & -1 & -2 & +8 \\
\hline
   & 1 & +2 & -8 & 0
\end{array}
$$

(If instead you use long division, divide by $x + 1$, and you get the same result, only not as quickly.) Therefore, the other factor is $x^2 + 2x - 8$, which factors into $(x + 4)(x - 2)$.

36. (A) 0.16666

If you didn't remember that $\frac{1}{6} = 0.16\overline{6}$, use your calculator. Then the answer is obviously answer choice (A). Answer choices (B) and (C) round the value *up*, and (D) equals $\frac{1}{6}$ exactly.

37. (D) $s = -16t^2 + 1{,}000$

The velocity (not the distance) at the moment the ball falls is given by $\frac{ds}{dt} = -32t$; it is negative because the ball is falling because velocity is change of distance per change in time. Then the distance from the ground at time t is $s = \int -32\, dt + C = -16t^2 + C$, where $C =$ the original 1,000 feet.

38. (D) Physical processes in which something is gradually dying away.

The equation is $y = ae^{-bt}$ when the independent variable $x = t$. Then as t increases, y decreases exponentially. At first the change could be quick, but over a period of time it becomes more and more gradual.

39. (C) green

This is a repeating cycle. One way to figure it out, since there are five colors in the cycle, is to realize that every 5th, 10th, 15th, etc., crayon is blue, so that must be true for the 55th crayon, and the 54th must be the color that comes before blue. Another way is to divide 5 into 54 and look for the color that is in the remainder (4th) place, which also is green. This last method involves modular math.

40. (C) $\frac{1}{4}, \frac{3}{10}, \frac{9}{26}$

Ascending order means the fractions get larger. All of the choices have the same three fractions. To find the lowest common denominator will be a time-waster because there is no obvious one. But two of the fractions are familiar: $\frac{1}{4} = .25$ and $\frac{3}{10} = .30$. So now the problem reduces to choosing the order that has $\frac{1}{4}$ before $\frac{3}{10}$, which occurs only in answer choices (A) and (C). So the question reduces to checking whether $\frac{9}{26}$ is less than $\frac{1}{4}$ or greater than $\frac{3}{10}$. Note that only one of these checks is needed since there are only two choices answer choices now. It should be obvious that $\frac{9}{26}$ is not less than $\frac{1}{4}$ (or use your calculator) so the correct answer is (C).

41. (D) $\dfrac{xy}{n}$ **cents**

The cost of one orange = $\dfrac{y}{n}$ cents. So the cost of x oranges is x times the cost of one, or $x\left(\dfrac{y}{n}\right) = \dfrac{xy}{n}$ cents.

42. (D) $\dfrac{ac}{a+c}$

The common denominator is abc. Multiply both sides of the equation by $\dfrac{abc}{abc}$ to get $\dfrac{bc}{abc} = \dfrac{ac}{abc} - \dfrac{ab}{abc}$, or $bc = ac - ab$. Solving for b:

$$ab + bc = ac$$
$$b(a + c) = ac$$
$$b = \dfrac{ac}{a+c}$$

43. 180

Just divide the miles by the time. Change the time to $4\dfrac{1}{6}$ hours. Then the calculation is $4750 \div \left(\dfrac{25}{6}\right) = 750 \times \left(\dfrac{6}{25}\right) = 30 \times 6 = 180$ miles per hour. Alternatively, change the time to minutes: 4 hours 10 minutes = $4(60) + 10 = 250$ minutes. Then the average speed is $\dfrac{750}{250} = 3$ miles per minute. Multiply by 60 to get 180 miles per hour.

44. (B) $(\infty, -2] \cup \left(\dfrac{1}{2}, \infty\right)$

Set the numerator and denominator equal to 0 and solve the resulting equations to find the critical numbers, which are $x = -2$ and $x = \dfrac{1}{2}$. Since $x = \dfrac{1}{2}$ makes the fraction have a zero denominator, which isn't allowed, it is not in the solution set of any answer choice. Answer choices (A), (C), and (D) include the interval between the critical values. Only one point in the interval needs to be checked. Let's check the point $x = 0$, which makes the fraction negative and the inequality false, so the interval between the critical points must be excluded. Therefore, answer choices (A), (C), and (D) are incorrect, and answer choice (B) must be correct. A check of answer choice (B) shows that any number to the right of $\dfrac{1}{2}$ and to the left of -2 makes the fraction positive.

45. (D) $\dfrac{15 + 3\sqrt{2}}{23}$

Rationalize the denominator by multiplying the given fraction $\dfrac{3}{5 - \sqrt{2}}$ by $\dfrac{5 + \sqrt{2}}{5 + \sqrt{2}}$:

$$\dfrac{3}{5 - \sqrt{2}} \times \dfrac{5 + \sqrt{2}}{5 + \sqrt{2}} = \dfrac{3(5 + \sqrt{2})}{25 - 2} = \dfrac{15 + 3\sqrt{2}}{23}.$$

46. (D) cylinder

The following figure shows the rotation, although it can be around any edge. Eliminate answer choice (A) because a circle is not three-dimensional. A cone (answer choice (B)) is formed by the rotation of a right triangle around one of its legs. The word *rotate* eliminates answer choice (C).

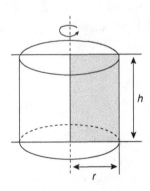

47. (C) Pythagorean identity

Although the Pythagorean identity is a result of the Pythagorean Theorem, in this case we use the identity, which is for trigonometric functions. Answer choice (D) isn't necessarily true.

48. $\boxed{B}, \boxed{C}, \boxed{D}$

Only answer choice $\boxed{A}$ is incorrect because the integral of a quotient is not the quotient of the integrals. Problems of this type need to use integration by parts. The actual answer thus becomes $\int \cot\theta \, d\theta = \ln|\sin\theta| + C$. Answer choices $\boxed{B}$ and $\boxed{D}$ come from the fundamental theorem of calculus. In answer choice $\boxed{C}$, $\cos^2 x + \sin^2 x = 1$ is the Pythagorean identity, and $\int dx = x + C$.

49. (A) 0

Using the quadratic formula $x = \dfrac{-b \pm \sqrt{b^2 - 4ac}}{2a}$, the discriminant $b^2 - 4ac$ signals the number of real solutions. If $b^2 - 4ac < 0$, the radicand is negative and solutions are imaginary. So there are no real roots.

50. (C) log 100*m*

If $x = \log m$, then $x + 2 = \log m + 2$. But $2 = \log 100$ (since $10^2 = 100$), so $\log m + 2 = \log m + \log 100$, but the sum of logs equals the log of the product, so $\log m + \log 100 = \log 100m$.

51. (A) $e^x \, dx$

If $\int xe^x \, dx = \int u \, dv$, and $u = x$, then dv must equal the rest of the integral, or $e^x \, dx$. You do not have to evaluate this integral to answer the question.

52. (D) $y = \sqrt{x - 3}, x \geq 3, y \geq 0$

Following the steps for finding the inverse of a function, rewrite the function in terms of x: $x^2 = y - 3$, or $x = \sqrt{y - 3}$. Use only the positive square root because the domain and range are the reverse of those for the function: $x \geq 3, y \geq 0$. Finally, switch the x and y, to get $y = \sqrt{x - 3}, x \geq 3, y \geq 0$.

53. (B) 0

This is an expression in which the power of the denominator is greater than the power of the numerator. The coefficients do not matter. Ultimately, the denominator is more "powerful" than the numerator, and the limit is the same as $\lim\limits_{x \to \infty} \dfrac{1}{x} = 0$.

54. (A) recursive

Any sequence for which the elements depend on prior elements is recursive. In this recusive sequence (the Fibonacci sequence), each element after the first two is the sum of the two elements before it. The other answer choices can be eliminated by checking the relationship between any two successive elements—they aren't repeated (except the first two), nor do they have a common ratio or a common difference.

55. (C) $\left(\dfrac{1}{2}\right)^8$

Each of the flips of the coin is independent of all the other flips, and each has a $\dfrac{1}{2}$ probability of landing heads up, so the probabilities are multiplied: $\dfrac{1}{2} \times \dfrac{1}{2} \times \ldots = \left(\dfrac{1}{2}\right)^8$.

56. (B) 2

There are exactly 2 numbers (7 and 9) that are in both circles.

57. (A) $400

At the end of 10 years with simple interest, the amount would be $P + i = P + Prt = \$5000 + (\$5000)(.04)(10) = \$7000$. At the end of 10 years with compound interest, the amount would be $P + Prt = \$5000 + (\$5000)(.04)(10) = \$7000$. The difference is $401, which is $400 rounded to the nearest hundred.

58. (A) .04

The probability is the ratio of the area of the bull's eye to the area of the whole target. The area of the whole target is found by using the formula for the area of a circle with a radius of 40 cm, or

$A_{\text{target}} = \pi r^2 = (40)^2 \pi = 1600\pi$ cm^2. To find the area of the bull's-eye, count the number of concentric circles to the bull's-eye, which is 4, each band being 8 cm wide. Then the radius of the bull's-eye is $40 - 4(8) = 8$ cm, and it has an area of $A_{\text{bull's eye}} = \pi r^2 = (8)^2 \pi = 64\pi$ cm^2. Then the probability is $\Pr_{\text{bull's eye}} = \dfrac{64\pi}{1600\pi} = .04$.

59. (B) $-m$

$\text{Log}(\cot x) = \log\left(\dfrac{1}{\tan x}\right) = \log 1 - \log(\tan x) = 0 - m = -m$.

60. (B) 6

The slope of the tangent line at a point on a curve is the instantaneous rate of change at that point, or the value of the first derivative at that point. For this function, $f'(x) = 6x$, so the slope at $x = 1$ is $6(1) = 6$.

Praxis Math
Content Knowledge
Practice Test 2

Praxis Math Content Knowledge
Practice Test 2 Answer Sheet

1. (A) (B) (C) (D) (E)

2. [＿＿＿＿＿＿]

3. (A) (B) (C) (D) (E)

4. (A) (B) (C) (D) (E)

5. (A) (B) (C) (D) (E)

6. (A) (B) (C) (D) (E)

7. (A) (B) (C) (D) (E)

8. (A) (B) (C) (D) (E)

9. (A) (B) (C) (D) (E)

10. (A) (B) (C) (D) (E)

11. (A) (B) (C) (D) (E)

12. (A) (B) (C) (D) (E)

13. (A) (B) (C) (D) (E)

14. (A) (B) (C) (D) (E)

15. [A] [B] [C] [D] [E]

16. (A) (B) (C) (D) (E)

17. (A) (B) (C) (D) (E)

18. [＿＿＿＿＿＿]

19. [＿＿＿＿＿＿]

20. (A) (B) (C) (D) (E)

21. (A) (B) (C) (D) (E)

22. (A) (B) (C) (D) (E)

23. (A) (B) (C) (D) (E)

24. (A) (B) (C) (D) (E)

25. (A) (B) (C) (D) (E)

26. (A) (B) (C) (D) (E)

27. [＿＿＿＿＿＿]

28. (A) (B) (C) (D) (E)

29. (A) (B) (C) (D) (E)

30. (A) (B) (C) (D) (E)

31. (A) (B) (C) (D) (E)

32. (A) (B) (C) (D) (E)

33. (A) (B) (C) (D) (E)

34. (A) (B) (C) (D) (E)

35. (A) (B) (C) (D) (E)

36. [A] [B] [C] [D] [E]

37. (A) (B) (C) (D) (E)

38. (A) (B) (C) (D) (E)

39. (A) (B) (C) (D) (E)

40. (A) (B) (C) (D) (E)

41. (A) (B) (C) (D) (E)

42. [＿＿＿＿＿＿]

43. (A) (B) (C) (D) (E)

44. (A) (B) (C) (D) (E)

45. [＿＿＿＿＿＿]

46. (A) (B) (C) (D) (E)

47. (A) (B) (C) (D) (E)

48. (A) (B) (C) (D) (E)

49. (A) (B) (C) (D) (E)

50. (A) (B) (C) (D) (E)

51. [A] [B] [C] [D] [E]

52. (A) (B) (C) (D) (E)

53. (A) (B) (C) (D) (E)

54. [＿＿＿＿＿＿]

55. (A) (B) (C) (D) (E)

56. (A) (B) (C) (D) (E)

57. (A) (B) (C) (D) (E)

58. [＿＿＿＿＿＿]

59. (A) (B) (C) (D) (E)

60. (A) (B) (C) (D) (E)

Praxis Math Content Knowledge
Practice Test 2

Time: 150 minutes for 60 items

> **Directions:** Answer each question by providing the correct response or responses. Most items on this test require you to provide the one best answer. However, some questions require you to select one or more answers, in which case you will be directed to respond with all answers that apply. Such response options are shown with squares around the letter choices to distinguish them from the questions with only one answer choice. Some questions are numeric-entry, requiring you to fill in a box or boxes with the correct answer.

To our readers: This printed practice test is designed to simulate as closely as possible the computerized Praxis Math test (5161). On test day, you will answer each question by either clicking on the correct response or inserting your answer into designated numeric-entry boxes. An on-screen calculator is available for the actual computerized Praxis Math test.

1. Which of the following statements about the roots of a polynomial is not true?

   (A) A polynomial of degree n has $(n - 1)$ roots if the polynomial equals zero.

   (B) The roots of a polynomial may be imaginary numbers.

   (C) The imaginary roots of a polynomial always come in pairs.

   (D) The product of a pair of imaginary roots of a polynomial yields an irreducible quadratic.

2. A pharmaceutical company wishes to test a new medication it thinks will reduce cholesterol. A group of 20 volunteers is formed and each has his or her cholesterol level measured. Half are randomly assigned to take the new drug and the other half are given a dummy pill, a pill with no active ingredients. After 6 months the volunteers' cho-

lesterol is measured again and any change from the beginning of the study recorded. This is a(n)

$$\begin{cases} \text{sample survey} \\ \text{experimental} \\ \text{observational} \end{cases} \text{type of study.}$$

3. The graph of the equation $y = 3x^2 - 7x + 5$.

   (A) is tangent to the x-axis.

   (B) intersects the x-axis in two distinct points.

   (C) intersects the x-axis in three distinct points.

   (D) has no points in common with the x-axis.

4. The limit of $s(t) = 6t - t^3$ as t approaches -2 is:

   (A) 4

   (B) -4

   (C) 20

   (D) -20

5. Express in simplest form: $\dfrac{\frac{a}{b} + c}{\frac{a}{c} + b}$.

    (A) $\dfrac{b}{c}$

    (B) $\dfrac{c}{b}$

    (C) $\dfrac{(a+bc)^2}{bc}$

    (D) $\dfrac{a+c}{a+b}$

6. The value of $\tan\dfrac{\pi}{3} + \cos\pi$ is

    (A) $\dfrac{\sqrt{3}+3}{3}$

    (B) $\dfrac{\sqrt{3}-3}{3}$

    (C) $\sqrt{3}+1$

    (D) $\sqrt{3}-1$

7. If $f(x) = 2x^0 + (x-1)^{-\frac{1}{2}}$, find the value of $f(5)$ as a mixed fraction.

    (A) $2\dfrac{1}{2}$

    (B) $10\dfrac{1}{2}$

    (C) $2\dfrac{1}{4}$

    (D) $1\dfrac{1}{2}$

8. When the product xy is differentiated with respect to x, the result is

    (A) $y\dfrac{dxy}{dx} + x\dfrac{dxy}{dx}$

    (B) $y^2 + xy$

    (C) $x\dfrac{dy}{dx} + y$

    (D) Cannot tell because x and y are both variables.

9. Is the graph of $ax^2 + by^2 = c$ always a circle?

    (A) Yes, that is the general form for a circle.

    (B) No, if $a \neq b$, it may be an ellipse or a hyperbola.

    (C) No, that is the general form for an ellipse.

    (D) Cannot tell without values for a and b.

10. The period of the curve $y = 2\sin x$ is

    (A) π

    (B) 2

    (C) 2π

    (D) $\dfrac{\pi}{2}$

11. In the following graph, the transformation from triangle ABC to triangle $A'B'C'$ is a

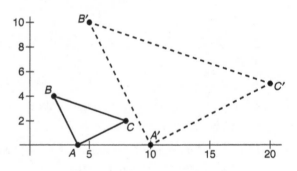

    (A) a translation of 6 units to the right

    (B) a dilation with a scale factor of 2.5

    (C) a dilation with a scale factor of $\dfrac{1}{6}$

    (D) a translation of 4 units to the right

12. The fraction $\dfrac{x^{-1}}{x^{-1} + y^{-1}}$ is equivalent to the fraction

    (A) y

    (B) $\dfrac{y}{x+y}$

    (C) $\dfrac{x+y}{x}$

    (D) $\dfrac{x}{x+y}$

13. If the roots of the equation $2x^2 - 3x + c = 0$ are real and irrational, then the value of c may be

    (A) 1
    (B) 2
    (C) 0
    (D) −1

14. What is the inverse of the function $y = x^2 + 4$?

    (A) $x = y^2 + 4$
    (B) $x = y^2 - 4$
    (C) $y^{-1} = \dfrac{1}{x^2 + 4}$
    (D) The inverse does not exist.

15. For a sample to be representative of a population, the sample must be _____. (Choose all of the correct answers.)

    $\boxed{A}$ unbiased
    $\boxed{B}$ random
    $\boxed{C}$ chosen only from members of the population
    $\boxed{D}$ of a sufficient size

16. The sum of an infinite geometric series with a fractional common ratio is given by $S_\infty = \dfrac{a_1}{1 - r}$, where a is the first term. The sum of the infinite geometric series $1 - \dfrac{1}{3} + \dfrac{1}{9} - \dots$ is

    (A) 0
    (B) ∞
    (C) $\dfrac{3}{4}$
    (D) $\dfrac{3}{2}$

17. If the median of 15 numbers is 20 and each of the numbers is decreased by 2, how is the new median affected?

    (A) It is increased to 22.
    (B) It is decreased to 18.
    (C) It stays the same.
    (D) It is decreased to 10.

18. If a number n is d greater than another number r, then $n + d$ $\left\{\begin{array}{c} \text{always} \\ \text{sometimes} \\ \text{never} \end{array}\right\}$ equals r.

19. If both the numerator and denominator of a proper fraction are increased by the same positive amount, the new fraction is $\left\{\begin{array}{c} \text{always} \\ \text{sometimes} \\ \text{never} \end{array}\right\}$ greater than the original fraction.

20. The length of a rectangular box is 5 inches more than its width, and its height is 1 inch more than its width. If the capacity of the box is 96 cubic inches, what are the dimensions of the box?

    (A) 3, 4, and 8 inches
    (B) 3, −4, and −8 inches
    (C) 2, 3, and 7 inches
    (D) 3, 15, and 4 inches

21. The number of subsets of {5, 6} is _____

    (A) 2
    (B) 3
    (C) 4
    (D) 5

22. What is the first derivative with respect to x of $y = \ln x^{e^x}$? (Remember that $\dfrac{d(e^x)}{dx} = e^x$ and $\dfrac{d(\ln x)}{dx} = \dfrac{1}{x}$.)

    (A) $y' = \dfrac{1}{x} + e^x \ln x$

    (B) $y' = e^x \dfrac{1}{x} + e^x \ln x$

    (C) $y' = e^x \dfrac{1}{x} + \ln x$

    (D) $y' = e^x \dfrac{\ln x}{x}$

23. A farmer has a total of 150 cows and chickens in his yard. Altogether, there are 480 legs. How many chickens are in the yard?

    (A) 30 chickens

    (B) 50 chickens

    (C) 60 chickens

    (D) 90 chickens

24. The tens digit of a two-digit number is 1 less than 5 times the units digit. The sum of the digits is 11. What is the number?

    (A) $9t + 2u$

    (B) 29

    (C) 92

    (D) $2t + 9u$

25. The length of one leg of a right triangle exceeds the length of the other leg by 5 inches. The hypotenuse is 25 inches. How long is the longer leg in inches?

    (A) 5 inches

    (B) 10 inches

    (C) 15 inches

    (D) 20 inches

26. What is the average value of the continuous function $f(x) = x^2$ between $x = 0$ and $x = 4$?

    (A) $\dfrac{64}{3}$

    (B) 16

    (C) 8

    (D) $\dfrac{16}{3}$

27. Two times a number x increased by 9 equals five times the number increased by 3. The equation to find this number is

    $$\left\{ \begin{array}{c} 2x + 9 = -3 + 5x \\ 2x + 9 = 5x + 3 \\ \text{Not enough information given} \end{array} \right\}.$$

28. Sandra's allowance is \$5 a week. She made the following proposition to her mother: "What if instead of giving me \$5 a week, you give me just one penny this week and then double my allowance every week?" On what week will Sandra's allowance be more than the initial \$5? (Count the first week, the one with a penny allowance, as week 1.)

    (A) 9 weeks

    (B) 10 weeks

    (C) 11 weeks

    (D) Cannot tell from given information

29. If S varies directly as the square of d, what change takes place in S when d is tripled?

    (A) S is tripled.

    (B) S is multiplied by $\sqrt{3}$.

    (C) S is multiplied by 9.

    (D) S is divided by 9.

30. Find the first derivative $\frac{dy}{dx}$ for $x^2 + y^2 = 9$.

    (A) $\frac{x}{y}$

    (B) $-\frac{x}{y}$

    (C) $\frac{y}{x}$

    (D) $-\frac{y}{x}$

31. In this figure (not drawn to scale), what is the measure of $\angle A$?

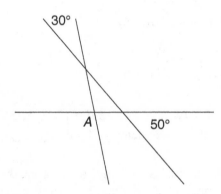

    (A) 100°

    (B) 80°

    (C) 20°

    (D) Cannot be determined with the information given.

32. Sonya is planning a business meeting for her company. She has a budget of $1,450 for renting a meeting room at a local hotel and providing lunch. She expects 26 people to attend the meeting. The cost of renting the meeting room is $300. Which inequality shows how to find the amount, x, Sonya can spend on lunch for each person.

    (A) $26x + 300 \geq 1,450$

    (B) $26x + 300 \leq 1,450$

    (C) $300x + 26 \geq 1,450$

    (D) $300x + 26 \leq 1,450$

33. If $i = \sqrt{-1}$, what is the value of $\frac{i^{10}}{i^2}$?

    (A) $\sqrt{-1}$

    (B) -1

    (C) $-\sqrt{-1}$

    (D) 1

34. Which set below contains *all* irrational numbers?

    (A) $\{(3+\sqrt{4}, \frac{\sqrt{10}}{3}, \cos 30°, \pi, \sqrt[3]{4}\}$

    (B) $\{(3+\sqrt{2}, \frac{\sqrt{10}}{3}, \cos 60°, \pi, \sqrt[3]{4}\}$

    (C) $\{(3+\sqrt{2}, \frac{\sqrt{10}}{3}, \cos 30°, \pi, \sqrt[3]{4}\}$

    (D) $\{(3+\sqrt{2}, \frac{\sqrt{10}}{3}, \cos 30°, \pi, \sqrt[3]{-8}\}$

35. Solve for x: $\log_4 \frac{1}{8} = x$.

    (A) $\frac{1}{2}$

    (B) $-\frac{1}{2}$

    (C) $\frac{3}{2}$

    (D) $-\frac{3}{2}$

36. What binary relations does $x \leq y$ have? (Choose *all* that apply.)

    A Reflexive

    B Transitive

    C Symmetric

    D Antisymmetric

37. If two integers have an even product and an odd sum, which of the following statements must be true?

    (A) The two integers are both odd.

    (B) The two integers are both even.

    (C) One of the integers is even and the other must be odd.

    (D) The two integers must be consecutive.

38. How many real solutions are there to the pair of equations $\begin{cases} y = x \\ y = x^2 - 4x + 9 \end{cases}$?

    (A) 0

    (B) 1

    (C) 2

    (D) 4

39. When a polynomial $f(x)$ of degree 3 is divided by the binomial $x - 4$ the result is a quadratic equation with a remainder of 2. What is the value of $f(4)$?

    (A) 2

    (B) 3

    (C) 4

    (D) Not enough information is given.

40. If a, b, and c represent the sides of a triangle, and if $\dfrac{a^2 + b^2 - c^2}{2ab} = 0$, the triangle is

    (A) acute

    (B) right

    (C) obtuse

    (D) impossible

41. The following table records the temperatures as a cold front moves through a city. What equation best represents the change in temperature as a function of time?

Time	Temperature
2:30 a.m.	57
4:30 a.m.	50
6:30 a.m.	43
7:30 a.m.	39.5
8:30 a.m.	36

    (A) $y = 3.5x + 57$

    (B) $y = -7.0x + 57$

    (C) $y = 7.0x + 57$

    (D) $y = -3.5x + 57$

42. If $A = \{1, 2, 3, 4\}$ and $B = \{2, 3, 5, 6, 7\}$ then the number of elements in $A - B$ is _____

43. Mercy puts $1000 into an account that pays 3% compounded continuously. How much will she have in the account after 5 years?

    (A) $1,150

    (B) $1,162

    (C) $1,030

    (D) Cannot tell from the information given

44. What is the value of $\lim\limits_{x \to -\infty} \left(\dfrac{-4x^3 + 7x - 4}{8x^3 + 2x^2 - 3x} \right)$?

    (A) ∞

    (B) $-\infty$

    (C) $-\dfrac{1}{2}$

    (D) $\dfrac{1}{2}$

45. Find two whole numbers, x and y, such that their sum is 8 and their product is a maximum.

   $x =$ _____ $y =$ _____

46. What is the equation of a circle whose center is at the origin and which passes through the point $(6, -8)$?

   (A) $x^2 + y^2 = 6^2$

   (B) $x^2 + y^2 = (-8)^2$

   (C) $x^2 + y^2 = 100$

   (D) $x^2 + y^2 = 10$

47. Given the projection function, $s(t) = -16t^2 + 100t + 5$, for a baseball thrown upward from an initial height of 5 feet above the ground with an initial velocity of 100 feet per second, what is the velocity of the baseball at $t = 1$ second?

   (A) 68 ft/sec

   (B) 73 ft/sec

   (C) 32 ft/sec

   (D) 5 ft/sec

48. Choose the correct reason for statement 2 in the proof that $\dfrac{1 - \sin x}{\cos^2 x} = \dfrac{1}{1 + \sin x}$ is an identity.

Statement	Reason
1. $\dfrac{1 - \sin x}{\cos^2 x}$	1. Given
2. $\dfrac{1 - \sin x}{1 - \sin^2 x}$	2. ?
3. $\dfrac{(1 - \sin x)}{(1 - \sin x)(1 + \sin x)}$	3. Factorization
4. $\dfrac{1}{1 + \sin x}$	4. Reduce the fraction
5. $\dfrac{1}{1 + \sin x} = \dfrac{1}{1 + \sin x}$	5. Proof of identity; true for all x.

(A) Substitution of the identity $\cos^2 x = 1 - \sin^2 x$.

(B) Sum and difference of squares.

(C) Cancellation

(D) Simplification

49. The graphs of the equations $x^2 + y^2 = 25$ and $y = x^2$ have how many points of intersection?

   (A) 1

   (B) 2

   (C) 3

   (D) 4

50. If someone tosses a six-sided die 4 times, what is the probability that it lands heads up all 4 times?

   (A) 6^4

   (B) $\left(\dfrac{1}{4}\right)^6$

   (C) $\left(\dfrac{1}{6}\right)^4$

   (D) $\dfrac{1}{6}$

51. $\text{Log}_3 25 = x$ is equivalent to which of the following. Choose *all* that apply.

   A $\dfrac{\log 25}{\log 3}$

   B $\dfrac{\ln 25}{\ln 3}$

   C $\log\left(\dfrac{25}{3}\right)$

   D $3^x = 25$

52. What mistake, if any, did Jordan make when he reduced the following fraction: $\dfrac{x+y+z}{x+y} = 1 + z$.

    (A) He canceled $x + y$ when it wasn't a factor in the numerator. The correct answer is z.

    (B) He should have canceled the x's and then the y's to get $\dfrac{1+1+z}{1+1} = \dfrac{2+x}{2}$.

    (C) He canceled $x + y$ when it wasn't a factor in the numerator. The fraction cannot be reduced.

    (D) Jordan didn't make a mistake; the answer is correct.

53. The members of the Fibonacci sequence are 1, 1, 2, 3, 5, 8, ... Which of the following is the formula for this sequence?

    (A) $a_n = a_{n-2} + a_{n-1}$

    (B) $a_1 = 1$, $a_n = a_{n-2} + a_{n-1}$

    (C) $a_1 = 1$, $a_2 = 1$, $a_n = a_{n-2} + a_{n-1}$

    (D) There is no formula for this sequence.

54. As x decreases, the value of $5 - \dfrac{1}{x}$, $\left\{\begin{array}{l} \text{increases} \\ \text{decreases} \\ \text{stays the same} \end{array}\right\}$.

55. Three-fifths of the weight of a ship is below the water. What is the ratio of the submerged weight to the exposed weight?

    (A) 2:3

    (B) 3:5

    (C) 2:5

    (D) 3:2

56. The root(s) of the equation $x + \sqrt{x-2} = 2$ are

    (A) both 2 and 3

    (B) only 2

    (C) only 3

    (D) neither 2 nor 3

57. For quadratic equation $ax^2 + bx + c = 0$, with $a \neq 0$, the value of $b^2 - 4ac = 0$. How many roots does the equation have?

    (A) 0

    (B) A real double root

    (C) An imaginary double root

    (D) Cannot tell without values for a, b, c.

58. The value of $\dfrac{n!}{(n-2)!}$ for $n = 57$ is _____.

59. The expression $\log \sqrt{\dfrac{x}{y}}$ is equivalent to the expression

    (A) $2(\log x + \log y)$

    (B) $\log x + \dfrac{1}{2} \log y$

    (C) $\dfrac{\log x - \log y}{2}$

    (D) $\log x + 2 \log y$

60. The function $y = (x + 1)^2$ is

    (A) an odd function

    (B) an even function

    (C) neither odd nor even

    (D) invertible

Praxis Math Content Knowledge
Practice Test 2 Answer Key

1. (A)

2. Experimental

3. (D)

4. (B)

5. (B)

6. (D)

7. (A)

8. (C)

9. (B)

10. (C)

11. (B)

12. (B)

13. (D)

14. (D)

15. $\boxed{A}$, $\boxed{B}$, $\boxed{C}$, and $\boxed{D}$

16. (C)

17. (B)

18. Sometimes

19. Sometimes

20. (A)

21. (C)

22. (B)

23. (C)

24. (C)

25. (D)

26. (D)

27. (B)

28. (B)

29. (C)

30. (B)

31. (A)

32. (B)

33. (D)

34. (C)

35. (D)

36. $\boxed{A}$, $\boxed{B}$, $\boxed{D}$

37. (C)

38. (A)

39. (A)

40. (B)

41. (D)

42. 2

43. (B)

44. (C)

45. $x = 4, y = 4$

46. (C)

47. (A)

48. (A)

49. (B)

50. (C)

51. $\boxed{A}$, $\boxed{B}$, $\boxed{D}$

52. (C)

53. (C)

54. Decreases

55. (D)

56. (B)

57. (B)

58. 3192

59. (C)

60. (C)

1. **(A) A polynomial of degree n has $(n-1)$ roots if the polynomial equals zero.**

    Every polynomial has as many roots as the degree of the polynomial, so answer choice (A) is not true. Even though some roots may be multiple roots, each root counts as one. The roots may be real or imaginary, but imaginary roots always come in pairs, so answer choices (B) and (C) are true. Answer choice (D) is also true because the product of an imaginary root and its conjugate (which is also a root) yields an irreducible quadratic: $(a + bi)(a - bi) = a^2 - b^2$.

2. **Experimental**

    The company is imposing conditions (new drug, dummy pill) on the participants in the study to determine their response (change in cholesterol) to the conditions.

3. **(D) has no points in common with the x-axis**

    Answer choice (C) can be eliminated right away because this is a second-degree equation and therefore has at most two solutions (a solution is the value of x when $y = 0$). One way to determine how many real roots, which is how many times the graph crosses the x axis, the quadratic has when $y = 0$, or $3x^2 - 7x + 5 = 0$. Using the quadratic formula with $a = 3$, $b = -7$, and $c = 5$, the discriminant is $b^2 - 4ac = 49 - 4(3)(5) = 49 - 60$, which is negative, so both roots are imaginary and the correct answer choice is (D). Another way to answer this question is to recognize that this parabola opens upward, and the x-value of the axis of symmetry is $x = -\dfrac{b}{2a} = \dfrac{7}{6}$. Substituting this value into the equation, if $y > 0$, the parabola will be completely above the x-axis and therefore not cross the x-axis at all. So we are interested in

    determining whether $3x^2 - 7x + 5$ evaluated at $x = \dfrac{7}{6}$ is greater than 0. We don't have to come up with a value, just whether it is positive. $3\left(\dfrac{7}{6}\right) - 7\left(\dfrac{7}{6}\right) + 5$ clearly is positive , so the parabola doesn't cross the x-axis.

4. **(B) −4**

    Since $s(t)$ is a polynomial function, the limit is $6(-2) - (-2)^3 = -12 - (-8) = -12 + 8 = -4$. Be sure to watch the signs of the terms.

5. **(B) $\dfrac{c}{b}$**

    Change the numerator and denominator into fractions, then divide the denominator into the numerator by inverting and multiplying: $\dfrac{\frac{a}{b} + c}{\frac{a}{c} + b} = \dfrac{\frac{a+bc}{b}}{\frac{a+bc}{c}} = \dfrac{a+bc}{b} \div \dfrac{a+bc}{c} = \dfrac{a+bc}{b} \times \dfrac{c}{a+bc} = \dfrac{c}{b}$.

6. **(D) $\sqrt{3} - 1$**

    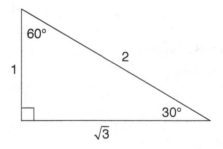

    If you forgot that $\tan \dfrac{\pi}{3} = \sqrt{3}$, you can figure it out by remembering that $\dfrac{\pi}{3} = 60°$, and figuring the functions by visualizing the 1–2–$\sqrt{3}$ (or 30°–60°–90°) trian-

gle and the definition of $\tan 60° = \dfrac{\text{opposite}}{\text{adjacent}} = \dfrac{\sqrt{3}}{1} = \sqrt{3}$.
$\cos \pi = -1$. So $\tan\dfrac{\pi}{3} + \cos\pi = \sqrt{3} - 1$.

7. (A) $2\dfrac{1}{2}$

Anything to a zero power equals 1, but only x is raised to the zero power, not $(2x)$. So $f(5) = 2(5^0) + (5-1)^{-\frac{1}{2}} = 2(1) + \dfrac{1}{\sqrt{4}} = 2 + \dfrac{1}{2} = 2\dfrac{1}{2}$.

8. (C) $x\dfrac{dy}{dx} + y$

Because x and y are both variables, the product must be differentiated by using the product rule (on the Praxis online formula sheet): $\dfrac{d}{dx}(xy) = x\dfrac{dy}{dx} + y\dfrac{dx}{dx} = x\dfrac{dy}{dx} + y$.

9. (B) No, if $a \neq b$, it may be an ellipse or a hyperbola.

$ax^2 + by^2 = c$ represents a circle only if $a = b$; otherwise, not. If a and b are unequal and both positive, the graph is an ellipse; if a and b are unequal and of opposite signs, the graph is a hyperbola. Answer choice (C) isn't true because if $a = b$, then it is a circle, not an ellipse.

10. (C) 2π

In trig equations, x is assumed to be measured in radians unless otherwise stated. The period of the sine curve is 2π. This period is unchanged because x is unchanged. (The "2" in the curve changes the amplitude, not the period.)

11. (B) a dilation with a scale factor of 2.5

A dilation can make a figure larger (scale factor >1) or smaller (scale factor <1, sometimes called a com-

pression). The scale factor is the factor by which all of the coordinate points are multiplied. In this figure, each vertex in triangle ABC is multiplied by 2.5 to get the corresponding vertices in triangle $A'B'C'$.

12. (B) $\dfrac{y}{x+y}$

$\dfrac{x^{-1}}{x^{-1} + y^{-1}} = \dfrac{\frac{1}{x}}{\frac{1}{x} + \frac{1}{y}} = \dfrac{\frac{1}{x}}{\frac{y+x}{xy}} = \dfrac{1}{x} \div \dfrac{y+x}{xy}$. Invert the divisor and multiply: $\dfrac{1}{x} \times \dfrac{xy}{y+x} = \dfrac{y}{x+y}$.

13. (D) -1

The determinant in the quadratic formula tells about the nature of the roots. For the roots to be real and irrational, the value of the determinant must be positive and not a perfect square. So for $2x - 3x + c = 0$, where $a = 2$ and $b = -3$, look at the values of the determinant ($b^2 - 4ac$): Answer choice (A) = 1, a perfect square; answer choice (B) = -7, negative; answer choice (C) = 9, a perfect square; answer choice (D) = 8, not a perfect square. So only answer choice (D) results in real and irrational roots.

14. (D) The inverse does not exist

The graph of this function is a vertical parabola, which means it doesn't pass the horizontal line test. A function has an inverse only if it is one-to-one, which is not true for any function for which any y value has more than one x value.

15. $\boxed{A}$, $\boxed{B}$, $\boxed{C}$, and $\boxed{D}$

These four choices are the conditions for a representative sample, and the sample must fulfill all of them.

16. **(C)** $\dfrac{3}{4}$

First, determine the common ratio, keeping in mind that this is a series in which the signs alternate. The common ratio is the ratio between the any term to the term before it, or $r = \dfrac{-\frac{1}{3}}{1}$ or $\dfrac{\frac{1}{9}}{-\frac{1}{3}} = -\dfrac{1}{3}$. Thus, the sum of the infinite series is $S_\infty = \dfrac{a_1}{1-r} = \dfrac{1}{1-\left(-\frac{1}{3}\right)} = \dfrac{1}{\frac{4}{3}} = \dfrac{3}{4}$. (Remember in the denominator that minus a negative becomes a positive, so $1-\left(-\dfrac{1}{3}\right) = 1+\dfrac{1}{3}$.)

17. **(B) It is decreased to 18**

Since all of the numbers are decreased by 2, the middle value, whatever it is, must also be decreased by 2. The old median is 20, so the new median must be 18.

18. **Sometimes**

This is generally false, since $n = r + d$, but it is true if $d = 0$.

19. **Sometimes**

For a positive proper fraction, it is always greater then the original, but for a negative proper fraction, the opposite may be true (e.g., if the original fraction is $\dfrac{-2}{3}$, the new fraction with 1 added to numerator and denominator would be $\dfrac{-1}{4}$).

20. **(A) 3, 4, and 8 inches**

Eliminate answer choice (B) because measurements aren't negative. Eliminate answer choices (C) and (D) because their product is not 96. That leaves only (A), which satisfies all criteria in the problem. Simply analyzing the problem and its possible answers is much quicker and easier than using algebra, such as in the following (time-consuming) solution.

The capacity of a rectangular box is length × width × height. The first sentence translates into width = w, length = $w + 5$, and height = $w + 1$, so the capacity is $w(w + 5)(w + 1) = 96$ cubic inches. So the problem is to solve the equation $w^3 + 6w^2 + 5w - 96 = 0$ for w. There are many possible roots (all of the factors of 96). Let's try 3 and use synthetic division:

3 $|$	1	+6	+5	−96
		+3	+27	+96
	1	+9	+32	0

So one root is 3, and the other roots are solutions to $w^2 + 9w + 32 = 0$, which factors into $(w + 4)$ and $(w + 8)$, with roots $w = -4$ and -8, so we reject these. If the width = 3 inches, the length is $3 + 5 = 8$ inches, and the height is $3 + 1 = 4$ inches.

21. **(C) 4**

The obvious subsets are {5}, {6}, and {5, 6}, but don't forget that the null set is a subset of every set.

22. **(B)** $y' = e^x \dfrac{1}{x} + e^x \ln x$

You do not have to take the log of both sides of the equation. First, using the exponent rule of logarithms, rewrite the problem as $y = e^x \ln x$ and just use the product rule (on the Praxis online formula sheet) to differentiate with respect to x. Then $\dfrac{dy}{dx} = \ln x \dfrac{de^x}{dx} + e^x \dfrac{d \ln x}{dx} = e^x \dfrac{1}{x} + e^x \ln x$.

23. **(C) 60 chickens**

To do this problem algebraically, let k = number of cows and c = number of chickens. Then the first sentence says $k + c = 150$, and the second says $4k + 2c = 480$ (assuming all cows have all four legs, and there are no one-legged chickens, of course). Solve this system of equations by either substitution or elimination to get

90 cows and 60 chickens. By substitution, the equation is $4(150 - c) + 2c = 480$, or $120 = 2c$, which yields 60 chickens. Or you can check each answer to eliminate the ones that don't agree with the problem's criteria.

24. (C) 92

Call the tens digit t and the units digit u. The first sentence says $t = 5u - 1$. The second sentence says $t + u = 11$. Solve these two simultaneous equations to find t and u. Substitute the first equation into the second one to get $(5u - 1) + u = 11$. Then $6u = 12$, $u = 2$, and $t = 5(2) - 1 = 9$. So the number is 92.

25. (D) 20 inches

The legs can be represented by x and $x + 5$. Then, according to the Pythagorean formula, $25^2 = x^2 + (x + 5)^2$, which becomes $2x^2 + 10x - 600 = 0$, or $x^2 + 5x - 300 = 0$. This factors into $(x + 20)(x - 15) = 0$, so the values for x are 15 and -20. So the shorter leg is 15 inches (remember to reject a negative value as a measurement), and the longer leg is 20 inches.

26. (D) $\dfrac{16}{3}$

The average value formula is $\dfrac{1}{b-a}\int_a^b x^2\,dx$.

For $f(x) = x^2$, this becomes $\dfrac{1}{4-0}\int_a^b x^2\,dx = \dfrac{1}{4}\left(\dfrac{x^3}{3}\right)\Big|_0^4 = \dfrac{1}{4}\left[\dfrac{64}{3} - 0\right] = \dfrac{16}{3}$.

27. (B) $2x + 9 = 5x + 3$

Just translate the sentence word for word into symbols:

Two times	a number	increased by	9	equals	five	times	the number	increased by	3
2	x	+	9	=	5	×	x	+	3

28. (B) ten weeks

Since Sandra's allowance is to be doubled every week, this is a geometric sequence with $r = 2$, and since she is starting with one penny, $a_1 = 1$. The answer can be found by just writing the values of 2^n and counting to find the number of weeks, such as 1, 2, 4, 8, 16, 32, 64, 128, 256, 512, which is the first number greater than 500 cents (= $5.00), and the tenth week. Formally, use the formula for the nth term of a geometric sequence, $a_n = a_1 \cdot r^{n-1}$, to find the first $a_n \geq 500$. This gives $(1)(2)^{n-1} \geq 500$, or $n - 1 = 9$, which gives $n = 10$.

29. (C) S is multiplied by 9

Since S varies directly as the square of d, $S = kd^2$. If we triple d, then the new $s = k(3d)^2 = 9kd^2$, so the original S is multiplied by 9.

30. (B) $-\dfrac{x}{y}$

Differentiating term by term with respect to x, we get $\dfrac{d}{dx}(x^2 + y^2 = 9) = 2x + 2y\dfrac{dy}{dx} = 0$. Solving this equation for $\dfrac{dy}{dx}$, we get $-\dfrac{2x}{2y} = -\dfrac{x}{y}$.

31. (A) 100°

Because vertical angles are equal, two of the angles of the triangle are 30° and 50°, which add up to 80°, leaving 100° for $\angle A$ because the sum of angles of a triangle is 180°. And since the third angle is 100°, so is its vertical angle, $\angle A$.

32. (B) $26x + 300 \leq \$1,450$

Since Sonya cannot spend more than $1,450, the total of the room cost ($300) plus the lunches for 26 people ($26x$) must be less than or equal to $1,450.

33. **(D) 1**

First, reduce the fraction to $\frac{i^{10}}{i^2} = i^{10-2} = i^8$. Recognizing that the powers of i follow a pattern where $i^n = 1, \sqrt{-1}, -1, -\sqrt{-1}, 1, \sqrt{-1}, \ldots$ where $n = 0, 1, 2, 3, \ldots$, the value of i^8 is the same as $i^0 = 1$.

34. **(C)** $\left\{ (3 + \sqrt{2}, \frac{\sqrt{10}}{3}, \cos 30°, \pi, \sqrt[3]{4} \right\}$

All answer choices are similar, but choices (A), (B), and (D) have one rational number in them: for (A), $3 + \sqrt{4} = 3 + 2$, for (B), $\cos 60° = \frac{1}{2}$, and for (D), $\sqrt[3]{-8} = -2$.

35. **(D)** $-\frac{3}{2}$

Use the change of base formula $\log_4 \frac{1}{8} = \frac{\log \frac{1}{8}}{\log 4} = -1.5$, evaluated with the online calculator. Another way to solve this is to set $4^x = \frac{1}{8}$ as $\left(2^2\right)^x = \frac{1}{2^3}$. Write the right fraction as a power of 2 to get $2^{2x} = 2^{-3}$. Then set the exponents equal: $2^{2x} = 2^{-3}$ and $x = \frac{-3}{2}$.

36. $\boxed{A}$, **Reflexive** $\boxed{B}$, **Transitive, and** $\boxed{D}$ **Antisymmetric**

The reflexive rule holds because of the equality sign in $x \leq x$. The transitive rule holds because if $x \leq y$ and $y \leq z$ then $x \leq z$. The antisymmetric rule holds, because if $x \leq y$ and $y \leq x$, then x must equal y. The symmetric rule does not hold because if $x \leq y$, then $y \geq x$, not $y \leq x$.

37. **(C) One of the integers is even and the other must be odd**

Eliminate answer choices (A) and (B) because if the product is even, at least one of the numbers must be

even, and if the sum is odd the numbers cannot both be even or both be odd. Answer choice (C), that one is even and the other odd, works in all cases. Answer choice (D) doesn't have to be true for all consecutive integers—consider 0 and 1. Zero is neither odd nor even.

38. **(A) 0**

If you graph the two equations on your calculator, you will see that they never meet. If you solve the two equations by substitution, the equation becomes $x^2 - 5x + 9 = 0$, for which the discriminant is $\sqrt{b^2 - 4ac} = \sqrt{25 - 36}$, which isn't real, so there are no real solutions common to both equations.

39. **(A) 2**

When a polynomial $f(x)$ (of any degree) is divided by a binomial of the form $x - c$, the value of $f(c)$ is the remainder of the division. Therefore, even without knowing what the polynomial $f(x)$ or the quadratic is, we know that $f(4) = 2$.

40. **(B) right**

There are two ways to figure this answer out. For the first, if we multiply both sides of the equation by $2ab$ gives the Pythagorean formula, $a^2 + b^2 = c^2$ after a little simple algebra. The other way is to use the law of cosines (a hint that this is how to solve this problem is the presence of the terms in the law of cosines formula), $c^2 = a^2 + b^2 - 2ab \cos C$. After some algebra, we get $\cos C = 0$, or $\angle C = 90°$; thus, the triangle is a right triangle.

41. **(D)** $y = -3.5x + 57$

From the table, we see that slope $= \frac{50 - 57}{2 - 0} = -3.5$. Answer choice (D) is the only one that has -3.5 as its slope. The first point is 57 for all answer choices.

42. 2

$A - B$ means all the elements in A that are not in B, or the two elements $\{1, 4\}$.

43. (B) $1,162

The original amount (P) is $1000, the interest rate (r) is 3%, or .03, and the amount of time (t) is 5. Since this is interest compounded continuously, the formula is $A = Pe^{rt}$. Substituting the known values into the equation gives $A = 1000e^{(.03)(5)} = 1000(1.162) = \$1,162$. Remember to use the "$e$" button on the calculator rather than 2,718, the decimal approximation for e.

44. (C) $-\dfrac{1}{2}$

Since the degrees of the numerator and denominator are equal, the limit is the ratio of the leading coefficients, or $\dfrac{-4}{8} = -\dfrac{1}{2}$.

45. $x = 4, y = 4$

If the first number is x, the second number is $y = 8 - x$, and the product, let's call it P, is $x(8 - x) = 8x - x^2$. The graph of this parabola on your calculator shows the maximum to be at $x = 4$. Then $y = 4$. Or, recognizing this as a parabola, the maximum can be obtained from $x = -\dfrac{b}{2a} = -\dfrac{8}{2(-1)} = 4$. A third option is to use calculus; the maximum would be at the point where the first derivative equals 0, or $P' = 8 - 2x = 0$, which occurs at $x = 4$.

46. (C) $x^2 + y^2 = 100$

The general form of the equation, since it is a circle whose center is at the origin, is $x^2 + y^2 = r^2$. Every point on the circle must satisfy this equation, so substitute $x = 6$ and $y = -8$ into the equation and solve for r^2: $(6)^2 + (-8)^2 = r^2 = 100$.

47. (A) 68 ft/sec

The velocity at any time t is the first derivative of the position function, or $v(t) = s'(t) = -32t + 100$. At $t = 1$, the velocity is $v(t) = -32(1) + 100 = 68$ ft/sec.

48. (A) Substitution of the identity $\cos^2 x = 1 - \sin^2 x$

To prove an identity, prove that the left side equals the right side, no matter what the value for the variable is. To go to $\dfrac{1 - \sin x}{1 - \sin^2 x}$ from $\dfrac{1 - \sin x}{\cos^2 x}$, use a variation of the identity $\sin^2 x + \cos^2 x = 1$.

49. (B) 2

There are several ways to get the answer this problem: (1) graphing by using the graphing calculator; sketching a circle with center at $(0, 0)$ and radius 5 and a parabola with vertex at $(0, 0)$; or (3) substitute $x^2 = y$ into $x^2 + y^2 = 25$ to get $y^2 + y - 25 = 0$, which has two real roots.

50. (C) $\left(\dfrac{1}{6}\right)^4$

Each toss of the die is independent of all the other tosses, and each number has a $\dfrac{1}{6}$ probability, so the probabilities are multiplied: $\dfrac{1}{6} \times \dfrac{1}{6} \times \dfrac{1}{6} \times \dfrac{1}{6} = \left(\dfrac{1}{6}\right)^4$.

51. $\boxed{A}\ \dfrac{\log 25}{\log 3}$, $\boxed{B}\ \dfrac{\ln 25}{\ln 3}$, $\boxed{D}\ 3x = 25$.

According to the change of base formula, a non-standard-base log can be converted to a fraction in which the numerator is the new log of the argument (here, 25), and the denominator is the new log of the on-standard base (here, 3). The new log can be anything, including $\log_{10}$ or ln, so answer choices $\boxed{A}$ and $\boxed{B}$ are true. Answer choice $\boxed{D}$ is just the exponential form of the log. Answer choice $\boxed{C}$ isn't true because $\log\left(\dfrac{a}{b}\right) = \log a - \log b$.

52. (C)

He canceled $x + y$ when it wasn't a factor in the numerator. The fraction cannot be reduced. You can cancel only common factors in *all* terms, so the x, y, and z cannot be canceled.

53. (C) $a_1 = 1$, $a_2 = 1$, $a_n = a_{n-2} + a_{n-1}$

If you don't recognize that each element after the first two in the Fibonacci sequence is the sum of the two elements before it, the answer can be found by checking the first three elements in each of the answer choices. Note that answer choice (A) is incorrect for a_1 and a_2, and answer choice (B) is incorrect for a_2, emphasizing the fact that for recursive sequences, the beginning element(s) must be defined.

54. Decreases

As x decreases, the fraction $\dfrac{1}{x}$ increases. Since an increasing amount is subtracted from 5, $5 - \dfrac{1}{x}$ decreases.

55. (D) 3:2

If $\dfrac{3}{5}$ of the weight is below the water (submerged), then the remaining $\dfrac{2}{5}$ must be above the water (exposed). Then, the ratio of submerged weight to exposed weight is $\dfrac{\frac{3}{5}}{\frac{2}{5}} = \dfrac{3}{5} \div \dfrac{2}{5} = \dfrac{3}{5} \times \dfrac{5}{2} = \dfrac{3}{2}$, which is the same as 3:2.

56. (B) only 2

Insert $x = 2$ and then $x = 3$ into the equation. For $x = 2$, $2 + 0 = 2$ is true; for $x = 3$, $3 + 1 \neq 2$.

57. (B) a real double root

The quadratic formula, $x = \dfrac{-b \pm \sqrt{b^2 - 4ac}}{2a}$, gives the roots to any quadratic equation. Here, the discriminant is $b^2 - 4ac = 0$, so the solution is the double root $x = \dfrac{-b}{2a}$.

58. 3192

Since $\dfrac{n!}{(n-2)!} = \dfrac{n \times (n-1) \times (n-2) \times (n-3) \times \ldots \times 1}{(n-2) \times (n-3) \times \ldots \times 1}$, and all of the factors from $(n-2)$ down cancel, the value is just $n \times (n-1) = 57 \times 56 = 3192$.

59. (C) $\dfrac{\log x - \log y}{2}$

$\log \sqrt{\dfrac{x}{y}}$ can be written as $\log \left(\dfrac{x}{y}\right)^{\frac{1}{2}}$. Exponents in a log expression become coefficients, so this can be written as $\dfrac{1}{2} \log \left(\dfrac{x}{y}\right)$, and the log of a division is equal to the difference of the numerator minus the denominator, so finally this can be written as $\dfrac{\log x - \log y}{2}$.

60. (C) neither odd nor even

A function is even if $f(x) = f(-x)$ for all x, and for this problem $f(x) = x^2 + 2x + 1$ but $f(-x) = x^2 - 2x + 1$, so it isn't even. A function is odd if $f(-x) = -f(x)$ for all x, and for this problem $-f(x) = -x^2 - 2x - 1$, which doesn't equal $f(-x)$, so it isn't odd. Therefore, it is neither odd nor even. The function is not invertible because the graph of $y = (x + 1)^2$ doesn't pass the horizontal line test, so it cannot have an inverse.

Practice Test 3
To cap off your preparation, go to the online
REA Study Center to take Practice Test 3.

(www.rea.com/studycenter)

GLOSSARY

absolute error   Amount of physical error in a measurement, or the actual amount you could be "off," or mistaken by, in a measurement; it is equal to ± the smallest unit of visible measurement.

absolute value function   A function that contains an absolute value.

absolute value   The value of the expression inside the absolute value signs, | |, changed to a positive value; used for expressing distance.

absorption laws for sets   For any two sets A and B, $A \cup (A \cap B) = A$ and $A \cap (A \cup B) = A$.

acceleration   The rate of change of velocity per unit time, given by the second derivative of the position function or the first derivative of the velocity function.

accumulation   A method for finding the area under a curve by accumulating the areas of rectangles of narrow width that approximate the curve.

accuracy   Comparison of measured value to a true value. See also degree of accuracy.

acute angle   An angle with a measurement between 0° and 90°.

acute triangle   A triangle with all acute angles.

addition rule for probability   Pr (A or B) = Pr(A) + Pr(B) − Pr(A and B) for overlapping events; the Pr(A and B) part equals 0 for mutually exclusive events.

addition rule of probability   "or" means add.

adjacent angles   Two angles that share a side; they need not share a vertex (e.g., consecutive angles in a polygon may be described as adjacent).

alternate exterior angles   Two angles formed when two parallel lines are crossed by a transversal; they are on opposite sides of the transversal and are exterior to the parallel lines, and they are equal.

alternate interior angles   Two angles formed when two parallel lines are crossed by a transversal; they are on opposite sides of the transversal and are interior to the parallel lines, and they are equal.

altitude   A line that is perpendicular to one side of a figure and ends at the opposite angle or vertex; also called the height.

amplitude of a periodic function   One-half the distance between the highest and lowest y values.

angle   The geometric object formed by two rays or line segments joined at their endpoints.

antiderivative   A general function $F(x)$ of $f(x)$ if $F'(x) = f(x)$.

antisymmetric property   If for any relation $\Re$ for all values of a and b, if $a \Re b$ and $b \Re a$, then $a = b$.

apothem   A line from the center of a regular polygon to the midpoint of a side.

arc   A portion of the circumference of a circle between two points.

area   The size of a surface; stated in square units.

argument in logic   An example of reasoning in which one or more statements are offered as support for another statement.

arithmetic sequence   A sequence of numbers in which a fixed number is added from each term to the next; also known as an arithmetic progression.

arithmetic series   The sum of a certain number of terms of an arithmetic sequence.

associative law for sets   For any three sets A, B, and C, $(A \cup B) \cup C = A \cup (B \cup C)$ and $(A \cap B) \cap C = A \cap (B \cap C)$.

associative property   The quality of changing the grouping of numbers does not affect the answer for a particular operation (e.g., for addition, $3 + (5 + 6) = (3 + 5) + 6$; for multiplication, $(25 \times 7) \times 4 = 25 \times (7 \times 4)$).

asymptotes   Lines that a curve gets closer and closer to but never crosses; the asymptotes are not part of the curve.

average rate of change   The average of all the rates of change between two designated points on a curve.

average   A measure of central tendency of a group of qualitative data calculated by totaling all of the data points and dividing by the number of points; also called the mean.

axes   The horizontal number line (x-axis) and the vertical number line (y-axis) on the coordinate plane. The axes intersect at the origin.

axis of symmetry   The line that separates two sides of a graph into mirror images of each other; the line is not a part of the graph.

bar graph   A method of presenting categorical data that shows categories versus number in each category; also called a bar chart.

base angles   The angles opposite the equal sides in an isosceles triangle.

base   The number or expression that is raised to a power expression (e.g., 2 in 2^6, x in x^3). Also, a name for a side of a closed two-dimensional figure, or the surface on which a three-dimensional object stands.

base   The side of a triangle to which the altitude is drawn; the unequal side of an isosceles triangle.

binary relations   Relations between two objects; also called equivalence relations; relates elements of one set to elements of another set.

binomial theorem   A method of finding the value of any power of a binomial, which can be done by the general formula $(x + y)^n = x^n + \frac{n}{1}x^{n-1}y + \frac{n(n-1)}{2}x^{n-2}y^2 + \ldots y^n$, or simplified by using Pascal's triangle.

binomials   Sum or difference of two terms (e.g., $x + 3$ or $y - 4$).

bivariate data   Data for two variables that are linked to each other.

cancellation   Eliminating like factors in the numerator and denominator of a fraction (e.g., $\frac{6}{8} = \frac{2 \times 3}{2 \times 4} = \frac{3}{4}$ or $\frac{x(x+2)}{(x-3)(x+2)} = \frac{x}{x-3}$); also called simplifying a fraction.

capacity   How much content a three-dimensional figure can hold.

Cartesian coordinate system   A coordinate system in which the domain axis (usually the x-axis) runs horizontally and the range axis (usually the y-axis) runs vertically.

Cartesian product   The set of ordered pairs of two sets that contains elements from each set as an ordered pair; for sets A and B, the set of ordered pairs (a,b)

such that a is an element of A and b is an element of B.

categorical data Data in the form of categories, such as yes/no, these are sometimes called qualitative data; best represented pictorially, such as on a pie chart or bar chart.

causation One event being the result of the occurrence of another event.

census A study that observes, or attempts to observe, every individual in a given population.

center The point inside a circle that is the same distance from every point on the circle. Also, the point inside a regular polygon that is the same distance from each vertex.

central angle An angle with its vertex at the center of a circle and two radii as its sides.

Central Limit Theorem As sample size increases, the distribution of the sample means of any population with mean μ and standard deviation σ will approach a normal distribution related to the mean $\bar{x}$ and standard deviation s.

central tendency A description of how a group of data tends to look; comprises three measure, the mean, median, and mode.

chain rule The first derivative of a composite function, $f(g(x))$, is given by $[f(g(x))]' = f'(g(x))g'(x)$.

change of base formula A formula for a logarithmic expression to any base that permits a change to an expression that involves the common log to base 10 (or e, the natural log).

characteristic The value of a logarithm before the decimal point, indicating the whole number of the power.

chord A line segment whose endpoints are on the circle.

circle graph A method of presenting categorical data that shows data as a percentage of the area of a circle shown as slices of a pie; sometimes called a pie chart.

circle All the points at a fixed distance from a certain point called the center.

circumference Perimeter of a circle.

clockwise Rotation in the same direction as the hands of a clock.

closed set A set for which some operation on the set of elements yields a result that is also in the set; the binary relation from one set to another is always a subset of the Cartesian product.

closure law for sets For any two sets A and B, $A \cup B$ and $A \cap B$ are each unique sets.

closure The property of a set of numbers for which the result of an operation is itself a member of the set.

cofunctions Pairs of trigonometric functions related to each other through phase shifts of 90°.

collinear Points along the same straight line.

combination The number of ways of choosing r objects out of n objects when order does not make a difference $_nC_r = \dfrac{n!}{r!(n-r)!}$.

common denominator A denominator that can be shared by the equivalents of several fractions (e.g., a common denominator of $\dfrac{1}{2}$, $\dfrac{3}{4}$, and $\dfrac{5}{8}$ is 16 because they can be written as $\dfrac{18}{16}$, $\dfrac{12}{16}$, and $\dfrac{10}{16}$, respectively. See also lowest common denominator.

common log Logarithm with base 10.

common ratio The ratio between any two consecutive terms in a geometric sequence.

commutative law for sets For any two sets A and B, $A \cup B = B \cup A$ and $A \cap B = B \cap A$.

commutative property The quality of changing the position of numbers does not affect the answer for a particular operation (e.g., for addition, $3 + 5 + 7 = 5 + 7 + 3$; for multiplication, $3 \times 5 \times 2 = 3 \times 2 \times 5 = 5 \times 3 \times 2$).

complement of a set All items in the universe not included in a particular set I, denoted as $\bar{I}$.

complementary angles Any two angles whose measures total 90°; they need not be adjacent.

complementary events Two events such that one or the other must occur, but not both at the same time.

completing the square A method to "force" a quadratic equation into a form that essentially is the equality of two squares, solved by taking the square root of each side.

complex conjugates Pair of complex numbers such that the real parts are the same and the "imaginary" parts differ only in sign (e.g., the complex conjugate of $a + bi$ is $a - bi$).

complex number system Numbers with two parts: a real part plus an imaginary part, symbolized as $a + bi$, where a and b are real numbers.

complex roots All roots of an equation, whether they are real or imaginary.

composite functions Applying one function to the results of a different function, or the output of one function becoming of input for a different function; also called a function of a function.

composite A non-prime number or factor; it may be divisible by several numbers or factors.

compound event An event for which there is more than one possible outcome; involves finding the sum of the probabilities of the individual events and, if necessary, removing any overlapping probabilities.

compression Changing the proportionality of two similar figures. Also, squeezing a function toward an axis.

concave polygon A polygon with one angle greater than 180°.

concavity The sign of curvature (positive for concave up, negative for concave down) of a function that is continuous at the point in question.

conclusion of an argument The statement being supported.

conditional (→) A connective that is true for all instances except when P is true and Q is false; relates to an "if-then" statement.

conditional probability Probability of an event happening dependent on another event already occurring; designated as $Pr(A|B)$, read as "the probability of A occurring when B has already occurred."

confidence interval An interval that approximates the population with a given degree of confidence given a sample mean and sample standard deviation.

congruent Description of figures for which all of the pairs of corresponding sides and corresponding angles are equal; the orientation may differ.

conic section The intersection of a plane slicing through a cone; includes circles, ellipses, parabolas, and hyperbolas.

conjugates Pair of binomials for which the unknown is a radical term constant terms are the same and the radical terms differ only in sign (e.g., the conjugate of $\sqrt{x} + 2$ is $\sqrt{x} - 2$); the product of conjugates eliminates the radical.

consistent equations Equations whose graphs intersect at a common point, the solution for all of the equations.

constant difference The difference between any two successive terms in an arithmetic sequence.

constant of integration The difference in value between indefinite integrals of a function that indicates that the antiderivative is a family of functions.

constraints A restriction on the value of a variable; indicated by using inequalities or interval notation.

constructions Historically, drawing a shape, line, or angle accurately by using a compass and straightedge (ruler); constructions are now drawn by computer.

contingency tables A representation of the possible relationships between two sets of categorical data whose values have been paired in some way; also called two-way frequency tables.

continuity Description of a function that has no holes, asymptotes, or breaks.

continuity For a function $f(x)$ at point a if $\lim_{x \to a} f(x)$ exists (which means it exists from the left and from the right) and is equal to $f(a)$.

contrapositive For the statement "if P, then Q," or $P \to Q$ is $\sim Q \to \sim P$, or "if not Q, then not P"; it is a combination of the inverse and the converse.

converse For the statement "if P, then Q," or $P \to Q$ is $Q \to P$, or "if Q, then P."

coordinates Points in the Cartesian coordinate system of the form (x, y) or (domain, range).

correlation coefficient A measure of the strength of the linear association between the variables; values range from +1 (perfect positive linear association) to 0 (no linear association) to −1 (perfect negative linear association).

correlation An indication of the extent to which two or more variables fluctuate together, or are associated in a systematic way.

corresponding angles Two angles formed in corresponding positions when two parallel lines are crossed by a transversal; corresponding angles are equal.

coterminal angles Two angles that share the same terminal ray; they have the same trigonometric values.

counterclockwise Rotation in a direction opposite to the hands of a clock.

counterexample Exception to a generality that is enough to prove the generality false.

counterexamples A method of disproving something, such as a statement, proposition, or theorem.

counting numbers Another word for natural numbers ($N = \{1, 2, 3, \ldots\}$) or positive integers.

counting principle If there are m ways to do one thing, and n ways to do another, then there are $m \times n$ ways of doing both.

Cramer's Rule A method for solving a system of equations by using matrices and determinants.

critical points Places where the graph of a function changes direction; a maximum or minimum can occur at a critical point.

critical value The value of the z-score in a standard normal distribution for a designated confidence interval, usually 90%, 95%, or 99%; also known as the maximum error of estimate.

cross-multiplication Multiplication a proportion in the shape of a cross to make a solvable equation (for example, $\frac{3}{1} \times \frac{x}{10}$ yields $3 \times 10 = x \times 1$).

cross-section method A method of using integrals to find volume that extends the method of using integrals to find area by adding a third dimension.

cube A three-dimensional right prism comprising six square faces.

cubed A power of 3, such as "four cubed" meaning 4^3.

cylinder   A three-dimensional figure in the shape of a can; the bases are circles aligned one directly above the other with a rectangle wrapped around the circles forming the side.

decimal   Equivalent of a fraction with a denominator of a power of 10; written with a integral part and a fractional part (actually, a decimal part) separated by a decimal point (e.g., 123.456).

deductive argument   An argument in which the premises claim to give conclusive grounds for the truth of the conclusion or the premises claim to necessarily support the conclusion.

definite integral   Integral with an upper and lower limit; in two dimensions, it represents the area between a function curve and the x-axis between the upper and lower limit.

degree of a polynomial   Largest exponent of the variable in the polynomial.

degree of accuracy   Usually, a half unit on each side of a measure (e.g., if measurement X is in inches, the degree of accuracy is a half inch, or $(X \pm 0.5)$ inches).

degree   A measure of an angle equal to $\frac{1}{360}$ th of a circle.

denominator   The bottom number of a common fraction; indicates the number of equal parts of the whole.

density   A measure of how closely the molecules of an object are packed together.

dependent equations   Equations that actually equal each other because one equation is multiplied (or divided) by the same quantity on both sides; they have an infinite number of solutions whose graphs are the same line.

Descartes' Rule of Signs   Determines how many roots of a polynomial can be positive or negative real numbers and possibly how many other roots there are.

determinant   A value found by applying a set of rules to a square matrix.

diagonal   A line from any vertex of a polygon to another vertex of the polygon.

diameter   A chord that passes through the center of a circle; it equals twice the radius.

difference laws for sets   For any three sets A, B, and C, $A - (B \cup C) = (A - B) \cap (A - C)$ and $A - (B \cap C) = (A - B) \cup (A - C)$.

difference of two sets   The set of all elements of one set that are not elements of another set, for sets S and T designated as $T - S$; also called the relative complement.

difference of two squares   An expression that can be written in the form $x^2 - y^2$, which factors into $(x + y)(x - y)$.

differentiability   The derivative of a function at a particular point as approached from the left and from the right are the same.

differentiation   The method to find a derivative.

dilation   Changing the proportionality of two similar figures. Also, stretching a function away from an axis.

dimensional analysis   An analysis that sets up equivalences of units, such as 1 foot = 12 inches, as ratios.

direct variation   A variation between variables such that when one variable increases, the other increases in proportion so that the ratio between the variables is unchanged (e.g., $y = kx$).

directrix   A fixed line used in describing a curve or surface.

discrete mathematics mathematics that deals with distinct items (e.g., the integers marked on a number line).

discriminant The value under the square root sign of the quadratic formula, $b^2 - 4ac$; the value of the discriminant determines whether the solutions of the quadratic equation are real, imaginary, or double roots.

distance A numerical description of how far apart one object (e.g., point) is from another object (e.g., another point, a line).

distributive law for sets For any three sets A, B, and C, $A \cup (B \cap C) = (A \cup B) \cap (A \cup C)$ and $A \cap (B \cup C) = (A \cap B) \cup (A \cap C)$.

distributive property The quality of multiplication over addition that distributes a factor to each number being added (e.g., $6(3 + 4) = (6 \times 3) + (6 \times 4)$).

domain The set of possible values of the independent variable(usually x) for which a function or relation is defined.

dot plot Similar to a tally in which each data point is graphed as a dot above its value.

double negation Reverse of a negation truth table.

double roots Roots of the quadratic equation that are real and identical; occurs when the discriminant is equal to 0.

eccentricity Measure of the curvature of a conic section; the ratio of the distance of any point on the conic section from the focus to its distance from directrix.

edges The lines on a three-dimensional figure where two faces meet.

element Each ordered pair in a relation.

elements of a set The individual objects in a set; also called members of a set; $x \in S$ means that x is an element of S.

elements Entries in a matrix.

ellipse A regular oval shape formed by the intersection of a cone is and an oblique plane that does not intersect the base.

empirical probability Probability resulting from experiment or observation.

empty set The set with no elements, designated $\varnothing$; also called the null set.

endpoint A point that terminates a line segment or ray.

equation A relationship among two or more mathematical expressions; whatever is on one side of the equal sign must equal what is on the other side, so whatever operation is done to one side, must also be done to the other side.

equiangular triangle A triangle with three equal angles; this triangle also has three equal sides.

equidistant At equal distances.

equilateral triangle A triangle with three equal sides; this triangle also has three equal angles.

equivalence ($\leftrightarrow$) A connective that is true if P and Q are both *true* or if P and Q are both false; otherwise, it is false; relates to an "if and only if" statement.

equivalence relations For binary relations, the symmetric, reflexive, and transitive properties together.

Euler's number, e The base of natural logarithms.

even function A function f for which every x in the domain, $f(-x) = f(x)$. Even functions are symmetric to the y-axis.

even number An integer that is divisible by 2.

expected value   The average of all possible outcomes, adjusted (or "weighted") for the likelihood that each outcome will occur.

experiment   A study in which the researcher deliberately influences individuals by imposing conditions and determining the individuals' responses to those conditions.

exponent   The quantity that represents the power of a given number or expression; it usually is expressed as a raised symbol beside the number or expression (e.g., 6 in 2^6, 3 in $(x + y)^3$).

exponential decay   Description of rapid decline in which the total value decreases by an equal factor over time.

exponential function   Function that grows or decays by an equal factor over equal intervals.

exponential growth   Description of a rapid increase when the total value increases by an equal factor over time.

expression   Mathematical phrase containing numbers, variables, and operation; equivalent to phrases in any language.

extrapolation   An estimation of a value outside of the known data based on extending the regression line at the same slope.

extremes of a proportion   The elements a and d in the proportion $\dfrac{a}{b} = \dfrac{c}{d}$.

extremum   A maximum or minimum in the graph of a function.

faces   Flat surfaces on a three-dimensional figure.

Factor Theorem   For a polynomial $f(x)$, if $f(c) = 0$, then $(x - c)$ must be a factor of $f(x)$, or if $(x - c)$ is a factor of a polynomial $f(x)$, then $f(c) = 0$.

factor   A number or quantity that when multiplied with another number or quantity produces a given number or expression.

factorial   The product of a positive integer n and every integer n down to 1, $n! = n(n - 1)(n - 2) \dots (2)(1)$

factoring   Finding two binomials that are factors of a quadratic equation; this is the reverse of the F-O-I-L method.

fair   Not biased (e.g., not weighted in the case of a coin or die).

fallacy   A bad method of argument.

Fibonacci sequence   The well-known recursive sequence is 1, 1, 2, 3, 5, 8, 13, 21, 34, . . .

finite sets   Sets with a countable number of elements.

first derivative   Denoted as $f'(x)$ or $\dfrac{d}{dx} f(x)$, tells whether the graph of a function is increasing $(f'(a) > 0)$, decreasing $(f'(a) < 0)$, or has a critical point $(f'(a) = 0)$ at a point a; If $f'(a)$ is indeterminate (e.g., the denominator is 0), the graph has a cusp at a.

F-O-I-L method   A method to multiply two binomials with any coefficients and any constants; the mnemonic stands for First-Outside-Inside-Last.

fraction   Value between the integers on the number line; composed of a numerator divided by a denominator.

fractional exponent   The indication of the root of a power such that $4^{\frac{1}{2}} = \sqrt{4^1} = \sqrt{4} = 2$ and $8^{\frac{2}{3}} = \sqrt[3]{8^2} = \sqrt[3]{64} = 4$.

frequency curve   For very large numbers of data or small intervals, a smoothed-out line graph in which the vertical axis can be frequency or percentage of the total and the horizontal axis shows the values of the data.

function A relation in which every element in the domain has one and only one element in the range applied to it.

Fundamental Principle of Counting If there are m ways to do one thing, and n ways to do another, then there are $m \times n$ ways of doing both; also called the counting principle or multiplication principle.

Fundamental Theorem of Algebra Any polynomial of degree n has n roots.

Fundamental Theorem of Calculus In part contains the definition of a definite integral: If $F(x)$ is any antiderivative of $f(x)$, where $f(x)$ is continuous on the closed interval $[a, b]$, then $\int_a^b f(x)\,dx = F(b) - F(a)$.

general form for conics $Ax^2 + Cy^2 + Dx + Ey + F = 0$; the coefficients of the squared terms tell the shape of the conic.

general information Information that is always true and is usually contained in the text of a problem.

geometric sequence A sequence of numbers with a constant ratio between any two consecutive terms; also called a geometric progression.

geometric series The sum of the first n terms of a geometric sequence.

height A line that is perpendicular to one side of a figure and ends at the opposite angle or vertex; also called the altitude.

heptagon Seven-sided polygon.

Heron's formula A method of finding the area of a triangle that isn't a right triangle, knowing the lengths of the three sides.

hexagon Six-sided polygon.

histogram A chart to show quantitative data as bars in a graph in which each interval is equal and the heights of the bars indicate quantity or frequency.

horizontal asymptote Values that a rational function approaches as the variable in the function approaches $+\infty$ or $-\infty$.

hyperbola A symmetrical open curve formed by the intersection of a circular cone with a plane with its axis at a smaller angle than the side of the cone.

hypotenuse The side opposite the 90° angle in a right triangle.

idempotent law for sets A set doesn't change value with the operations of union or intersection by itself. for set A, $A \cup A = A$ and $A \cap A = A$.

identity element The element for which the identity property for a number holds (for addition, it is 0; for multiplication, it is 1).

identity property The quality by which a number doesn't change when the number and its identity element are combined by an operation (e.g., for addition, the identity element is 0, so $a + 0 = a$ for all a; for multiplication, the identity element is 1, and $a \times 1 = a$ for all real a).

imaginary numbers Numbers that aren't real numbers.

imaginary roots Roots of a quadratic equation of the form that aren't real; occurs when the discriminant is negative. If a root is imaginary, it is also complex.

implication An "if-then" statement.

improper fraction Fraction with a numerator that is greater than the denominator (e.g., $\frac{20}{17}$).

inconsistent equations Equations that have no solution that holds for all of the equations; Their graphs are parallel lines.

indefinite integrals Integrals with no upper or lower limits.

independent events   Any string of events that each don't influence the others; the probability of an event doesn't affect the probability of another event.

indeterminate   Description of a mathematical expression that has one value at one time and also another value at the same time (e.g., 0^0, which can equal 0 or 1 at the same time).

index   The value k in the radical expression $\sqrt[k]{a}$; no value of k indicates a square root.

inductive argument   An argument that claims that its premises support but do not guarantee its conclusion.

inequalities   Relation between two expressions that are not equal, based on the notations $\pm$ "not equal to," $>$ "greater than," or $<$ "less than" (e.g., $-4 < x \le 3$ means "all values of x greater than -4 and less than or equal to 3."

infinite geometric series   The sum of a geometric sequence for which $n \to \infty$.

infinite set   Sets with an infinite number of elements, usually defined by describing the properties that define it.

inscribed polygon   A polygon inside a circle such that all of its vertices are on the circumference.

instantaneous rate of change   The rate of change at a particular moment, or the value of the derivative of a function at a particular point; this is the same as the slope of the line tangent to the curve at the point, or the slope of the curve at the point.

integers   Numbers belonging to the set $\mathbb{Z} = \{\ldots, -3, -2, -1, 0, 1, 2, 3, \ldots\}$.

integral   Another name for antiderivative, generally of the form $\int f(x)\,dx$.

integration by parts   The antiderivative of the product rule for differentiation, or $\int u\,dv = uv - \int v\,du$,

using the notation for functions $u = f(x)$ and $v = g(x)$.

Intermediate Value Theorem   If $f(x)$ is continuous on the interval $[a, b]$ and has values $f(a)$ and $f(b)$ at each end of the interval, then direct substitution will find the value of $f(c)$ for any c such that $a < c < b$.

interpolation   An estimation of a value within the data set by using the regression line.

intersection of sets   All the elements of one set that are also elements of another set; $S \cap T$ means all the elements of set S that are also elements of set T.

interval notation   Representation of the possible values of a variable as a pair of numbers, which are the endpoints, where parentheses indicate the exclusion of the endpoint and brackets indicate the inclusion of the endpoint (e.g., a domain of $[2, 6)$ indicates the interval of real numbers between 2 and 6, excluding 6, which can also be written as $2 \le x < 6$).

invalid   Describing an argument that is not valid.

inverse of a function   A function that undoes the action of another function.

inverse property   The quality of an operation that "undoes" another operation, yielding the identity element for that operation (the additive inverse of a is $-a$, so $a + (-a) = 0$; the multiplicative inverse of a is $\frac{1}{a}$, so $a \times \left(\frac{1}{a}\right) = 1$, $a \ne 0$).

inverse trigonometric functions   Notation that indicates the principle angle that has the given function value; the designation "arc" before a function means "the angle whose function is."

inverse variation   A variation between variables such that when one variable increases, the other decreases in proportion so that the product of the variables is unchanged (e.g., $y = \frac{k}{x}$, or $xy = k$).

inverse   For the statement "if P, then Q," or $P \rightarrow Q$, is $\sim P \rightarrow \sim Q$, or "if not P, then not Q.

invertible   Adjective used when the function and its inverse exist and are both functions.

invertible   Description of any matrix that has a "non-zero" determinant.

irrational numbers   Numbers that are not rational (e.g., π or $\sqrt{2}$).

isosceles trapezoid   A quadrilateral in which two sides are parallel and the other two sides are equal.

isosceles triangle   A triangle with two equal side lengths.

joint frequencies   Frequencies within a contingency, or two-way frequency, table.

law of cosines   A method to find the third side of a triangle that isn't a right triangle, knowing the lengths of the other two sides and the angle between them.

Law of Large Numbers theorem   As the number of trials of a probability experiment increases, the empirical probability will approach the theoretical probability.

law of sines   A method of finding the other measures of a triangle that isn't a right triangle, knowing the measurement of two angles and a third side.

legs   The two shorter sides of a right triangle; they are not necessarily equal. Also, the two equal sides of an isosceles triangle.

limit   The value of y that the function approaches as x approaches a given value.

line graph   A line constructed by connecting the midpoints of the bars of a histogram with a line.

line of best fit   The best-fitting straight line through a group of data points such as in a scatter plot; also called a regression line.

line segment   A portion of a line that has two endpoints and a definite length, written as, for example, $\overline{CD}$.

line   A geometric object with only one dimension, length, formed by an infinite number of points; it may be straight or curved, and has no endpoints, so it is often written as $\overrightarrow{AB}$, for example, with the double-headed arrow showing that a line goes on forever.

linear equation   Equations with two unknowns, usually x and y each to the first power (e.g., $y = mx + b$).

linear quadratic systems   System of two equations in which one is a linear equation and the other is a quadratic.

locus   A set of points that obeys some sort of rule or rules.

logarithm (log)   Defined by $\log_a x = b$ means $a^b = x$.

logarithmic function   A function that contains a logarithm.

logic   The study of argument.

logical conjunction (∧)   A conjunction that is true when components P and Q are both true, and false otherwise.

logical disjunction (∨)   A disjunction that is true when either or both of the components P and Q are true, and false only if both P and Q are false; also called an inclusive disjunction.

logically equivalent (↔)   A connective that is true if P and Q are both *true* or if P and Q are both false; otherwise, it is false; relates to an "if and only if" statement.

lowest common denominator   The lowest denominator that is shared by the equivalents of several fractions (e.g., the lowest common denominator of $\frac{1}{2}$, $\frac{3}{4}$, and $\frac{5}{8}$ is 8 because they can be written as $\frac{4}{8}$, $\frac{6}{8}$, and $\frac{5}{8}$, respectively.

major axis   The line segment that contains both foci and has its endpoints on an ellipse.

mantissa   The value of a logarithm after the decimal point, indicating the fractional part of the power.

mapping   Taking the points of one space into the points of the same or another space.

marginal frequencies   Frequencies in the margins of a contingency, or two-way frequency, table.

mass   The amount of matter in an object.

matrix   A way to organize data in columns and rows to form an array of numbers or other mathematical objects for which operations, such as addition and multiplication, are defined.

Mean Value Theorem   There is at least one value c, between a and b in the open interval (a, b) for which the instantaneous rate of change (slope of the tangent line) equals the average rate of change of $f(x)$ over the closed interval $[a, b]$.

Mean Value Theorem for Integration   For any continuous function $f(x)$ over the interval $[a, b]$, there exists a c, $a \le c \le b$, for which $\int_a^b f(x)\,dx = f(c)(b - a)$.

mean   A measure of central tendency of a group of qualitative data calculated by totaling all of the data points and dividing by the number of points; also called the average.

means of a proportion   The elements b and c in the proportion $\frac{a}{b} = \frac{c}{d}$.

median of a triangle   A line from the midpoint of one side of a triangle to the opposite vertex.

median   The middle data point in a group of qualitative data when the data are arranged in order.

members of a set   The individual objects in a set; also called elements of a set.

metric system   System used outside of the United States and in the scientific, medical, and international trade communities; also called the International System of Units (SI) (the units are kilometer, centimeter, gram).

midpoint rule   A variation of accumulation that uses the midpoints of the rectangles.

midpoint   The middle point of a line segment, exactly equidistant from the endpoints. The point that divides a line segment into two equal parts.

midsegment   A line that joints the midpoints of two sides of a triangle.

minor axis   A line segment perpendicular to and bisecting the major axis in an ellipse.

mixed number   A number with an integer part and a fractional or decimal part (e.g., $2\frac{2}{3}$, 4.32).

mnemonic   A device to assists in remembering something, such as a pattern of letters, ideas, or associations (e.g., PEMDAS for the order of operations).

mode   The data point with the highest frequency.

modular mathematics   A way of expressing the remainder (a) when dividing an integer by the modulus (m) expressed as $a = n(\text{mod } m)$, where $0 \le a < m$.

modulus   A fixed quantity in modular mathematics after which numbers restart (e.g., 12 on a clock face).

multiple   The numbers obtained when a particular number is multiplied by an integer or integers.

multiplication rule of probability   "and" means multiply.

mutually exclusive events   Events that cannot occur at the same time; not the same as independent events.

natural log   Logarithm with base e.

natural numbers Whole numbers belonging to the set $N = \{1, 2, 3, \ldots\}$.

negation (~) The opposite of a statement; if statement P is true, its negation $\sim P$ is false.

net A two-dimensional pattern traced on paper, cut, and folded to make a three-dimensional figure.

normal curve A bell-shaped curve in which the horizontal axis shows the data with the center point being the mean of the data, and the vertical axis is the frequency of the data points, with the maximum corresponding to the mean; the degree to which actual data points vary from a normal distribution allow statisticians to make their analyses.

null set The set with no elements, designated $\varnothing$; also called the empty set.

number line A continuous straight line with integers marked at definite intervals; useful for showing relations among numbers and for visualizing positive and negative numbers as well as distances between numbers.

numerator The top number of a common fraction; tells how many parts of the whole denominator.

numerical data Another name for quantitative data.

observation A study that attempts to determine relationships between variables without imposing any conditions on the individuals (e.g., a survey).

obtuse angle An angle with a measurement between $90°$ and $180°$.

obtuse triangle A triangle in which one of the angles is obtuse.

octagon Eight-sided polygon.

odd function A function for which $f(-x) = -f(x)$ for all x.

odd number An integer that is not divisible by 2.

one-tailed distribution A distribution in which the values of the maximum error of estimate either above or below the mean but not both are considered.

one-to-one (1-1) function Any function whose inverse is also a function, or a function for which every element of the range of the function corresponds to exactly one element of the domain; the function passes the vertical and horizontal line tests.

optimization Maximization or minimization of a particular quantity.

order of magnitude A comparison of size between values; one order of magnitude means the values differ by 10^1, and two orders of magnitude means the values differ by $10^2 = 100$.

order of operations The rule that operations must be done in the order of parentheses, exponents, multiplication and division (left to right), and addition and subtraction (left to right); abbreviated as PEMDAS.

ordered pair Another name for coordinates, so-called because order makes a difference in coordinates, (x, y).

origin The point where the axes meet in a coordinate system.

overlapping events Events that have outcomes in common, or one or more outcomes occur at the same time; these events aren't mutually exclusive.

parabola A symmetrical open plane curve formed by the intersection of a cone with a plane parallel to its side; the path of a projectile under the influence of gravity.

parallel lines Two lines that never intersect.

parallelogram A quadrilateral with two pair of parallel sides; the parallel sides are equal to each other.

particular information Information that is true only at the instant of a problem, usually contained in the final question; it must not be used until the last step of solving a problem.

Pascal's triangle A triangle of numbers (the first four rows shown below)

$$
\begin{array}{ccccccccccc}
& & & & & 1 & & & & & \\
& & & & 1 & & 2 & & 1 & & \\
& & & 1 & & 3 & & 3 & & 1 & \\
& & 1 & & 4 & & 6 & & 4 & & 1 \\
& 1 & & 5 & & 10 & & 10 & & 5 & & 1
\end{array}
$$

in which the all the edges are 1's, and all the numbers in the middle are the sums of the two numbers above them; used to find the value of any power of a binomial.

pattern sequence Sequences aren't arithmetic or geometric or recursive (e.g., the sequence of integer squares, 1, 4, 9, 16, 36, 49, 64).

PEMDAS Abbreviation for order of operations.

pentagon Five-sided polygon.

percentage A dimensionless number or ratio expressed as a fraction of 100 (e.g., $12\% = \dfrac{12}{100}$).

perfect square Any number with an integer square root (e.g., 16 is a perfect square; 17 is not).

perimeter The sum of the sides lengths of a two-dimensional figure.

periodic functions Functions that repeat their output values at regular intervals, or periods.

permutation The number of ways of choosing r objects out of n objects when order makes a difference: $_nP_r = \dfrac{n!}{(n-r)!}$.

perpendicular lines Two lines that intersect at a right (90°) angle.

phase shift Horizontal translation of a periodic function with no dilation.

pi (π) The ratio of the circumference (perimeter) of a circle to its diameter.

pictograph Similar to dot plots, but using icons instead of dots; each icon can represent a multiple of the data.

pie chart A method of presenting categorical data that shows data as a percentage of the area of a circle shown as slices of a pie; sometimes called a circle graph.

piecewise function Pieces of different functions defined for a particular scenario and graphed all on one set of coordinates.

point of inflection A point on a curve at which the sign of the curvature changes.

point A geometric object with no dimensions, used for defining positions.

polar coordinates A two-dimensional (r, θ) coordinate system that describes a point (x, y) according to its distance r from a reference point and an angle θ from the horizontal.

polygons Closed, straight-line figures.

polyhedron A solid figure with many plane faces.

polynomial function A function of degree n of the form $f(x) = a_n x^n + a_{n-1} x^{n-1} + \ldots + a_1 x + a_0$, where all a_i are real numbers and $a_n \neq 0$.

polynomial An expression of more than two algebraic terms that contain different powers of the variable(s).

population The collection of all items under consideration.

power rule The first derivative $f'(ax^n) = \dfrac{d}{dx}(ax^n) = (n \bullet a)x^{n-1}$.

power A shorthand for the number of repeated factors, expressed as an exponent (e.g., the power 8 in $2 \times 2 \times 2 \times 2 \times 2 \times 2 \times 2 \times 2 = 2^8$).

precision Comparison of measured value to another measured value.

premises of an argument The statements that support an argument.

prime A number or factor that is not divisible by any positive number except 1 and itself.

prime factorization The operation for which all of the factors of the original quantity are primes.

probability The chance that something will occur, or the number of ways that an event can occur divided by the total number of possible outcomes; it is a fraction between 0 (impossible) and 1 (inevitable).

probability distribution A table or equation that links each outcome of a statistical experiment with its probability of occurrence; sometimes called an experimental probability distribution.

problem solving The process of finding solutions to difficult or complex issues.

product rule The first derivative of a product of functions, $f(x)g(x)$ is given by $(f(x)g(x))' = f'(x)g(x) + f(x)g'(x)$.

proper subset All the elements of are elements of another set but it is not the same as the other set (e.g., set $S = \{1, 2, 3, 4\}$ is a proper subset of set $T = \{1, 2, 3, 4, 5\}$);.

properties of binary relations Includes reflexive, transitive, symmetric, and antisymmetric; similar to the same properties for number.

properties A quality, such as commutative, associative, identity, distributive, for mathematical entities.

proportion Equivalence of two ratios.

Pythagorean identities A trigonometric relation expressing the Pythagorean theorem in terms of trigonometric functions.

Pythagorean Theorem Pertains to right triangles: The square of the hypotenuse is equal to the sum of the squares of the other two sides. Common Pythagorean triples are 3-4-5, 5-12-13, 8-15-17, and their multiples.

Pythagorean triples The sides of a right triangle that are whole numbers that satisfy the Pythagorean Theorem.

quadratic equation An equation in which the unknown is squared and there is no higher power of the unknown (e.g., $x^2 + x - 6 = 0$, $x^2 - 9 = 0$, and $x^2 + 3x = 0$).

quadratic formula A formula for finding the roots of all quadratic equations of the form $ax^2 + bx + c = 0$:
$$x = \frac{-b \pm \sqrt{b^2 - 4ac}}{2a}.$$

quadrilaterals Four-sided closed figures.

qualitative data Another name for categorical data.

quantitative data Data are numbers, these are sometimes called numerical data; can be analyzed by standard statistical methods.

quantitative reasoning Using basic mathematical skills, understanding elementary mathematical concepts, being able to reason quantitatively, and having the ability to model and solve problems with quantitative methods; in short, "doing math correctly."

quotient rule The first derivative of a quotient of functions, $\frac{f(x)}{g(x)}$ is given by $\left(\frac{f(x)}{g(x)}\right)' = \frac{f'(x)(g(x) - f(x)g'(x)}{(g(x))^2}$, if $g(x) \neq 0$.

radian A measure of an angle related to the measure of a central angle of a circle that intercepts an arc equal to the radius of that circle.

radical function A function that contains a radical.

radical sign ($\sqrt{}$)   The sign that indicates taking a root of a quantity; an index in the radical sign indicates the root (e.g., an index of 3 indicates a cube root. $\sqrt[3]{64} = 4$, but without an index, the radical sign means square root, $\sqrt{64} = 8$).

radical   The inverse of powers expressed as the root of an expression or number; indicated by $\sqrt[k]{a}$, expressed as "the kth root of a." See also root.

radicand   The value a in the radical expression $\sqrt[k]{a}$.

radius   The fixed distance from the center to a circle; plural is radii.

range   A measure of quantitative data that is simply the highest value minus the lowest value.

range   The complete set of all possible results of the dependent variable (usually y), after substituting the values of the domain. Also, in statistics, the difference between the lowest and highest values of a set of data.

ratio   A way to quantitatively compare two quantities.

rational decimal   Decimal that either terminates (.75) or repeats ($0.3\overline{3}$).

rational expressions   Expressions that can be written in fraction form, where the numerator and denominator are themselves expressions.

rational function   The quotient of two polynomials.

rational numbers (Q)   Numbers that can be written as fractions, repeating decimals, or terminating decimals.

Rational Roots Test   Gives a list of relatively easy possible numbers to try to factor a polynomial.

raw scores   The values of x of a distribution.

ray   A portion of a line that has only one endpoint, written as $\overrightarrow{EF}$, for example, to emphasize that it goes on forever in only one direction, away from the endpoint.

real numbers   Numbers that can be found on the number line, including both rational numbers and irrational numbers.

reciprocal trigonometric functions   Pairs of trig functions that are reciprocal of each other: sine-cosecant, cosine-secant, tangent-cotangent.

rectangle   A quadrilateral with two pair of parallel sides and all four angles are equal.

recursive sequence   A list of numbers in which each number depends on the values of previous numbers (e.g., the Fibonacci sequence).

reducible fraction   A fraction with a numerator and denominator that have factors in common that can cancel out.

reference angle   The acute angle formed by the terminal side of a given angle and the negative or positive x-axis on a unit circle.

reflection   Creating a mirror image of a geometric figure across an axis or a line.

reflex angle   An angle with a measurement greater than 180°.

reflexive binary property of equality   Any value is equal to itself.

regression line   The best-fitting straight line through a group of data points such as in a scatter plot; also called the line of best fit.

regular polygon   A polygon with all sides equal and all angles equal.

regular pyramid   A three-dimensional figure in which one base is a regular polygon and the other end is a point that is above the center of the polygon base; all of the faces are identical triangles.

related rates Generally, if z is related to y and y is related to x, then z is related to x by using the following first derivatives: $\dfrac{dz}{dx} = \left(\dfrac{dz}{dy}\right)\left(\dfrac{dy}{dx}\right)$.

relation A set of ordered pairs.

relative complement The set of all elements of one set that are not elements of another set; for two sets S and T, designated as $T \setminus S$, also called the difference of two sets.

relative error Compares the absolute error against the size of the object being measured.

relative frequencies A way to compare frequencies in relation to the rest of the data.

Remainder Theorem When a polynomial $f(x)$ is divided by a binomial $x - c$, the remainder r equals $f(c)$.

repeating decimal A decimal that repeats a pattern, often indicated by a bar over the repeating digits (e.g., $0.3\overline{3}$, $0.1287\overline{312873}$).

repeating decimals A decimal that has a digit, or a block of digits, that repeat over and over again without ever ending (e.g., $\dfrac{1}{3} = .333333\ldots = .\overline{3}$).

residue The remainder in modular mathematics.

rhombus A quadrilateral with two pair of parallel sides and all four sides are equal.

Riemann sum A method for finding the area under a curve by adding the areas of rectangles of narrow width that approximate the curve; sometimes referred to as an accumulation.

right angle An angle with perpendicular sides; the measure is 90°.

right circular cone Similar to a cylinder, with a point as one of the bases.

right prism A prism that has bases aligned one directly above the other and has lateral faces that are rectangles meeting the bases at right angles.

right triangle A triangle with one 90° angle.

root A number multiplied by itself a given number of times to produce a given value (e.g., the second root of 9 is 3 because $3 \times 3 = 9$).

root Values of x for which a function $f(x) = 0$; also called zeros. Graphically, locations where the graph of the function crosses the x-axis.

roster method Explicitly listing each of the elements of a finite set.

rotation method A method of using integrals to find volume by rotating an area about a line or axis.

rotation Turning a plane figure or point around a fixed center point. Also, a method by which a two-dimensional figure can become a three-dimensional shape.

rounding errors Errors encountered by rounding too early in a calculation; rounding should be confined to the final step in a calculation.

rounding Altering a number to a less exact but more convenient number for calculations; if the digit to the right of the one to be rounded is less than 5, drop that digit and all the ones to the right (inserting zeros if necessary), and if that digit is 5 or more, add "1" to the one being rounded.

sample A selected subset of a population from which data are gathered.

sample space The total number of ways an event can and cannot happen.

sample survey A study that collects information from part of a population in order to determine one or more characteristics of the population.

sampling error The standard deviation of the distribution of sample means, which is not an error but just reflects the variability in the data; interpreted as the error in a statistical analysis due to the sample being unrepresentative of the data;.

scalar   Description of quantities that have only magnitude.

scale factor   The value of the proportion between two similar figures; also called a size transformation.

scalene triangle   A triangle in which the lengths of all of the sides are different.

scatter plots   Plots of ordered pairs on Cartesian coordinates for which the horizontal axis represents the independent variable and the vertical axis represents thee dependent variable.

secant   The extension of a chord in both directions. Also, a trigonometric function.

second derivative   Denoted as $f''(x)$ or $\frac{d^2}{dx^2}f(x)$, tells whether the graph of a function is curving upward ($f''(a)>0$), downward ($f''(a)<0$), or has a possible point of inflection ($f''(a)=0$) at a point a.

sector   An area of the circle with three sides comprising two radii and an arc.

semicircle   A half circle.

semi-major axis   Half the major axis.

semiperimeter   Half the perimeter of the triangle.

sequence   A set of things that have some rule for their order; it can be finite or infinite.

series   The sum of a finite sequence.

set builder notation $\{x : x$ has property $P\}$, which indicates a set of objects x having property P (e.g., $S = \{x : x$ is an even integer$\}$ is the set of all even integers).

set   Any collection of objects restricted only by the definition of the set.

significance level   The rest of the probability after the confidence percentage is determined; also called the alpha value (e.g., for a 95% confidence interval, the alpha value is 5%).

significant   A statistical term for an actual difference (one not just due to chance) between a data point and what is to be expected; statistical significance plays the primary role in statistics.

similar   Description of figures for which all of the pairs of corresponding angles are equal, and the lengths of the corresponding sides are proportional and not necessarily equal.

simplifying a fraction   Rewriting a fraction in lowest terms (*see* cancellation) with no radicals in the denominator.

simultaneous equations   A group of two or more equations that share one solution; also called system of equations.

size transformation   The value of the proportion between two similar figures; also called a scale factor.

skew   The condition whereby one or a few anomalously high or low values pull the mean too far in one direction or the other.

slant asymptote   An oblique, or slanted, line similar to the horizontal asymptote of a rational function.

slant height   The measure from the point of a pyramid to the midpoint of a side of the regular polygon base.

slope   Relationship between x and y indicating how y changes in relation to x (the rate of change of the relationship); usually indicated by $m = \frac{\Delta y}{\Delta x}$.

slope-intercept form   Of a linear equation, $y = mx + b$, where m is the slope and b is the y-intercept of the line.

speed   Velocity without direction (as on the speedometer of a car).

sphere A three-dimensional figure in which every point on the surface is the same distance from the center of the sphere.

square matrix A matrix with the same number of rows and columns.

square A quadrilateral with two pair of parallel sides, all four sides are equal, and all four angles are equal.

squared A power of 2, such as "four squared" meaning 4^2.

standard deviation A measurement of the spread of data from the mean; square root of the variance.

standard form Of a linear equation, $Ax + By = C$, where A, B, and C can be any numbers.

standard form The most commonly accepted form of an equation.

standard normal distribution A neater and easier to understand variation of the normal distribution in which the mean is normalized to 0, one standard deviation is 1, and the area under the whole curve above the x-axis is 1. The standard deviations are called z-scores.

standard scores The values of z that determine how many standard deviations from the mean a data value lies in a standard normal distribution; also called a z-score, a negative z-score indicates standard deviations below the mean, and a z-score of 0 indicates a raw score that is equal to the mean, and a positive z-score indicates standard deviations above the mean.

statistics Collecting and analyzing numerical data in large quantities, especially for the purpose of inferring proportions for a whole population from those in a representative sample; involves collecting, analyzing, presenting, and interpreting data.

straight angle An angle with a measurement of 180°.

subset A set in which all of its elements are elements of another set; it said to be a subset of that set.

substitution property of binary relations If $x = y$, then x may be replaced by y in any equation or expression.

superset The same as a proper subset; "S is a superset of T" is denoted as $T \supset S$; whereas $S \subset T$ means "S is a proper subset of T."

supplementary angles Any two angles whose measures total 180°; they need not be adjacent.

support in logic Justification, grounds, reasons, or evidence.

surface area The total area of all the faces of a three-dimensional figure.

symmetric binary property of equality Both sides of an equal sign are equal no matter which side of the equal sign they are on.

symmetric functions Functions that can be reflected around a specific location; can be even odd, or neither.

synthetic division A method that simplifies long division of a polynomial by the binomial of the form $x + c$ or $x - d$.

system of equations A group of two or more equations that share one solution; also called simultaneous equations.

table of values A table of x values with their corresponding y values.

tangent A line that touches a curve at one and only one point, even when extended.

tangent A line that touches the circle at just one point with all of its other points outside the circle. Also, a trigonometric function.

terminating decimal A decimal that has an end, and doesn't go on forever (e.g., 0.5, 0.75).

theoretical probability The usual way probability is perceived; the number of ways that an event can occur divided by the total number of possible outcomes.

three-dimensional figures Shapes with length, width, and depth.

transformation The manipulation of the shape of a point, line, or shape involving a change of variables or coordinates in which a function of new variables or coordinates is substituted for each original variable or coordinate; types of transformation are translation, reflection, and rotation.

transitive binary property of equality If one value is equal to another value, and that second value is equal to a third value, then the first value is also equal to the third value.

translation Movement of an object from one place to another; the size and orientation are not changed.

transversal A line that intersects two or more other lines.

trapezoid rule A variation of accumulation that uses trapezoids instead of rectangles.

trapezoid A quadrilateral in which two of the sides are parallel.

trend estimation A statistical technique that helps to describe and analyze data to make and justify statements about the data.

trend A pattern of change in a series of data points to move in a certain direction over time.

triangle A closed two-dimensional figure composed of three line segments.

trigonometric functions A function of an angle that defines relationships among the sides and angles of a triangle; includes sine, cosine, tangent, cotangent, secant, and cosecant.

trigonometry The branch of mathematics dealing with the relations of the sides and angles of triangles and with the relevant functions of any angle.

truth table A table of connectives of a statement in logic, including negation (~).

truth An attribute of the premises of an argument.

two-dimensional figures Shapes with length and width but no depth.

two-tailed distribution A distribution in which the values of the maximum error of estimate both above and below the mean are considered.

two-way frequency tables A representation of the possible relationships between two sets of categorical data whose values have been paired in some way; also called contingency tables.

union of sets All the elements of two sets together; $S \cup T$ means all the elements of set S and set T together.

unit circle A circle with radius = 1 and center at (0, 0) used to define trigonometric functions.

unit conversion The result when any dimension is multiplied by its equivalence (e.g., 1 minute = 60 seconds), so the resultant value is unchanged.

universe Population of interest in probability.

US standard system System of units used mainly in the United States; also called the customary system (the units are, for example, mile, yard, ounce).

validity An attribute of the reasoning in support of the premises of an argument.

variance Tells how much variability exists in a distribution; it is the average of the squared differences between the data values and the mean.

variation Relationship between two variables that involves proportions. See also direct variation and inverse variation.

vector Description of quantities that have magnitude and direction.

velocity Rate of change of position per unit time, or speed in a given direction; given by the first derivative of the position function. It is also the antiderivative of the acceleration function.

Venn diagrams A diagrammatic method of showing whether events overlap; all of the space within the borders represents the universe, or population of interest.

vertex The point at which the two or more curves, lines, or edges meet to form an angle; the plural of vertex is vertices.

vertical angles Two angles formed across from each other when two lines intersect; vertical angles are equal.

vertical asymptote A vertical line that a rational function may approach but never cross.

vertical shift A graph that is raised or lowered; a vertical translation with no dilation.

volume How much space a three-dimensional figure takes up.

weighted means A method to find the mean of a set of data by multiplying values times frequencies rather than entering each data point individually.

whole numbers Integers belonging to the set W = $\{0, 1, 2, 3, \ldots\}$.

y-intercept The location where a function crosses the y-axis, $(0, y)$.

zeros of an equation The values of the variable for which the equation has a value of zero; these are the roots or factors of the equation.

zeros of a function The real solutions where a function crosses the x-axis $(x, 0)$.

INDEX

Self-Assessment Guide by Topic

Practice Test 1 Topic Coverage*

Number and Quantity

Questions: 7, 33, 36, 40, 43

Algebra

Questions: 3, 4, 6, 9, 11, 12, 21, 24, 27, 29, 30, 35, 41, 42, 45, 49

Functions

Questions: 13, 14, 20, 22, 31, 44, 52, 57, 60

Functions: Logarithms

Questions: 17, 38, 50, 59

Calculus

Questions: 1, 2, 37, 48, 51, 53

Geometry

Questions: 19, 28, 32, 46

Geometry: Trigonometry

Questions: 8, 10, 16, 47

Probability and Statistics

Questions: 23, 55, 56, 58

Discrete Mathematics

Questions: 5, 15, 18, 25, 26, 34, 39, 54

Practice Test 2 Topic Coverage*

Number and Quantity

Questions: 18, 19, 34, 37, 54

Algebra

Questions: 5, 12, 13, 23, 24, 27, 29, 32, 33, 41, 42, 45, 52, 55, 57

Functions

Questions: 1, 3, 7, 11, 14, 38, 39, 44, 56

Functions: Logarithms

Questions: 35, 43, 51, 59

Calculus

Questions: 4, 8, 22, 26, 30, 47, 60

Geometry

Questions: 9, 20, 25, 31, 40, 46, 49

Geometry: Trigonometry

Questions: 6, 10, 48

Probability and Statistics

Questions: 2, 15, 17, 50, 58

Discrete Mathematics

Questions: 16, 21, 28, 36, 53

---

*We've provided a topic breakdown here so you can readily pinpoint where you need further work. Of course, you'll want to measure your overall performance and estimate your score as well. ETS recommends that the passing score on the Praxis Mathematics Content Knowledge (5161) test should be 32 out of a possible 50 raw-score points. This equates to 64%, or a scaled score of 160 on the final Praxis test scale, which runs from 100 to 200. We recommend that your goal should be at least 35 correct on each of our practice tests, equivalent to at least 70% correct on test day. Be sure to consult the agency or institution requiring your test for the passing score it has set.

...wo intersecting circles on a Venn diagram contain the following numbers: R = {5, 6, 7, 8, 9}; and S = {2, 7, 9, 10, 11}, how many numbers will be in the intersection of R and S?

(A) 0

(B) 2

(C) 7

(D) 9

57. What is the difference (rounded to the nearest hundred dollars) between the simple interest and compound interest at the end of 10 years on $5000 compounded annually at 4%?

(A) $400

(B) $800

(C) $2000

(D) $2400

58. A target is in the form of an 80-cm diameter circle with concentric circles, that form 8-cm wide circular bands. What is the probability that someone's arrow lands on the innermost circle (bull's-eye)?

(A) .04

(B) .4

(C) .08

(D) .8

59. If $\log (\tan x) = m$, then $\log (\cot x)$ is equivalent to

(A) $\dfrac{1}{m}$

(B) $-m$

(C) $1 - m$

(D) $-\dfrac{1}{m}$

60. For the function $f(x) = 3x^2 + 4$, what is the slope of the tangent line at $x = 1$?

(A) 3

(B) 6

(C) 7

(D) 10